Praise for
Walter R. Borneman's
Iron Horses

Winner of the 2011 Colorado Book Award in Biography/History

"A riveting history of the frenetic race to construct a railroad across the great American Southwest following the Civil War. Borneman is masterful at writing seamless narrative. Every page sings with fine writing."

—Douglas Brinkley, Professor of History at
Rice University and author of *The Wilderness Warrior:
Theodore Roosevelt and the Crusade for America*

"In this richly detailed and sprightly narrative, Walter Borneman paints a compelling portrait of one of the great chapters in American history. Readers puzzled by the pace of technological change in our own time will learn in these pages that there is nothing new under the sun."

—Jon Meacham, author of
Thomas Jefferson: The Art of Power

"Brisk, colorful, and exciting.... A worthy look at a less-publicized aspect of railroad construction."

—Jay Freeman, *Booklist*

"Borneman's telling of this story is admirable foremost because of its detail and historical accuracy; his extensive research is put to good use. But he also is a gifted storyteller, and he introduces his readers to an array of characters who are part of this transcontinental treasure hunt.... Borneman's book is an enjoyable read for railroad buffs, Old West aficionados, serious-minded historians, and anyone who finds romance in the sound of a train whistle in the night."

—*BookPage*

Atchison, Topeka and Santa Fe locomotive no. 280, a 2-8-0 consolidation with balloon stack, attracted a crowd on the turntable atop Glorieta Pass; this section between Lamy and Las Vegas, New Mexico, was tough mountain railroading, and helper engines were routine. *(Denver Public Library, Western History Collection, A. Frank Randall, Z-5460)*

IRON HORSES

For Dad
Christmas 2016

IRON HORSES

America's Race to Bring the Railroads West

WALTER R. BORNEMAN

BACK BAY BOOKS
Little, Brown and Company
New York   Boston   London

From
Pennie

Back Bay Books / Little, Brown and Company
Hachette Book Group
1290 Avenue of the Americas, New York, NY 10104
littlebrown.com

Originally published in hardcover by Random House, September 2010
First Back Bay paperback edition, November 2014

Back Bay Books is an imprint of Little, Brown and Company.
The Back Bay Books name and logo are trademarks of Hachette Book Group, Inc.

Maps by David Lambert
Locomotive drawings by Henry Comstock

The publisher is not responsible for websites (or their content)
that are not owned by the publisher.

The Hachette Speakers Bureau provides a wide range of authors for speaking events.
To find out more, go to hachettespeakersbureau.com or call (866) 376-6591.

ISBN 978-0-316-37177-3
LCCN 2014940604

10 9 8 7 6 5 4 3 2 1

RRD-C

Printed in the United States of America

For
Alexander C. Hoyt,
with cause

Contents

Part I:
Opening Gambits (1853-1874)

Part II:
Contested Empire (1874–1889)

Part III:
Santa Fe All the Way (1889–1909)

List of Maps

Introduction

❖

Railroad Battleground

Among my earliest memories are those of being down at the railroad depot with my grandfather, watching the trains come in. It was the 1950s, and I wish I had realized then what an era was passing before my eyes. I grew up dreaming of airplanes and space travel, but my fascination with railroads never left me. Ironically, fifty years later, there has been a great resurgence in America's dependence on rails. It will never be the same as the Santa Fe Super Chief, of course, or the California Zephyr that I rode west from Chicago with Grandpa and Grandma, but America's commerce still rides the rails—no more so than on the direct Los Angeles-to-Chicago super route across the American Southwest.

Much has been written about America's first transcontinental railroad, but driving the golden spike at Promontory Summit in 1869 signaled merely the beginning of the transcontinental railroad saga. The pre–Civil War notion that only one rail line would cross the continent vanished on the prairie winds. The rest of the country was suddenly up for grabs. Dozens of railroads, all with aggressive empire builders at their helms, raced one another for the ultimate prize of a southern transcontinental route that was generally free of snow, shorter in distance, and gentler in gradients.

The Denver and Rio Grande Railway's gentleman general, William Jackson Palmer, put his railroad's three-foot narrow gauge rails up against the big boys. The Atchison, Topeka and Santa Fe's William Barstow Strong and Edward Payson Ripley made sure that the routes were staked and won, and then created a textbook example of efficiency upon them. Collis P. Huntington, having already won half the West for the Central Pacific, determined to control the other half for the Southern Pacific. Above them all floated the shadowy hand of Jay Gould, a man who bought and sold railroads as readily as some men traded horses.

Meanwhile, tens of thousands of ordinary men waged a different type of war: the herculean task of constructing the bridges, tunnels, cuts, and fills of these empires and hurriedly flinging track across wild and wide-open country. Among their challenges were vast distances, high elevations, tortuous canyons, unruly rivers, and two towering walls of mountains. The better routes were often not to be shared—admitting no passage wider than the ruts of a wagon or the steel rails of a single track of railroad.

From wagon ruts to a railroad empire, this is the story of the battles to control the heavily contested transportation corridors of the American Southwest and to build America's greatest transcontinental route through them. When the dust finally settled, the southern route linking Los Angeles and Chicago had become the most significant of the nation's transcontinental railroads.

Railroads and Railroaders

———◆———

A Cast of Characters

RAILROADS

There are hundreds, perhaps thousands, of railroad names scattered about the American West. The vast majority were "paper" railroads, incorporated legally to hold a route, bluff an opponent, or appease local economic interests—all without laying a single railroad tie. Many of the companies that incorporated and actually laid track went through a succession of names because of mergers, acquisitions, and reorganizations after bankruptcy. Sometimes the change was no more than for *Railroad* to become *Railway* or vice versa. Many of these, too, drifted into oblivion or became part of larger enterprises. Finally, the principal contenders were frequently forced by state or territorial laws to incorporate separate corporations within certain boundaries.

References herein are usually to the major railroads without distinction to their numerous controlled affiliates, subsidiaries, or joint ventures. This list is by no means definitive—nor even comprehensive of the railroads in this book—but it is an effort to identify the key roads.

A note about ampersands: The ampersand (&) is a staple of railroading, but its usage was varied and highly inconsistent. Consequently, *and* is used herein in railroad names to avoid confusion.

ATCHISON, TOPEKA AND SANTA FE—Organized in 1860, the railroad finally started construction in 1868 and eventually became the dominant transcontinental system in the southwestern United States.

ATLANTIC AND PACIFIC—Forced into early receivership, the Atlantic and Pacific Railroad emerged as a joint venture of the Santa Fe and Frisco railroads and eventually became the key link in the Santa Fe's main line across Arizona.

CALIFORNIA SOUTHERN—With capital from Santa Fe investors, the California Southern built north from San Diego to San Bernardino and eventually over Cajon Pass.

CENTRAL PACIFIC—The western end of the first transcontinental, the Central Pacific was the foundation of the "Big Four" 's (Crocker, Hopkins, Huntington, and Stanford) empire and became an important part of the Southern Pacific system.

CHICAGO, BURLINGTON AND QUINCY—Known most readily as "the Burlington," the railroad had pre–Civil War origins but became a transcontinental contender when it built west to Colorado and later pioneered the Zephyr streamliners.

COLORADO MIDLAND—Built by mining tycoon J. J. Hagerman from Colorado Springs to Aspen, this road through the heart of Colorado was sold to the Santa Fe just before the panic of 1893.

DENVER AND RIO GRANDE—Initially a narrow gauge incorporated by William Jackson Palmer to run south from Denver and serve as a north-south feeder line, the Denver and Rio Grande developed its own transcontinental ambitions.

DENVER AND RIO GRANDE WESTERN—Incorporated in 1881 and known simply as the Rio Grande Western after 1889, this segment between Grand Junction, Colorado, and Ogden, Utah, remained under William Jackson Palmer's control until sold to the Denver and Rio Grande in 1903. After a reorganization in 1920, the entire Rio Grande system was called the Denver and Rio Grande Western Railroad.

DENVER, SOUTH PARK AND PACIFIC—This was a feisty narrow gauge with which founder John Evans and Denver investors hoped to tap the mineral riches of central Colorado and then connect Denver to the Pacific.

GULF, COLORADO AND SANTA FE—This railroad made halfhearted progress north through Texas from Galveston until it was absorbed into the Santa Fe system, giving that road access from the Midwest to the Gulf of Mexico.

KANSAS PACIFIC—Begun as the Union Pacific, Eastern Division, its completed line between Kansas City and Denver eventually became part of the Union Pacific.

MEXICAN CENTRAL—A standard gauge concession granted by Mexico to Santa Fe interests, its main line stretched from El Paso, Texas, to Mexico City.

MEXICAN NATIONAL—A narrow gauge road built under concession to William Jackson Palmer and his associates, it ran from Laredo, Texas, to Mexico City.

MISSOURI PACIFIC—A sleepy local road until bought by Jay Gould, the Missouri Pacific evolved into the centerpiece of the Gould empire, extending west to Colorado and south to the Gulf of Mexico via the Texas and Pacific Railway.

ST. LOUIS AND SAN FRANCISCO—Despite transcontinental dreams, the Frisco, as it was called, remained a Midwest regional road, but its western land grants made the Atlantic and Pacific possible.

SOUTHERN PACIFIC—Acquiring a number of small Bay Area railroads, the Southern Pacific built east across Arizona and New Mexico and was the domain of Collis P. Huntington.

TEXAS AND PACIFIC—Saved from early bankruptcy by Thomas A. Scott, who later sold it to Jay Gould, the road built across Texas to link up with the Southern Pacific.

UNION PACIFIC—The eastern end of the first transcontinental, the Union Pacific slipped into receivership before becoming a powerhouse under E. H. Harriman.

UNION PACIFIC, EASTERN DIVISION—Always a separate entity from the original Union Pacific, this road became the Kansas Pacific and reached Denver by 1870.

WESTERN PACIFIC—Not to be confused with an early Bay Area venture absorbed into the Southern Pacific, this was George Gould's twentieth-century effort between Ogden and Oakland via the Feather River Canyon.

RAILROADERS

MARY JANE COLTER (1869–1958)—Architect and designer whose buildings and interiors tied the Atchison, Topeka and Santa Fe to the landscape it served.

CHARLES CROCKER (1822–1888)—One of the Central Pacific's Big Four and the construction expert behind the effort to build the Southern Pacific across the Southwest.

JOHN EVANS (1814–1897)—Principal founder of the Denver, South Park and Pacific Railroad and the Fort Worth and Denver City Railway between Colorado and Texas.

GEORGE GOULD (1864–1923)—Jay's son and ruler of his own considerable empire of the Missouri Pacific, Denver and Rio Grande, and Western Pacific.

JAY GOULD (1836–1892)—Wall Street banker who at one time or another controlled the Union Pacific, Texas and Pacific, Denver and Rio Grande, Frisco, and Missouri Pacific.

E. H. HARRIMAN (1848–1909)—New York banker turned rail baron, he revitalized the Union Pacific and began an acquisition program that included the Southern Pacific.

FRED HARVEY (1835–1901)—The Santa Fe's marketing ace in the hole as the purveyor of solid, reliable food in Harvey House restaurants and hotels up and down the Santa Fe line.

CYRUS K. HOLLIDAY (1826–1900)—Visionary behind the Atchison, Topeka and Santa Fe, and a longtime member of its board of directors.

MARK HOPKINS (1813–1879)—Big Four accountant and money counter whose attention to detail and underlying conservatism made them all millionaires.

COLLIS P. HUNTINGTON (1821–1900)—The Big Four's insatiable expansionist who championed the Southern Pacific and extended a railroad empire across the continent.

WILLIAM RAYMOND MORLEY (1846–1883)—The Santa Fe's man on the scene at the pivotal battles for Raton Pass and the Royal Gorge.

THOMAS NICKERSON (1810–1892)—Sea captain turned railroad investor, he led the Santa Fe through its turbulent expansion during the 1870s.

WILLIAM JACKSON PALMER (1836–1909)—Construction manager of the Kansas Pacific's drive across the plains and guiding light of the narrow gauge Denver and Rio Grande.

EDWARD PAYSON RIPLEY (1845–1920)—Foremost an "operations" man, he guided the Santa Fe out of the panic of 1893 with steady expansion and sound management.

A. A. ROBINSON (1844–1919)—The engineer and implementer of much of the Santa Fe's expansion, he made the decision to seize Raton Pass.

WILLIAM S. ROSECRANS (1819–1898)—Civil War general who went west to seek his fortune in railroads and real estate, particularly in Southern California and Mexico.

THOMAS A. SCOTT (1823–1881)—Thomson's right-hand man at the Pennsylvania Railroad, he sought to extend its network with the Texas and Pacific.

LELAND STANFORD (1824–1893)—More politician than railroader, he handled the political strings of the Big Four as California governor and U.S. senator.

WILLIAM BARSTOW STRONG (1837–1914)—The president of the Santa Fe from the battle for Raton Pass through the completion of its line across Arizona and into California.

J. EDGAR THOMSON (1808–1874)—The man many call "the father of the modern railroad network," he led the Pennsylvania Railroad with the mantra "Build west."

Major Events in Building the Southwestern Transcontinental System

AT&SF—Atchison, Topeka and Santa Fe Railroad
D&RG—Denver and Rio Grande Railway
SP—Southern Pacific Railroad

1853 U.S. Army Corps of Engineers leads railroad surveys of the West.
      Gadsden Purchase ensures U.S. control of 32nd parallel route.

1858 Butterfield Overland Mail begins.

1860 Cyrus K. Holliday and others incorporate AT&SF.

1862 Congress passes Pacific Railroad Act.

1864 Amendments to Pacific Railroad Act increase land grants.

1865 Civil War ends; railroad construction renews with a flurry.

1866 Union Pacific reaches the 100th meridian, in mid-Nebraska.
      Congress approves land grants for still-trackless SP.

1867 William Jackson Palmer surveys 35th parallel for Kansas Pacific.

1868 AT&SF begins construction southwest from Topeka, Kansas.

1869 Completion of first transcontinental railroad at Promontory, Utah.

1870 Denver Pacific reaches Denver from Cheyenne, Wyoming.
      Kansas Pacific completes line to Denver at Comanche Crossing.
      Collis P. Huntington consolidates Bay Area railroads into SP.
      William Jackson Palmer incorporates D&RG.

1872 AT&SF reaches Colorado-Kansas line, earning Kansas land grant.

1873 Panic of 1873 slows all railroad construction.

1874 AT&SF gains access to Kansas City, Missouri.

1876 SP completes Tehachapi Loop.
      SP completes San Fernando Tunnel, on San Francisco-to-L.A. line.

1877 SP reaches Colorado River at Yuma and forces crossing.

1878 AT&SF seizes Raton Pass and blocks D&RG advance south.
      D&RG and AT&SF contest Royal Gorge and route to Leadville,
      Colorado.
      Fred Harvey opens restaurant and sleeping rooms, Florence,
      Kansas.

1879 Raton Pass Tunnel opens to AT&SF traffic.

1880 "Treaty of Boston" resolves "Royal Gorge war."
      SP reaches Tucson, Arizona.
      AT&SF reaches Albuquerque, New Mexico.
      John Evans sells Denver, South Park and Pacific to Jay Gould.

1881 AT&SF makes connection with SP at Deming, New Mexico.
      Tom Scott sells Texas and Pacific to Jay Gould.
      D&RG crosses Marshall Pass and reaches Gunnison, Colorado.
      AT&SF and Texas and Pacific join rails at Sierra Blanca, Texas.

1882 Denver, South Park and Pacific completes Alpine Tunnel.
      AT&SF completes Cañon Diablo bridge; first train to Flagstaff,
      Arizona.

1883 SP Sunset Route completed, San Francisco to New Orleans.
      Atlantic and Pacific (AT&SF) meets the SP at Needles, California.
      D&RG completes line to Ogden through Colorado.
      California Southern connects San Diego and San Bernardino.

1884 Georgetown Loop completed by Jay Gould.

1885 California Southern builds line over Cajon Pass.

1887 AT&SF joins the Gulf, Colorado and Santa Fe to its system.
      AT&SF builds its own line from Kansas City to Chicago.
      AT&SF completes its own line into Los Angeles.

1889 William Barstow Strong leaves presidency of AT&SF.

1890 Reporter Nellie Bly races from San Francisco to Chicago via SP and
      AT&SF.

1892 AT&SF inaugurates California Limited, Chicago to Los Angeles.

1893 Panic of 1893 forces many railroads into receivership.

1895 Edward Payson Ripley becomes president of AT&SF.

1897 SP and AT&SF swap the Sonora and Mojave lines.
       First section of double track laid on AT&SF in Kansas.

1898 AT&SF acquires the San Francisco and San Joaquin.

1900 E. H. Harriman acquires control of SP from Huntington estate.

1901 George Gould acquires control of D&RG.

1905 El Tovar Hotel and Hopi House open to rave reviews at Grand
       Canyon.
       Walter "Death Valley Scotty" Scott rockets from Los Angeles to
       Chicago.

1908 AT&SF completes Belen Cutoff, final link in Los Angeles–Chicago
       straightaway.

The Kansas prairie was largely treeless and trodden mostly by Plains Indians and vanishing buffalo herds when the Union Pacific, Eastern Division, pushed west of Hayes, Kansas; the date is October 19, 1867. *(Kansas State Historical Society, Alexander Gardner photo)*

Part I

Opening Gambits

(1853–1874)

*If the section of which I am a citizen has the best route, I ask who
that looks to the interest of the country has a right to deny to it the road?
If it has not, let it go where nature says it should be made.*

—SENATOR JEFFERSON DAVIS
TO THE UNITED STATES SENATE, DECEMBER 14, 1858

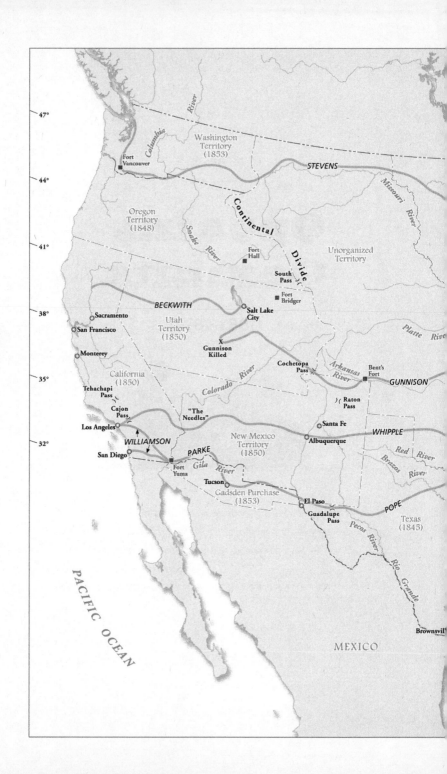

General Routes of the
Pacific Railroad Surveys
of 1853

1

Lines upon the Map

T he wind makes a mournful moan as it roars through the canyons and arroyos of West Texas. But on the afternoon of September 28, 1858, a new sound pierced the air. The tinny call of a bugle announced the impending arrival of the first westbound Butterfield Overland Mail stagecoach at the Pinery Station near the crest of 5,534-foot Guadalupe Pass.

Eighteen months earlier, Congress had authorized the postmaster general to establish regular overland mail service between San Francisco and the Mississippi River. When bids were opened, the route was awarded to John Butterfield for the then staggering sum of $600,000 per year. The *New York Times* promptly termed the entire enterprise a waste of government money.

Butterfield's contract required twice-weekly service and a transcontinental schedule of twenty-five days or less. The 2,795-mile route converged from St. Louis and Memphis at Fort Smith, Arkansas, and then dipped south across Texas, the Gila River country, and Southern California before swinging north to San Francisco. The Pinery was but one of 141 stations that Butterfield initially constructed to accommodate the numerous horses, mules, stagecoaches, and men required to put the line into operation.

When the coach creaked to a halt at the Pinery that September day, a sole passenger alighted and brushed the alkali dust from his clothes. If the station workers eyed him as an eastern dude, they were right. His name was Waterman Lily Ormsby III, and he was a twenty-three-year-old special correspondent for the *New York Herald.* He had been enticed west by John Butterfield to record the glories of transcontinental mail service. Butterfield himself had elected to depart the inaugural run at Fort Smith.

While four fresh mules were attached to the coach, Ormsby wolfed down a hasty meal of venison and baked beans. Then the young newsman climbed back inside. The driver and conductor remounted their swaying perch, and with a flick of the reins they bounced westward across Guadalupe Pass.

That evening, as Ormsby's coach descended the pass, there was a commotion on the trail ahead. The first eastbound coach from San Francisco came into sight and pulled to a stop alongside its westbound twin. After historic pleasantries, both drivers urged their teams forward in their respective directions at speeds averaging five miles an hour.[1]

Brief though it was, this encounter proved that the American coasts had been joined—however tenuously—and the neophyte Butterfield Overland Mail unleashed a huge national appetite for transcontinental connections. Whether by stagecoach, Pony Express, or iron rails, this obsession with bridging the continent would consume the American nation for the next century.

Only a half century before John Butterfield's enterprise, the American West was largely unmapped. Native Americans in much of the region lived a seminomadic lifestyle with fluid territorial boundaries. These changed over the years with intertribal warfare and pressures stirred by newcomers chased out of their indigenous homelands east of the Mississippi.

By the 1820s, the rivers flowing eastward from the Rocky Mountains had become trails into their midst. Mountain men trapping beaver were followed by traders—the risk-taking entrepreneurs of their day—who forced groaning wagons loaded with goods along the river valleys. Among the earliest and most famous of these routes was the Santa Fe Trail linking Independence, Missouri, and Santa Fe, New Mexico.

But as the Santa Fe trade swelled during the 1830s, the problem in the eyes of many Americans was that Santa Fe and the entire Southwest, from California to Texas, belonged to Mexico. Once the Republic of Texas was born in 1836, this decidedly American presence looked covetously at Santa Fe and the land beyond.

The tide of American expansionism running westward along the Santa Fe Trail soon exploded under the banner of Manifest Destiny. When the Mexican-American War ended in 1848, the Mexican provinces of Upper California and New Mexico—essentially, the future American states of California, Nevada, Arizona, New Mexico, Utah, and more than half of Colorado—belonged to the United States.

Some thought the new territory quite worthless. Others who had been in the vanguard to Santa Fe or lusted in a similar vein for California knew better. Now the race to build an empire here would not be between Americans and Mexicans but among Americans themselves.

Mountain men and traders found the routes into the Rockies, but it was a succession of military topographers who put those routes down on paper as lines upon the map of the West. It did not take long for visionaries to see those lines as logical extensions of the railroads that were beginning to extend their spidery webs about the East.

To show the importance the federal government placed on such mapping, the U.S. Army Corps of Topographical Engineers was established in 1838 and put on equal footing with the army's other departments. Its first major project was the survey of the new border between the United States and Mexico after the Treaty of Guadalupe Hidalgo ended the Mexican-American War. The man who knew this country as well as anyone was Major William H. Emory, who had ridden west as a topographical engineer at the war's outbreak.

Even then, Emory was thinking far ahead. "The road from Santa Fe to Fort Leavenworth [Kansas]," Emory reported, "presents few obstacles for a railway, and if it continues as good to the Pacific, will be one of the routes to be considered over which the United States will pass immense quantities of merchandise into what may become, in time, the rich and populous states of Sonora, Durango, and Southern California."[2]

Reaching California, Emory confirmed that as a transportation corridor, the route west from Santa Fe did indeed "continue as good to the Pacific." His resulting map of the Southwest showed a moderate, all-weather railroad route linking the Great Plains and Southern California along the still-nebulous U.S.-Mexican border.

Such a railroad was deemed by many to be essential to holding on to the fruits of the recent war. "The consequences of such a road are immense," Colonel John J. Abert, the taciturn, no-nonsense chief of the Topographical Engineers, asserted. "Unless some easy, cheap, and rapid means of communicating with these distant provinces be accomplished, there is danger, great danger, that they will not constitute parts of our Union."[3]

But as the boundary survey neared completion, Emory and certain southern politicians argued that the most promising railroad route to California lay along the 32nd parallel—decidedly south of the proposed international border. One of the southern politicians who held that view was among Emory's closest friends, both from their family connections and from their days together at West Point. His name was Jefferson Davis.

In 1845 Davis had won a seat in the U.S. House of Representatives as a Democrat from Mississippi. When war with Mexico broke out, he resigned from Congress and accepted command of a regiment of Mississippi volunteers. Davis returned wounded but a hero and was appointed to a vacancy in the United States Senate. But Davis supported states' rights so staunchly that he soon tendered another resignation and returned to Mississippi to run unsuccessfully for governor as a States Rights Democrat.

When Democrat Franklin Pierce of New Hampshire won the presidency in 1852, he appointed Davis his secretary of war in an effort to balance his cabinet geographically and reunite the Democratic Party politically. As secretary of war, Davis was immediately involved in two controversies: remedying the geographic deficiencies of the Treaty of Guadalupe Hidalgo and surveying routes for a transcontinental railroad.

Driven by proponents of Emory's recommended railroad route along the 32nd parallel, U.S. ambassador to Mexico James Gadsden succeeded in purchasing from Mexico the southwestern corner of New Mexico and the southern watershed of the Gila River in what is now southern Arizona. The Gadsden Purchase stoked political controversies on both sides of the border, but at least it was a decisive event. The railroad surveys would prove to be an entirely different matter.

Even before the dust of the Mexican-American War settled, railroad conventions with all the best chamber-of-commerce trappings had been held in key cities up and down the Mississippi Valley. Each would-be metropolis espoused itself the only logical choice for the eastern terminus of a transcontinental railroad. In reality, the competition among Mississippi Valley locales was already round three of America's railroad sweepstakes.

When the iron horse was new in the 1830s, the East Coast cities of Boston, New York, Philadelphia, Baltimore, Charleston, and Savannah competed to become the first railroad hubs. In the 1840s, with railroad technology here to stay, the inland cities west of the Appalachian Mountains—Buffalo, Pittsburgh, Wheeling, Cincinnati, Chicago, Detroit, Nashville, Chattanooga, and Atlanta—lobbied hard to become the next hubs in the spreading web of steel. By the 1850s, it was the would-be Mississippi Valley hubs of Minneapolis, Davenport, St. Louis, Cairo (Illinois), Memphis, Vicksburg, Natchez, and New Orleans that all wanted to sit astride railroads leading still farther west.[4]

Each city and corresponding geographic route had its particular political champion. Senator Stephen Douglas of Illinois liked the idea of the Great Lakes as an eastern terminal and wanted the rail line to run west from Chicago to Davenport, Council Bluffs, and across the plains to Wyoming's South Pass. The Memphis Railroad Convention of October 1849 wholeheartedly declared its support for a route from that city west across Arkansas and Texas. A Missouri faction led by Congressman John S. Phelps wanted Springfield in the southwestern part of that state as the gateway to a route that would run west across Indian Territory to Santa Fe.

St. Louis interests were well represented by Senator Thomas Hart Benton, who for decades had trumpeted Missouri as the logical gateway to the West via the central Rockies. The St. Louis Railroad Convention heard the indomitable Benton urge Congress to build a western railroad and do so in order to have "the Bay of San Francisco at one end, St. Louis in the middle, and the national metropolis and great commercial emporium at the other end."[5] And on it went.

With such hometown boosterism and concomitant sectional rivalries, it was little wonder that a national railroad bill got nowhere in the United States Congress. This was despite the presumption—often rebutted in antebellum days—that *national* interest should come first in such matters. Part of the reason for the strong sectional rivalries that attached themselves to the vigorous debate about a transcontinental route was that even the most visionary assumed there would be only *one* western railroad—*one* railroad that would make or break the geographic section it embraced or bypassed.

So when after lengthy debate Congress finally passed the Pacific Railroad Survey Act on March 2, 1853, it was not to designate one grand railroad to the Pacific but to authorize extensive explorations along the contested routes. Secretary of War Jefferson Davis was charged with ordering army expeditions into the field and completing the gargantuan task within eleven months.[6]

By looking at the routes through the eyes of the Corps of Topographical Engineers, Congress hoped—as did Davis—that one route would emerge with qualities so apparent as to stifle sectional rivalries. Thus, the surveys "promised to substitute the impartial judgment of science for the passions of the politicos and the promoters."[7]

The great equalizer in this impartial judgment was to be grade, the yardstick by which all railroad routes are ultimately measured. Grade is a critical limiting factor in railroad operations because locomotives simply stagger to a halt if they are unable to pull their load up a particular incline. The lower the grade, the more efficiently loads can be moved along it. Consequently, finding the most direct route with the lowest possible grade was the key to building a competitive railroad.[8]

Jefferson Davis couldn't be sure, but based on everything that William Emory had already reported, there was an excellent chance that their favored southern route would outshine them all. Davis promptly tapped Emory to oversee the surveys. Given the unrealistic timetable and the vast terrain to be covered, these efforts became general reconnaissance surveys rather than mile-by-mile grade surveys. Still, by the standards of the day, they were costly undertakings. Congress appropriated an initial $150,000, added $40,000 a year later, and then put another $150,000 on the table to complete the work and publish the reports.[9]

Emory saw to it that in addition to army topographers and engineers, each contingent included a wide array of scientists: anthropologists, botanists, cartographers, geographers, geologists, meteorologists, paleontologists, and zoologists, as well as illustrators and artists. "Not since Napoleon had taken his company of savants into Egypt," historian William H. Goetzmann later observed, "had the world seen such an assemblage of scientists and technicians marshaled under one banner."[10]

Initially, four parties were dispatched along specific parallels of latitude: the northern route between the 47th and 49th parallels leading west from St. Paul, Minnesota, to the upper Missouri; a south-central route up the Arkansas River through the central Rockies to the Great Salt Lake along the 38th parallel; the 35th parallel route from Fort Smith, Arkansas, to Albuquerque, northern Arizona, and California; and investigations in California for passes through the Sierras between the 32nd and 35th parallels.

There were two obvious omissions. No work was ordered on Stephen Douglas's proposed north-central line from Council Bluffs to South Pass or on Davis and Emory's favored line along the 32nd parallel. In the final report of the surveys, Davis himself brushed off the absence of work on the South Pass route and merely referenced the earlier reports of surveyors John C. Frémont and Howard Stansbury through that general vicinity.[11]

As to the southern route, perhaps Davis thought that Emory's work had already identified the merits of the 32nd parallel. Perhaps he simply delayed sending a contingent to this area while negotiations for the Gadsden Purchase were under way. Davis may even have wanted to demonstrate some measure of sectional impartiality by dispatching the northern expeditions first. Whatever the reasons, it was October 1853 before Davis ordered a two-prong look at the 32nd parallel. So, amidst the politics, the parties took to the field in the summer of 1853 to see if science could declare a sure winner in the transcontinental sweepstakes.

.   .   .

If there was any survey commander apt to be overly biased in favor of his appointed route, it was Isaac I. Stevens, formerly an officer in the Corps of Engineers but now, thanks to political connections with President Pierce, the freshly appointed governor of newly created Washington Territory. Stevens was charged with examining the northern route and ultimately linking the watersheds of the Missouri and Columbia rivers. While the governor's main party moved westward from St. Paul across Minnesota, the Dakota plains, and the headwaters of the Missouri, a detachment under Captain George B. McClellan probed the Cascade Mountains at the western end of the route.

Following in the footsteps of Lewis and Clark, Stevens located possible passes across the Continental Divide and then met up with McClellan's troops in the Bitterroot Valley south of what would later become Missoula, Montana. Young McClellan, who would go on to frustrate Abraham Lincoln as his dilatory commander of the Army of the Potomac during the Civil War, showed his lifelong disposition to glory without risk when he decidedly overestimated the snow depth on passes through the Cascades and twice refused to cross them. Civilian engineers subsequently made the trips without incident.[12]

Stevens's command numbered more than two hundred and was by far the largest of the parallel surveys. And, as might have been expected, given his political appointment, the governor's report was the most enthusiastic. When it came to reporting any negatives, Stevens was decidedly understated if not outright misleading. The new governor went so far as to assert that the snow here "would not present the slightest impediment to the passage of railroad trains."[13]

In the end, this unbridled boosterism hurt the credibility of the Stevens survey, and many agreed with the expedition naturalist George Suckley, who noted, "the Governor is a very ambitious man and knows very well that his political fortunes are wrapped up in the success of the railroad making its Pacific terminus in his own territory."[14] It would be a while before railroads followed the Stevens route to the Northwest.

Governor Stevens's large entourage was definitely the exception and not the rule. Captain John W. Gunnison, an 1837 graduate of West Point and one of Colonel Abert's topographical engineers, led a company west along the 38th parallel that numbered several dozen men, among them Lieutenant E. G. Beckwith and civilian artist R. H. Kern.

This was the south-central route so ardently championed by Thomas Hart Benton and the one upon which Benton's son-in-law, John C. Frémont, had already met with disaster when his party got lost in the San Juan Mountains of Colorado in the winter of 1848–49. Gunnison's key goal was to find a railroad pass through or around the San Juans in the vicinity of Frémont's wintry ordeal.

Gunnison was no stranger to the West. In 1849 he had accompanied Captain Howard Stansbury along the Platte River trails from Fort Leavenworth to Fort Bridger in the western reaches of Wyoming. Stansbury was under orders to survey the area between Fort Bridger and the Great Salt Lake, giving particular emphasis to the gold rush trails leading westward across the Great Basin to California.

On their return east the next year, Stansbury and Gunnison struck a beeline across southern Wyoming, well south of their outbound trace along the established trails over South Pass. In the process, they crossed the wide open flats of the Great Divide Desert, snaked between the Laramie and Medicine Bow mountains, and emerged on the high plains near the upper reaches of Lodgepole Creek, a tributary of the South Platte.

Stansbury and Gunnison didn't know it at the time, but in extensively mapping the Great Salt Lake Basin and investigating a transportation corridor directly eastward from there, they had done on a small scale what the topographical engineers would soon be ordered to do throughout the West.[15]

In 1853 Captain Gunnison was supervising harbor improvements in Milwaukee when he received orders to head west again. He led his men from Fort Leavenworth and up the Arkansas River, eventually crossing Sangre de Cristo Pass into Colorado's San Luis Valley. The view from the crest of the Sangre de Cristo Mountains made it clear that any route directly west led into the labyrinth of the San Juan Mountains. Frémont had already been there and floundered.

Instead Gunnison and his party followed a Ute Indian trail that ran toward the low hills between the northern end of the San Juans and the high points of Mount Antora and Mount Ouray. At first it seemed too good to be true. The approach "by the Sahwatch creek," noted the expedition report, "opens very favorably for the construction of a railroad."

The gentle grades continued, and the column crossed the Continental Divide atop 10,032-foot Cochetopa Pass, said to mean "pass of the buffalo" in Ute. But the ease of this crossing on September 2, 1853, was deceptive of the terrain that lay ahead.[16]

From Cochetopa Pass, the route led down the river that would soon bear Gunnison's name. When the river disappeared into a deep and dark canyon—"Black Canyon" would be an apt description—the party crossed the Blue Mesa and Cerro Summit divides and descended into the arid Uncompahgre Valley.

By now Gunnison had his doubts about the feasibility of a railroad through such terrain. "For a railroad route," Gunnison wrote of his course through central Colorado, "it is far inferior to the Middle Central [route] by Medicine Bow River and the Laramie plains" and would require an "enormous expense" of tunneling, bridging, and spanning gullies. So skeptical did Gunnison become of the Colorado route that he noted it would have been "a waste of labor to add even a crude estimate of the cost of so impracticable an undertaking."[17]

But an even deadlier blow than Gunnison's frank assessment struck Benton's 38th parallel dream as the Gunnison party crossed the deserts of Utah. Early on the morning of October 26, in the valley of the Sevier River, Paiute Indians, who had recently been victimized by a California-bound wagon train, attacked the survey party. Gunnison, Kern, and six others were killed.

Lieutenant Beckwith did an admirable job of salvaging the expedition, but the tragedy overshadowed its results. After wintering in Salt Lake City, Beckwith surveyed passes through the Wasatch Mountains to the Wyoming plains, tying into the route that Stansbury and Gunnison had taken east in 1850. Then Beckwith continued westward across the Great Basin along the 41st parallel all the way to California.

Combining this route with Stansbury and Gunnison's earlier reconnaissance across southern Wyoming and comparing it to the eventual route of the Union Pacific and Central Pacific railroads shows Beckwith to be about as prescient as anyone could possibly be. His achievement, however, caused little stir at the time.

For one thing, the expedition's star topographer, Captain Gunnison, lay dead. For another, the strongest proponent of the 38th parallel route, Thomas Hart Benton, was not pleased that the party detailed to confirm his choice should end up espousing a route so far north. Finally, Beckwith was an artilleryman with little topographic training, and he did not include construction cost estimates in his final report because Gunnison himself had questioned their worth.

So with Gunnison's own words damning the Cochetopa Pass–38th parallel route through Colorado, and with Beckwith lacking the political and scientific clout to champion the southern Wyoming–41st parallel route, this survey, too, failed to rise above the others.[18]

Command of the third major survey—the 35th parallel between Fort Smith and California via Albuquerque and the pueblos of the Zuni Indians—was given to another topographical engineer, Lieutenant Amiel W. Whipple. Initially this route may have been more important politically than it was geographically. If the topography of this route proved at all acceptable, it might offer the perfect political compromise between north and south.

The 35th parallel route was far enough south that the various southern interests championing Springfield (Missouri), Memphis, Vicksburg, and New Orleans might be willing to rally behind it. Stephen Douglas and the Chicago crowd might be placated because the Illinois Central Railroad running from Chicago to points south would likely connect with any eastern terminus as a north-south feeder line. Senator Benton would grumble and thunder, of course, but even he would find it preferable to a more northerly route than the one he advocated. What might convince supporters of the extreme northern route to support it was evidence that Governor Stevens's assessment of snow conditions in the Northern Rockies and Cascades was overly optimistic.

So Lieutenant Whipple's party traipsed west from Fort Smith, Arkansas, in July 1853, staffed with the normal contingent of surveyors and scientists. The initial leg between Fort Smith and Albuquerque along the Canadian River was by now both well known and well traveled as a southern alternative to the Santa Fe Trail. The real questions lay west of Albuquerque.

Joined by an additional escort commanded by Lieutenant Joseph C. Ives, the combined party marched west from Albuquerque and then picked its way along the Little Colorado River, across a divide south of the San Francisco Peaks, and down the Bill Williams River to the main Colorado River. It was a route that steered well clear of the yawning Grand Canyon a short distance to the north.

From the mouth of the Bill Williams River, Whipple turned north and crossed the Colorado near spindly rock pinnacles called "the Needles." Then the column struck west across the Mojave Desert and eventually came upon the Old Spanish Trail, which it followed south across Cajon Pass. Lieutenant Robert S. Williamson had already scouted Cajon Pass as part of his survey work in California and pronounced it difficult for a railroad. Whipple concurred, but overall he was quite pleased with the 35th parallel route.

Compared to the overt boosterism of Governor Stevens for the northern route and Captain Gunnison's decided disdain for the central Colorado Rockies, Whipple's report was well balanced. Recognizing that a more detailed analysis of his findings was required, even Whipple, however, could not refrain from being caught up in the excitement of a possible railroad.

"There is no doubt remaining," he concluded, "that, for the construction of a railway, the route we have passed over is not only practicable, but, in many respects, eminently advantageous." The main drawback seemed to be Whipple's highly inflated cost estimate: a whopping $169 million, almost double later revised numbers.[19]

That left Jefferson Davis's and William Emory's first love: the southern route along the 32nd parallel. For reasons already mentioned, Davis was slow in commanding a more detailed look at this terrain. With time running out in the fall of 1853, he divided the task between two parties. The western half fell to Lieutenant John G. Parke, who had been assisting Lieutenant Williamson in scouting California passes.

Receiving his orders a few days before Christmas 1853, Parke led fifty-eight men east to survey the southern tributaries of the Gila River. In general, Parke stayed well south of the main river and passed through Tucson and the Chiricahua Mountains—American territory subsequent to the signing of the Gadsden Purchase treaty.

By the time Parke reached the Rio Grande, he confirmed Emory's first impression of this pathway and reported generally gentle terrain without the rigors of high mountain passes or steep grades. The major drawbacks to the route were a lack of timber for construction and water for operating thirsty steam locomotives. Parke recommended that experiments to drill artesian wells be commenced immediately.[20]

The eastern half of the southern route was left to Kentuckian John Pope. Leaving the Rio Grande near present-day Las Cruces, New Mexico, on February 12, 1854, Pope's first order of exploration was to find a suitable pass through the Guadalupe Mountains. Two and a half weeks later, the terrain became rocky as the route wound up a narrow canyon. But Guadalupe Pass proved short, and "from the summit, the view over the surrounding country was at once grand and picturesque—the southern peak of the Guadalupe [El Capitan] towering majestically above all." By nightfall, Pope and his men were encamped at a green oasis they called "the Pinery," thankful that there was "an abundance of everything requisite for camping at this place."[21]

East of the Guadalupes, Pope kept to the southern edge of the vast mesas of the Llano Estacado and made for the Red River, some 50 miles north of the hamlet of Dallas. Pope found conditions similar to those in the western section. The grades were quite manageable. The arid plains would have to be tapped with artesian wells, but the climate was milder and less fickle than along the northern routes.

Perhaps because he understood the political benefits of Lieutenant Whipple's 35th parallel route, Pope noted that an eastern terminus of the 32nd parallel route at Fulton, Arkansas (in the extreme southwest corner of the state), might just as easily satisfy the various interests of Cairo, Memphis, Vicksburg, and New Orleans.[22]

Indeed, the only major drawback to the southern route came from the work that Lieutenant Williamson conducted in California. It seemed that there was no easy direct route between Yuma, at the mouth of the Gila on the Colorado River, and the port of San Diego. This meant that the California portion of the southern line might end up running along Lieutenant Whipple's Mojave route and thus make sleepy Los Angeles its western terminus rather than San Diego.

So what had the surveys accomplished? Their stated goal had been to find the most practical and economical route for a railroad from the

Mississippi to the Pacific Ocean. Despite all that was learned about the western landscape, science did not provide one clear and overriding choice of railroad route. Because it did not—perhaps could not—the issue of a western railroad was thrown back into the cauldron of sectional rivalries that was slowly coming to a boil. Before steel rails were laid far west of the Mississippi, there would be war.

One of the few who might have stopped it—or at least removed the transcontinental railroad question from the list of fractious issues—was Jefferson Davis. With New Englander Franklin Pierce as his presidential ally, might Davis have been able to broker a compromise that joined his fellow southerners with Stephen Douglas's Illinois interests in support of the 35th parallel route?

It is an intriguing question. In 1858, when once more a senator from Mississippi, Davis appears to have eschewed the sectional politics of the issue, although by then it was too late. "In Congress, with all due respect to my associates," Davis told the Senate, "I must say the location of this road will be a political question. It should be a question of engineering, a commercial question, a governmental question—not a question of partisan advantage, or of sectional success in a struggle between parties and sections."

Congress's attempting to fix a route, Davis argued, "revives political dissensions and sectional warfare, of which, we surely have enough on other questions. If the section of which I am a citizen has the best route, I ask who that looks to the interest of the country has a right to deny to it the road? If it has not, let it go where nature says it should be made."[23]

The results of the surveys were initially published in 1855 in a three-volume summary and then in a complete report of thirteen volumes. Save for the deceased Captain Gunnison, the major participants were all strong advocates for their own routes. Turned loose to resolve a political debate, the topographers and scientists of the surveys fanned it further with their individual enthusiasms. But they put the lines down upon the map of the West, and in time, transcontinental railroads would be built along them.

And despite its inability to agree on *one* railroad route to the Pacific, Congress took a significant step toward tying together the country's far-flung coasts when it authorized regular overland mail service. The highest of the stations that winning bidder John Butterfield built to operate the line was at the Pinery—the desert oasis that John Pope's men found so inviting beneath the sentinel of Guadalupe Peak. John Butterfield, however, was not the only one looking to span the continent.

2

Learning the Rails

Leipsic, Delaware, was an unlikely place for a mountain railroader to be born, but Quaker roots ran deep there and nurtured in the townspeople an inner strength and quiet self-assurance. In 1836, at Kinsale Farm on the outskirts of town, Matilda Jackson Palmer gave birth to her first son, who was christened William Jackson—a good Quaker name matched with her own maiden name.

When William Jackson Palmer was five, his family moved to what were then the outskirts of Philadelphia. In 1840 greater Philadelphia was the second largest urban area in the country and no stranger to the acrimonious abolitionist debates already percolating throughout the North. The Palmers' circle of friends included many ardent abolitionists, among them Charles Ellet, Jr., one of the most accomplished civil engineers of the day.

In 1853 Ellet's work as chief engineer of the Hempfield Railroad got young Palmer his first job, that of a rod man on a surveying party locating the line. Later gobbled up by the Baltimore and Ohio Railroad, the Hempfield was being built in southwestern Pennsylvania to serve that region's developing coal mines.

"Nothing stops us," Palmer reported to a boyhood friend, "for a railroad line must be a straight one . . . it cannot avoid a hill or go round a pond or choose its own walking. It must tramp right over the one and ford the other and walk by the points of the compass."[1]

Palmer's apprenticeship on the Hempfield Railroad lasted two years. In the spring of 1855, when he was eighteen, his mother's brother, Frank H. Jackson, appears to have been his chief sponsor in loaning funds and arranging a trip to England and the Continent. Palmer's letters of introduction included one from J. Edgar Thomson of the Pennsylvania Railroad.

The chief engineer of the London and North Western Railway was a large shareholder of the Pennsylvania Railroad, and, thanks to Thomson's letter, he gave Palmer the freedom of the road. The young man made the most of it, "spending the time principally on the locomotives, and in visiting towns and famous places along the line."

By the time Palmer returned to the United States in June 1856, the satisfaction of railroading that he had first experienced on the Hempfield was thick in his blood. After a brief stint with the Westmoreland Coal Company, twenty-one-year-old William Jackson Palmer went to work for J. Edgar Thomson as his confidential secretary at the then generous salary of $900 a year.[2]

If one sought a mentor in building fledgling railroad systems, it would have been difficult if not impossible to find one more astute than J. Edgar Thomson. Born in 1808 in Delaware County, Pennsylvania, Thomson learned engineering from his father, a civil engineer who counted among his credits work on the Delaware and Chesapeake Canal.

Early on, young Thomson showed a genius for planning and an eager curiosity about anything new. Through his father's influence, he cut his teeth on the preliminary surveys for the Philadelphia and Columbia Railroad and by the age of twenty-two was in charge of locating the line of the Camden and Amboy Railroad across New Jersey. After more formal civil and mechanical engineering studies in Great Britain, Thomson became chief engineer of the Georgia Railroad, which proposed to build west across Georgia.

Clearly seeing the future, Thomson pointed the railroad toward the isolated, upland cotton country in the northern part of the state. The tiny town of Thomson just west of Augusta was named for him, but better known is the town site that he laid out as the western terminus of the Georgia Railroad. It became the transportation hub of the inland Deep South and retained the name that Thomson gave it: Atlanta.[3]

Meanwhile, Philadelphia was determined to retain its position as the commercial hub of the mid-Atlantic states. Between 1830 and 1835, more railroad construction was undertaken in Pennsylvania than in any other state. By and large, this construction was in short lines that linked would-be metropolises, without much thought to a unified statewide system.

This provincial planning began to change when the Pennsylvania Railroad was incorporated on April 13, 1846. The choice of a chief engineer was easy, and J. Edgar Thomson returned north to assume responsibility for the railroad's construction and direction. No matter how daunting the terrain or how queasy the financiers, Thomson came up with a simple refrain: Build west, build west, build west.

On September 1, 1849, the Pennsylvania Railroad inaugurated service on its first section between Harrisburg and Lewistown, 60 miles to the west. A year later, Thomson had succeeded in pushing the line a similar distance west to Hollidaysburg—soon to be dwarfed by Altoona. There it connected with the Allegheny Portage Railroad.

To Thomson, the moves on the chessboard were clear. He was determined to complete a unified system of railroads between Philadelphia and Pittsburgh and in the process thwart the rival Baltimore and Ohio to the south and the New York Central to the north in a race for the Ohio River country and, in time, Chicago itself.

When Thomson found his vision of a "great national enterprise" at odds with more parochial views of a road "built by the business community for the benefit of trade," it was Thomson who prevailed. The shareholders of the Pennsylvania Railroad elected a slate of directors supportive of Thomson, and they unanimously elected him to the Pennsylvania's presidency, a post he would hold for the next twenty-two years.

By the time William Jackson Palmer came under Thomson's tutelage, the Pennsylvania was beginning to gobble up little branch lines with what would become an insatiable appetite. On July 18, 1858, a Pennsylvania Railroad train rode its own tracks all the way from Philadelphia to Pittsburgh.[4]

Another Thomson protégé in the thick of the Pennsylvania Railroad's expansion was Thomas A. Scott. Born in Franklin County, Pennsylvania, in 1823, Scott was the son of a tavern keeper at a stagecoach stop. Young Scott worked in country stores and then got a clerkship in the office of the collector of tolls for the state's system of public roads and canals. In 1850 he went to work for the Pennsylvania Railroad as a station agent at Hollidaysburg.

In the following decade, Scott rose quickly through the corporate ranks. He was soon in charge of the Allegheny Portage Railroad segment and the western division of the state canal. When Pennsylvania Railroad tracks were completed to Pittsburgh, Scott became general superintendent of the Philadelphia-Pittsburgh line. In 1860 Thomson tapped him to be vice president of the company.

Thomson himself was rather humorless and reserved. He cast the perfect image of a conservative and thoughtful corporate leader, but when it came to lobbying legislators or putting an exuberant public face on plans for expansion, Scott was the man to carry the flag. "Quick-witted, dapper, handsome, and well-met," Scott was perfect in the role of Thomson's alter ego. Much later, when Scott had arguably become a more powerful rail baron than his mentor, he would emulate Thomson's style and prefer to play a shadowy role while pulling strings through subordinates.

One of the more important lessons that Scott learned from Thomson—other than Thomson's mantra of "Build west"—was the business principle that "the best investment a thriving railroad can make of its operating profits is in *itself,* and not in large dividends." At the time, many businessmen viewed the reinvestment of profits as a rather radical step that hurt their pocketbooks, but Thomson took the longer view. Part of Scott's responsibility was to double-track heavy traffic sections of the Philadelphia-Pittsburgh main line even before it was completed to Pittsburgh.[5]

. . .

But J. Edgar Thomson, Thomas A. Scott, and William Jackson Palmer were not the only men learning the rails in Pennsylvania. Cyrus K. Holliday was born in 1826 in Carlisle, the youngest of seven children. He graduated from the Methodist enclave of Allegheny College in Meadville in 1852, expecting to become a lawyer. One of his first tasks was to prepare the incorporation papers for a branch line railroad near Meadville. Taking an equity interest in lieu of a fee, Holliday reportedly realized a profit of $20,000—a significant sum in those days—when the little line was acquired by outside interests.

Holliday resolved to look west for a place to invest his new fortune, and he made a tour of Cleveland, Chicago, and St. Louis before taking a steamboat up the Missouri River to Fort Leavenworth, Kansas Territory. By the end of 1854, he had purchased a few shares in the Lawrence Town Company, a real estate promotion to develop the town of Lawrence, but he was already looking farther west.

On New Year's Eve 1854, Holliday wrote to his wife, Mary, back in Meadville, that he had been elected president of the city association of the Topeka Land Company. Assuming the persona of an old-timer, the twenty-eight-year-old asserted to his recent bride, "You Pennsylvania people would be greatly surprised could you have a view of us as we find ourselves situated in this new territory."

Holliday confessed that he had been wearing the same shirt for two weeks and "scarcely know when I will get a clean one." But he was sold on Kansas, and he told Mary, "I would not exchange Kansas and its dirty shirt for Pennsylvania with all its elegance and refinement." Holliday devotedly wrote hundreds of letters to Mary until she eventually joined him in Topeka.

Town promotion, abolitionist politics, and a quest to make Topeka the territorial capital consumed the next few years. But railroad plans were afoot here, too, and Holliday, no doubt inspired by his early success in Pennsylvania, became convinced that a railroad linking Topeka with Atchison on the Missouri River was the key to the town's success.

In late January 1859, Holliday was in Lawrence as a member of the territorial legislature when he scribbled out a charter for the Atchison and Topeka Railroad. Well aware of wider domains, Holliday provided for its westward extension beyond Topeka in the direction of Santa Fe. The legislature approved the charter, and the territorial governor signed it on the last day of the blissfully short legislative session, February 11, 1859.

But these were tough years for Kansas. A dreadful drought and open warfare between abolitionists and slaveholders made Kansas bleed. Many settlers simply packed up and headed back east with signs proclaiming, "In God we trusted, in Kansas we busted."

Holliday persevered through these maelstroms, however, and finally, in September 1860, accompanied by future senator Edmund G. Ross and two others, he rode in a buggy from Topeka to Atchison for the organizational meeting of the Atchison and Topeka Railroad. Thirteen directors, many of them the future leaders of the state of Kansas, each subscribed $4,000 in stock. Fortunately for most, only 10 percent was to be paid immediately. Some of these would-be rail barons were so strapped for cash that Holliday elected to ford the Kansas River en route to Atchison rather than pay the ferry fee. It would be a while before iron rails crossed the Kansas prairies.[6]

Far to the west of Kansas, there was another would-be rail baron getting his first taste of the business. Collis P. Huntington was born in 1821 in Connecticut. The sixth of nine children, he left home early and wandered rather aimlessly around the East as the proverbial Yankee peddler. But the tall, broad-shouldered lad also showed his business acumen by routinely buying defaulted notes at a heavy discount. The creditor merchants were glad to get a few cents on the dollar, and Huntington frequently made money when he chanced upon the debtor in the course of his travels.

Shortly after his twenty-first birthday, Huntington settled in Oneonta, New York, and went to work for his older brother, Solon, in his general store. By 1844, the brothers were partners, and Collis purchased a little house for his new bride, Elizabeth Stoddard. Such domestic tranquility was interrupted early in 1849 when news of gold discoveries in California excited the town. Collis joined an eager group of Oneonta men and headed west, intending from the start to open a branch of the Huntington store and make his money from trade with the miners and not directly from the hills.

Anxious to get a jump on the hordes, the Oneonta group opted for the expensive passage across the Isthmus of Panama. Among the passengers on the paddle wheel steamer *Crescent City* outbound from New York was Jessie Benton Frémont, the twenty-five-year-old daughter of Senator Thomas Hart Benton and wife of explorer John C. Frémont. The only woman on board besides her six-year-old daughter and her maid, Jessie was on her way to California to rendezvous with Frémont, who, unbeknownst to her, had been delayed by his wintry ordeal in the San Juan Mountains.

There is no record that the glamorous Jessie exchanged even so much as a glance with the burly Collis, who was ensconced in steerage, but Huntington would always be among the controversial explorer's admirers. Decades later, when Huntington's railroad empire spanned many of the passes that Frémont had mapped, Huntington would gallantly assist the Frémonts on another journey.

As it was, Jessie's standing got her first-class treatment in Panama and better connections for the voyage up the West Coast. Huntington and his fellow Oneonta residents languished amidst assorted tropical fevers and dysentery. Finally, an overloaded Dutch bark, hastily converted from a coal carrier to a transport, took them north to San Francisco after a squalid 102 days at sea. A month later, in September 1849, Huntington arrived in the booming little town of Sacramento.

The first year was tough. Huntington was plagued by illness, interminable mud, and exorbitant freight costs. By the following fall, he was eastward bound, but not to turn tail and run. After a respite in Oneonta, he packed up Elizabeth, ordered more goods from wholesalers in New York, and once more headed for California via Panama. Upon hearing of the horrors of Collis's first year in Sacramento, Elizabeth had been skeptical, but even she pronounced the jungle passage "a fine trip."

But Sacramento was little improved, and the hardware business was momentarily suffering from a glut of merchandise as early placer operations in the gold fields ebbed. Huntington nonetheless managed to build a brick residence for Elizabeth, only to suffer its loss in a November 1852 fire that leveled much of downtown Sacramento.

Out of the ashes eventually came a partnership with the merchant next door, who had also suffered a loss and quickly rebuilt. The neighbor's name was Mark Hopkins and he too was a New Yorker. Eight years Huntington's elder, Hopkins was the antithesis of Huntington physically—reed thin, perhaps even scrawny—but Hopkins possessed an even sharper financial mind than did Huntington. They were a pair, and the firm of Huntington-Hopkins Hardware, which they decided to evolve from general merchandise into heavy equipment, would be just the beginning.

Among the other business ventures in Sacramento that Huntington and Hopkins watched with interest was the budding Sacramento Valley Railroad Company. The company harnessed the energies of a young engineer named Theodore Judah and in just two years managed to build from the wharves of Sacramento up the American River toward Folsom, California.

Rail service commenced on February 22, 1856, but Judah was soon dreaming of destinations beyond the Sierra Nevada foothills. On his own, he incorporated the California Central Railroad and announced that he had found a pass through the mountains that would allow it to reach Nevada—perhaps run even farther east. When San Francisco financiers showed little interest in the venture, Judah turned to Sacramento's merchants in hopes of a more favorable response.

Collis Huntington and Mark Hopkins listened to Judah's sales pitch, by one version of the story, on the second floor of Huntington-Hopkins Hardware. Two other merchants in attendance were Charles Crocker, who sold dry goods, and Leland Stanford, whose firm specialized in groceries. The four had already been working together in Republican Party politics; why not a railroad? Before the meeting broke up, Huntington, Hopkins, Crocker, and Stanford were among those agreeing to pay their share of a preliminary survey to validate Judah's proposition.[7]

Meanwhile, "confidential secretary" hardly begins to explain the nature of William Jackson Palmer's work for J. Edgar Thomson. At five foot nine, with reddish brown hair and a dapper mustache, Palmer was slight of frame and somewhat wiry. He quickly became Thomson's trusted aide and inveterate troubleshooter, overseeing a number of special assignments, including the Pennsylvania Railroad's transition from wood to coal as a fuel source for its locomotives.

Palmer built on his experiences in Great Britain and with Westmoreland Coal, and he readily experimented with this new way to increase the Pennsylvania's fuel efficiency. "The experiment made during the year 1859 with coal-burning engines," Thomson wrote in the railroad's annual report, "has demonstrated the entire practicability of substituting bituminous coal as fuel for locomotives instead of wood, providing as it does, a much more reliable article at a greatly reduced cost. In a short time all passenger trains on this road will be moved with coal-burning engines, at a saving in cost of fuel of about 50 percent."[8]

This transition to coal meant that as the Pennsylvania and other railroads pushed westward, they sought to serve areas with good coal deposits—both for their own locomotive needs and as a profitable commodity to be shipped over their developing lines to other markets.

In Thomson's behalf, Palmer made his first trip west in 1859—if only to Chicago and St. Louis. "I find the name of J. Edgar Thomson a passport wherever I go," Palmer wrote his parents, "and believe, with his letter of credit, I could travel from Maine to Texas without the unpleasant necessity of putting my hand in my pocket for the pewter."[9]

But even as the network of the Pennsylvania Railroad spread toward Chicago, J. Edgar Thomson was looking farther west. Palmer probably had a hand in a letter that Thomson drafted but for some reason never sent, urging Congress to get behind a unified Pacific Railroad plan. The intended addressee or addressees is not entirely clear, but it appears to have been Georgia congressman Alexander Stephens, with whom Thomson was probably well acquainted from his days on the Georgia Railroad.

"A railway to connect the valley of the Mississippi with the Pacific Ocean, passing through the territory of the United States, must now be viewed by every thinking person as a great national necessity," the draft began. "To secure the completion of such an enterprise within a reasonable period, the aid of the general government seems to me to be essential, and cannot be longer withheld, without a sacrifice of the best interests of the country."

Recognizing the obvious, Thomson continued: "It is alleged that sectional interests prevent action at this session of Congress upon any particular route and that the credit of the Nation would scarcely be sufficient to compass the construction of all the lines that have been proposed."

There was, however, a solution, Thomson maintained. "Fortunately for the early completion of this national thoroughfare," there was a "narrow belt of country . . . *so situated that any line traversing it, can with equal facility, accommodate the northern and southern sections of the Union*" [underlined in original].

Thus did J. Edgar Thomson argue for a line between the 32nd and 35th parallels, essentially some combination of Lieutenant Whipple's compromise route. "To ensure the early completion . . ." Thomson concluded, "a liberal capitalization of the pay for transporting the United States mails is all that is required."[10]

What motivated Thomson to draft this in the first place is debatable. Perhaps he did so as a favor to Alexander Stephens. What caused him to have second thoughts and not send it is even more problematic. Perhaps Thomson looked at the map and saw the logical extension of the Pennsylvania Railroad and its connections straight west from Chicago and lost whatever enthusiasm he may have initially professed for a compromise southern route.

Whatever Thomson's reasoning, by the following spring, Palmer was writing to his own contacts in behalf of the latest Pacific Railroad bills before Congress. "You can say to Mr. Thomson," Charles Ellet, Jr., replied to Palmer, "that if he thinks my name or aid would serve to forward the work he has on hand, I will cheerfully contribute either . . ."

Ellet weighed in on the route question by noting, "my own prepossessions are in favor of the more southern of those two routes . . . though I think that there ought to be two, and that two roads will find support by the time they can be made."[11]

But the success of even one transcontinental railroad, let alone two, was still highly in question. "Remember boys," John Butterfield had admonished his first drivers, "nothing on God's earth must stop the United States mail!" But now a number of things threatened to do just that: escalating political acrimony, still struggling new technologies, and the gathering clouds of civil war.

"We think ourselves fast," Palmer wrote to a friend in March 1861, "but those to come after us, will rank us 'slow old coaches,' and wonder how we ever were satisfied to creep along at 30 miles an hour behind such lumbering old machines . . ."[12] In time, the political uncertainties would be resolved and the technological frontiers pushed wildly with unbridled determination, but first there would have to be an interruption of war.

3

An Interruption of War

The drumbeats of sectional rivalry that had been heard in the debate over a transcontinental railroad route became a call to arms when South Carolina seceded from the Union in December 1860. A banner headline in the *Charleston Mercury* screamed the news—"The Union Is Dissolved"—while out in Charleston Harbor, a garrison of seventy-odd Union artillery troops under the command of Major Robert Anderson awaited its fate.

Confederate batteries led by fiery Pierre Gustave Toutant Beauregard began a bombardment of Fort Sumter on April 12, 1861. Two days later, Major Anderson, who had once been Beauregard's artillery instructor at West Point, surrendered the post. Meanwhile, Jefferson Davis, whose call for reason over politics had gone unheeded when it came to selecting a transcontinental railroad route, had been elected president of the Confederate States of America.

The outbreak of war had an immediate impact on the Pennsylvania Railroad. William Jackson Palmer's high-level errand-running for

J. Edgar Thomson suddenly became much more dangerous. Maryland's status as a border state was tenuous at best, and Southern sympathies ran high there. When normal communications and train traffic through the state were disrupted, Thomson feared that Washington, DC, would become totally isolated from the North.

"The suspension of intercourse between this place [Philadelphia] and Washington," Thomson wrote Lincoln's secretary of war, Simon Cameron, "has caused an intense feeling here in relation to the safety of the capital, and there is great eagerness to rush to its assistance."[1]

Thomson offered the full services of his railroad to the federal government, but orders for troop displacements were painfully slow in coming. Noting the lack of troops moving south from Philadelphia despite his arrangements for transporting five regiments per day, Thomson grew caustic. "We infer from this," he scolded Cameron, "that you must feel entirely safe at Annapolis and at Washington."[2]

Meanwhile, Cameron was busy raiding Thomson's corporate pocket for talent. Because telegraph lines were down, Palmer hand-carried a dispatch from Cameron to Thomas A. Scott, the Pennsylvania Railroad's vice president. Cameron wanted Scott's managerial skills in the War Department, and within days, Scott was assistant secretary of war for transportation. He soon became the Union army's railroad czar.

"This morning we open three daily passenger lines to and from Baltimore," Scott wrote Palmer shortly thereafter, "also one daily freight train—from all of which you will perceive that the U.S. Military Routes are progressing towards the P.R.R. [Pennsylvania Railroad] standard."[3]

As the railroads struggled with their new roles, the nation as a whole—both blue and gray—found that there would be no quick end to the war. Cries of "On to Richmond!" aside, General Irvin McDowell's neophyte Union army smacked into the stone wall of Jackson and his compatriots at a creek called Bull Run and was sent fleeing back to Washington. Realization sunk in that this would not be a short family quarrel but rather the testing piece of a generation.

William Jackson Palmer reluctantly put aside his Quaker upbringing and recruited a special troop of cavalry from among the gentlemen class of Pennsylvania. And who better to identify with than that hero of Fort Sumter, Major Anderson? Thus was born the Anderson Troop.

Palmer wrote to his circle of friends throughout Pennsylvania and to business associates of J. Edgar Thomson, urging them to nominate suitable young men for the outfit. While he originally disclaimed interest in the position, Palmer, to no one's surprise, was elected captain of the troop.[4]

Their first battle came soon enough. Early in 1862, Ulysses S. Grant began a concerted drive south up the Tennessee River. Fort Henry fell to him, and the capture of Fort Donelson on the Cumberland River earned him the sobriquet "Unconditional Surrender." With the lower Cumberland in Union hands, Palmer and the Anderson Troop went with General Don Carlos Buell's headquarters staff to Nashville.

As Grant plunged onward toward the critical rail junction of Corinth, Mississippi, Buell's Army of the Ohio moved south from Nashville to protect his left flank. The climax came on April 6 at a little church called Shiloh, a stone's throw from Pittsburg Landing on the Tennessee River. While Palmer's cavalry saw no direct action, Palmer averred as to how "Buell has undoubtedly saved Grant's army," albeit with frightful losses on both sides.[5]

Until Shiloh, the horror of what the war would become had not yet sunk into the national consciousness. Despite the war—both boldly and perhaps a little naively—the United States Congress resolved to do in war what it had been unable to do in peace.

Old-line Whigs and new Republicans in the North had long advocated the expenditure of federal dollars for what were characterized as "internal improvements": roads, canals, and river and harbor facilities. The Republican Party platforms of 1856 and 1860 added railroads to this category and not only called for a railroad to the Pacific but also urged government aid in its construction. In 1860 Democrats also supported a railroad to the Pacific, but the party maintained its longstanding opposition to the direct use of federal dollars for the effort, particularly if the route was to be one of the more northerly choices.

Now, relieved of southern Democrats, the remaining Republican majority in Congress once again considered the construction of a transcontinental railroad. Colonel John J. Abert's 1849 assertion that the "integrity of the Union" demanded such a road was trumpeted anew with an increased sense of urgency.

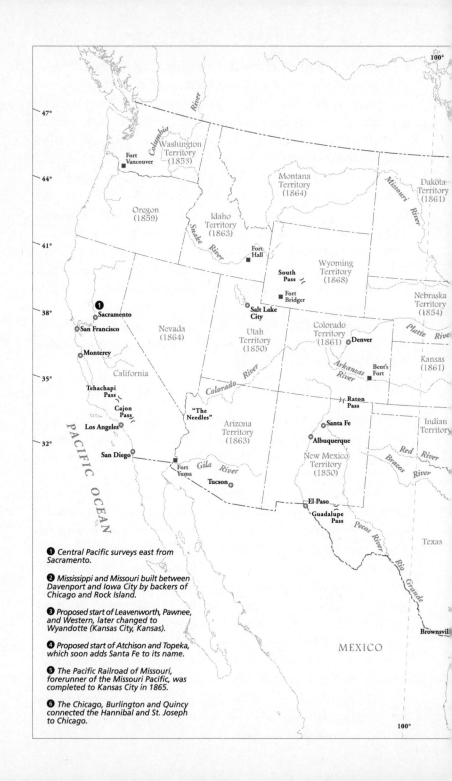

❶ Central Pacific surveys east from Sacramento.

❷ Mississippi and Missouri built between Davenport and Iowa City by backers of Chicago and Rock Island.

❸ Proposed start of Leavenworth, Pawnee, and Western, later changed to Wyandotte (Kansas City, Kansas).

❹ Proposed start of Atchison and Topeka, which soon adds Santa Fe to its name.

❺ The Pacific Railroad of Missouri, forerunner of the Missouri Pacific, was completed to Kansas City in 1865.

❻ The Chicago, Burlington and Quincy connected the Hannibal and St. Joseph to Chicago.

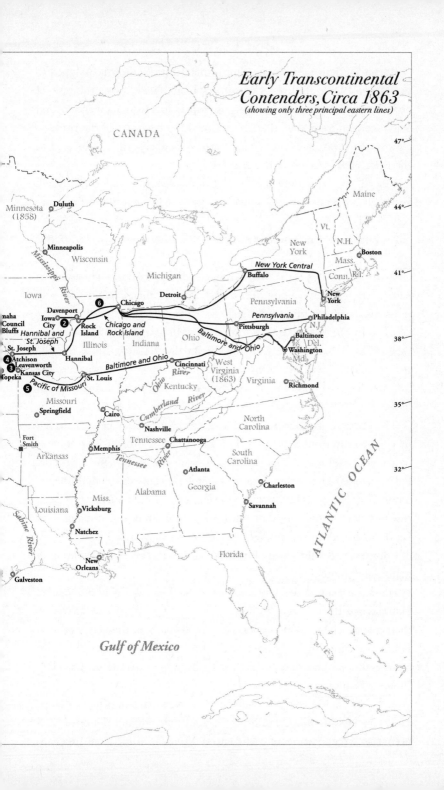

Early Transcontinental Contenders, Circa 1863
(showing only three principal eastern lines)

Aaron Sargent, a freshman congressman from California assigned to the House Pacific Railroad Committee, unabashedly made the case. "I now conceive it my duty . . . to arouse this House from its inaction, and convince it, if I am able, that this railroad is a necessity of the times— a great war measure—to be inaugurated now, if regard is to be paid to the most vital interests of the country."[6]

Indeed, the remaining northern regional rivalries were diminished, although certainly not extinguished, by the argument of "military necessity." There was jockeying for position by real and paper railroads alike, but three companies seemed to enjoy a leg up on their competition.

Chartered in 1852, the Mississippi and Missouri Railroad had taken halting steps to build along the eastern leg of Stephen Douglas's favored transcontinental route from Chicago to South Pass. Connected to Chicago by the Rock Island Railroad, the Mississippi and Missouri ran west across Iowa from Davenport, bound for Council Bluffs. In the spring of 1862, with its railhead some 50 miles west of Iowa City, the line was experiencing one of its frequent halts due to financial problems.

The Leavenworth, Pawnee, and Western Railroad had been chartered in 1855 to run from Leavenworth, Kansas, on the Missouri River, west past Cyrus Holliday's Topeka, for a total of about 100 miles to Fort Riley, Kansas. This was more or less along the transcontinental line intended by Thomas Hart Benton. Seven years later, a survey had been run but not a single mile of track laid. That, however, did not stop Leavenworth, Pawnee, and Western lobbyists from making the rounds of Congress and wildly distributing stock certificates in anticipation of major land grants.[7]

But a third contender appeared out of the West. Railroad proponents Douglas and Benton were both now dead, but they must have stirred in their graves when it was announced that the clerk of the newly created House subcommittee charged with drafting one railroad bill from among the various contenders was to be none other than Theodore Judah of California.

Judah had completed the preliminary survey that Huntington, Hopkins, Crocker, Stanford, and others had authorized, and the result had been the incorporation of the Central Pacific Railroad on June 28,

1861. Leland Stanford—to Huntington's undying dismay—was elected president, while Huntington settled for vice president. Mark Hopkins was elected treasurer, and Judah was named chief engineer. Clearly, the Central Pacific Railroad would be a major player in any ensuing legislation.[8]

Determined to avoid the geographic debates of the past, Judah's committee reported a bill that was very specific both about who would build the Pacific railroad and the route it would take. Principally, the Central Pacific got the nod in the West from Sacramento across the Sierra Nevada to Nevada. Cries in California of nepotism were futile because in business, politics, or railroads, there were fewer and fewer people who could challenge the muscle of the quartet of Huntington, Hopkins, Crocker, and Stanford. On the eastern end, thanks in no small measure to those free-flowing stock certificates, the Leavenworth, Pawnee, and Western secured the major franchise.

Along the broad middle ground of the Rockies, the exact route was still to be determined. Here a new entity was to be incorporated to build between the eastern border of Nevada and the presumed terminus of the Leavenworth, Pawnee, and Western at the western border of Kansas. The new entity would be called the Union Pacific Railroad.

But Iowa was not pleased with this decision, and those with a stake in the future of the Mississippi and Missouri scurried to do something about it. By the time the Pacific Railroad bill passed the House of Representatives, a coalition of interests along the line eastward from Iowa to Chicago, New York, and Boston had succeeded in amending the route. The eastern terminal was now placed at an unnamed location somewhere on Iowa's western border—presumably, the western terminal of the unfinished Mississippi and Missouri—rather than the Kansas terminus of the Leavenworth, Pawnee, and Western.[9]

Over in the Senate, a similar coalition prevailed. The result was that the first transcontinental corridor would have its axis through Council Bluffs, Davenport, Chicago, and New York rather than Topeka, Kansas City, St. Louis, Pittsburgh, and Philadelphia. The Senate bill also authorized the Union Pacific to build between the western boundary of Kansas and the Mississippi and Missouri Railroad at the Missouri River. After the Senate version passed, the House concurred, and President Lincoln signed the Pacific Railroad Act of 1862 into law on July 1, 1862.

Collis Huntington, who had spent much of the previous winter in Washington lobbying its passage, was elated. Decades later, he told historians that he cabled his partners with the news: "We have drawn the elephant. Now let us see if we can harness him up."

Colorful though it was in hindsight, this quote was also attributed to Theodore Judah. In truth, Huntington was in Sacramento with his partners when Aaron Sargent telegraphed a more perfunctory sentiment: "The President has signed the Railroad Bill. Let California rejoice."

Perhaps most significant about this show of national resolve in the face of the Civil War was the fact that cloaking the railroad enterprise in cries of "military necessity" led Congress to extraordinary extremes. To support the venture, it set aside twenty million acres of public domain for land grants and provided a $60 million loan. Then Congress entrusted both to comparatively obscure businessmen who had yet to prove themselves or, in some cases, lay a single mile of track.[10]

As the Pacific Railroad Act of 1862 slowly wound its way through Congress, George B. McClellan's Union Army of the Potomac ground to a halt on Virginia's James-York Peninsula. McClellan, now a major general, got within spitting distance of the gates of Richmond but proved as timid there as he had once been as a young captain surveying railroad routes across snowy mountain passes in the Cascades. It was going to be a long summer.

Out in the West, William Jackson Palmer and the Anderson Troop were at Huntsville, Alabama, with General Buell, whose Army of the Ohio was ostensibly advancing on the pivotal southern rail junction of Chattanooga, Tennessee. Quite pleased with the performance of the Anderson Troop, Buell asked Palmer to raise three additional companies for what would become the Fifteenth Pennsylvania Cavalry. Palmer went east to recruit, and when he returned, the army was still advancing on Chattanooga, but it had a new commander, Major General William S. Rosecrans.

On September 9, 1863, Rosecrans finally entered Chattanooga unopposed. Buoyed by this success, the general quickly pushed southeast into Georgia before realizing that far from fleeing before him, the Confederates were massing to counterattack. Soon thereafter, all hell broke loose along a creek called Chickamauga.

Rosecrans hastily gathered his army along the western bank of Chickamauga Creek and established his headquarters at the Widow Glenn's cabin, Palmer and elements of the Fifteenth Pennsylvania with him. The battle opened on the morning of September 19, with General Braxton Bragg and his Confederates determined to turn Rosecrans's left flank and push the Union army into Missionary Ridge. These attacks faltered, but by the morning of the following day, the reason for Bragg's newfound tenacity became evident.

In an amazing display of mobility, a patchwork network of southern railroads had transported upward of ten thousand men from General James Longstreet's corps of the Army of Northern Virginia over 700 circuitous miles via a dozen railroads and deposited them at Catoosa Station, Georgia, just south of the Chickamauga battlefield. It was the longest and most extensive troop movement by rail ever undertaken by the Confederates, and it proved a testament to the growing military power of railroads.[11]

On the morning of the second day, as Bragg again pressured Rosecrans's left, Longstreet's troops poured into a hole in the middle of the Union line. By afternoon, as Union troops fled toward Chattanooga through gaps in Missionary Ridge, General Rosecrans and what was left of his staff came to a crossroads. One road led northwest to Chattanooga, a route most of the army seemed to be taking. The other struck east toward General George Thomas's stand atop Snodgrass Hill. Initially, Rosecrans ordered his chief of staff to take the road to Chattanooga and rally a defensive perimeter while he, Rosecrans, rode toward the sound of the guns.

Somehow at the intersection of two dusty roads, those roles became reversed. It was Rosecrans who rode in an ever-deepening stupor toward Chattanooga while his chief of staff, Brigadier General James A. Garfield, turned east and reached Thomas after a wild ride. Reputations are made or lost on much less. Rosecrans became the general who had deserted his army; Garfield continued his ride all the way to the White House.[12]

When the remains of Rosecrans's army were besieged in Chattanooga, Secretary of War Edwin Stanton prevailed upon Thomas A.

Scott to once more take a leave of absence from the Pennsylvania Railroad and hurry to Louisville, Kentucky, to coordinate the movement of troops south by rail to Rosecrans's relief.

It was Grant who lifted the siege at Chattanooga and was soon called east to show similar resolve against Robert E. Lee. As Grant plodded toward Richmond in the spring of 1864, Congress once again debated the Pacific railroad question. On July 1 it passed an amendment to the Pacific Railroad Act of 1862.

Some said that its measures were a necessary economic stimulus to prod the construction of the line despite the continuing uncertainties of the war. Others, like Illinois congressman E. B. Washburne, claimed that it was "the most monstrous and flagrant attempt to overreach the Government and the people that can be found in all the legislative annuals of the country," brashly designed to fill further the pockets of a select and unproven few under the guise of national emergency.[13]

In essence, the 1864 amendment doubled the land grants and gave the fledgling Central Pacific and Union Pacific railroads authority to float their own first-mortgage thirty-year construction bonds paying 6 percent in addition to the previously authorized government bonds, which were now subordinated to a second lien. These additional amounts were not to exceed the three issue levels—depending on terrain—spelled out in the original act. Across the prairies, the railroads could sell $16,000 of their own bonds per mile; on the high plains, $32,000 per mile; and in the mountains, $48,000 per mile, making the total indebtedness per mile double that.

Not only would the government guarantee the interest on these bonds but also it would pay the first year's interest outright. Despite the rigors facing the Central Pacific in the Sierra Nevada and the endless sweep of prairie ahead of the Union Pacific, it was the sweetheart deal of the century.[14]

One other thing was certain. Such economic rewards were more than enough to fan the fires of friendly, nay, cutthroat, competition. When a Senate version of the 1864 amendments proposed to give the Central Pacific the authority to build only to the California-Nevada border and not Nevada's eastern boundary, that railroad's directors saw red. They were paying the price in California's Sierras by doggedly blasting out some of the toughest miles of mountain railroads in the world, and they were not about to be left out of the financial prize that came with the easier miles across the Great Basin.

An irate Collis Huntington of the Central Pacific confronted the Union Pacific's wily Dr. Thomas Durant in the backrooms of Washington. "How dare you try to hog all the continent?" exploded Huntington. "Well, how much do *you* want?" demanded Durant. "Give me Nevada," Huntington supposedly replied. For the moment, the two compromised on 150 miles of it, but it was clear that when the war was finally over, the first of many races would be on.[15]

By the fall of 1864, much of the wartime uncertainty that had attended the passage of both the original Pacific Railroad Act and its 1864 amendment was past. Atlanta fell, Lincoln was reelected, Grant tightened the noose around Richmond, and Sherman went marching through Georgia. By April 1865, to all but the most diehard of Southerners, it was over. Confederate president Jefferson Davis fled his capital and was reported to be heading west for Texas with five hundred veteran cavalry to continue the fight.

Among those detailed to pursue Davis was a brigade of Union cavalry under the command of newly appointed Brevet Brigadier General William Jackson Palmer. Never mind that he was only a *brevet* brigadier general of *volunteers,* or that for all intents and purposes the war was over. Still shy of his twenty-ninth birthday, he would be *General* Palmer for the remainder of his life.

But now the pursuit of Jefferson Davis—in whom, under different circumstances, Palmer might have found a railroad mentor to rival J. Edgar Thomson—became a frenzied game of cat and mouse. Davis was reported leaving Charlotte, North Carolina, with wagons loaded with Confederate gold. The purported amount of the treasure and the number of his cavalry grew with every mile that the Confederate president traveled—$2 million, $5 million, and eventually $10 million.

By vigorous marches, Palmer and his cavalry succeeded in gaining two days on Davis and his escort and then got ahead of them by crossing the Savannah River, effectively cutting off their line of escape to the West. Fearing that Davis might simply abandon his escort and try to slip through with a small party, perhaps via rail, Palmer ordered the line of the Georgia Railroad—one of J. Edgar Thomson's early projects—cut at Madison, about 20 miles south of Athens, Georgia.[16]

Meanwhile, the net was growing tighter. The Confederacy's vice president, Alexander Stephens, to whom Palmer had once helped Thomson draft a letter urging a southern transcontinental route, had gone to his home in Crawfordville, just east of Madison. Here he waited for a detachment from Palmer's brigade to ride into his yard.

But where were Davis and his reported treasure? On the morning of May 8, while searching for Davis near the forks of the Appalachee and Oconee rivers, the Fifteenth Pennsylvania came upon seven wagons hidden in the woods. They contained $188,000 in coin, $1,588,000 in negotiable paper, and about $4 million in Confederate money, the latter of dubious value. This treasure, however, was the property of the Georgia Central Railroad and Banking Company, spirited away from Macon in advance of Union troops. Reports of a Confederate treasure had been grossly exaggerated, and Davis's coffers were as empty as his cause.

Two days later, on May 10, Davis himself was captured by elements of the Fourth Michigan Cavalry of General James H. Wilson's corps at Irwinton, about 25 miles east of Macon. "General Wilson held the bag," General George Thomas remarked to his staff, but "Palmer drove the game into it."[17]

Now the war was really over. One day Palmer's command was riding headlong after Jefferson Davis, and the next it was on its way home. "I was mustered out with my regiment on Wednesday last," Palmer wrote his uncle, "and am consequently now in the full enjoyment of the beatitude of being a citizen . . . and I suppose, jobless for the first time in nearly four years." But he would not remain so for long.[18]

The Civil War transformed American railroads just as World War I would later transform the airplane. When America looked up from the carnage of four bitter years, it found that railroads had dramatically increased its mobility, become the arteries of its growing industrial strength, and stood poised to replace covered wagons as the vessels of its western expansion, quickly making good prewar boasts of Manifest Destiny.

Between 1850 and 1860, the number of miles of railroads in the United States had more than tripled, from 9,000 to 30,000. While many railroads in the South now lay in ruins, most would be quickly rebuilt, and the number of miles of track in the United States would reach 53,000 by 1870.

This mileage would include the completion of the first transcontinental railroad, but as the guns fell silent, that line's speedy completion was still not assured. And it soon became clear that while the Central Pacific and Union Pacific were the leading contenders to finish first, they would not have the field to themselves.

Prewar, regional fears that there would be only one transcontinental line were rapidly disappearing. For starters, with almost lightning speed in the weeks after Robert E. Lee's surrender at Appomattox, Virginia, effectively ending the Civil War, there was a new breed of observer heading west. These were not the stalwart scientists of Colonel Abert's Corps of Topographical Engineers but rather the vanguard of capitalism itself. These were people who either would bankroll the ventures or were in positions of political or media power to fan the fires and convince others to ante up for the cause.

No less a personage than Schuyler Colfax, ex-newspaperman from Indiana and lately Speaker of the U.S. House of Representatives, hopped a stagecoach with Samuel Bowles, a Massachusetts newspaper editor, and headed west. From the Missouri to Denver took less than five days. "It was a magnificent, uninterrupted stage ride of six hundred and fifty miles," wrote Bowles, "much more endurable in its discomforts, much more exhilarating in its novelties, than I had anticipated."

Colfax, who would soon have Denver's main east-west street named for him, was transfixed by the railroad possibilities. By the time the party reached Virginia City, Nevada, the ex-Speaker told a crowd, "I believe the Pacific Railroad to be a national and political and military necessity."[19]

In the depths of civil war, Secretary of State William Seward had strenuously agreed. Long a proponent of a transcontinental railroad, Seward saw its importance to national unity: "When this [railroad] shall have been done, disunion will be rendered forever after impossible. There will be no fulcrum for the lever of treason to rest upon."[20]

Indeed, the first transcontinental railroad and the competing lines that raced to network the rest of the West would become the very fulcrum upon which the settlement of half a continent was based and the sanctity of the Union made secure. With an interruption of war, railroads had come of age, and now, so too would the country.

4

Transcontinental by Any Name

While Speaker Colfax's entourage completed its grand tour of Denver and points west, William Jackson Palmer spent a few weeks luxuriating in the amenities of Newport, Rhode Island. He gave little thought to his decision to leave the army, and events quickly proved the wisdom of his choice. On May 1, 1865, there were 1,052,038 men under arms in the Union forces. Six months later, more than 800,000 had been mustered out, and there was no denying that the army had an abundance of brevet brigadiers.

But the influence of the Fifteenth Pennsylvania Cavalry and the leadership skills that Palmer honed at its head would stay with him all his life. He would always be "General" Palmer, but railroading and not the army would be his first love. No doubt his patrons, J. Edgar Thomson and Thomas A. Scott, would have gladly accorded him a new role with the Pennsylvania Railroad, but Thomson and Scott were themselves looking west.

Palmer's Newport interlude was cut short by a terse telegram from Scott. "Can you meet me here {Altoona, Pennsylvania} on Saturday next. I go west for several weeks on Monday next. When you come, make your arrangements to go to Missouri permanently." Palmer promptly accompanied Scott to St. Louis and arrived there on August 6, 1865. Two days later, he headed west to Kansas to inspect the initial 41 miles of the Leavenworth, Pawnee, and Western Railroad.[1]

Few railroads changed their name as many times as did the Leavenworth, Pawnee, and Western. Originally incorporated in Kansas Territory in 1855, the railroad was a winner in the Pacific Railroad Act of 1862, although the Mississippi and Missouri was accorded the main eastern terminus. For its part, the Leavenworth, Pawnee, and Western secured the right to build west to a junction with the Union Pacific at the 100th meridian—roughly the middle of Nebraska—and the same government subsidies and land grants for each mile of track laid that were awarded to the Union Pacific and Central Pacific.

In 1863 a group that included John C. Frémont gained control of the line. With thoughts of immediate political gain, they changed its name to the Union Pacific Railway, Eastern Division. This was a mouthful that had nothing to do with the original Union Pacific—except for sharing the plums of Congress's bonds and land grants—but it was calculated to attract investors because of the confusing similarity of names.

When the 1862 act was amended in 1864, the Eastern Division's land grants were also doubled, and it was given the right to link up with the Central Pacific if it could reach the 100th meridian before the Union Pacific. Prior congressional victories by the Iowa-Chicago axis aside, such a linkup would have tilted the proposed transcontinental back toward Kansas and Missouri.

Frémont's chief partner in the venture was a boisterous self-promoter named Samuel Hallett. Without Frémont's knowledge, Hallett unabashedly cancelled an existing construction contract, awarded the work to his own company, and then negotiated a series of corporate loans with which to pay himself. While Frémont fumed, Hallett's new firm hastily laid track from Wyandotte (now Kansas City, Kansas) west to Lawrence and then asked the government for payment.

But this first section of track proved a shoddy piece of work. When the railroad's chief engineer, Orlando A. Talcott, refused to certify the first 20 miles of track as complete and ready for the government subsidy, Hallett fired him. Not to be outdone, Talcott wrote directly to President Lincoln and claimed that Hallett's substandard construction was "the biggest swindle yet"—a statement that would prove hyperbolic considering the railroad construction schemes to come.

Lincoln referred Talcott's charge to his secretary of the interior, John P. Usher, a Kansan who was siding with Hallett in his feud with Frémont. Usher showed Talcott's letter to Hallett, who was in Washington seeking payment. The contractor promptly wired his burly brother back in Kansas to find Talcott and "slap" him. Thomas Hallett took the order to the extreme and beat the bookish engineer senseless.

Talcott, who was partially crippled from a stroke, waited patiently for his revenge. On the morning of July 27, 1864, Samuel Hallett returned to Wyandotte. As he approached company headquarters, Talcott limped out from the cover of an alley and shot him in the back with a rifle. Hallett died within minutes, and Talcott fled west to Colorado. He eluded capture for some fifteen years, and when finally tried for the murder, he was acquitted by a sympathetic jury.

This left the Union Pacific, Eastern Division—née Leavenworth, Pawnee, and Western—in shambles, both as to its corporate structure and its physical roadbed. John D. Perry, a banker from St. Louis who had made some of the loans to Hallett, sorted through the mess, bought out Frémont, and repudiated Hallett's construction contract. The roadbed was put in working order, and trains began regular service between Wyandotte and Lawrence in December 1864.[2]

By the summer of 1865, as William Jackson Palmer inspected these first miles of track, the railhead of the original Union Pacific was still within sight of Omaha, 220 miles east of the dividing point of the 100th meridian. The Eastern Division's railhead at Lawrence was about 260 miles east of the line. No wonder that the Union Pacific's confusing namesake was quick to attract national attention.

It added to the confusion of names and the importance of reaching the 100th meridian that for a time the Union Pacific *main* line was considered to be only that segment west from the 100th meridian to the proposed junction with the Central Pacific. This was initially thought to be 150 miles east of the California-Nevada border—Huntington's "Give me Nevada" compromise.

The Union Pacific *branch* line was that portion between the 100th meridian and Omaha. When Congress removed the 150-mile Nevada limit in an 1866 amendment, the Central Pacific was free to build east as far as it could. The Union Pacific was forced to race westward, not only to beat the Central Pacific to as much ground as possible but also to beat the Eastern Division to the 100th meridian and ensure itself the main line.

From the start, John D. Perry had no interest in the Eastern Division being merely the tail of the Union Pacific dog. There is no better evidence of this than the alliance he made with J. Edgar Thomson and Thomas A. Scott of the Pennsylvania Railroad. Scott had watched and learned from Thomson's consolidation of the Pennsylvania across the Keystone State during the 1850s. His own experiences with the Union war effort had further convinced him of the necessity of a transcontinental line under the control of one company. Thomson's mantra, "Build west," resounded anew.

A quick look at the map of the United States told the story. The Pennsylvania Railroad was already knocking at the gates of St. Louis through control of a number of subsidiaries. There were several Missouri lines that might be acquired to span that state between St. Louis and Kansas City. West from there, the Eastern Division promised a direct connection with the Central Pacific if it could beat the Union Pacific to the 100th meridian. Failing either that or coming to terms with Huntington and his Central Pacific cohorts, there was the lure of the independent continuation of the Eastern Division toward California.

To restart the Eastern Division, Thomson and Scott agreed to raise $1 million in eastern capital to match another $1 million that Perry was contributing from his St. Louis contacts and the value of the initial construction. The St. Louis parties thought "Scott drove a pretty hard bargain" by requiring an indemnity for his investors against any claims that might still arise from Hallett's construction shenanigans. But that was only the beginning. By the time Scott concluded his negotiations with Perry, J. Edgar Thomson held the power to name the odd director to the Eastern Division's board, otherwise equally split between westerners and easterners.

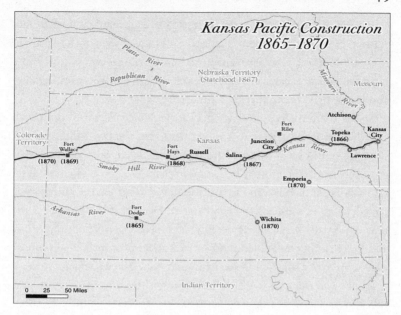

To look after their investment, Scott arranged for the appointment of William Jackson Palmer as the new treasurer of the Eastern Division. Quite suddenly, within a week of his arrival in Kansas, Palmer had become Thomson and Scott's man on the ground in the West. For his part, the not quite twenty-nine-year-old seems to have understood his role perfectly.

"Young men without money can only make a fortune by connecting themselves with capitalists," Palmer wrote his uncle shortly afterward. "The heaviest of these reside in the East where they can look after their own affairs. But the best place to invest capital is in the West. Eastern capitalists must therefore have representatives here to attend to their interests if they wish to invest heavily in the West."[3]

Thomson and Scott's representative that he was, Palmer keenly watched the Eastern Division come to life and sputter west from Lawrence. The railroad reached Topeka, another 20 miles farther, early in 1866. Topeka town father Cyrus K. Holliday no doubt celebrated, but his own railroad enterprise had yet to lay a single mile of track. By fall, the Eastern Division had completed its tracks another 60-some miles past Fort Riley to Junction City, as well as a spur from Lawrence to Leavenworth.

By the spring of 1867, the Eastern Division had reached Salina, Kansas, but it was still more than 100 miles shy of the 100th meridian. Meanwhile, the Union Pacific, spurred on by the specter of losing any race, had laid an exhausting 247 miles of track in just 182 working days and reached the 100th meridian in October 1866.[4]

So the Eastern Division's race to beat the Union Pacific to the 100th meridian and build west to connect with the Central Pacific proved short lived. But by now it was clear to any knowledgeable observer that the West would be crossed by far more than just one transcontinental railroad. From the Eastern Division's railhead at Salina, the railroad was confident of its route all the way west to Denver. If the Union Pacific now appeared to control its destiny *north* of Denver, Thomson, Scott, and Perry simply redoubled their interest in a transcontinental route of their own to the south of Denver through New Mexico and Arizona.

Those who thought to call John D. Perry shrewd would suggest that the Eastern Division's destiny bent in that direction as early as 1864, when he chose to stake its line through western Kansas along the more southerly Smoky Hill drainage rather than the Republican River to the north. This may well have contributed to Thomson and Scott's interest in the line.

In the spring of 1867, Thomson made a request of Perry. Presuming that few of the eastern directors would journey west for the annual meeting, Thomson nonetheless noted that the expanding company could use a vice president. He suggested William Jackson Palmer for the position and expressed "the personal knowledge which we of the East possess of him would make such a choice especially agreeable to us." Just so Perry had no doubt that Thomson's courteous suggestion was in fact a command, all of the controlling eastern directors signed the letter to "heartily concur in his views."[5]

Once appointed, their new vice president was charged with the task of organizing a comprehensive survey of their transcontinental options. Palmer's primary objective was "to ascertain the best general route for the extension of the company's road from the end of the track . . . by a southern parallel, through New Mexico and Arizona, to the Pacific Ocean." This general direction bespoke the obvious learned from at least four decades of Southwest travel. The initial objective must be

Santa Fe and/or Albuquerque and the Rio Grande Valley and thence west via either the 35th or 32nd parallels.

Lieutenant Amiel W. Whipple, of course, had been over much of the 35th parallel route in 1853 and reported positively on it, although without the benefit of detailed measurements. What Palmer thought of Jefferson Davis's long-touted southern route along the 32nd parallel—particularly in light of his wartime pursuit of the Confederate president—would become clear only upon publication of his final report.

Early in July 1867, while Palmer was completing business in the East, the Eastern Division survey party left Fort Wallace, near present-day Sharon Springs and the Kansas-Colorado border. Santa Fe was the goal, and three major routes with a half dozen variations were to be explored.

The first followed the general corridor of the well-established Mountain Branch of the Santa Fe Trail southwest across the Raton Mountains, past Fort Union, and on to Santa Fe from the south. A second route continued up the Arkansas to the Huerfano River, along its headwaters to Sangre de Cristo Pass, and into the upper Rio Grande Valley to reach Santa Fe from the north.

The third route followed the Arkansas through its Grand Canyon—later known as the Royal Gorge—to the north side of Poncha Pass, and then south across it to the upper Rio Grande Valley. This latter route was the longest of the three and at first glance appeared wildly circuitous. A closer look, however, showed its advantages in tapping any mineral potential in the Colorado Rockies and in securing a future transit between the headwaters of the Arkansas and Colorado rivers.

But for the moment, these Colorado considerations were minor, and the main attention focused on crossing the volcanic mesas of the Raton Mountains directly to Santa Fe. Raton Pass just south of Trinidad at the foot of Fishers Peak was the proven route of the Mountain Branch—perhaps a little steep for a railroad, but passable.

Thirty-five miles to the east was a second possibility: 7,079-foot Trinchera Pass. When General Palmer caught up with the survey at a camp on its northern approaches, some in the expedition were already singing its praises. An English investor and self-styled adventurer

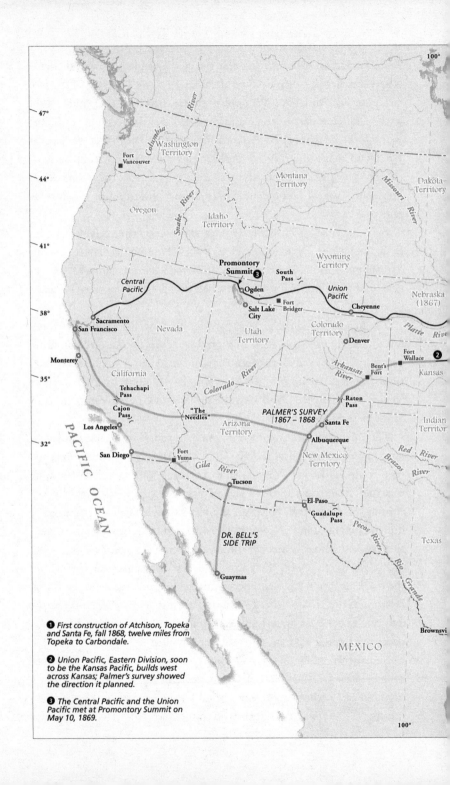

❶ First construction of Atchison, Topeka and Santa Fe, fall 1868, twelve miles from Topeka to Carbondale.

❷ Union Pacific, Eastern Division, soon to be the Kansas Pacific, builds west across Kansas; Palmer's survey showed the direction it planned.

❸ The Central Pacific and the Union Pacific met at Promontory Summit on May 10, 1869.

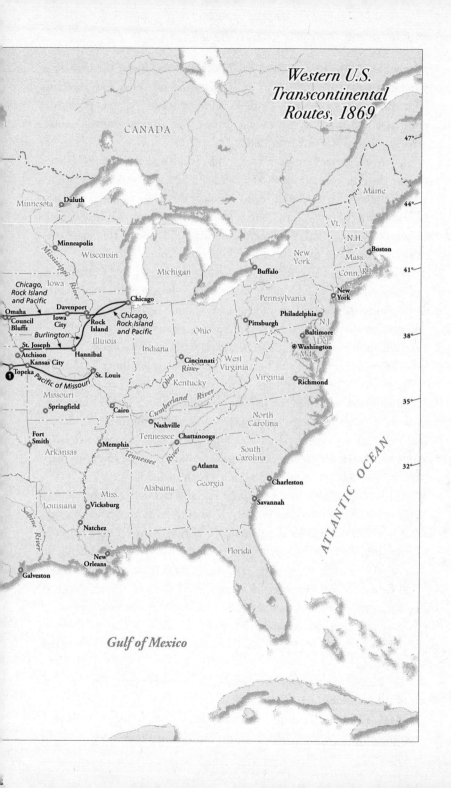

Western U.S. Transcontinental Routes, 1869

CANADA

Maine

47°

Minnesota

Duluth

Vt.

44°

Minneapolis

Wisconsin

N.H.

Mass.

Boston

Michigan

New York

Conn. R.I.

41°

Buffalo

Chicago, Rock Island and Pacific

Davenport

Chicago

Pennsylvania

New York

Omaha

Council Bluffs

Iowa City

Rock Island

Chicago, Rock Island and Pacific

Ohio

Pittsburgh

Philadelphia

N.J.

Burlington

Illinois

Indiana

Baltimore

Del.

38°

St. Joseph

Hannibal

Washington

Md.

Atchison

Cincinnati River

West Virginia

Kansas City

Topeka

Pacific of Missouri

St. Louis

Ohio

Kentucky

Cumberland River

Virginia

Richmond

Missouri

35°

Springfield

Cairo

Nashville

North Carolina

Fort Smith

Tennessee

Chattanooga

Arkansas

Memphis

Tennessee River

South Carolina

Atlanta

32°

Charleston

Miss.

Alabama

Georgia

Louisiana

Vicksburg

Savannah

Natchez

Florida

New Orleans

Galveston

ATLANTIC OCEAN

Gulf of Mexico

Mississippi River

Iowa

Sabine River

named Dr. William A. Bell called Trinchera Pass "by far the best natural highway across the range." It had never been crossed with wagons,
but there was "no doubt"—in Bell's mind, at least—"that a very small
outlay would make it, not only a shorter, but a better route . . . than
that via Trinidad and Raton Pass."

Lastly, there was Cimarron Pass at the eastern end of the range. It was
lower than the others by almost a thousand feet and sat on a direct line
from Kansas City to Albuquerque. Much of this route followed the ruts
of the main Santa Fe Trail. But between the Arkansas River and Fort
Union—as many Santa Fe–bound caravans could attest—this route traversed almost 300 miles of "dry and inferior country."

Palmer worried that it "does not follow the line of settlements, and
of mineral, arable and timber wealth," but he conceded that if the
Cimarron line was "not adopted at first, it must be built eventually, to
economize the transportation of *through* passenger and freight traffic—
including all that will originate west and south of Fort Union."[6]

The next major stop was Santa Fe itself. "General Palmer held quite
a levee here," Dr. Bell reported. "His rooms were always crowded with
men either interested in the railway or well acquainted with some portion of the country to the westward." All possible information was obtained about the 32nd and 35th parallel routes, and, according to Bell,
"the relative advantages seemed from the reports to be so evenly balanced" that Palmer decided to examine both in detail.

If Bell is a reliable source, Palmer initially favored Jefferson Davis's
assertion that "the decided preference" should go to the 32nd parallel.
But having heard the local testimonials, he now wasn't so sure. At Fort
Craig, about 30 miles south of Socorro on the Rio Grande, Palmer split
his survey into three divisions. Two were to continue south down the
Rio Grande: one following the known route through Cookes Canyon
and into the upper reaches of the Gila River, the other charged with
finding any more direct cutoffs. Palmer went with the Third Division,
which backtracked to Albuquerque and then struck westward along the
35th parallel.[7]

Dr. Bell joined the southern party exploring for cutoffs. This led him
into the Mimbres Mountains north of Cookes Canyon at a passage that
he named Palmer's Pass. But the Burro Mountains farther west proved
too steep for a railroad grade, and the cutoff party moved south. They

joined the main party after crossing the Continental Divide on the broad plateau between present-day Deming and Lordsburg.

To the west, all acknowledged that the established emigrant trail through Apache Pass past Fort Bowie was too steep for rails. But to the north, between the twin summits of Dos Cabezas and Mount Graham, there was a wide depression that offered a gradual ascent on both sides. This was the key to getting into the drainage of the San Pedro River, a tributary of the Gila. Back in 1853, Lieutenant John Parke had prematurely named it Railroad Pass. Now Palmer's survey confirmed the worth of Parke's work.

From Railroad Pass, while the main survey worked west across the broad salt flats of the Sulphur Springs Valley, Dr. Bell elected to make a wide detour south into Sonora. Considering Palmer's later exploits in building Mexican railroads, it is reasonable to assume that Bell had more than a passing interest in gaining "information as to the best way to reach the Port of Guaymas in the Californian Gulf." One affable Englishman was likely to be far better received than a large party overweight with recently discharged Union officers.

So Dr. Bell trekked southward to Hermosillo and then on to Guaymas, commenting in his diary about everything from making tortillas to the influences of Moorish architecture. While this region was somewhat removed from the unrest of Mexico's fight against its recent French invaders, Bell found its inhabitants in utter despair and poverty. Perhaps with a mind to more than just a railroad connection, Bell observed, "they seemed to me to look upon annexation to the United States as their destiny, and one to be hoped for with as little delay as possible."

But Bell's report to Palmer on railroad possibilities was not encouraging. If anything, it would confirm the general's growing bias in favor of the 35th parallel route. Finding the harbor at Guaymas too small and too far up the Gulf of California for easy Pacific access, Bell came to the conclusion that whatever trade there might be in Sonora was best served by local railroads "radiating from the coast inland." So the good doctor boarded a steamer and sailed north with plans to rejoin his companions.[8]

While Bell made this detour, the main party along the 32nd parallel followed the Gila westward, arriving at its confluence with the Colorado River opposite Fort Yuma. Here, Arizona City, described as "a very small place with a very big name," was nonetheless acknowledged as "an excellent bridging point, the river being confined between rocky bluffs." Those who gaze at the Colorado at Yuma today might doubt the claim that it was "472 feet wide, and from 12 to 37 feet deep, with a very rapid current," but it then flowed unchecked to the sea.[9]

Meanwhile, General Palmer moved west from Albuquerque along the 35th parallel. His survey passed Inscription Rock (now El Morro National Monument), where in 1853 Lieutenant Whipple added his name to those of numerous Spanish travelers. Then it was west past the Pueblo of Zuni and into the mostly dry headwaters of the Little Colorado River.

Determined to avoid a line too high on the pine-covered slopes of the San Francisco Peaks, Palmer pushed ahead of his main group and traversed the upper canyons of the Verde River. Backtracking to take a second look, his party dropped into the canyon of Sycamore Creek. An ascent upstream looked impassable for his pack animals; downstream only slightly less so. Then the rattle of Apache muskets and a flurry of arrows made escape all the more necessary.

From the comparative safety of the cedars lining the canyon rim, the Apaches hollered threats and rolled rocks that resounded "like heavy ordnance." Palmer got a little melodramatic when he recounted the fray later, writing that the cries of their largely unseen attackers called out, "This country belongs to us—the whole of it; and we do not want your people here, nor your soldiers, nor your railroad."

Palmer led a detachment of the accompanying cavalry troop on foot up one side of the canyon in an attempt to outflank them. The Apache seemed more intent on harassment than frontal combat, and, miraculously, no one was hurt. But in the process, Palmer's group got separated from the main force. When they finally rejoined the column the next day, Palmer learned that as the main force had slowly worked its way out of the canyon via a narrow and precipitous path, the general's prized gray horse, Signor, had lost his footing and tumbled to his death.

After Sycamore Canyon, the slopes of the San Francisco Peaks didn't look so bad. Rather than the tortuous canyons of the Verde, they promised gentle, rolling country and the added benefit of bountiful timber. "The grades up to this place are easy," Palmer reported, "and the line runs for nearly 150 miles through a dense forest of fine tall pines, which will of themselves be a great advantage to the railroad in many ways."[10]

Hugging the San Francisco Peaks had the effect of pointing the survey due west toward Fort Mojave on the Colorado River rather than a more southerly crossing near the mouth of the Bill Williams River (present-day Parker Dam), as Palmer had originally planned. But this proved fortunate. Their survey line crossed the Colorado 3 miles above the rocky spine of the Needles and proved it almost as good of a crossing of the Colorado as that surveyed at Yuma.

Then an interesting encounter occurred. Once again, Palmer had gone ahead in the vanguard. He aimed almost due west across the Mojave Desert toward Tehachapi Pass. But the expedition's botanist, Charles C. Parry, met a man along the Colorado River who claimed to have traversed the Grand Canyon on a raft. This was James White. It was two years before John Wesley Powell's epic passage, but Parry, and later both Palmer and Bell, were inclined to believe White.

Historians and Colorado River rats will forever debate the claim, but if nothing else, White's story shed some light for Palmer on the terrain north of the 35th parallel. It also prompted him to contemplate Grand Canyon railroad routes. In his published report of the survey, Palmer was among the first to call what had previously been known as simply the "Big Canyon" by its much more superlative name.

"If the Grand Canyon of the Colorado," Palmer theorized, " . . . should be ascertained to be narrow enough at the top to be spanned by a suspension bridge at any point on the Colorado Plateau . . . the temptation of a possible saving of 5,000 feet of rise and fall would warrant a reconnaissance westward in California, to ascertain if this point of crossing could be favorably connected with Tehachapi Pass."

That statement wasn't as outlandish as it now appears, because Lieutenant Joseph C. Ives, coming upriver from the Gulf of California in 1857, had reported the canyon "to be not over 50 yards wide at the bottom, with very precipitous walls." Palmer, however, quickly went on to say what was the obvious: "The innumerable side cañons, of great depth, with which this plateau everywhere in the vicinity of the 'Grand Cañon' appears to be furrowed, might, in any event, render such a line impracticable."[11]

From Tehachapi Pass, Palmer pushed on down the San Joaquin Valley to San Francisco and rendezvoused with the irrepressible Dr. Bell. By now it was January 1868, and the general was anxious to return east and report his findings to his nominal superior, John D. Perry, and to those who held the real power, Thomson and Scott. But he had one important call to make first.

Months before, out on the Colorado plains just shy of Trinchera Pass, Palmer had bluntly written to Perry what had long been obvious when it came to the confusing name of their railroad. "We can never get along with the Eastern Division, it looks subordinate on the face of it, and leads to constant misunderstanding." The replacement name that slowly came into usage, and that was officially changed in 1869, was far more descriptive as to both origin and planned destination. The ill-fitting Union Pacific Railway, Eastern Division, became the Kansas Pacific Railway.

That name and Palmer's enthusiasm for a transcontinental route spoke volumes when the general paid a call in California on Judge E. B. Crocker, Charley's older brother and nominally the fifth member of the Big Four. Hearing Palmer voice the Kansas Pacific's transcontinental intentions, Judge Crocker suggested that a southern branch of the Central Pacific might agree to meet the Kansas line at some point on the California border. Palmer was quick to reply that the Kansas Pacific intended to build right on to San Francisco by itself. "I, of course," Crocker reported to Huntington, "had no reply."

While Huntington pondered this news, Palmer hurried east from Sacramento via the Central Pacific. He had not yet publicly committed to either the 35th or 32nd parallel, but his journey across the snowy Sierra Nevada must have convinced him that either was preferable to the line the Central Pacific was still building.

By the time Palmer arrived back at Fort Wallace, Kansas, on the morning of March 10, 1868, he had been on the trail eight months. In the meantime, the Kansas Pacific railhead, which he had left at Salina, had pushed 100 miles farther west and spawned the new towns of Ellsworth and Hayes, Kansas.[12]

While Palmer focused on the route west, it was these towns that provided the Kansas Pacific with much-needed revenue from the growing cattle trade. Texas longhorns were driven to Louisiana in small quantities before the Civil War, but in its aftermath, hundreds of herds with hundreds of thousands of cattle were driven north toward the meatpacking center of Chicago. The Kansas Pacific rails at Abilene, Kansas, welcomed the first herd up the Chisholm Trail in 1867. Abilene got most of the bad press for being a rowdy cow town, but Ellsworth and Hayes weren't far behind.

When the full report of Palmer's Kansas Pacific survey was published the following year, it acknowledged four "practicable and good general routes" from the Kansas Pacific's growing main line to the vicinity of Albuquerque. Westward from Albuquerque and the Rio Grande, the choice was clearer, essentially Whipple's 35th parallel modified by straightening the route in western Arizona and crossing the Sierras via Tehachapi Pass.

When Palmer finally said it publicly, he left no doubt. "The results along the thirty-fifth parallel proved to be of such a favorable character that, with its great advantage in distance and accessibility from nearly every section of the Union to start with, its claims have been found decidedly to outweigh those of the extreme southern line."

Palmer trumpeted anew Whipple's thesis that such a route might indeed please both northern and southern interests. The latter had not been thought too important of late—Jefferson Davis had only recently been released from a Union prison—but this would change as war wounds healed. Palmer also shared Bell's view about the future of northern Mexico. Among his pleas for government assistance to the Kansas Pacific was the assertion that "the Government should give its assistance, because a railroad is the cheapest and most efficient means of defense to our southern border, until Mexico becomes a part of the United States."[13]

The details of Palmer's more immediate personal report to Perry and Scott can be surmised by the actions they took as Palmer returned east in March 1868. Perry had already been trying to obtain an additional land grant from Congress for the Kansas Pacific that would extend from

Colorado to California. Learning of Palmer's conversation with Judge Crocker and the general's enthusiasm for the 35th parallel route, Perry—no doubt with Scott's concurrence—decided that it was time to sit down with Collis P. Huntington and further divide up the continent.

Perry and Scott were keenly aware that Huntington's support, or lack of it, was critical to any favorable land grants for the Kansas Pacific. Indeed, Judge Crocker's report to Huntington of Palmer's western visit only strengthened Huntington's resolve to work behind the scenes to thwart any Kansas Pacific aid. He found willing allies in the Union Pacific who did not like the Kansas Pacific competing with it across the plains.

To change Huntington's position, Perry offered the Central Pacific the California portion of any land grant the Kansas Pacific might acquire along the 35th parallel. Huntington bluntly refused, saying that the Central Pacific "would not think of it" and wanted no part of what "would only be a small feeder line to their road." Instead he countered with a proposal to build the entire western half of the route between Colorado and the Pacific. If Perry wanted Huntington's support, that was his price.

Huntington's seemingly preposterous proposition—after all, under that scheme the Kansas Pacific would have gained little ground—may have been designed to lure in the other players. If so, it worked perfectly because several weeks later, on March 21, Perry again met with Huntington, this time in the company of Thomas A. Scott.

Scott candidly laid out the pieces of the Pennsylvania Railroad–Kansas Pacific transcontinental plan for Huntington. "Their proposition was that we come in with them and build the road under one organization," Huntington reported to Judge Crocker. "I of course refused," Huntington added, saying that he had already ruled out a branch line relationship and in any event "was not aware before that they had anything to give west of Denver." That, of course, was a dig that the Kansas Pacific's desired land grants west of Denver would not budge out of Congress without his support.

Huntington's intransigence left Perry and Scott with little to negotiate. The meeting ended with them saying that they had to confer with their engineer (Palmer) who was due in Washington in a day or two.

But then a few minutes later, Scott, whom Huntington described as "very sharp," reappeared at Huntington's door alone. If Huntington's version is correct, Scott "said if I would give a certain party a small interest in our part of the line, he thought he could carry it with his people." Presumably, Scott was alluding to J. Edgar Thomson or perhaps even himself as the one who could "carry" the deal with the Perry crowd.

Now Huntington really flaunted his power. Playing the likeable friend who was saddled with intractable partners, Huntington told Scott that he didn't think that his California associates would agree to any dilution of control. Then Huntington may have held the door open just a crack and suggested that he might be able to offer a small portion of the construction proceeds.

This wasn't what Scott was after, and he left Huntington a second time, asking him not to mention this subsequent meeting to anyone. If nothing else, Huntington, whose Central Pacific partners still had their hands full meeting the Union Pacific in Utah, had become interested in a second southern transcontinental line. By the end of March 1868, Huntington boasted to Mark Hopkins that before it was over, Scott's crowd would "agree to what we want, which is: to have the line between, say Denver and San Francisco . . ."[14]

But when Huntington next called on Scott in Philadelphia, it was Scott's turn to be firm. "Since General Palmer's return, they have been very stiff," Huntington told Hopkins. "I could do nothing with him," Huntington continued with rare exasperation. By the time Huntington got up to leave, he was reduced to bluffing Scott that he would secure his own land grant in California and let Scott fend for himself. This had the desired effect, and Scott replied that he did not want to see that done. Instead he promised to meet Huntington again the next week in New York and to bring Perry with him.

The trio met at the Fifth Avenue Hotel until midnight on April 16. Once again, maps of the West were unrolled and the horse-trading began. It continued the next day at the Central Pacific's New York office. When Huntington, Scott, and Perry were finally finished, they had agreed to meet at the Colorado River and work together to secure congressional aid for the entire route.

Unbeknownst to Scott and Perry, Huntington's partners were already beginning to question his unbridled expansion, but a few days after their deal, Huntington was certainly not regretting it. He wrote Judge Crocker, avowing as how "I think we have got to a point now where, with care, we can control the west end of the three Pacific roads, which I think will be built, and that the west end of all three of them will be in San Francisco, California."[15]

The following spring, the Union Pacific and the Central Pacific completed their headlong rush across the continent and joined rails at Promontory Summit, Utah, on May 10, 1869. Along many miles on both roads, the last sprints of construction left unballasted track, rickety trestles, and improbable grades. But the deed had been done and the claim to be America's first transcontinental railroad won.

Meanwhile, the Kansas Pacific continued its march across Kansas, reaching the Colorado border in January 1870. It had come out of the gates first, but now, as the Kansas Pacific was transfixed by Palmer's survey and potential battles with Collis P. Huntington farther west, there was a new competitor nipping at its flanks. The race to the Southwest was just beginning.

5

The Santa Fe
Joins the Fray

Cyrus K. Holliday's railroad dreams did not come easily. After the incorporation of the Atchison and Topeka Railroad in September 1860, Holliday's enterprise languished in the uncertainty of civil war. The most positive development occurred when the Republican majority in Congress—only too glad to have two more Republican senators after Kansas was granted statehood in 1861—eventually provided for substantial land grants.

On March 3, 1863, Abraham Lincoln signed a land grant bill that had been instigated by Holliday and introduced by Senator Samuel C. Pomeroy of Kansas. Designed to foster railroad construction throughout the state, it promised alternate sections of land, ten sections deep on both sides of the route—6,400 acres of land for every mile of track laid. The principal beneficiary was the Atchison and Topeka Railroad, which was to build from Atchison west to the Kansas-Colorado state line.

Lands were to be conveyed upon the completion "in a good, substantial, and workmanlike manner" of 20-mile segments of "a first-class railroad." If previously granted homestead lands—a particular concern in the eastern part of the state—preempted a full conveyance of 6,400 acres per mile, the railroads could select other "preemption lands" within 20 miles of their route. These were to be conveyed upon completion of the *entire* line. In return, construction had to be completed within ten years.[1]

At the Chase Hotel in Topeka the following November, Atchison and Topeka shareholders elected Senator Pomeroy president of the company as a vote of thanks for his efforts in securing the land grant. They also voted to change the company's name. Given the vast western lands to be had and Holliday's continued exhortations that the company's future lay in the West, the name Atchison and Topeka seemed far too limiting. Thus, the company became the Atchison, Topeka and Santa Fe Railroad. As the company grew, eastern capitalists would continue to call the road the Atchison, but to anyone west of the Missouri, it was simply the Santa Fe.

And to Santa Fe, the railroad was bound. But prospective land grants in the unpopulated western reaches of Kansas were one thing; immediate capital for initial construction quite another. In August 1865, the company ordered three thousand tons of iron rails at $100 per ton, but Holliday, Pomeroy, and their East Coast agents were unable to raise the required funds. The rail order was cancelled, and the next two years saw no better results.

What the railroad desperately needed was developable land closer to Topeka. The problem was that some of the most fertile and well-watered ground was on the Potawatomi Indian Reservation northwest of town. Led by Senator Pomeroy, the railroad entered into negotiations that resulted in an 1868 treaty approved by Congress whereby the railroad purchased 338,766 acres from the Potawatomi at $1 an acre with easy six-year, 6 percent terms.

The Santa Fe turned around and put this land on the market to settlers for 20 percent down and the balance in five equal installments. Some tracts were sold for as much as $16 per acre, but others went to insiders like Pomeroy and his brother-in-law at only $1 per acre. It was a rather dubious way to fund railroad construction, but the Santa Fe had its first inflow of construction capital.

Once again, Cyrus K. Holliday was the unflagging cheerleader. "The child is born and his name is 'Success,' " crowed Holliday to the *Kansas State Record* from his fund-raising perch in New York City. "Let the Capital City rejoice. The Atchison, Topeka and Santa Fe Rail Road will be built beyond a peradventure [uncertainty]. Work will commence immediately."

"To no one man in Kansas," the *Record* went on to say, "can the praise be awarded more surely for fostering and encouraging the various railroad schemes now making every farmer in the State richer than he was, than to Col. Holliday. While others have abandoned the project as chimerical, the Col. has never faltered."[2]

Holliday was definitely a cheerleader for Topeka and his railroad, but he was also never shy about boasting of his efforts in their behalf. When a local bond issue failed and momentarily derailed his development plans for Topeka, he "almost resolved that I would quit the town." Writing to Mary, who was traveling in Europe, Holliday grumbled, "I have given the place eighteen years of my life and a great deal of money—as you well know—and without my unceasing and untiring efforts Topeka, today, would be no better than the small communities around her."[3]

But when the first shovel of dirt was turned later in the fall of 1868, Atchison residents thought something terribly amiss. The grade did not start in Atchison or even lead northeast out of Topeka *toward* their city. Instead it ran south from Topeka toward coal deposits at Carbondale, a dozen miles away and a ready market. And when construction started in the opposite direction, it was not to reach Atchison but merely to drive pilings for a bridge across the Kansas River on the outskirts of Topeka and make a connection with the Kansas Pacific Railway.

The neophyte Santa Fe could hardly call the established Kansas Pacific its competitor—yet—and in the interim, the Kansas Pacific provided an easy route over which construction materiel from the East could reach the Santa Fe's railhead. The 1,400-foot bridge over the Kansas River was opened to traffic on March 30, 1869, and the first Santa Fe locomotive over the new line was christened the Cyrus K. Holliday.

Compared to the smoke-belching behemoths that would one day roar over the Santa Fe line, the "Holliday" was a decidedly dainty ma-

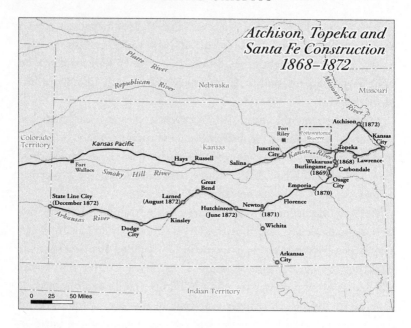

Atchison, Topeka and Santa Fe Construction 1868–1872

chine. It had a pointy cowcatcher, balloon smokestack, and a 4-4-0 wheel configuration—the four drivers being five feet tall. Originally built in Cincinnati for the Ohio and Mississippi Railroad, the locomotive arrived in North Topeka via the Kansas Pacific and was soon pulling flatcars loaded with rails across the new bridge.

More locomotives and rolling stock quickly followed, including a rickety wooden coach purchased used from the Indianapolis and Cincinnati Railroad. By July 1, the Santa Fe was operational into Carbondale, and coal shipments contributed important freight revenue. Ten weeks later, another 27 miles of track was completed to Burlingame in western Osage County. The town went wild.

The *Osage Chronicle* boasted that "old earth slowly careened in the direction of Emporia, changing her center from the poles to Burlingame . . ." (Never mind that a caricature of a steam engine accompanying the story looked more like the original Tom Thumb of the Baltimore and Ohio than the Cyrus K. Holliday.) "Rival papers, please 'toot!' " the *Chronicle* concluded.[4]

Now there was a little momentum behind the line. It became easier to attract eastern capital, and the grade was pushed farther southwest. Emporia took the Santa Fe's arrival in July 1870 in stride—largely because since the prior December it had been connected to the Missouri, Kansas and Texas Railroad (fondly called "the Katy"). But for the Santa Fe, reaching Emporia was significant. This was the first of the cattle towns it would encounter. Now both cattle and coal rolled into Topeka on the little road.

These revenues and the promise of more cattle the farther west the line built encouraged Santa Fe stockholders. But the townspeople of Atchison—still waiting for the Topeka-Atchison link to be completed—were becoming increasingly disgruntled. Their anger grew when a large order of rails arrived in St. Louis, bound not for Atchison but for the railhead at Emporia.

Atchison grumbling aside, the Santa Fe's directors soon realized that they could no longer afford to benefit the Kansas Pacific by turning freight over to it in North Topeka. It was finally time to build its own line to Atchison. There the Santa Fe had a choice of three railroads not in direct competition with it for access to Chicago and St. Louis, including the Rock Island, and the Chicago, Burlington and Quincy. Even so, delayed by a lack of rails, the first through train between Atchison and Topeka did not operate until May 13, 1872.[5]

Meanwhile, survey crews had been moving rapidly west of Emporia toward Fort Dodge. The first major stop was the new town of Newton. It was a typical railhead boomtown. One day there was nothing but wide-open prairie and a few survey stakes marking the proposed right-of-way. Almost overnight, a hodgepodge of buildings sprang up.

Few locations marked the line of the frontier as heavily as the railhead. By their very nature, railhead construction camps were rough and rowdy places, populated by men who needed to blow off steam after a week of heavy work. But behind the advancing iron horse, its tracks stretched as a conduit, not only of construction men and materiel but also the rush of civilization itself: farmers, ranchers, merchants, and more.

Sometimes the railhead was a mobile mass of tents, wagons, and people inching its way across the plains. At other times, construction delays caused by lack of supplies or financing forced a pause in one location. But one thing was certain. The coming of the railroad would change the landscape forever. As one report from the Kansas plains prophesied: "Settlers are fast coming into the valley. Town lots are selling fast. The change that will take place within one year, even in this town and surrounding country, is hardly to be realized."[6]

The *Kansas Daily Commonwealth* of Topeka noted Newton's arrival as "an enterprising railroad town, situated on the [railroad] and the intersection of the great Texas cattle trail." Four weeks after the first building was commenced, there were "twenty houses almost finished, with lumber on the ground for the speedy erection of many more."

Seventy-eight miles of new track were opened between Emporia and Newton, and the first passenger train chugged into the infant town on July 17, 1871. Along with it came a raucous mob that rode the crest of the railroad's advance.

"It must be borne in mind that the state of society in that town [Newton] is now at its worst," the neighboring *Emporia News* lamented. "The town is largely inhabited by prostitutes, gamblers and whisky-sellers. Pistol shooting is the common amusement. All the frequenters of the saloons, gambling dens and houses of ill-fame are armed at all times, mostly with two pistols."

And when this element of railhead riffraff collided with the cowboys moving cattle north to the railroad, there was bound to be trouble. A month after the railroad reached Newton, five men were killed and another six wounded in a wild shooting spree that came to be called the Newton General Massacre. When a hastily assembled coroner's jury returned an unpopular charge of manslaughter against an alleged instigator, the jurors were promptly advised to leave town lest they themselves be lynched.

But soon it was the railhead that was moving on. The cattle business held sway in Newton only for that first year of 1871, when forty thousand head were shipped via the Santa Fe to eastern markets. By the next trail driving season, the spur of the Wichita and South Western Railroad had been built south from the Santa Fe main line, and Wichita— not Newton—assumed the laurels and pitfalls of being a major cow town.[7]

Construction west out of Newton began in earnest in the early spring of 1872, but now the calendar came into play. Despite a brisk business between Newton and points east, for the Santa Fe to secure its total land grant, the remaining 330 miles of track to the Colorado border had to be completed in another year to meet the ten-year construction deadline.

With the clock ticking, Senator Pomeroy tried to get a congressional extension. But Congress, once the dispenser of unbridled largesse to the railroads, was feeling pressure from the exposure of the Crédit Mobilier scandal, in which promoters of the Union Pacific Railroad had incorporated an allied company and awarded themselves construction contracts at huge profits. But the real scandal occurred when certain congressmen attempted to expose the scheme and then were themselves readily silenced by receiving Crédit Mobilier stock at bargain prices.

No doubt leery of the growing political fallout from the Crédit Mobilier situation, only sixty members of the House of Representatives voted in favor of even allowing debate on Pomeroy's extension request, and it failed. In this contest, the Santa Fe would be racing the clock.

The railroad's fate rested in the hands of a hard-driving, hard-swearing construction boss named J. D. "Pete" Criley and his experienced gang of largely Irish laborers. Working for about $2 per day, good money then, they pushed the line west at more than a mile a day during the summer of 1872. Thirty-three miles between Newton and Hutchinson were opened on June 17; another 74 miles on past Great Bend to Larned on August 12. Almost all the route followed in or near the ruts of the Santa Fe Trail.

Along the way, the *Kansas Daily Commonwealth* reported that on one day alone, Criley's crews laid 3 miles and 400 feet of track. "This beats anything in the previous history of track-laying in the west," the paper cheered, apparently oblivious to the Central Pacific's 1869 record of 10 miles and 56 feet.

With the rush on to extend the railhead with all haste, this early tracklaying was not very refined. Surveyors staked the route, and horse-drawn scrapers hurriedly followed, clearing away the prairie topsoil. Across this rolling terrain, cuts and fills were relatively simple excavations, neither the deep incisions nor high mounds that would be required in mountainous country farther west. Men with shovels and wheelbarrows followed the scrapers to smooth out any ridges or holes.

Next ties were distributed along the right-of-way and then "bedded" into a loose ballast of sand and dirt—a far cry from the tamped gravel ballast of later operations. Because the roadbed was not entirely smooth and the ties were not entirely uniform in size, workers then had to tamp down those ties that were above grade and raise those that were too low by throwing dirt under them.

The clang of rails followed as laborers gripped the long strands with giant tongs and carried them into place from a flatcar inching its way close behind. The rails were dropped at the command of "Down!" and then joined together with tie bars. The rhythmic twang of spikes being driven into wood announced the completion of another thirty-foot section of track.

One thing that Kansas lacked for easy railroad construction was a handy supply of ties. Some were shipped from the more wooded eastern sections of the state and others cut from groves along nearby riverbanks. But as the railroad got farther west, the mountains of Colorado offered a major source, and the Arkansas River—at least when running high in the spring and early summer—promised a ready conduit.

As the Santa Fe advanced past the new town of Great Bend, tie contractors under contract to the railroad for delivery of two hundred thousand ties built an 805-foot containment boom on an angle across the river just east of town. This structure was intended to corral ties that were cut high in Colorado's mountains and floated some 600 miles downstream.

The plan was to send about twenty thousand ties at a time downstream and have tie wranglers follow the flotilla in small boats and by horseback to herd them along. How successful this particular operation was is not readily known, but hundreds of thousands of ties made their way by water or wagon out of the mountains of Colorado and into the construction camps on the plains.

By now, Holliday's enterprise—which had started with one locomotive—boasted 15 engines, 19 passenger cars, and a variety of 362 stock, coal, and revenue freight cars. When regular passenger service began between Atchison and Larned, trains covered 291 miles between the two towns in a published timetable of 17 hours and 40 minutes—an average of 16.5 miles per hour. Cost for a one-way ticket was $16.[8]

Another 60 miles of track put the railhead at Dodge City. No doubt construction boss Criley shuddered for the safety and sobriety of his

Irishmen, because the heady times of Newton paled in comparison to the distractions offered by Dodge City.

For starters, "the law" was a rather nebulous concept in Dodge City. The town itself—briefly called Buffalo City after the rapidly vanishing herds—was scarcely a few weeks old when the railroad arrived. According to one observer, it consisted of a dozen frame houses, two-dozen tents, a few adobe houses, several stores, a gunsmith's establishment, and a barbershop. "Nearly every building has out the sign, in large letters, 'Saloon.' "

Establishing a civil government was far down the list of priorities, but that meant people frequently took matters into their own hands. Witness the case of Jack Reynolds. When Reynolds, described as a "notoriously mean and contemptible desperado," caused trouble on a train, the conductor "tackled the brute, took the six-shooter away from him and pitched him off the train." Unfortunately, in the process, the conductor suffered a broken arm that somehow proved fatal. But Reynolds soon got his due. When he tried to bully one of Criley's men, the track-layer "put six balls, in rapid succession, into Jack's body" and he "expired instantly."[9]

Dodge City suffered through far worse and more prolonged violence several years later when the Santa Fe opened major cattle pen operations there. Among the leading players then were two brothers named Bat and Ed Masterson. They had arrived in town with the railroad, working to grade 4 miles of the Santa Fe's line in surrounding Ford County between Fort Dodge and infant Buffalo City in the summer of 1872. But when it came time for Raymond Ritter, one of the many grading subcontractors, to pay them, the brothers received only a few dollars and a promise that Ritter would return shortly with the balance—the sizeable sum of some $300.

As time went by and Ritter failed to reappear, the Mastersons realized that they had been duped. They hunted buffalo and did odd jobs to make ends meet. Then in the spring of 1873, Bat heard that Ritter had been seen farther west at the Santa Fe's most recent railhead. The rumor was that he was headed east on the next train with quite a roll of cash.

When the eastbound train steamed into Dodge City, young Bat boarded the cars alone, marched Ritter off the train at gunpoint, and soon recovered his overdue account. Ritter was quick to scurry back on board and head out of town, while Bat "led the way to Kelley's to set up drinks for the cheering, back-slapping crowd" of new admirers. After that, Bat Masterson was "considered a man to be reckoned with" in Dodge.

With a growing reputation, Bat was elected county sheriff in November 1877, defeating a three-hundred-pound tough named Larry Deger by only 3 votes, 166 to 163. Ed Masterson was appointed city marshal a few weeks later. The Masterson boys—Ed was twenty-five and Bat barely twenty-four—were eager to prove themselves.

They got their chance a few weeks later when six armed men tried to hold up Santa Fe trains on the line east of Dodge City. The gang's first attempt at a water tank east of Kinsley failed when the eastbound passenger train did not stop to take on water as they had expected. The robbers then rode into Kinsley and waited at the depot for the westbound Pueblo Express. In the process, they held the station agent on the platform at gunpoint, but overlooked some $2,000 in the company safe.

As the train pulled into the station, the agent broke free from his captors and shouted a warning to the train crew. As he did so, he leaped across the tracks just in front of the slowing locomotive and used it to shield himself from a hail of gunfire. The train robbers attempted to board the locomotive, but the engineer opened the throttle and sped down the track.

The holdup had been foiled, but the Santa Fe wanted to send a strong message that it would not tolerate such lawlessness. The railroad promptly circulated posters "offering one-hundred-dollar rewards for the capture, dead or alive, of each of the outlaws."

Bat Masterson organized a posse and captured two of the robbers, Dave Rudabaugh and Ed West, in a blinding snowstorm near Crooked Creek, south of Dodge City. Two other gang members were arrested in town when they showed up with thoughts of busting their comrades out of Bat's jail. By then the Santa Fe had dispatched a special train to haul the prisoners to the jail in Kinsley. Bat tried unsuccessfully to capture Mike Rourke, the reputed ringleader, but Rourke was arrested in Ellsworth, Kansas, some months later. The sixth gang member was never caught.

In the end, Dave Rudabaugh avoided prison by turning state's evidence against his captured accomplices, who all served time in Leavenworth. His protestations of turning over a new leaf were without merit, however, and Rudabaugh would go on to a lawless spree in New Mexico—crossing paths with Pat Garrett and Billy the Kid—before being killed by outraged citizens in Chihuahua, Mexico, in 1886.

Bat Masterson's dogged pursuit of the train robbers added to his reputation and placed him in good stead with the Santa Fe, which would soon have cause to call on his talents again. Ed Masterson was not so lucky. In April 1878, he was summoned to quell a disturbance by Texas cowboys at one of Dodge City's ubiquitous dance halls. Ed was gunned down when he tried to disarm one of the rowdies, a cowboy named Jack Wagner, but he managed to return fire and mortally wound his assailant.

Bat did not arrive on the scene until a few minutes later. Tall tales to the contrary, he did not go on a wild spree of revenge but lawfully arrested possible participants. They were later released when the dying Wagner confessed to killing Ed.[10]

Just how wild and lawless Dodge City really was during those cattle years will always be debated, but there is one oft-told story to sum it up. There are as many versions as there were saloons in Dodge City, but the general line has a surly and at least slightly inebriated cowboy boarding a train somewhere along the Santa Fe line through Kansas. When the conductor demanded his ticket and asked where he was going, the fellow retorted that he had no ticket and was going to hell. "Give me a dollar," replied the conductor, "and get off in Dodge."

As winter approached the plains in the fall of 1872, Pete Criley's construction crews pushed the Santa Fe line westward from Dodge City, laying more than 100 additional miles of track. In mid-December they reached the state line—or so they thought. Behind them was a construction season of 303 tough days and almost 300 miles of track since they had struck west from Newton.

But while the men celebrated in the most recent railhead boomtown, "State Line City," federal surveyors announced that according to their measurements, the state line and the certainty of the railroad's land grants was still 4 miles away. Criley quickly gathered up those who were sober—and undoubtedly some who were not—and went to work once more.

" 'State Line City' is being removed four miles farther west," the *Hutchinson News* reported, "in consequence of the government survey establishing the State line that far from the estimate of the A. T. & S. F. R. R. Company. As the city is built out of tents, we presume that no great difficulty is experienced."

But with construction materiel running low, Criley had to scavenge assorted rails and ties from back down the line, even tearing up a couple of sidings to get the required rails. Finally, on December 28, 1872, the construction boss was able to wire Topeka rather grandly: "We send you greeting over the completion of the road to the State line. Beyond us lie fertile valleys that invite us forward . . . The mountains signal us from their lofty crests, and still beyond, the Pacific shouts amen! We send you three cheers over past successes, and three times three for that which is yet to come."[11]

But what was yet to come? With its herculean advance across Kansas, the Santa Fe had cut off the parallel Kansas Pacific line some 50 miles to the north from the lion's share of the cattle trade. But as other railroads built directly into Texas, the Santa Fe itself could not rely on the likes of boisterous Dodge City and other cow towns as its profit centers for very long.

"The road cannot remain on the prairie in the Arkansas valley, but must be pushed on to a profitable terminus in the cattle regions of southern Colorado, and the silver mines of the territory," the *Kansas Daily Commonwealth* declared as the state line was reached. "The A. T. & S. F. road will not be completed until it is stopped by the waves of the Pacific, and has been made the fair weather transcontinental route of the nation."[12]

But for the moment, the Atchison, Topeka and Santa Fe was financially exhausted by the demands of its frenzied 1872 construction season. While building to the Pacific sounded grand, tapping the markets of Colorado and reaching the New Mexico town of its name were its immediate priorities. Neither would be easy. Up ahead, the Colorado railroad scene was becoming quite crowded.

6

Straight West from Denver

Denver in the 1860s was still a dusty, bawling infant of a town. In 1858, reports of a few light pans of placer gold from nearby creeks had somehow mushroomed out of proportion. Wildly overstated and nowhere near Zebulon Pike's grand peak, the find nonetheless encouraged tens of thousands to paint "Pikes Peak or Bust!" on their wagons and head west, hopeful of duplicating the success of the California Gold Rush a decade earlier. Disappointment and despair swept many back across the plains, but enough stayed along the foothills of the Rockies to stake out a future.

A group of Kansans laid out a town site where Cherry Creek empties into the South Platte River and named it after James W. Denver, the governor of Kansas Territory, in whose jurisdiction they were. In 1861 Kansas became a state, and its far-flung western county was split off as Colorado Territory—organized less on its own merits than to permit a clean western boundary to Kansas. Four years of civil war in the East, declining placer operations in the mountains to the west, and a disastrous flood took their toll, but Denver was still there to welcome the vanguard of the postwar rush. The town quickly figured in the plans of railroads with transcontinental goals.

Arriving in Denver in May 1862 as Colorado Territory's second governor, John Evans wasted no time in promoting a railroad connection with the East. A medical doctor by training and a real estate investor in Chicago, Evans had helped to organize the Fort Wayne and Chicago Railroad in 1852. Then, as a member of Chicago's city council, he'd been instrumental in getting its right-of-way into the city. It would not be the only time that Evans would mix politics and railroads.[1]

Prospects for Colorado looked quite promising, the new governor told a large gathering from the balcony of his Denver hotel upon his arrival. This was because Congress was completing the Pacific Railroad Act of 1862, and it had not one but two railroads pointed toward them.

Noting that Kansas was subject to severe droughts and Nebraska occasionally beset by drowning rains, Evans claimed that the railroad bill safeguarded Colorado in either event because it provided two routes from the Missouri River—what would become the Union Pacific from Council Bluffs and the Kansas Pacific from Kansas City. "Whether famine reigns in Kansas, or drenching storms farther north, you will always have a source of supply," Evans boasted.[2]

Indeed, the governor's railroad enthusiasm knew no bounds. On one of his early trips from Denver, Evans inspected Berthoud Pass, a high passage in the Continental Divide, about 50 miles west of Denver. When a surveyor reported that a wagon road was feasible, but a railroad would require a 3.5-mile tunnel, Evans optimistically suggested that gold might be discovered during the tunnel's construction.

A few months later, Evans was back in Chicago trying to convince the other 157 members of the unwieldy board charged with organizing the Union Pacific that the railroad should build through Colorado because of its mineral prospects. In return, he received only a gratuitous statement acknowledging that the development of settlements in *all* the western territories was a welcome impetus to the construction of the road.[3]

By the time Evans returned to Colorado in November 1862—this time he brought his family along as permanent residents—the growing territory was on a collision course with the Arapaho and Cheyenne tribes that roamed the eastern plains. Tensions culminated two years later when, without warning, army and militia units attacked a peaceful Cheyenne camp on Sand Creek, killing over 150, more than half of them women and children. The role that Governor Evans played personally in this atrocity would be long debated, and ensuing recriminations were enough to force him from office.

Despite this, Evans was only getting started with Colorado politics and its railroads. The ex-governor asked John Pierce, one of the assistants on the 1862 Berthoud Pass survey, to take a second look at the pass in the hope that a temporary track might be laid across its heights prior to the construction of a tunnel.

Sure, said Pierce, a temporary track could be run over the pass by a series of switchbacks "with no trouble," but if Evans was determined to reach the Pacific through Colorado, there was an even better route. It would also require a tunnel under the Continental Divide, but it would be less than half the length of the Berthoud bore.

Pierce's suggested alternative ran southwest up the South Platte River from Denver, crossed the wide basin of South Park, hopped across the upper Arkansas River, and burrowed under the divide at the headwaters of Chalk Creek. "The richness of the country and the abundance of fuel on the line through Colorado," Pierce concluded, " . . . demand that these passes should at least be surveyed in a thorough manner."

But the Union Pacific was not interested in either route—Berthoud Pass or Chalk Creek. In fact, the Union Pacific's chief engineer, General Grenville Dodge, had little interest in traversing Colorado by *any* route. John C. Frémont's wintry folly lost in the San Juans, John Gunnison's grim assessment of the Black Canyon as a railroad route, and Dodge's own personal experience in a November blizzard atop Boulder Pass (now called Rollins Pass) had convinced him to stay well clear of Colorado's mountains. No doubt the Central Pacific's challenges in the Sierra Nevada only added to his conviction.[4]

Try as he might, Evans couldn't budge the Union Pacific crowd. Its main line would be built across Wyoming and only nick the corner of Colorado Territory at Julesburg. Denver despaired, but rallied to organize the Denver Pacific Railroad to build from Denver to the Union Pacific at Cheyenne. It might have been only a short line, but Denver was determined to have a railroad with transcontinental connections. With the Kansas Pacific still deep in Kansas, and the Atchison, Topeka and Santa Fe not yet out of Topeka, a connection with the Union Pacific was the logical and most promising choice.

John Evans joined the Denver Pacific's board of directors, and four months later, in March 1868, he was elected its president. The first task of the president of any paper railroad was to raise funds for construction. Without a federal land grant or deep-pocketed investors, the most likely source was county bonds. Local voters were asked to approve a bond issue; the county willingly exchanged its bonds for unmarketable railroad stock because it wanted a railroad built; and then the railroad sold the county bonds—marketable securities instead of unmarketable stock—to finance its construction.

There was, of course, an inherent element of lobbying in this process. Sometimes it went far beyond mere arm-twisting. When a representative of the Kansas Pacific pointedly suggested that the advancing railroad would bypass Denver and head south unless surrounding Arapahoe County floated $2 million in bonds to support it, the locals responded with outrage at the apparent blackmail.

No doubt William Jackson Palmer would have finessed the proposal better, but at the time, he was completing his western survey and brashly telling the Big Four that the Kansas Pacific planned to build to San Francisco with or without them. Indeed, that southern bent by the Kansas Pacific may have been what Denver feared most. With the Union Pacific wedded to Wyoming, if the Kansas Pacific bypassed Denver to the south, instead of two transcontinental railroads—as Governor Evans had boasted back in 1862—Denver might end up with none.

Thanks in part to the indelicate demands of the Kansas Pacific, Arapahoe County turned to the Denver Pacific as its railroad savior and voted $500,000 in bonds for the construction between Denver and Cheyenne. But even these county bonds proved difficult to sell. Eastern capital markets were salivating over the U.S. government bonds from the Central Pacific and Union Pacific with their government-guaranteed interest, and there was no rush to buy Arapahoe County bonds no matter what the yield.[5]

Finally, Evans went hat in hand to Sidney Dillon and Thomas Durant, who along with brothers Oakes and Oliver Ames were the princi-

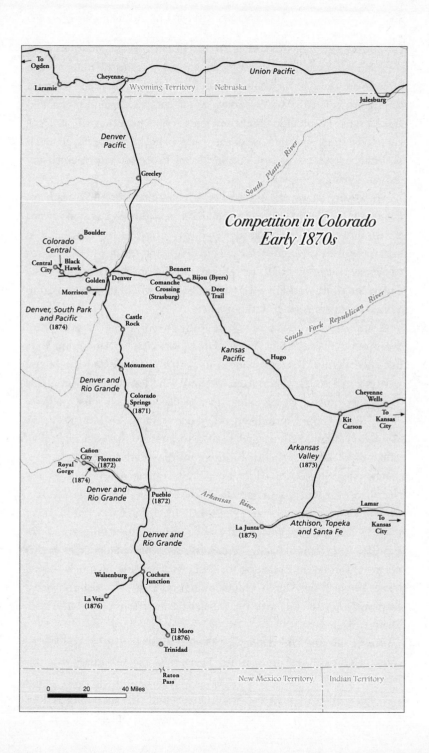

Competition in Colorado
Early 1870s

To Ogden

Laramie

Cheyenne

Wyoming Territory

Nebraska

Union Pacific

Julesburg

Denver Pacific

South Platte River

Greeley

Boulder

Colorado Central

Central City

Black Hawk

Golden

Morrison

Denver

Bennett

Comanche Crossing (Strasburg)

Bijou (Byers)

Deer Trail

Denver, South Park and Pacific (1874)

Castle Rock

Kansas Pacific

Hugo

South Fork Republican River

Monument

Denver and Rio Grande

Colorado Springs (1871)

Cheyenne Wells

Kit Carson

To Kansas City

Cañon City

Royal Gorge (1874)

Florence (1872)

Denver and Rio Grande

Pueblo (1872)

Arkansas Valley (1873)

Arkansas River

La Junta (1875)

Atchison, Topeka and Santa Fe

Lamar

To Kansas City

Denver and Rio Grande

Walsenburg

Cuchara Junction

La Veta (1876)

El Moro (1876)

Trinidad

Raton Pass

New Mexico Territory

Indian Territory

0   20   40 Miles

pal powers building the Union Pacific. When their negotiations were complete, the fledgling Denver Pacific agreed to grade the right-of-way, provide and lay the ties, and build the bridges. Dillon and Durant, through their Crédit Mobilier construction company, would supply and lay the rails and provide the rolling stock—this for a majority of Denver Pacific stock and the lease of the road to the Union Pacific. So much for local control, but Evans and the Denver Board of Trade deemed any railroad preferable to none.

There were, however, two additional requirements in the agreement. Evans and his Denver railroad would have to build an extension toward the mining camps—that was in everyone's best interests—but they also had to apply to Congress for a land grant for the main Denver-to-Cheyenne route. After all, for Dillon and Durant, the masters of the Crédit Mobilier, working without a land grant would have been akin to a high-wire performance without a net.

"I am very busy with my R. R. bill," Evans wrote his wife from Washington in July 1868, but his efforts to secure the land grant were not encouraging. Bills introduced in both the Senate and the House were referred to the Committee on the Pacific Railroad and promptly died quiet deaths. Recognizing that he needed much more political clout, Evans turned to unlikely allies. He went to see John D. Perry, William Jackson Palmer, and their associates at the Kansas Pacific, which was still pondering its future in western Kansas.

The two railroads joined forces, and after some complicated legislative maneuverings, Congress granted the Denver Pacific alternate sections of land for 20 miles on either side of its right-of-way from Denver to Cheyenne and the right to sell $32,000 of bonds per mile. As part of the deal, the Kansas Pacific relinquished its prior land grant rights north of Denver in exchange for $32,000 per mile of much-needed bonds between the Kansas-Colorado line and Denver. It also received a perpetual right-of-way over the Denver Pacific tracks to be built from Denver to Cheyenne.

Wait a minute, said Dillon and Durant. Competitive Kansas Pacific trains operating over its planned Denver Pacific subsidiary was not what they had in mind. The specter of traffic east of Cheyenne being split between the Union Pacific to Omaha and the competing Kansas Pacific to Kansas City via Denver was frightening. But Dillon and Durant were themselves broke at the moment as they raced the Central Pacific to Utah. They had no way to stop Evans from working with the Kansas Pacific. Instead they backed out of the Denver Pacific construction deal. The result for the Union Pacific was that it would wring its hands over Kansas Pacific competition for the next decade.[6]

As Dillon and Durant bowed out, the Denver Pacific's board of directors collectively threw up its hands and offered John Evans all the road's assets and full control if he would just get the road built. Evans agreed and formed a construction company that soon assigned a half interest to R. E. Carr, a director of the Kansas Pacific, who then parceled that half out among Kansas Pacific backers, including a 7 percent interest to Palmer.

The result was that the Denver Pacific was once again a subsidiary, but this time the controlling interest was the Kansas Pacific, not the Union Pacific. Evans remained president of the Denver Pacific, but its reorganized board of directors counted many Kansas Pacific men, including J. Edgar Thomson, Thomas A. Scott, and Palmer.

With Kansas Pacific support, the rails of the Denver Pacific started south from the Union Pacific line at Cheyenne on September 13, 1869, and were completed to Denver for last spike ceremonies on June 24, 1870. "Everybody and wife, sweetheart, etc. etc., was there" to watch the construction of the last few miles into town. Meanwhile, the Kansas Pacific, with Palmer as its construction superintendent, rushed its completion to Denver from the east.[7]

The Kansas Pacific started west from Sheridan, Kansas, with a vengeance late in the fall of 1869 after the Evans-Carr construction arrangement was finally completed. "Our long agony of negotiation with Gov. Evans is over and the contract agreed upon," Palmer sighed, as the Kansas Pacific advertised for 50,000 to 75,000 ties to be delivered to its railhead. That was only a fraction of the 2,500 ties per mile that would ultimately be needed, and on the largely treeless plains, they had to come from hundreds of miles away in Colorado's foothills.

Located just east of present-day Sharon Springs, Sheridan had enjoyed the boom of being a railhead while the Kansas Pacific paused there and negotiated the Denver deals. But once the Kansas Pacific line crossed into Colorado and reached the towns of Cheyenne Wells and Kit Carson in March 1870, Sheridan soon disappeared. "Poor Sheridan!" wrote Palmer to his fiancée. "There is very little of it left now and there will be less on your arrival. It has gradually and silently taken wings and flown away to Kit Carson."

Kit Carson boomed as a railhead and had a "brisk and lively appearance," but the new town was not without its problems. "The water about town is scarce and bad, and is the very worst I have ever had to drink in my life," a correspondent for Denver's *Rocky Mountain News* reported. "It makes one pause before he washes his face in the morning, and leaves him as dirty as before; renders your coffee black and dark, spoils the color and flavor of your tea, obscures the brilliancy of your morning 'cock tail,' ruins the taste of our whisky, and as a beverage, generally, is unpalatable, unhealthy, and disgusting. May a kind providence preserve those who have to use it this summer."[8]

By mid-April, the telegraph line along the Kansas Pacific right-of-way had reached Denver. As the rails followed it west from Kit Carson, it was reported, "the business men of the town don't like this," but the railhead was moving on.

Ties and rails were always in short supply, but now the Plains Indians made a last gasp effort to stop the iron horse. Palmer reported "fighting along our line," and in one attack west of Kit Carson, eleven graders were killed and another nineteen wounded. Several days later, a raiding party tore down the Kansas Pacific water tank 4 miles east of town. Among the troops hastily assigned to protect the construction crews were cavalry from Fort Wallace (near Sheridan) under the command of George Armstrong Custer.[9]

By the end of May, the threat had eased, and with the Denver Pacific closing in on Denver from the north, grading crews began work east from there to meet the advancing Kansas Pacific. Completion was in sight by early August, but the final rush of materiel to the converging railheads was not without mishap. About ten o'clock at night on August 9, a fourteen-car construction train eastbound from Denver and loaded with rails got away from the engineer of number 31. Reportedly, his two brakemen were unable to club down the brakes on the flatcars because the iron rails had been stacked in such a way that it was impossible to operate the brake wheels fully.

The runaway train raced downgrade at an estimated speed of forty miles per hour, with the engineer frantically whistling "down brakes" to no avail. Up ahead, a string of worker-filled boarding cars was parked in a cut near the end of track. Here the grade reversed and ran uphill, but the combined weight of the iron and the speed of the train were too much to control. The engineer threw his locomotive into reverse and jumped.

The locomotive struck the first car of the boarding train, and it telescoped into the next two cars. Six tracklayers—including four workers who were sleeping under the cars—were killed and eleven others injured. A special train carrying three doctors, including pioneer Denver physician Frederick J. Bancroft, raced to the scene from Denver.

Surviving tracklayers were quick to blame the engineer and conductor for the crash. Loose talk of hanging them inched toward action until construction superintendent Leonard Eicholtz intervened and eventually convinced the angry workers that the accident had been "unavoidable." A hurriedly convened coroner's jury concurred with that verdict.[10]

By the next morning, a wrecker from Denver had the locomotive back on the track and the tangled mess of cars off the main line. Tracklayers continued laying rail eastward and reached Bennett on the morning of August 11. Two days later, crews building westward paused at Bijou (soon renamed Byers) because of a shortage of rails. Now only 10.25 miles remained between the two railheads.

It would have been a simple matter to keep laying rail eastward from Bennett, but superintendent Eicholtz had something else in mind. The year before, he had witnessed the Central Pacific's tracklaying record in its final sprint to meet the Union Pacific at Promontory Summit—10 miles and 56 feet of track in less than twelve hours—on April 28, 1869. Determined to beat it, Eicholtz had teamsters haul iron to the eastern end of the gap while his tracklayers got a Sunday to rest.

Early on Monday morning, August 15, 1870, an American flag— and by some reports, a keg of whiskey—was placed at the midway point. At five in the morning, with dawn just lighting the eastern sky, the two crews went to work. Eicholtz personally directed the western crew, but by midmorning, they were a half mile behind their eastern competitors. An hour later, the eastern crew was ahead 4 miles to 3.

Inexplicably, Eicholtz's team on the western end lost more time when it ran out of rail shortly after noon. More iron was hurried forward while the pace on the eastern end slowed as its own supply of iron grew thin. Finally, at 2:53 p.m., the rails touched at Comanche Crossing, just east of present-day Strasburg. No record remains of who claimed the keg—if indeed there was one—but the westbound workers had laid 5.25 miles and 400 feet of track, and their eastbound cohorts, 5 miles, less 400 feet. The Kansas Pacific was complete to Denver, and Eicholtz's tracklaying record secured: 10.25 miles in less than ten hours.

With unbridled enthusiasm, John D. Perry wired General Palmer congratulations from St. Louis. "In the name of the company, I thank you and those under you for the able manner in which the important work under your charge has been brought to a successful terminus. I do not know of anything in the history of railroad construction in this or any other country to equal the splendid success exhibited by you yesterday," Perry concluded, as he made plans to host an opening excursion gala from St. Louis to Denver.

"The coach has given way before the palace car, and staging for the overland traveler is a thing of the past," the *Rocky Mountain News* proclaimed. "For eleven years these coaches have been run with a regularity unparalleled, and afforded our only means of travel . . . But 'their occupation is gone.' The bright coaches will soon be dusty, the shining harness will soon become rusty, and the handsome prancing fours in-hand will descend to the more common-place position of farm or draft horses. The 'overland boys' will be known no more for they too will have become scattered."

Alongside this nostalgic obituary, there were advertisements boasting the new Kansas Pacific Railway. Its Smoky Hill route was pronounced the best connection to the East and "the only road that has unbroken connections with all points East via the great iron bridge over the Missouri River at Kansas City." Not only would passengers save time by using the Kansas Pacific instead of journeying northward to the Union Pacific, the railroad claimed, but also they would avoid the expense and annoyance of crossing the Missouri River by boat.[11]

By boat? Yes, it was true. The claim of the Central Pacific and Union Pacific to have completed the first transcontinental railroad at Promontory Summit, Utah, on May 10, 1869, contained several qualifiers. To be sure, it was a grand achievement, but one could not yet ride rails without interruption from the Atlantic to the Pacific. There was a 1,500-foot gap across the Missouri River between Omaha, Nebraska, and Council Bluffs, Iowa, and another gap between Sacramento and Oakland, California.

While the Union Pacific ferried passengers and freight across the Missouri at Omaha, the Hannibal and St. Joseph Railroad (soon to become part of the Chicago, Burlington and Quincy) completed its tracks into Kansas City via a bridge across the Missouri on June 30, 1869. (At the time, this was the only bridge across the Missouri from the Mississippi upstream to Fort Benton, Montana.) At Kansas City, the Hannibal and St. Joseph linked up with the Kansas Pacific and provided uninterrupted rail service eastward into Chicago, crossing the Mississippi over a bridge at Quincy, Illinois.

A few months later, the California gap on the Central Pacific was closed when the Big Four–controlled San Francisco and Alameda Railroad completed rails into Oakland. That left the 1,500-foot span on the Union Pacific across the Missouri. This gap was closed for sixty-six days in January and February 1870, when temporary track was laid across the frozen river. That lasted until the ice broke up on March 14, and ferry service was resumed. A similar arrangement was made during the winters of 1871 and 1872. The Union Pacific did not complete its massive $2.87 million bridge across the Missouri River at Omaha until March 22, 1872.

In the meantime, transcontinental rail service on the Kansas Pacific via Kansas City and its bridge was about 300 miles longer than on the Union Pacific via Omaha and its river crossing. No one seems to have been too troubled by the latter, and both lines got plenty of business. However, the fact remains that the final spike of the Kansas Pacific Railway driven at Comanche Crossing, Colorado, on August 15, 1870, marked the completion of the first *uninterrupted* transcontinental railroad between the Atlantic and Pacific oceans.

It ran from the Pennsylvania Railroad at Jersey City, New Jersey, west to Chicago; the Chicago, Burlington and Quincy to Kansas City; the Kansas Pacific to Denver; the Denver Pacific to Cheyenne; the Union Pacific to Promontory Summit; and the Central Pacific to Oakland. This route remained the only complete transcontinental until the

Union Pacific's bridge opened at Omaha nineteen months later. Even so, the golden spike at Promontory Summit garners history's accolades, while the joining of the rails at Comanche Crossing rates scarcely a footnote. At the time, the Atchison, Topeka and Santa Fe had barely made it from Topeka to Emporia.[12]

With the joint Denver Pacific–Kansas Pacific line operational, neither John Evans nor William Jackson Palmer was content to rest on his laurels. Evans was still transfixed—as were many Colorado railroaders of his and the following generation—with the idea of a direct rail link straight west from Denver. The Denver Pacific ran to the north and the Kansas Pacific still eyed Santa Fe to the south, but not even the rocky heights and rugged canyons west of Denver could shake his notion that it was feasible to lay rails directly through this labyrinth.

When the Colorado Central Railroad blocked the most direct route west along Clear Creek, Evans remembered John Pierce's description of the route up the South Platte and across South Park. Evans sold his Kansas Pacific stock, and on October 1, 1872, he incorporated the Denver, South Park and Pacific Railroad. Doing so put him on a collision course with his onetime Kansas Pacific ally, William Jackson Palmer.[13]

Palmer, too, was now looking to his own interests. Even before the completion of the Kansas Pacific to Denver, the general had served notice that he was resigning from the company. In the short term, he had personal concerns. The handsome and quite eligible bachelor was to be married to one of the East's most alluring prospects. With wavy hair and a button nose, she was just turning nineteen when they met in a railcar in St. Louis. Her name was Mary Lincoln Mellen, but everyone called her "Queen," a testament to how she expected to be treated.

Queen's father was William Proctor Mellen, a former law partner of Abraham Lincoln's first secretary of the treasury, Salmon P. Chase, and well connected in eastern financial circles. With Queen accompanying him, Mellen was in St. Louis tending to client interests when they first met Palmer in March 1869. Mellen readily embraced the relationship and aided his future son-in-law with East Coast contacts while availing himself of western investments in Palmer's enterprises. Palmer and Queen became engaged almost immediately—she persisted in addressing him as "General" for several months until he chastised her to do otherwise—and planned a November 1870 wedding to be followed by the requisite European honeymoon.

But in the long term, beyond romance, the general also had his own railroad in mind, and he would combine nuptial bliss with fund-raising while in Europe. The object, as he confessed to Queen, was "a little railroad of a few hundred miles in length all under one's own control with one's friends, to have no jealousies and contests and differing policies, but to be able to carry out unimpeded and harmoniously one's views in regard to what ought and ought not to be done."

Poor Palmer. To entertain such an idealistic view, he must have been severely infected by the love bug. Surely his prior experiences at J. Edgar Thomson's elbow and throughout the Kansas Pacific campaign had taught him the folly of any such talk of railroad harmony. But Palmer was a young man on a mission, and when Queen responded enthusiastically, if somewhat naively, to what her beau characterized as his "dream at the car window," he was off and running.

Early in February 1870, Palmer told Queen that he had "laid the smallest first flooring . . . for an organization independent of the Kansas Pacific" that would run north and south along the foothills of the Rockies from Denver south to Santa Fe and beyond. It would go right past their planned homestead at Monument, Colorado, "but not near enough to make it noisy . . . It won't hurt—when it is our own railroad, will it?" he teased her.[14]

So, on October 27, 1870, in between the completion of the Kansas Pacific to Denver and his marriage to Queen Mellen, William Jackson Palmer filed the certificate of incorporation for the Denver and Rio Grande Railway. Among those joining him as a director was his soon-to-be father-in-law. The next day, the directors elected Palmer the company's president and authorized him to contract for the construction of the road.

Aside from its north-south axis, the Denver and Rio Grande was to be quite different from its competitors in one significant respect. For reasons that probably went back to his youthful visits to the mountainous railroads of Wales, in the United Kingdom, Palmer decided to construct the Denver and Rio Grande as a narrow gauge.

Gauge, in railroad parlance, is the distance between the inside edges of the rails and the corresponding wheel span of the locomotive and cars. Prior to the Civil War, American railroads used various gauges, the interchange of which created havoc when moving shipments from one road to another. The Pacific Railroad Act of 1862 mandated that the entire length of the Pacific railroad and its branches be of uniform width so that cars could be "run from the Missouri River to the Pacific coast." The president of the United States was charged with determining what that gauge would be.

As might be expected, Lincoln came under intense lobbying from all sides. Collis P. Huntington favored a 5' gauge because that is how the initial tracks of the Central Pacific were laid. The Mississippi and Missouri also favored the 5' gauge. Among other roads, the New York Central and the Baltimore and Ohio advocated their own 4' 8½" gauge, which was widely used in Great Britain.

Lincoln called for a secret ballot among his advisors and then announced for the 5' gauge without divulging the vote. Urged on by New York congressman Erastus Corning, who by no small coincidence was also president of the New York Central, Congress quickly overruled Lincoln and established the uniform gauge at 4' 8½"—what thereafter was termed standard gauge.[15]

Technically, narrow gauge was anything smaller than standard gauge, although Palmer and others built their narrow gauge lines to a specified width of three feet. Palmer chose the narrow gauge because it could climb steeper grades, turn tighter curves, and in general was less expensive to construct than standard gauge. The flip side, of course, was that the tonnage that could be hauled on any given narrow gauge trip was less than that of comparable standard gauge trains. Time would tell whether Palmer's decision to build "a baby road" was the correct one.

The projected routes of the Denver and Rio Grande were both decidedly linear—a direct north-south main line from Denver to El Paso and into Mexico—and territorially expansive: no less than seven branch lines spreading out like tentacles and tapping perceived local markets. Beyond Palmer's musings to Queen about "how fine it would be to have a little railroad," the general and his investors thought that they held a distinct competitive advantage over the east-west lines.

In addition to mining prospects in the Colorado and New Mexico mountains, Palmer foresaw a continued flow of homesteaders like those who had fueled the Kansas Pacific and Santa Fe. But Palmer also was somewhat visionary in anticipating a rush of tourists that he felt certain would seek out the region's dry climate and grand scenery. Finally, Palmer saw his road as the logical north-south connecting link between the east-west transcontinental lines and the cities that would spring up at those junctions.[16]

To a large extent, Palmer was right on these counts, but he was dead wrong on his overall thesis that his little road would somehow be free from competition. If the lucrative traffic that Palmer forecast came to pass, it was simply not reasonable to assume that men like John Evans, Cyrus K. Holliday, or Collis P. Huntington would turn aside simply because one railroad had already occupied the field.

The Denver and Rio Grande Railway began grading south of Denver early in 1871. By October, its rails were complete to Colorado Springs, a town founded and developed by the same cadre of Palmer associates who controlled the railroad and its construction company. These interests sponsored an excursion for the Denver press to see the completed line and boast of the splendor of their new town. The general and his young bride were on hand to greet them, and Queen initially embraced life here. She organized a school, presided over the budding social scene—a queen indeed—and supervised the construction of the Palmer home west of town.

By the spring of 1872—the year of the Santa Fe's sprint west from Newton to the Colorado-Kansas line—the Rio Grande had graded another 44 miles to Pueblo. Rails would reach the town that summer and then be extended west to Labran, Colorado (present-day Florence), to tap nearby coal deposits. But in the meantime, General Palmer and Queen embarked on a trip to Mexico, where Palmer began protracted negotiations with the Mexican government to secure a franchise for the line south from El Paso. It was evidence that the magnitude of Palmer's own transcontinental plans had not diminished.[17]

But while Palmer looked far afield from Colorado, the Denver and Rio Grande was not nearly as free from competition as the general boasted. John Evans still had designs on the South Park region. The Atchison, Topeka and Santa Fe stood poised to cross the Colorado border and build up the Arkansas River toward Pueblo. The Kansas Pacific was looking south from its main line at Kit Carson, once again thinking of the southern route to Santa Fe. Lastly, any railroad heading into the Southwest did so at its peril if it failed to take into account the designs of Huntington and his California cohorts. Competition was one thing of which there was plenty.

7

"Why Is It We Have So Many Bitter Enemies?"

It was a long way between Colorado's mountains and California, but ever since his first conversations with John D. Perry and Thomas A. Scott, Collis P. Huntington was taking no chances that out of squabbles there might come a railroad streaking into California's backdoor. He had too much at stake to do otherwise.

Few men saw their own power increase more dramatically than Huntington and his partners, Stanford, Crocker, and Hopkins, did in the decade of the 1860s. From four merely prosperous merchants, the Big Four were becoming the political and business fulcrum of California, if not the western United States.

Leland Stanford served a two-year term as California's governor, became a mainstay of Republican Party politics, and enjoyed the prestige of being front and center as a railroad president. Charles Crocker ramrodded the flow of men and materiel to the railhead, whether that be in the snows of the high Sierras or later in the deserts of Nevada and Utah. Quiet Mark Hopkins stayed out of the limelight but presided over the myriad of financial details that would someday pay off in millions for each of them.

Huntington's role was twofold: one assigned, the other assumed.

Huntington was the designated rainmaker, the partner whose wheeling and dealing—and sometimes outright bribing—ensured the associates access to government land grants, foreign and domestic investment capital, and proceeds from the sale of largely unproven railroad bonds. But Huntington was also the inveterate railroad builder of the group. The other three were keenly interested in their holdings, but for them it was business. For Huntington, railroading became an insatiable obsession.

There is no question that Huntington was also the driving empire builder of the group. He had little patience in his manner and no wasted motion in his methods. "Had he been a soldier," one newspaper editor observed, "he would not have depended upon tactics . . . he . . . would have struck directly at the enemy's center."[1]

In the beginning, the Big Four had their hands full with the Central Pacific and did not lack for competition in California. In 1860 a competing group of San Francisco businessmen incorporated the San Francisco and San Jose Railroad. After the usual false starts in the transition from paper railroad to construction, track was completed to San Jose in 1864.

Overshadowed by transcontinental aspirants, the San Francisco and San Jose was not accorded federal subsidies or land grants in the Pacific Railway acts. Nonetheless, the railroad raised local financing from the city of San Francisco and surrounding counties and extended almost 30 miles farther south to Gilroy. By then, the San Franciscans backing the venture had seen the growing power of federal land grants, and they readily incorporated another line with a less regional identity.

Called the Southern Pacific Railroad Company, its declared objective was to link San Francisco with Los Angeles and San Diego along the coast and then build east from San Diego to the eastern border of the state. In July 1866, Congress approved its right-of-way and land grants of ten alternate sections per mile on the condition that the railroad connect with the proposed Atlantic and Pacific Railroad near present-day Needles on the California-Arizona border. This had the effect of bending the Southern Pacific's attention eastward from its stated route south to Los Angeles and San Diego, but as it had yet to lay a mile of track, there was plenty of time for maneuvering.[2]

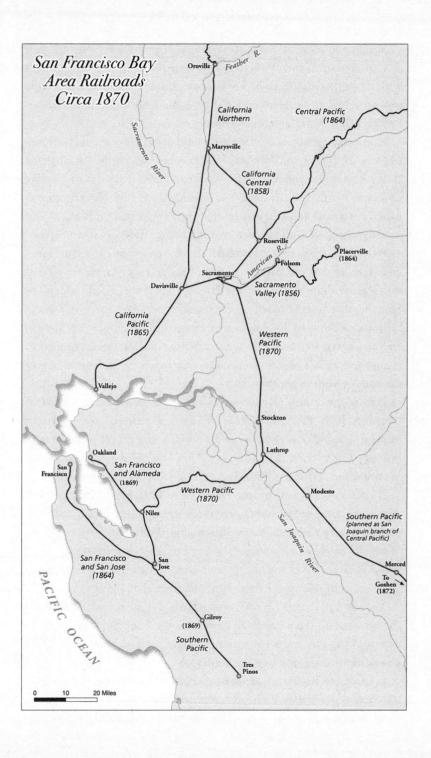

San Francisco Bay
Area Railroads
Circa 1870

Oroville

Feather R.

California
Northern

Central Pacific
(1864)

Marysville

California
Central
(1858)

Sacramento River

Roseville

American R.

Placerville
(1864)

Folsom

Sacramento

Davisville

Sacramento
Valley (1856)

California
Pacific
(1865)

Western
Pacific
(1870)

Vallejo

Stockton

Oakland

Lathrop

San
Francisco

San Francisco
and Alameda
(1869)

Western Pacific
(1870)

Modesto

Niles

San Joaquin River

Southern Pacific
(planned as San
Joaquin branch of
Central Pacific)

San Francisco
and San Jose
(1864)

San
Jose

Merced

To
Goshen
(1872)

PACIFIC OCEAN

Gilroy

(1869)

Southern
Pacific

Tres
Pinos

0   10   20 Miles

Meanwhile, essentially the same group of San Francisco businessmen also incorporated the Western Pacific Railroad—not to be confused with a twentieth-century line of the same name. This Western Pacific was projected to build from San Jose around the eastern side of San Francisco Bay to Sacramento via Stockton.

In a complicated transaction they would come to regret and later rectify, the Big Four initially assigned the Central Pacific's land grant rights west of Sacramento to the Western Pacific. They did so in order to secure San Francisco's financial backing to their broader transcontinental enterprise and as a gesture that their line's final terminus would be somewhere on San Francisco Bay and not up the Sacramento River.

But no matter who controlled it, the San Francisco–San Jose– Stockton–Sacramento route was circuitous at best. A competing all-water grade route was incorporated as the California Pacific along the Sacramento River. It relied on ferries across the bay and avoided the hilly divide between San Jose and Stockton. Other competition loomed for the Central Pacific north of Sacramento. Indeed, there appeared to be no shortage of California railroad ventures—some with actual track, many more with paper charters.[3]

But by the spring of 1868—as Huntington was having his initial meetings with Perry and Scott—California railroads were coming under increasing criticism over rates from the very people who had once been so eager to cheer their advances. After Mark Hopkins made a point of noting such criticism, Huntington was quick with a rejoinder.

"I notice that you write that everybody is in favor of a railroad until they get it built, and then every one is against it, unless the railroad company will carry them and theirs for nothing," Huntington wrote. "In all of which I think you are quite right; but I have about made up my mind that it is about as well to fight them on all the railroads in the State, as on our road, as it is not much more fight and there is more pay . . ."

Then in a postscript, Huntington added: "I wish you would send me the names of all the railroads in California, the length of them, and the names of the officers, stating starting point and terminus." Hopkins knew that Huntington was not kidding.[4]

In truth, the Big Four had already purchased their earliest competitor, the Sacramento Valley Railroad from Sacramento to Folsom, as well as its extension east toward Placerville. To the south, the Big Four's construction company ended up building the Western Pacific, and that route was soon back in their hands. Then, on August 25, 1869, the Central Pacific purchased the San Francisco and Alameda Railroad that ran from Niles on the Western Pacific straight into the heart of Oakland.

Frenzied development ensued on the Oakland waterfront, including a wharf over 2 miles in length, and, with the completion of the Central Pacific–Union Pacific earlier that year, there was no longer any doubt that the Big Four had secured their window on the Pacific. But what about the southern half of the state?[5]

Even before Huntington's request to Hopkins for a list of the state's railroads, there was talk that the emerging Central Pacific–Western Pacific alliance exerted influence, if not outright control, over the trackless Southern Pacific. As president of the Central Pacific, Leland Stanford denied these rumors so vehemently in the *San Francisco Bulletin* in March 1868 that for many it was a case that all his smoke had to conceal at least a little fire. Those flames became a public record the following September when it was Collis P. Huntington who signed the letter transmitting the Southern Pacific's annual report to Congress as required by its land grant. Of course, the Big Four had interests south of San Francisco.[6]

The Southern Pacific's original charter called for it to run south between the coast and the Coast Ranges to reach Los Angeles and San Diego. From the latter, it would angle northeast and complete a transcontinental link with the projected Atlantic and Pacific at the Needles crossing of the Colorado River. But when it became clear that prior Mexican land grants limited the amount of public lands available along that path in the southern third of the state, the Southern Pacific remapped its route.

Now it led southeast from the San Francisco and San Jose's terminus at Gilroy, down the western edge of the Coast Range to Hollister and Tres Pinos, and then east across the Coast Range to the San Joaquin Valley. If a transcontinental connection at Needles was the objective, this was certainly the shorter, more direct route.

This hardly left commercial interests in Los Angeles and San Diego very pleased, but they soon found an unlikely hero. General William S. Rosecrans, who had chosen the wrong road at Chickamauga and ridden to ridicule, had nonetheless emerged from the Civil War determined to resurrect his career in California. He started by buying considerable real estate between Los Angeles and San Diego, flirted with running for the California governorship, and then settled on a brief appointment as ambassador to Mexico.

Rosecrans became convinced that yet another railroad promotion by John C. Frémont—this one to build the Memphis, El Paso, and Pacific along the 32nd parallel—stood half a chance of success. (Frémont was enthralled with the route's warmer climates after his snowy experiences in Colorado.) Consequently, Rosecrans incorporated the California Southern Railroad to run from Frémont's projected Pacific terminus at San Diego, north up the coast to San Francisco.

Though flaunting only a paper railroad, Rosecrans caught the attention of the Big Four when he boasted that if the Southern Pacific altered its route and bypassed Los Angeles and San Diego, he would build up the coast route. If the Southern Pacific stuck to the coast, Rosecrans threatened to cross into the San Joaquin Valley and challenge the Southern Pacific's contemplated hookup with the Atlantic and Pacific, as well as tap the valley's developing agricultural markets.

"Huntington," his biographer David Lavender later wrote, "had heard many people talk about more railroad than they were able to build"— Huntington himself sometimes had more railroad than he could build— but Rosecrans seemed to have widespread support among the locals of Southern California and to be a credible threat. The general also had certain influence among former comrades in arms in Washington.[7]

Consequently, Huntington and his associates would take no chances. In exchange for an undisclosed sum and a vague promise to build a coastal line to San Diego, Rosecrans delivered the paper California Southern into the hands of the Big Four. The loosely held myth that the Central Pacific and Southern Pacific somehow answered to different masters was swept away on October 12, 1870, when Huntington next consolidated the Southern Pacific, the San Francisco and San Jose, and the California Southern under the name of the Southern Pacific Railroad Company. Huntington became its president.

Rosecrans later had second thoughts and tried to maneuver into the combined company. When Huntington suggested a substantial cash payment as a prerequisite for entry—he had enough partners, but cash for his highly leveraged operations was another matter—Rosecrans balked. In a huff, the general incorporated the California Southern *Coast* Railroad and tried to attract another offer. This time, having been to the well once before, he came up dry.[8]

But now Huntington faced an adversary waving more than incorporation papers. While stymied in Colorado with the Kansas Pacific, Thomas A. Scott was far from finished with railroading. Out of the quagmire of the eastern roads, Scott managed to resurrect the land grants to Frémont's Memphis, El Paso, and Pacific that had lapsed for lack of construction.

In March 1871, Congress approved Scott's new company, the Texas Pacific Railroad Company, building from Marshall, Texas, just west of Shreveport, Louisiana, west through Fort Worth and El Paso, and on across the 32nd parallel to San Diego. (A year later, its name would be changed to the Texas *and* Pacific Rail*way* Company.)

Huntington was concerned, but his own machinations with Congress succeeded in including a little present for the Southern Pacific amidst the Texas Pacific authorization. Bolstered with a land grant of twenty sections of land per mile, the Southern Pacific was granted an additional right-of-way "from a point at or near Tehachapi Pass, by way of Los Angeles, to the Texas Pacific Railroad at or near the Colorado River."[9]

Now the question was asked of Los Angeles, what inducements might that small town of 5,728 people offer an advancing railroad? Federal land grants aside, what would persuade the Southern Pacific to breach the San Gabriel Mountains and descend into the Los Angeles Basin, rather than skirt it and head straight east toward the Colorado River?

The answer was anything that the railroad demanded. California law limited a bond issue in support of railroads to 5 percent of a county's assessed valuation. For Los Angeles County in 1872, that amount was $610,000. But even that wasn't enough for the Big Four. Huntington also demanded $250,000 in bonds that Los Angeles held in the little Los Angeles and San Pedro Railroad. Completed in October 1869, the 22-mile line was the town's commercial outlet to the Pacific. Giving up local control of its rail link to the coast proved such a hotly debated topic that the matter was placed on the November 1872 ballot.

But the election contest quickly shaped up to be about more than a subsidy to one railroad. Who should show up in Los Angeles that summer but Thomas A. Scott. The Pennsylvanian was in nearby San Diego—then less than half the size of Los Angeles—to get his own share of concessions from the proposed terminus of the Texas and Pacific. Scott came bearing a promise that he would extend the Texas and Pacific line north to Los Angeles from San Diego if the people of Los Angeles would subsidize his efforts—not for the full $610,000 demanded by Huntington but for only $377,000.

No matter Scott's Pennsylvania Railroad connections, this was still rather bold talk for a railroad executive whose Texas and Pacific railhead was some 1,200 miles east of San Diego at Fort Worth. And despite Scott's personal appeal, the Southern Pacific argument was persuasive. Which would Los Angeles rather be, Huntington's man on the scene asked, a stop on the Southern Pacific's line with its transcontinental aspirations one way and fixed connections to San Francisco the other, or merely the end of a branch line from the Texas and Pacific at San Diego? The latter, after all, was hardly going to give up any trade from its fine harbor to its neighbor. So, on Election Day 1872, while California voted for President Ulysses S. Grant's reelection to a second term, Los Angelenos voted for the Southern Pacific over Scott and the Texas and Pacific, 1,896 to 650.[10]

But Los Angeles was going to have to wait awhile for a rail connection from either north or south. National economic concerns intervened. Even before what came to be called the panic of 1873, the fortunes of California railroading had never had smooth financial sailing. Cash was always tight, in large part because of the insatiable demands of Huntington's relentless construction on so many fronts.

No wonder that Huntington's partners tried to halt it from time to time, and no wonder that Huntington himself advised them to go slow with their own expenditures unless they knew "where the money was coming from. I certainly do not," the rainmaker confessed.[11]

Decades later, when the Southern Pacific had become a colossus and Collis P. Huntington one of America's undisputed industrial leaders, the depth of his despair and the narrow margin by which the Big Four prevailed would be downplayed. But suffice to say that in 1872 and

1873, they were on the ropes. So much so that Huntington did the unthinkable and not only sought buyers for the Southern Pacific but also actively courted Thomas A. Scott to be among them.

"It is possible that we could sell the So. P. road to Tom Scott," Huntington mused to Hopkins as early as October 1872. "Give me your views on this, and as to the least amount that we should take."

With short-term debt of about $5 million and interest on long-term bond coupons due semiannually, Huntington went begging to everyone. Yet somehow, the onetime peddler stayed the fox and did not become a chicken.

Scott met Huntington in November in New York to discuss the sale, but when the Pennsylvanian later telegraphed Huntington and asked him to come to Philadelphia to continue the negotiations, Huntington demurred. He told Hopkins, "I thought it would be better that he should come here to buy than for me to go there to sell."

Only ten days before, Huntington had reported to Hopkins, "I have been out to see if I could borrow some money with which to pay January interest, and as yet have not been able to get any."[12]

But playing cagey with Scott despite the Big Four's desperate straits appeared to work. On January 17, 1873, Scott called on Huntington in New York and offered $16 million for the Southern Pacific, essentially the right to the unbuilt western half of his Texas and Pacific–Pennsylvania transcontinental supersystem.

Huntington's answer is telling. Sixteen million dollars—albeit not all in cash—would have answered Huntington's plea to get out of debt. But instead of jumping at the offer immediately, the fox tried to get as much cash out of the deal as possible, telling Hopkins afterward, "*while I think the property* worth much more, I should sell it if the pay is good, but I am fearful that he will fail in that."

After Scott left to confer with his investors, Huntington was left to ponder a deal not made. More than a month later, Huntington was still urging Hopkins to "sell anything that we have that will bring money," while assuring him, "I am doing all I can to close this trade with Scott for the sale of the So. P."[13]

But as the year went on, Scott too began to suffer from a tightness of credit. The more time that went by, the less ability he had to consummate the Southern Pacific purchase even at his original offer. Cyrus K.

Holliday and the Santa Fe interests might well have stepped into Scott's shoes to negotiate on their own behalf, but their road was financially exhausted from the frenzy of its 1872 construction to reach the Colorado-Kansas line.

With no other suitors for the Southern Pacific, Huntington told Leland Stanford at the end of February that he had "made up my mind to get out of all active business" and encouraged Stanford to sell his own Central Pacific stock below par, if necessary—which it definitely was—and simply "retire and enjoy it."

Meanwhile, lenders continued to hound Huntington. "I have never seen so blue a time for money here before," he wrote in despair on March 8. "Something must be done, and that at once." Two days later, Huntington wrote again. "You know," he told Hopkins, "that when I have made up my mind to do a thing, dollars and cents have but little to do with it. I have got tired and am going to quit."[14]

That statement—dollars and cents having little to do with it—concerned a possible sale of the Central Pacific, but it may well be read both ways. On the one hand, Huntington damned the dollars and pushed the construction, not just of his western railroads, but the Chesapeake and Ohio and other ventures in the East as well. But conversely, if he had indeed made up his mind to sell his western railroads, why had he tried to squeeze more ready cash out of Tom Scott? Even at the bottom, the builder in Huntington could not quit.

By the middle of March, it was getting too late to make a deal with anyone. Scott came to New York again, but it was to attend to his own finances and not to call on Huntington. "It looks a little as though he were playing us," Huntington reported to Hopkins, "but his hands are very full."

"If we do not trade with him [Scott]," Huntington bemoaned, "we must trade with someone, for we have to pay here, between this and the first of June, $1,033,903.23, a little over half of which is in gold, and this does not include what we owe F. & H. [Fisk and Hatch], which is, say, $1,700,000, all on call; and then come the bills for material, which is very considerable. So, you will see the necessity of doing *something at once.*"

By March 26, Huntington despaired that he had "been out today to borrow some money, and I could not get any." Reluctantly, he acknowledged that Scott had been back in New York yet again without calling and that "he cannot do anything now." Scott, too, was "a large bor-rower," and the deal was off. But then things got worse.[15]

Two events shook the national economy during 1873 and rendered the tightness of credit that Huntington and Scott felt the norm throughout the country. The first was the infamous Crédit Mobilier scandal. There had been plenty of innuendo floated during the 1872 presidential cam-paign that numerous Republican members of Congress had accepted stock in the Union Pacific's construction company under less than cash-on-the-barrelhead terms. Vice President Schuyler Colfax, long a pro-ponent of a transcontinental railroad, was caught in the mess, as were two congressmen who would follow Grant to the White House: Ruther-ford B. Hayes and General Rosecrans's ex-aide, James A. Garfield.

Congress did the usual and appointed a committee to investigate. While attention focused on the Union Pacific, Congress wanted to know how *all* railroads had used their government subsidies. In the course of the hearings, Collis P. Huntington was put on the stand and grilled about the operations of the Central Pacific's own construction company, the Big Four–controlled Contract and Finance Company. His reception was far from friendly. "Why is it," Huntington bristled to Hopkins as the California press added its criticisms, "that we have so many bitter enemies in California?"

Huntington was loath to open the Big Four's books to outside eyes—what their profits were and how they applied them to their expanding empire was, in their minds, their private business. But he was also very nervous about showing the ownership of so vast a transportation net-work in the hands of only four men. For them, it really had been the sweetheart deal of the century.

Huntington had no choice but to appear before "these hellhounds," as he characterized the congressional investigators. But that did not mean that he had to tell them much—"the truth, but nothing more," as he put it.

The first to fall under the congressional inquisition was Republican congressman Oakes Ames of Massachusetts, one of the chief promoters of the Union Pacific. Ames and Congressman James Brooks, Democrat from New York, were offered up as the requisite scapegoats, Ames because he had sold Union Pacific stock to members of Congress at bargain prices and Brooks because he was one of the major purchasers. The House initially recommended their dismissal, but settled for a resolution of censure.

The Central Pacific, for which Huntington himself had done the bulk of the "stock promotion" and outright cash payments that Mark Hopkins listed on the books as "legal expenses," was even more immune. Huntington and Hopkins produced a figure of what it had cost to build the Central Pacific. This figure was well in excess of the subsidies reported by the government and thus was offered as evidence that far from skimming the public trough, the associates had contributed considerable private capital to it.

By the time the committee put Huntington back on the stand in late July 1873 and asked to see the records of the Contract and Finance Company to corroborate his earlier testimony, Huntington was able to say with a straight face that they didn't exist. Its work completed, the company was being dissolved, Huntington testified, and Mark Hopkins had burned the fifteen volumes of records in an effort to save space in the company's cramped offices.[16]

The bottom line of the Crédit Mobilier scandal was that all railroad stocks and bonds were suspect, and it became very difficult to market them. What made their sale next to impossible was the collapse on September 18, 1873, of the banking firm of Jay Cooke and Company—the second major blow to railroads across the country.

The Cooke firm was heavily invested in railroads, but it had bet an inordinate amount of its cash on the unmarketable securities of the Northern Pacific Railroad, extending huge loans for the railroad's construction west from Duluth, far in excess of the railroad's ability to repay. When Cooke managers begged funds from other banks to stay liquid, their pleas were refused because Cooke had no remaining assets with which to secure them.

Feeling the credit tightening on the Santa Fe, Cyrus K. Holliday put his finger on the nub of the problem. Jay Cooke's demise was the immediate cause of the panic, he told his wife, Mary, but "the *remote* cause was the widespread apprehension that if so strong a house as Jay Cooke's should fail, how many others would be carried down with the crash!"

By the following day—one of many Black Fridays on Wall Street—

news of Cooke's insolvency triggered a domino effect of cash shortages. The ensuing panic of 1873 staggered postwar economic expansion and hit America's railroads particularly hard. Most had used easy credit to push their expansion beyond any reasonable model of economic stability. When credit tightened or dried up, many roads found themselves unable to service their burgeoning debt.[17]

Among the casualties was Thomas A. Scott's Atlantic and Pacific. Barely more than a paper railroad, the Atlantic and Pacific went into receivership, and Scott chose instead to save the Texas and Pacific. It was hardly knocking at the gates of Los Angeles, but it had constructed some track in Texas.

In a story related somewhat anecdotally by Grenville Dodge, Scott summoned his principal investors and asked whether they should "save the property or ourselves." The unanimous answer was that they would "save the road and let the individuals go to the wall." Thus, Scott and his associates assumed the Texas and Pacific's entire debt in excess of $10 million, and the railroad remained afloat.[18]

For a time in the fall of 1873, it looked as if similar action by Huntington and his associates would not be enough to save their own railroads. They simply couldn't do it; they were already mortgaged to the hilt. At the end of October, Huntington spent two days borrowing $48,150 to pay small notes that were due. No banking firm would consider the loan, so Huntington begged and borrowed from friends in amounts of about $5,000 each.

In return, Huntington pledged the only remaining collateral he had left: his personal guarantee. He made up the difference with $14,000 that belonged to Huntington-Hopkins Hardware and paid the last note with forty minutes to spare before it went to protest. "I would not go through another panic like this for all the railroads in the world," he told Hopkins.[19]

Across the country, it was a similar story. Whether on Palmer's Denver and Rio Grande or Holliday's Atchison, Topeka and Santa Fe, construction slowed to a crawl or ground to a halt in the economic morass. But one thing was certain: No matter the dismal present, half a continent still remained to be won. The pause would be temporary. It would weed out the lightweights, and when the races renewed, the entire Southwest would be a contested empire.

Downstream from the Hanging Bridge, Denver and Rio Grande engine no. 206 pauses for the requisite photo; the locomotive with caboose suggests this may have been an excursion for photographer William Henry Jackson, who was frequently accorded special trains. *(Colorado Historical Society, scan 20102192, W. H. Jackson Collection)*

Part II

—◆—

Contested Empire

(1874–1889)

A railroad cannot stand still; it must either get or give business; it must make new combinations, open new territory, and secure new traffic.
—WILLIAM BARSTOW STRONG, *ANNUAL REPORT OF THE ATCHISON, TOPEKA AND SANTA FE RAILROAD,* 1884

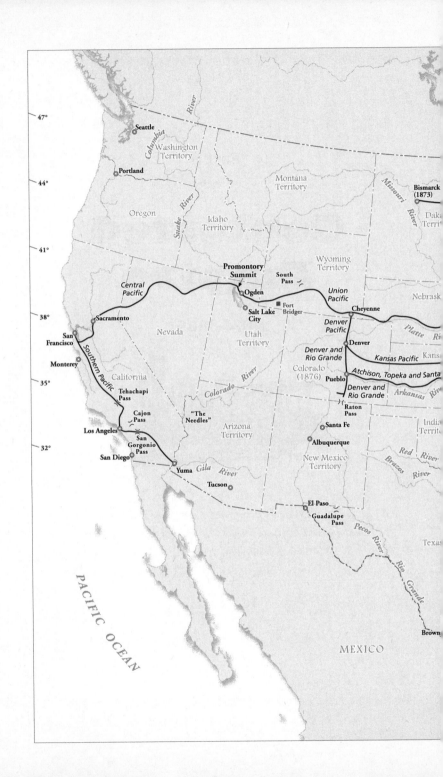

Western U.S.
Transcontinental
Routes, 1877

CANADA

Minnesota
(rgo
871)
orthern Pacific
Duluth

Minneapolis

Mississippi River

Wisconsin

Michigan

Chicago,
Rock Island
and Pacific
Davenport
Omaha
Council
Bluffs
Burlington
St. Joseph
Atchison
Kansas City
Topeka
Pacific of Missouri
Missouri

Iowa

Iowa
City
Rock
Island

Chicago,
Rock Island
and Pacific

Chicago

Detroit

Buffalo

New York

Pennsylvania

Ohio

Indiana

Illinois

Hannibal

St. Louis

Springfield

Cairo

Ohio River

Cumberland River

Kentucky

Cincinnati

West
Virginia

Virginia

Tennessee River

Nashville

Chattanooga

Memphis

Tennessee

North
Carolina

Atlanta

South
Carolina

Fort
Smith

Arkansas

Alabama

Georgia

Charleston

Louisiana

Miss.

Vicksburg

Savannah

Natchez

New
Orleans

Florida

Galveston

Gulf of Mexico

Maine

Vt.
N.H.
Boston
Mass.
Conn. R.I.

New
York

Philadelphia
Pittsburgh
N.J.
Baltimore
Del.
Washington
Md.

Richmond

ATLANTIC OCEAN

47°
44°
41°
38°
35°
32°

8

Showdown at Yuma

Amidst the gloom of the panic of 1873, the Big Four's treasurer announced some rather startling news. While Collis P. Huntington had been aggressively spending money, steady Mark Hopkins had been making it. Despite construction costs on many fronts and the national depression, the Central Pacific had begun to generate substantial profits.

In 1873 the Central Pacific and its branches earned gross revenues of $13.9 million and a resulting net income before bond interest of $8.3 million. After interest on the long-term bonds was paid, a handsome profit of almost $4.8 million remained. This surplus saved the Big Four, corporately as well as individually. Hopkins promptly declared the company's first dividend of 3 percent, payable in hard currency and not speculative stocks or bonds.

Even Huntington was caught off guard by this timely payout. "The figures are large," he confessed to Hopkins as bills, too, continued to rise, "but I have gotten used to large figures, and I have more faith that all will yet be well than I had one year ago . . ."[1]

. . .

By the summer of 1874, the Big Four and their expanding web of rail-roads roared out of the panic of 1873 full steam ahead. Back in Colorado, the Atchison, Topeka and Santa Fe and the Denver and Rio Grande were also stirring, and there was no time to lose. Earlier, Leland Stanford had visited the Southern Pacific railhead at Tres Pinos and pronounced the surrounding San Benito Valley sadly lacking in trade and requiring expensive construction. Because the railroad was required to lay 20 miles of track a year to maintain its land grant, Stanford recommended that the Southern Pacific simply skip over to Goshen in the more promising San Joaquin Valley and build the required miles south from there.

Goshen was the terminus of the San Joaquin Valley branch of the Central Pacific. That line cut off from the Western Pacific at Lathrop, just south of Stockton. It was a confusing mix of railroad names, but the ownership was quite simple. All were owned outright or otherwise controlled by Huntington, Stanford, Hopkins, and Crocker.

Once the panic of 1873 was weathered, the direct rail link to the Oakland waterfront provided a steady stream of men and materiel, as tracks were extended up the San Joaquin Valley at a frantic pace. (The San Joaquin River flows generally north between the Sierra Nevada and Coast Ranges, so going south is indeed *up* the valley.)[2]

The lure, however, was certainly not local traffic. There wasn't much in the San Joaquin Valley either. Nor was the Big Four's promise to the people of Los Angeles enough to drive them on. What led to this flurry of construction was the threat once again posed by Thomas A. Scott. Having gone "to the wall" to save the Texas and Pacific, Scott was determined to push it westward.

Scott's original charter for the Texas and Pacific anticipated a direct route west along the 32nd parallel from El Paso to Yuma and on to San Diego. Closer inspection, however, showed that endless miles of blazing desert and rugged mountains lay between Yuma and San Diego. Scott asked Congress to approve a change in route that would avoid this terrain, skirt the depths of the Imperial Valley, and arrive in Los Angeles from the east via San Gorgonio Pass.

The problem, of course, was that this was the projected route of the Southern Pacific *out* of the Los Angeles Basin. When Scott met with Huntington and rather casually suggested that the Southern Pacific

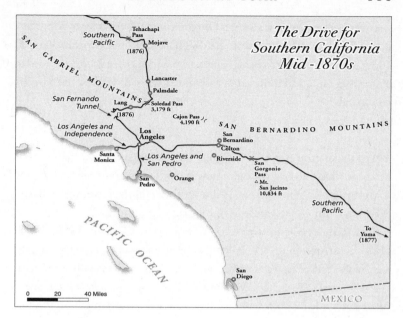

The Drive for
Southern California
Mid-1870s

should join the Texas and Pacific at San Gorgonio Pass rather than the Colorado River at Yuma, as previously agreed, Huntington's response was predictable.

If Rosecrans's paper railroad with solely California ties had caught Huntington's attention, Scott's continuing bid for direct transcontinental access to the ports of Los Angeles and San Diego was a call to arms. No one knew what Pacific trade might develop in these sleepy little towns, but Huntington knew for certain that whatever the amount, it would pass through Southern California to the detriment of the San Francisco Bay waterfront that he and his associates controlled.

Huntington countered Scott with an offer to provide the Texas and Pacific access to Los Angeles and San Diego over the Southern Pacific's rails from Yuma. Huntington made it quite clear to Scott that the Southern Pacific's destination was Yuma and that Huntington would adamantly oppose Scott's congressional request for any land grant change west of that point.

Characteristically, Scott stood his ground. With his own railhead still at Fort Worth, some 1,200 miles to the east, Scott replied that if this were the case, he and Huntington would be running competing lines

not just between Yuma and San Gorgonio but all the way to San Francisco. That was the same thing that William Jackson Palmer had said to
Judge Crocker in Scott's behalf almost a decade earlier. Thus, the race to
Yuma was on, and Huntington responded with all the resources at his
command.[3]

First Huntington had to make good on the Los Angeles vote—as well
as collect his subsidies—and connect the Southern Pacific main line
with the Los Angeles and San Pedro short line in the Los Angeles Basin.
To do so required two marvels of railroad engineering.

The initial challenge was to get out of the San Joaquin Valley. Much
of the construction up the valley had been across open country on gentle grades, but at its head at Caliente, the railroad was confronted with
the wall of the Tehachapi Mountains. This range continued the Sierra
Nevada Divide and blocked easy access between the San Joaquin Valley
and the comparable flats of the Mojave Desert leading east to Needles.

The key to the divide, Tehachapi Pass, rose almost 3,000 feet above
Caliente in only a few miles. William F. Hood, the Southern Pacific's assistant chief engineer, took one look and knew that the only solution
was plenty of curves and tunnels. So, upward from Caliente the line
snaked along knobby, auburn-colored hills studded with piñons and
junipers and through narrow, rocky canyons lined with scrub oaks and
cottonwoods.

After more than 6 miles of track and six tunnels, Caliente was still
plainly visible below, only one air mile away. Two more tunnels, 532
feet and 690 feet, respectively, were drilled by hand, blasted with dynamite, and cleared with shovels. Many of the workers were veteran Chinese laborers, some well seasoned from years of working for Charley
Crocker on the Central Pacific.

Above Keene (the station there was later called Woodford), at 2,700
feet in elevation, the valley narrowed even more. Holding to a maximum grade of 2.2 percent, the roadbed crossed Tehachapi Creek and
then recrossed it in the process of making a climbing semicircle loop.
After a rising left curve, Hood lined up the roadbed on a short straightaway and called for tunnel no. 9. It was only 126 feet in length, but it
was to be the centerpiece of what came next.

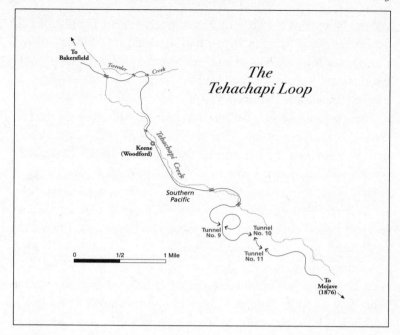

Once through the tunnel, the grade circled steadily left, ascending around a conical hill until it had made a complete 360-degree loop and passed over the track through tunnel no. 9. The design made for a hard-won elevation gain of 77 feet and set up the line for the second half of the climb to the Tehachapi summit.

Above the loop, eight more tunnels were constructed to reach the high point of the pass. It was 28 tortuous track miles from Caliente, almost 1.5 miles of which was through a total of seventeen tunnels. From the pass, construction continued down the relative ease of Cache Creek to the sagebrush flats of the town of Mojave, arriving there on August 8, 1876.

More than a century later, the Tehachapi Loop remains as William F. Hood designed it. Trains over 4,000 feet in length pass over themselves when climbing or descending the route. Dozens of trains wind around the loop daily on what is routinely the busiest single track of mountain railroad in the United States.[4]

South of Mojave at Palmdale, the Southern Pacific confronted a second barrier to the Los Angeles Basin. Rising above 10,000 feet, the San

Gabriel Mountains blocked easy access to Los Angeles from the north. To the northeast, the San Bernardino Mountains culminated in the 11,502-foot San Gorgonio Mountain above the pass of the same name, but this eastern gateway to Los Angeles was almost 100 miles out of the way and intended as the railroad's exit.

There was one other possibility. A geologic fault between the San Gabriel and San Bernardino mountains had the effect of creating a natural ramp between the Los Angeles Basin and the Mojave Desert. Attention had long focused on a route from the Mojave across the 35th parallel, *south* of the Grand Canyon. But as more became known about the Colorado Plateau, some looked at the map and thought it plausible to connect Southern California with the Union Pacific at Salt Lake City by building *north* of the Grand Canyon.

One proponent of such a venture was Senator John P. Jones of Nevada. Jones began by building a narrow gauge line from the piers at Santa Monica, which he helped to develop, to downtown Los Angeles. This provided the town with a second rail link to the ocean, and, after Huntington and the Southern Pacific wrestled control of the Los Angeles and San Pedro Railroad away from local interests, Jones's line became the hometown favorite. But his Los Angeles and Independence Railroad had bigger plans than simply providing competition for Huntington.

Jones, who had made a princely fortune in silver from Nevada's Comstock Lode during the 1860s, was interested in developing mining properties around Death Valley, principally near Panamint and Independence, California. The natural ramp between the San Gabriel and San Bernardino Mountains, called Cajon Pass, not only offered a direct route from Los Angeles to Death Valley, but by following the eastern edge of the Mojave Desert, it pointed straight north to Salt Lake City.

"Join hands with our natural allies [Jones's Los Angeles and Independence] and carry that narrow gauge through the Cajon Pass at a gallop," cried a local newspaper. "Time is everything, the Southern Pacific operates against us."

Even without this railroad threat, John P. Jones was not a favorite of the Big Four. The senator was also trying to tax the Central Pacific's land grant holdings in Nevada—no small thing considering that seven million acres were involved.

While Huntington worked in Congress to amend the Southern Pacific's land grant to include Cajon Pass, Jones hired a young engineer named James U. Crawford away from Tom Scott's Texas and Pacific and sent him into the mountains to survey the Cajon route. Making a cursory inspection by horse and buggy, Crawford determined that with 20 miles of track and an 1,800-foot tunnel punched through the sandstone atop the pass, he could be out of the Los Angeles Basin and streaking toward Salt Lake City.

By November 1874, survey stakes lined the pass, but the work was not easy. "We are camped on the summit of the Cajon, about 31 miles north of San Bernardino," Crawford reported. "It is very cold. Snow among the pines reaches down close to our camp. Bears are numerous, and frequently interrupt our surveying."

A month later, a crew of rival Southern Pacific engineers and surveyors fresh from the Tehachapi Loop arrived on the Cajon scene. By then, Crawford had laborers felling trees and blasting rock. A wintry rain began to fall, and it pummeled the pass for three days, turning the area into a quagmire of bottomless salt flats and sluice box gullies. By the time falling temperatures and ferocious winds lashed a blizzard across the pass, Crawford's men were secure in makeshift huts, but the Southern Pacific crew was literally blown out of the pass, tents and all. Score one for Senator Jones's Los Angeles and Independence.

While Huntington fumed, Crawford's men drilled their way 300 feet into Cajon's rocky spine before coming to a stop. Cajon Pass didn't defeat Senator Jones, but the declining silver prices of the 1870s did. While the Big Four chuckled, Huntington bought the Los Angeles and Independence from Jones for a meager $100,000 in cash, a $25,000 note, and $70,000 in Southern Pacific bonds. Once again, there might be railroads with different names in Los Angeles, but they all had the same owners.[5]

Meanwhile, Huntington had been taking no chances on reaching Los Angeles from the north—with or without Cajon Pass. Even as work progressed on the Tehachapi Loop, Huntington had workers laboring away at the second of the Southern Pacific's twin engineering feats. This one was to be a single tunnel over a mile long.

From Palmdale in Antelope Valley, the Southern Pacific's route climbed to the head of Soledad Canyon and then wound down the Santa Clara River, looking for a way through the western end of the San Gabriel Mountains. Finding none, Hood chose to tunnel through the range just south of Santa Clarita.

Day and night, 4,000 men and 300 animals labored through a mountain of crumbly rock and subsurface water that required extensive redwood timbering. A shaft was sunk near the middle of the tunnel to permit work on four faces at once—inward from each portal and outward in opposite directions from the shaft. When the headings met on July 14, 1876—almost fifteen months after work began—the San Fernando Tunnel was 6,966 feet in length and the longest railroad bore in the world.

On September 5, a special train of five cars loaded with 350 invited guests left Los Angeles and headed north to inspect the results. It took a long ten and a half minutes at about 7.5 miles per hour to make the pitch-black passage, and "time dragged heavily" through what one reporter called "the dark abyss." But the train emerged to bright sunshine, and at Lang in Soledad Canyon, its passengers found "an army of about 3000 Chinamen standing at parade rest with their long-handled shovels" in a line on either side of the roadbed.

Charley Crocker greeted the Los Angeles contingent, and an hour later a similar special arrived from the north carrying Leland Stanford and dignitaries from San Francisco. They all watched as two crews working from opposite directions laid the remaining 500 feet of track in a contest that lasted all of eight and one-half minutes.

Crocker then drove a golden spike to signal the completion of the line from San Francisco, around the Tehachapi Loop, through the San Fernando Tunnel, and into downtown Los Angeles. The Southern Pacific men, the *Los Angeles Evening Express* enthused, "have not only lived up to the letter of their promises, but in the face of difficulties that were fairly gigantic, they have reached Los Angeles sooner than the most sanguine of us expected." The next day, regular service was inaugurated between San Francisco and Los Angeles, with express trains making the run in twenty-four hours.[6]

.   .   .

Amidst half-hearted pledges of cooperation between San Francisco and Los Angeles—and while San Diego interests eagerly awaited their turn—the question was, where next? What to do with the seasoned crews that had just bested the Tehachapi Mountains and bored through the San Gabriels?

The answer was obvious to any interested observer. San Diego could wait. While Tom Scott plugged away in Texas, and Colonel Holliday's Santa Fe still struggled in Colorado, the Southern Pacific would build east out of Los Angeles, control San Gorgonio Pass for itself, and race southeast across relatively open country to the Colorado River crossing at Yuma.

To counter competitors' claims—Scott was the most vocal—that the Southern Pacific's advances amounted to nothing short of a railroad monopoly in the West, Huntington tapped a California businessman named David D. Colton to be his lieutenant and, for a time, the figurehead president of the Southern Pacific. Red haired, heavy set, and with a mercurial temper, Colton was an odd choice. But he had Charley Crocker's blessing, and in the press of business, Huntington concurred.

Colton's tenure with the Big Four was to be tumultuous and short lived. He would die in 1878, and for years his widow would carry on a highly public feud with the Big Four for his alleged interests. But for the present, Huntington was Colton's alter ego, and Colton pushed the Big Four's plans as strenuously as anyone. This was particularly true when it came to besting Tom Scott, whether in the halls of Congress or among the sand dunes of Yuma.

In trying to jumpstart the Texas and Pacific after the panic of 1873, Scott sought to add a federal subsidy to the land grant that the railroad had already received. Shrewdly, he tied his request to the growing reconciliation with the South and lobbied for southern congressional support by arguing that a subsidy for a southern road was but a narrow slice of the federal largesse that had been benefiting northern railroads since the end of the war.

Huntington countered by saying that the Southern Pacific would build the South a southern transcontinental between Yuma and El Paso without subsidies other than the land grant already awarded to the Texas and Pacific. Scott dug in his heels, of course, and firmly opposed any transfer of the land grant as well as any authority for the Southern Pacific to expand outside its present charter limits of California.

"Scott is making a very dirty fight, and I shall try very hard to pry him off," Huntington told his new front man Colton, "and if I do not live to see the grass growing over him I shall be mistaken."

Huntington was quite capable of planting his own innuendo. Scott could play the monopoly card against the Big Four, but Huntington countered that what Scott was really after was the formation of a Pennsylvania Railroad–dominated transcontinental system such as Scott had sought earlier with the Kansas Pacific.

All Scott had to do, Huntington told his southern friends, was turn the eastern axis of the Texas and Pacific northeast and point it toward St. Louis instead of Memphis, and the South would be left without a transcontinental link. Huntington, on the other hand, promised that if the Southern Pacific were given free rein to race east, it wouldn't stop until it reached New Orleans.

"We must split Tom Scott wide open if we can and get rid of him . . ." Colton told Huntington. "He is the head and front at this time of all the devilment against the C.P. & S. P. . . . He is today the most *active* and *practical* enemy, we have in the world."[7]

And Scott appeared to hold a powerful advantage in at least one respect. The Southern Pacific's own 1866 congressional land grant extended eastward only to the California-Arizona border, presumably the middle of the Colorado River. There was no hope for similar land grants in Arizona and New Mexico as long as Scott and the Texas and Pacific were opposed.

So instead Huntington used all means possible to secure a franchise from the Arizona legislature for a simple right-of-way across the territory. There was no land grant involved because almost all land was federally owned, but the territorial legislature could convey a right-of-way for public purposes across such land under authority granted to states and territories by the Right-of-Way Act of 1875.

Wanting no delays, Charley Crocker inspected the Yuma crossing in the spring of 1877 and selected sites for a bridge. Several miles downstream from its confluence with the Gila, the Colorado cut through a low line of sandy-colored bluffs. While generally flowing north to south, the big river was making one of its many twists and turns and was actually running east to west at this point. Just below the bluffs, the river was still somewhat constrained by high banks that offered suitable abutments for a bridge.

To cover all bases, Crocker obtained a bridge charter from both the state of California and the territory of Arizona. But reaching the crossing with rails from the California side presented its own set of legal problems. The Fort Yuma Military Reservation occupied the California bank, and in order to access the bridge site, Southern Pacific tracks had to cross military land, something that required the permission of the secretary of war.

Crocker started up the chain of command with General Irvin McDowell, who sixteen years earlier had been the Union's scapegoat at the First Battle of Bull Run. Now McDowell was in charge of the army's Department of the Pacific, with headquarters in San Francisco. Showing McDowell the plans for the bridge, Crocker argued that it would be of little value unless track could be laid across the reservation to reach it.

McDowell passed the request on to Secretary of War George McCrary, who immediately came under intense lobbying pressure—for and against—from Huntington and Scott. Deciding to pass the buck, McCrary ruled that only Congress could permanently decide the issue. But in the interim, he gave the Southern Pacific permission to lay temporary tracks across the reservation, so long as the railroad agreed to remove them if Congress denied the right-of-way. In order not to show favoritism to the Southern Pacific, McCrary accorded the same arrangement to the Texas and Pacific, even though its railhead was 1,000 miles away.

While McCrary's action created some uncertainty for the Southern Pacific, Huntington was not one to hesitate. He had long believed that it was far better to ask for forgiveness afterward than to sit idly waiting for permission beforehand. So, in July 1877, work started on the Yuma bridge from the California side. It was to be 667 feet long and include a swinging drawbridge that would allow steamships to pass up or down the Colorado River.

About this time, the majority of troops at Fort Yuma were ordered north to Idaho to join the pursuit of Chief Joseph and his Nez Perce Indians. Only Major T. S. Dunn, one sergeant, and two privates were left

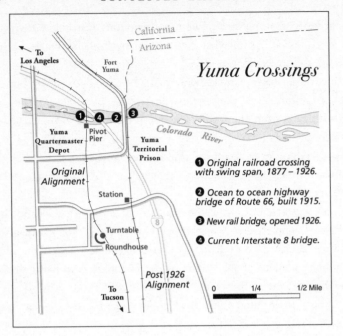

Yuma Crossings

❶ Original railroad crossing with swing span, 1877 – 1926.

❷ Ocean to ocean highway bridge of Route 66, built 1915.

❸ New rail bridge, opened 1926.

❹ Current Interstate 8 bridge.

at the fort. Early in August, Dunn inspected the Southern Pacific's "temporary" tracks as they were being laid across the reservation. They certainly had a look of permanence about them, and Dunn reported that fact to Secretary of War McCrary. In reply, the secretary telegraphed an order to halt all construction on the tracks *and* the bridge immediately. By that time, however, rails were within a few yards of the half-built bridge.

Not to be denied, Crocker insisted to General McDowell that the half-built bridge was likely to be destroyed by the river's current unless the Southern Pacific was able to salvage it. More telegrams were exchanged, and on September 6, McCrary authorized enough work on the bridge structure to protect it from destruction. Crocker intended to do just that, but rather than pulling up piles, he secured the bridge from damage by rapidly completing the structure and anchoring it firmly to the Arizona bank of the river.

"So far as going on and finishing the bridge is concerned," Crocker wrote Huntington, "we have given orders to our men there not to quit till they feel the point of the bayonet in their rear. . . ."[8]

The completed bridge had six spans of 80-foot wood trusses supported by piers and pilings driven into the hardpan of the riverbed. On the Arizona side, the draw span was 93.5 feet in length. It rested on the final pier of the truss sections and pivoted on another pier near the shore to allow boats to pass through the deepest part of the channel. Toward the Arizona shore from this pivot pier, which would later be replaced with a circular concrete foundation, a wooden truss ran to the riverbank.

Once the bridge decking was in place, spiking rails across it could be done in a few hours. Under orders from Secretary McCrary, poor Major Dunn was forced to mount a rotating guard with his four-man garrison to prevent that from happening. But it was Crocker who had ready and effective reinforcements close at hand. Surmising that the U.S. Army would not interfere with a civilian train carrying mail and passengers— particularly if it were to be wildly welcomed by the citizens of Yuma— he dispatched just such a special from San Francisco.

Major Dunn and his outnumbered troops stood guard on the bridge until eleven o'clock on Saturday night, September 29. Assuming in the manner of the time that no laborers would work on Sunday, Dunn and his men then retired. But their sleep was interrupted a few hours later by the dull thuds and throaty clangs of rails being dropped into place. Crocker's crew had no such apprehension about toil on the Sabbath.

Dunn and his troopers hurried back to the bridge, but they were literally bowled out of the way by a carload of rails being pushed ahead of a Southern Pacific locomotive. Recovering, Major Dunn ordered the foreman placed under arrest. The man's reply was less than courteous and certainly not compliant. Outnumbered by the construction crew as they were, Dunn and his three soldiers could do little but stand aside as another half mile of track was spiked down into the center of Yuma.

Dawn Sunday morning, September 30, 1877, was announced by the shrill blasts of the first locomotive in Arizona. Yuma's citizens poured into the streets to give it a hearty reception. After a crew on a handcar inspected the new track, Crocker's San Francisco Express, gaily bedecked with American flags, rolled into town to a similar reception. Crocker telegraphed Huntington with the news: "Bridge across Colorado complete and train carrying United States mails, passengers and express crossed over to Arizona side of river this morning. People of Yuma highly elated over the event."

While Yuma cheered, the battle with the army reverted to the tele-graph wires. General McDowell, who may have been feeling as snookered here as at Bull Run, ordered all the reinforcements that he could muster— "one officer, twelve soldiers and a laundress" from San Francisco—and dispatched them posthaste to Yuma. By train.[9]

But how could the U.S. Army declare war on the very institution that was winning the West? In a flurry of support that Southern Pacific operatives no doubt encouraged, if not outright orchestrated, Yuma's mayor, town council, and leading merchants, as well as Arizona's terri-torial governor, besieged Washington with pleas not to deprive them of their railroad.

"By the completion of the Southern Pacific Rail Road to Yuma a new era seemed to have dawned upon the Territory," almost one hundred Yuma residents petitioned Secretary of War "McCreary," spelling his name wrong in the process. "By prohibiting the completion of the bridge at Yuma," they asserted, "our goods are landed on the California side of the Colorado river without shelter from the sun or storms." They considered it "an outrage to be put to the inconvenience and delay of an expensive and dangerous ferry" when trains could be run into the city.[10]

The San Francisco *Daily Alta California* added its voice to the fray. In the face of this accomplishment, what was the government to do, the paper demanded with due sarcasm, order "Stanford and Company to work pulling up those piles with their teeth" or " . . . set us back to the days of Forty Nine, when we crossed the river in a basket covered with the skin of a dead mule?"

The answer was, hardly. "I do not believe they [the government] will interfere with the mail and passengers, after the track is completed," David Colton wrote to Huntington, "*but at any rate I think it is a good cli-mate on the Arizona side in which to winter an S. P. locomotive,* should they cut us off, & it will be a check to our friend Thos. A. Scott."[11]

It was Huntington who got the government's answer firsthand and at the highest level. The bridge matter was debated in two cabinet meet-ings, and Secretary of War McCrary's referral to Congress affirmed, but on October 9, Huntington called at the White House to see President Rutherford B. Hayes.

"I think I have the bridge question settled," he reported to Colton af-terward. "I found it harder to do than I expected." According to Huntington, Hayes was at first angry and scolded Huntington that the Southern Pacific had defied the government.

But then Hayes asked, "What do you propose to do if we let you run over the bridge?" Why, push the road right on through Arizona, Huntington replied. "Will you do that?" the president queried. "If you will, that will suit me first rate." Hayes promptly issued an order to permit train service across the reservation and into Yuma.[12]

But there would be no rapid construction eastward across Arizona. This time, the nemesis was not the government, nor the terrain, nor even Tom Scott. This time Huntington's partners simply refused to fund another wild expansion. Having gotten a whiff of the dividends that came from an operating profit, all but Huntington were strongly opposed to extending the Southern Pacific until their enormous Central Pacific debt could be brought under control.

Despite his enthusiasm in reaching Yuma, Crocker was quick to assure Huntington that "taking all things into consideration, I feel that we have all the railroad property that we can well afford to own, and that I would like to get a few eggs in some other basket."

Huntington did not give up the idea, of course, but by January 1878, Crocker's resolve had hardened. "I notice what you say about the importance of doing some work on the Southern Pacific road east of Yuma," he told Huntington. "I answered that proposition in a late letter which I wrote you. We have no money to spend there now."

Even Huntington's old hardware store partner, Mark Hopkins, shook his head when Huntington asked Hopkins, Stanford, and Crocker to endorse a stack of blank promissory notes so that Huntington might fill them in as required—the ultimate "blank checks." For the moment, Yuma was the end of the line. Huntington had to be content to control the river crossing there and wait to see what rival might emerge from the chaos in Colorado or the financial woes of Tom Scott in Texas.[13]

But there was to be one indirect casualty from the bridge battle at Yuma. Mark Hopkins had not been well for much of the preceding year, complaining in particular of rheumatism. A Chinese herb doctor treated his maladies, and as he showed some improvement, he chose to escape the damp winter cold of the Bay Area and head for warmer climes. Perhaps because Huntington had routinely criticized his partners for never having seen entire sections of their expanding empire, Hopkins decided to combine his desire for hot, dry air with an inspection of the bridge that had caused so much fuss.

There was no question that Hopkins would be accorded a private car. Accompanied by some Southern Pacific bigwigs, including the railroad's chief physician, his train chugged south and arrived at Yuma. On the evening of March 28, 1878, while his private car sat on a siding there, Hopkins stretched out on a couch and appeared merely to take a little after-dinner nap. One of the company's construction engineers later heard Hopkins give a deep sigh and, knowing that it was close to the punctual man's bedtime, tried to rouse him. The doctor was hastily summoned, but the detail person of the Big Four was dead a few months short of sixty-five.[14]

9

---◦---

Impasse at Raton

While his associates momentarily shackled Collis P. Huntington from further expansion, the other southwestern railroads slowly emerged from the economic hangover of the panic of 1873. During this time, the Atchison, Topeka and Santa Fe secured its own rail access eastward from Topeka into the railroad hub of Kansas City. The moves were complex and the number of subsidiaries involved was mind numbing, but the resulting connection was as significant of a transcontinental step as any the Santa Fe had taken previously. In time, it would look to extend even farther east.[1]

Out west, after a two-year pause just inside the Colorado border, the Santa Fe continued construction up the Arkansas Valley toward Pueblo, reaching La Junta in 1875 and Pueblo itself early in 1876. After a similar construction hiatus, the narrow gauge Denver and Rio Grande built south from Pueblo and extended 50 miles to Cuchara Junction (near present-day Walsenburg). Here the Rio Grande line forked with the western leg following the Cucharas River to La Veta, and the other leg, continuing south toward coalfields near Raton Pass.

It would have been an easy matter for the Rio Grande to build into the town of Trinidad at the foot of Raton Pass. Certainly Trinidad

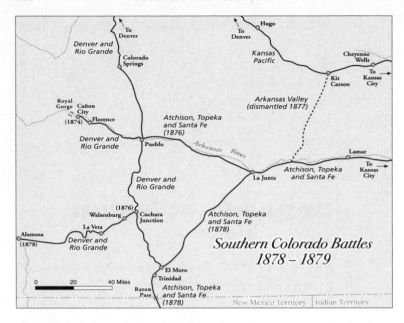

To Denver

Denver and Rio Grande

Colorado Springs

To Denver

Hugo

Kansas Pacific

Cheyenne Wells

Kit Carson

To Kansas City

Royal Gorge Cañon City (1874) Florence

Arkansas Valley (dismantled 1877)

Denver and Rio Grande

Atchison, Topeka and Santa Fe (1876)

Pueblo

Arkansas River

Lamar

To Kansas City

Denver and Rio Grande

La Junta

Atchison, Topeka and Santa Fe

(1876)
Walsenburg
La Veta

Cuchara Junction

Atchison, Topeka and Santa Fe (1878)

Alamosa (1878)

Denver and Rio Grande

Southern Colorado Battles 1878 – 1879

0   20   40 Miles

El Moro
Trinidad

Raton Pass

Atchison, Topeka and Santa Fe (1878)

New Mexico Territory | Indian Territory

cheered the railroad's advance. But William Jackson Palmer had other ideas. Fresh from his land development successes at Colorado Springs, the general chose to halt the Rio Grande about 4 miles north of Trinidad and establish the new town of El Moro. It was a development strategy that he would employ time after time. But while Palmer and his circle of investors profited from the resulting land speculation, the technique hardly endeared them to the existing towns that were left without a railroad.

In the case of El Moro, the town fathers of Trinidad were outraged. Some saw the founding of the new town as outright blackmail by the Rio Grande to induce Trinidad and surrounding Las Animas County to vote bonds to aid the railroad's construction. Even as the Rio Grande paused at El Moro, Trinidad was hotly debating just such a bond issue to support the Kansas Pacific in building to Trinidad.

The third railroad with its eyes on Trinidad was the Santa Fe. Holliday's road had made no bones about its ultimate destination since adding the town of Santa Fe to its Atchison and Topeka moniker before it had laid a single rail. Now its management saw an opportunity en route to be welcomed into Trinidad as heroes. After Las Animas County rejected the Kansas Pacific bond issue and local sentiment turned against the Rio Grande because of its halt at El Moro, the Atchison, Topeka and Santa Fe became the hometown favorite in Trinidad.

The Denver and Rio Grande was completed to El Moro on April 20, 1876. Regular passenger and freight service was inaugurated within a week, and the railroad-sponsored town promoted itself as the logical terminus of stage and freighting operations to and from New Mexico— to the detriment of Trinidad. By the end of the summer, three hundred people were living in El Moro, and several companies had built freight warehouses there.

Palmer, however, was not pleased with the overall results. Too many freighters continued to haul goods by wagon over the old Santa Fe Trail between Trinidad and La Junta directly to and from the Santa Fe Railroad. Some freighters from the San Luis Valley did the same thing, avoiding the Rio Grande's La Veta branch and hauling goods to and from the Santa Fe's railhead at Pueblo instead.

The advance of the Santa Fe up the Arkansas River to Pueblo had already disrupted the cozy relationship that Palmer and the Rio Grande had with the Kansas Pacific for connecting east-west traffic. Before the Santa Fe's encroachment, the Rio Grande funneled traffic along Colorado's Front Range to and from the Kansas Pacific at Denver. Thanks to the Santa Fe's recent direct connections to Kansas City, it could now compete head-to-head with the Kansas Pacific for east-west traffic.

In theory, Palmer and the Rio Grande should have been in the catbird seat. By adjusting its rate structure between Denver and Pueblo, the railroad could direct traffic either northward to the Kansas Pacific at Denver or southward to the Santa Fe at Pueblo. But as the Santa Fe got more and more of the southern Colorado traffic directly, the Kansas Pacific cried foul.

Somewhat warily, the three roads entered into a pooling arrangement that required the Denver and Rio Grande to divide its business between the Kansas Pacific and the Santa Fe with the understanding that the Kansas Pacific would not build to Pueblo and the Santa Fe would not build to Denver. This arrangement proved short lived, however, and was soon "crumbling beneath the pressures of mutual distrust and conflicting ambitions."[2]

A major source of the friction was Colorado's slumbering mining prospects. They were finally beginning to attract attention. A muddy impediment to placer gold mining proved to be residue from silver ore, and by 1877, a rush began for Leadville and a host of other silver mining camps in Colorado's mountains.

There would be no lack of competitors attempting to build out of Denver to tap this bonanza—John Evans's Denver, South Park and Pacific, and William Loveland's Colorado Central among them—but one major name was to be absent from the race. In fact, it also disappeared from the contest to reach Santa Fe.

The Kansas Pacific's construction deal with the Denver Pacific had been calculated to speed the road to Denver and a connection with the Union Pacific, not permanently dissuade it from a southwestern bent toward Santa Fe. But the panic of 1873, growing competition from the Santa Fe, and the Kansas Pacific's failure to secure Las Animas County bonds had taken their toll. Instead of racing the Santa Fe and the Rio Grande to Pueblo or Trinidad, or heading south into New Mexico, the Kansas Pacific simply abandoned the field and waited for the Union Pacific eventually to absorb it.[3]

The Kansas Pacific's retreat left the Denver and Rio Grande and the Santa Fe to slug it out for both Colorado traffic and the long-sought gateway to New Mexico and beyond. Although owing certain subservience to his East Coast investors, General Palmer was clearly in command of the Rio Grande. As a confrontation with the Santa Fe loomed, that railroad had two equally forceful and effective leaders at its helm. In some respects, their relationship and roles resembled those of J. Edgar Thomson and Thomas A. Scott.

The senior member of the Santa Fe team was Thomas Nickerson, a leading member of the railroad's "Boston crowd" of investors. Born in Brewster, Massachusetts, in 1810, Nickerson came from a long line of New England sailors. He spent almost thirty years at sea before investing his profits on land. By 1870, he was a major Santa Fe shareholder. Nickerson became the railroad's vice president in 1873, and a year later, the board of directors decided that the seasoned sailor was the man to serve as president and lead them out of the financial woes of the panic of 1873. Both cautious and tenacious, Nickerson was slow to change course, but unafraid to sail into the wind.

Nickerson's conservatism sometimes frustrated his right-hand man, but once William Barstow Strong received go-ahead orders, Strong knew that he had Nickerson's full support. Born in Vermont, Strong was almost twenty-seven years Nickerson's junior. After business college in Chicago, he went to work as a station agent and telegraph operator for the Chicago, Milwaukee and St. Paul Railroad. Progressively more responsible jobs with Midwest railroads followed, including two tours with the Chicago, Burlington and Quincy. The Santa Fe hired Strong away from the Burlington to become its general manager in 1877, and six weeks later, Strong was also named vice president. Between the two of them, Nickerson and Strong would see the Santa Fe through a far-flung expansion.[4]

If Nickerson's and Strong's names are not as well known to later generations as those of rail barons Huntington or Jay Gould, it is not because their accomplishments were any less but rather that they undertook them with less bravado. Aside from Holliday's occasional crowing of his founding role, the Santa Fe management was much more of a team effort than many other roads. While Huntington roared between Washington politics and New York finances, and Gould fixated the high and the mighty of Wall Street with his deals, Nickerson and Strong stayed largely out of the public eye—quiet, efficient, and determined of purpose, but no less calculating.

And so the battle was joined. Long after the conflict at Raton Pass, George S. Van Law, who at the time was a young surveyor with the Santa Fe, termed the Denver and Rio Grande as having been "cocky and resolute." Van Law recalled that the railroad "believed in a future life and believed in setting its stakes in the beyond, and doing it first."

To be sure, "cocky and resolute" was probably an apt description of Palmer and his associates. After all, they had pretty much been given free rein over a sizeable chunk of Colorado. Certainly their interest in a railroad across Raton Pass dated back to Palmer's 1867 survey for the Kansas Pacific. But somewhere along the line, their bold plans and long-held dreams ran afoul of the Right-of-Way Act of 1875.

This was the same act that had permitted Huntington and his Southern Pacific cohorts to secure a right-of-way on the Arizona side of the Colorado River from Arizona Territory. Under the act, any state or territory could grant a railroad a right-of-way across the public domain, but such company was required to file a plat (survey) and profile of its intended route with the U.S. General Land Office to establish its priority over subsequent claimants. Otherwise the first party to begin actual construction controlled the route.

Well after the Right-of-Way Act became law, Palmer cabled his close friend and business associate Dr. William A. Bell what amounted to his manifesto. "It is understood you understand," Palmer wrote, "that we stop not until San Luis Park is reached, and I hope not until Santa Fe although for manifest reasons we hold open question of route to New Mexico whether from Trinidad south [Raton Pass] or Garland south [La Veta Pass]."[5]

Why then did Palmer fail to file the required plat for the Raton Pass route? With his own railhead at El Moro within sight of the pass and the Santa Fe still 60 miles away at La Junta, Palmer may well have tried too hard to outfox the Santa Fe by masking his intentions. He may have thought that his earlier explorations there preempted the field, or he may have been distracted from the details by his many other ventures: land speculation, coal mines, and even railroads in Mexico.

None of this, however, seems to excuse what in hindsight appears as both a monumental corporate blunder and the first of two history-changing moments in western transcontinental railroad construction. Palmer, who was so meticulous in so many things, overlooked or chose to ignore the filing requirements of the Right-of-Way Act. Too late, the general realized that he had to take immediate steps on the ground to seize the key passage at Raton.

The Santa Fe approached the matter very differently. First, William Barstow Strong secured a charter from New Mexico for construction south from Raton Pass. Then one of the Santa Fe's engineering assistants, William Raymond Morley, spent several weeks surveying the Raton slopes disguised as a Mexican sheepherder.

Ray Morley was, in fact, the quintessential railroad surveyor. As his obituary opined, "he was no respecter of rules until he had proved them in his own way" and "he asked no man to go where he was not willing to lead."

Morley was born in Massachusetts in 1846. Orphaned quite young, he ended up with an uncle in Iowa, where he later lied about his age and joined the Ninth Iowa Volunteer Regiment of the Union army during the Civil War. He got an early look at the business of railroads—albeit destroying them—while following General William Tecumseh Sherman through Georgia. Back in Iowa, he entered Iowa State University but was forced to drop out after his second year for lack of funds.

Morley found work as a land surveyor around Sioux City and on the Iowa Northern Railroad. Then he went to work for William Jackson Palmer on the Kansas Pacific. The general must have had his eye on the young ex-private, because when Palmer's wide-flung interests came to include the sprawling Maxwell Grant in northern New Mexico, a vestige of historic Spanish land grants, Palmer offered Morley a surveying job there. By November 1872, Morley had been promoted to manager.

With this respectable job in hand, Morley hurried back to Iowa and married Ada McPherson. After a five-year courtship of mostly letters, this genteel, golden-haired twenty-year-old followed her new husband to the headquarters house of the Maxwell Grant in Cimarron, New Mexico. Ada quickly took to the lifestyle, and the couple was soon involved in the rough and tumble of territorial politics.

When the Maxwell Grant changed ownership yet again, Morley spent the summer of 1876 surveying for the Denver and Rio Grande on its line over La Veta Pass, including laying out the corkscrew of Mule Shoe Curve. Exactly when and why he came to throw his allegiance to the Santa Fe is uncertain. It seems probable, however, that Morley disdained Palmer's heavy-handed rival town techniques and thought that the Santa Fe was likely to have a larger role in New Mexico than the Rio Grande. So the wiry figure wrapped in a serape carefully avoided the Rio Grande surveyors who were also at work on Raton and quietly made his own calculations.[6]

On February 20, 1878, William Barstow Strong and President Thomas Nickerson met in Pueblo to map out their next course of action. That Nickerson should be so far from Boston and out on the road in the middle of winter is evidence that the Santa Fe viewed these next steps as critical to the railroad's future. "Of course we have no certain means of knowing what was going on," Pueblo's *Colorado Weekly Chieftain* reported of the two men's joint appearance in town, but "it is predicted by those who know that the Atchison, Topeka & Santa Fe company will make a big jump when it does start."

A week later, while acknowledging, "The air is full of railroad rumors, but nothing reliable," the *Chieftain* wryly noted that the Santa Fe had appointed a superintendent of construction, and, "as railroad companies do not appoint superintendents of construction unless they mean to construct something, this looks like business."[7]

It was. Nickerson authorized Strong to build south from the Santa Fe main line at La Junta in whatever manner Strong thought best. Rather than starting at La Junta, Strong chose to secure the entire route into New Mexico by immediately undertaking the first flurry of construction in the section of Raton Pass that would admit only one set of tracks. Thus began one of the most oft-repeated episodes of the western railroad wars—a story in which it has always been difficult to sort fact from fiction.

Upon receiving the go-ahead, Strong immediately ordered construction engineer A. A. Robinson to take a grading crew and seize what Ray Morley had determined to be the key stretch of the Raton route. Robinson was in Pueblo at the time, and he sent a telegram in cipher to El Moro ordering Morley to assemble a Santa Fe work crew in secret. Ironically, Robinson then took the Denver and Rio Grande train from Pueblo to El Moro, arriving there shortly after midnight in the wee hours of February 27.

On the same train was the chief engineer of the Denver and Rio Grande, J. A. McMurtrie. Reports vary as to whether the two men were aware of each other's presence on the train and who went to sleep upon arriving in El Moro and who didn't. McMurtrie is thought to have slept for several hours, while Robinson reportedly secured a horse and immediately rode through the night to Uncle Dick Wootton's place on the northern slope of the pass.

Richens Lacy "Uncle Dick" Wootton was one of those truly legendary characters. Call him Indian fighter, scout, trader, rancher, self-promoter, moonshiner—he was at least a little of each. Wootton had earned his familiar sobriquet of Uncle Dick by arriving in the fledgling town of Denver at Christmas 1858, promptly breaking open two barrels of "Taos Lightning" whiskey, and offering the welcome refreshment to any and all takers free of charge. By evening, he was everyone's favorite uncle.

In 1865 Wootton secured charters from the territorial legislatures of both Colorado and New Mexico for a toll road from Trinidad to Red River, New Mexico, via Raton Pass. (The latter half toward Red River was certainly not a railroad route, but it was one way to get travelers to the Rio Grande above Taos and Santa Fe.) By some accounts, the Santa Fe tried to buy Wootton's toll road, but Uncle Dick turned them down. In exchange for a right-of-way, he simply asked the railroad to give him and his wife free passes and a lifetime credit of $50 per month at the general store in Trinidad.

Arriving at Wootton's place after his nighttime ride, Robinson met Morley, and with Uncle Dick along, the men organized the gang of workers who had gathered on Robinson's orders. By five o'clock in the bitter cold of the dark, wintry morning, they began to pick at rocks and to shovel dirt by lantern light "at three of the most difficult points in the pass."

Rio Grande engineer McMurtrie, whether he had slept or not, assembled a similar work gang in El Moro and headed south toward the slopes of Raton at an equally early hour. By some accounts, his party arrived on the scene not more than thirty minutes after Robinson's crew had begun to scrape away at the mountainside. How many threats were exchanged between the rival groups—apparently there were armed men on both sides—varies with the telling, but the fact remained that there was only enough room in the canyon for one railroad grade, and the Santa Fe men were in possession of it. If the Rio Grande was going to dislodge them, McMurtrie's workers would have to resort to force.

Some secondary accounts report that veteran Dodge City marshal Bat Masterson was in the employ of the Santa Fe and soon arrived on the pass with a gang of gunslingers to support the Santa Fe position. This seems unlikely and a confusion with Masterson's later role in the Royal Gorge war. Bat's brother, Ed, was killed that April in Dodge City, and Bat was present there. Masterson was certainly a Santa Fe ally, but his reported appearance at Raton may have been confused with only boastful threats of his *pending* arrival that Santa Fe men may have made to bolster their position.

With the numbers in each party about equal, a tense standoff continued until the Denver and Rio Grande crew finally withdrew, hurling a few last threats over their shoulders. McMurtrie had them make a halfhearted effort to excavate in nearby Chicken Creek (present-day Galli-nas Creek) before deciding that it was not a suitable alternative.

The Denver and Rio Grande had lost its long-planned route to Santa Fe. But one more question must be asked of Palmer's tactics. Having been blocked at Raton Pass, why didn't he build across the Raton Mountains via Trinchera Pass, some 35 miles to the east? Given its rail-head at El Moro, the Rio Grande was poised to skirt Fishers Peak in that direction, and quick construction might have leapfrogged the Santa Fe as it wrestled with the upper slopes of Raton. Dr. Bell and others had viewed Trinchera Pass favorably on the 1867 Kansas Pacific survey, al-though Palmer never seemed enamored with it.

Most likely, once the Rio Grande arrived at El Moro, Palmer saw Trinchera Pass as too great a detour east on the line toward Santa Fe and assumed that he would be able to reach the New Mexico capital by ex-tending the La Veta Pass line down the upper Rio Grande. Of even greater concern, perhaps, was the fact that the increasing lure of the Leadville and San Juan mining trade focused his attention in that direc-tion rather than eastward around Raton.[8]

Having won the field, the Santa Fe set about building its line across Raton Pass. Construction started in earnest from La Junta, and when the first Santa Fe train chugged into Trinidad on September 1, 1878, the town that had been spurned by the Denver and Rio Grande cele-brated with great enthusiasm. More than a century later, Trinidad re-mains bound to the Santa Fe.

The arrival of the Santa Fe main line in Trinidad brought heavier equipment for the difficult work higher on Raton Pass. A. A. Robinson laid out the grade up the canyon of Raton Creek and then just at the Colorado–New Mexico line—a stone's throw from Uncle Dick Woot-ton's place—he called for a tunnel to burrow under the crest of the pass. Traffic could either wait for its completion or a temporary track would have to be built.

The urgency the Santa Fe felt in building into New Mexico dictated that while work went forward on the tunnel, Robinson lay out an inge-nious ladder of switchbacks that permitted trains to stair-step their way over the pass. Coming upgrade from Trinidad, the main line passed a

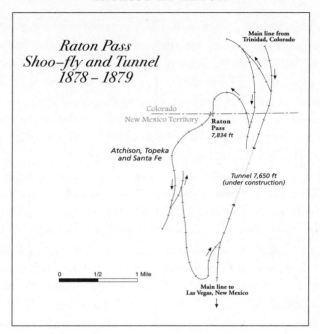

Raton Pass
Shoo–fly and Tunnel
1878 – 1879

Main line from
Trinidad, Colorado

Colorado
New Mexico Territory

Raton
Pass
7,834 ft

Atchison, Topeka
and Santa Fe

Tunnel 7,650 ft
(under construction)

0   1/2   1 Mile

Main line to
Las Vegas, New Mexico

siding and then entered a deep cut leading to where crews were excavating the tunnel. Then a switch was thrown behind the train, and it backed up a switchback until it had passed over another switch and onto the leg of a Y. This switch was thrown, and the train moved forward to a second Y where another change in direction left it backing up around a curve and over the summit.

On the New Mexico side of the pass, with the train still backing but now going downgrade, it came to another Y and backed in. When that switch was thrown, the locomotive steamed forward and downhill to the second Y on the New Mexico side. It pulled to the end of that leg. Then once that switch was thrown, the train backed down the remaining grade and around a curve and over a switch onto the main line, where it would emerge from the southern end of the proposed tunnel.

This laddered run-around—a "shoo-fly," as railroaders call it—above the Raton Tunnel site hardly made for an express run, but it did permit passengers and freight to ride rails all the way from Kansas City to the advancing railhead in New Mexico. More important, it allowed men and materiel to push the railhead forward while the tunnel was still under construction.

With grades of 6 percent, it also required the Santa Fe to expand its motive power. The lighter American-type locomotives that had served the road well across the plains of Kansas lacked the power to move heavy cars over this mountainous terrain. To meet the demand, the Baldwin Locomotive Works built consolidation-type locomotives. The first model bore the number 204, but in consideration of the locale in which it was to serve, the name "Uncle Dick" was soon emblazoned on its cab in honor of Raton Pass's most famous resident.

The Uncle Dick was the largest locomotive yet built by Baldwin. It had a wheel configuration of 2-8-0—a set of two pilot wheels, four sets of two drivers, and no trailer wheels under the cab. (By comparison, the American types had 4-4-0 wheel configurations, providing only four driving wheels.) But there was one other special adaptation. While the total wheelbase of the drivers was fourteen feet, nine inches, the first and third sets were equipped with tires instead of flanges so that the rigid wheelbase between the second and fourth sets was less than ten feet. This meant that the locomotive could more readily follow the tighter curves on the line.

Not only was the beefier Uncle Dick more than equal in pulling capacity to two standard road engines, but also its operating costs were only a little more than that of one American-type locomotive. These innovations and their resulting efficiencies cemented a long relationship between the Baldwin Locomotive Works and the Santa Fe, and in time, Baldwin built more than one thousand steam locomotives for the railroad.

Meanwhile, work continued on the tunnel. Railroad tunnel work was no job for the faint of heart. One journalist, afforded a tour of the Raton construction operation, reported climbing through a narrow opening at the south portal. Far into the darkness, he could see dimly twinkling candlelight and hear the steady clank of sledgehammers striking drills. Working in unison, the sledge men had to trust their partners as they each swung away in a regular rhythm. But the true hero was the holder of the drill. With each clang of a striking blow, the holder turned the drill a few degrees and trusted that the hammer to follow would be square and not come crashing down on his hands.

Once the drillers had done their work, dynamite was stuck in the holes and exploded to break down the rock face one foot at a time. Then the resulting debris was cleared, and another round of drilling began. On the north end, the rock in the Raton Tunnel was loose and crumbly, and the passage required substantial timbering, but on the south end, the bore was blasted through rock so solid that it needed no timbers. After the tunnel was opened to through traffic on September 7, 1879, the temporary system of switchbacks was abandoned.[9]

Regular operations over Raton Pass brought the Santa Fe squarely into the realm of mountain railroading. Gone were the easy grades of the plains. At high altitude, on steep hills and tight curves, in frequently harsh weather, everything was more difficult to do on mountain railroads. Brakes were just one example.

The locomotive was the beating heart of a train, but brakes were the circulatory system that allowed it to function. In the very early days of railroads, stopping a light train of one or two cars on a moderate grade was usually a matter of slowing down and then reversing the locomotive. As trains added more cars and heavier loads, individual cars were outfitted with brake wheels at one end. When these wheels were tightened, the connecting rigging clamped brake shoes against the running wheels and created enough friction to slow their revolutions, thus slowing the train.

Operating these brake wheels gave rise to the most dangerous job in railroading. At a whistle signal from the engineer, nimble brakemen ran atop the cars—jumping from one swaying car to another—and frantically set the brakes. Because it was frequently difficult to turn the brake wheel, even strong-armed brakemen carried a baseball bat–sized club of wood to give them more leverage. Hence, the term "club down the brakes." When the train was past the downgrade, this process was reversed to release the brakes.

Railroad braking began to change in the 1870s when George Westinghouse patented the air brake. Operated from an air compressor on the locomotive, air pressure, rather than brawny arms, applied the force to press the brake shoes against the wheels. Initially, this was a straight-air system; that meant that if a coupling anywhere along the train became loose or blew out, the brake system for the entire train ceased to function. This either sent brakemen back atop the cars hurriedly setting brakes by hand or caused a runaway.

Westinghouse soon solved these straight-air problems by creating an automatic brake system. Each car was equipped with an air cylinder, and when the lines were full of air, the brakes were released; when air was bled off, the brakes engaged. Thus, should cars separate, the locomotive compressor lose pressure, or something else malfunction to reduce air pressure, the brakes would set automatically and in theory stop the train. But automatic air was not standard on the Santa Fe across Raton until 1885, and in the meantime, there were many instances of horrendous runaway wrecks.

Helper engines were the other mainstay and frequently the unsung heroes of mountain railroading. More correctly, the men who labored through heat and cold, wind and water, and a host of mechanical challenges to operate the helpers were the heroes. Depending on the route and their tonnage, trains were assigned helper engines to boost them over a divide. Once atop the hill, the helpers were disconnected and either dispatched back to their starting point or sent down the other side in front of the train to where they were needed next. Often a heavy freight would have the regular engine and a helper pulling in double-header fashion, with another helper or two pushing at the rear of the train. Sometimes longer trains were divided into sections for the pull over a pass.

All signals passed between the engineers of the helpers by whistle, and it took a great deal of coordination for three or four locomotives to move in tandem. More than one conductor and rear brakeman became nervous when watching a pounding helper locomotive pushing with all its might against their wooden caboose. The best they could hope was that the lead engines were indeed pulling upgrade and not suddenly backing down.

With the Santa Fe in command of Raton Pass, speculation was rampant about the railroad's next move. The *Colorado Weekly Chieftain* of Pueblo reported quite assuredly that with the prize of Raton won, the Santa Fe would abandon its proposed line up the Arkansas River toward

Leadville and "devote all of their resources and energies to the construction of their great transcontinental line." Others thought that the Santa Fe was simply taking advantage of cheap Mexican labor "to play a game of bluff" at Raton and that the railroad's true destination lay in the mountains of Colorado.

For his part, Rio Grande engineer McMurtrie, who had seen the Santa Fe's determination in action, never believed that Raton was a bluff. McMurtrie bluntly told Palmer that the Rio Grande should either find a way to skirt its impasse at Raton or build south immediately from its La Veta branch in the San Luis Valley. McMurtrie was convinced that the Santa Fe would be across Raton Pass and en route to El Paso within the year.

In case McMurtrie was wrong and the Santa Fe was bluffing at Raton, Palmer incorporated a Colorado subsidiary to build from El Moro to the New Mexico line. But before any construction began, Palmer acknowledged that his little line had been both outfinanced and outfought. As McMurtrie later put it, there was no sense in pursuing a "cutthroat policy of building two roads into the same country when there was hardly business enough to support one."[10]

But the overriding reason that Palmer did not press the Raton fight is that having wrestled control of Raton Pass away from the Rio Grande, William Barstow Strong and the Santa Fe were now threatening to deliver Palmer's road a death knell by going for its jugular. Strong was indeed determined to extend the Santa Fe toward transcontinental destinations, but he was not about to give up the mining country of Colorado that looked all the more promising in the wake of the rich silver strikes at Leadville. What that meant was that the Denver and Rio Grande and the Santa Fe would soon be locked in a battle royal.

10

Battle Royal
for the Gorge

The fight between the Atchison, Topeka and Santa Fe and the Denver and Rio Grande for Raton Pass was only a prelude to a much more heavily contested affair. Transcontinental stakes were rising, and enticing regional markets further fueled the competition. Once again, the rugged landscape of the American West would play a major role in how this battle was fought and won.

For 55 miles above Cañon City, Colorado, the Arkansas River cuts a twisting canyon. The narrowest, deepest, and most spectacular section is the 8 miles immediately upstream from the mouth of Grape Creek, which empties into the Arkansas about a mile above Cañon City. Here the canyon walls rise more than 1,000 feet above the river and in places constrict it to a rocky defile less than 50 feet wide. While initially labeled the Grand Cañon of the Arkansas, this slender passage has long been called the Royal Gorge.[1]

Explorer Zebulon Pike peered into the eastern end of the gorge late in 1806 and promptly detoured around it—only mistakenly to follow the Arkansas River back downstream to it a few weeks later. Subsequent travelers also avoided the gorge. In time a wagon road was built around it over Eight Mile Hill, so named because it was eight miles from Cañon City.

But the direct route *through* the Royal Gorge held one undeniable attraction for a railroad. Yes, the gorge was narrow; yes, construction would be difficult. But the river through the gorge led 100-some miles upstream to the mines of Leadville on an uncannily constant water grade of about 1 percent. Even through the Royal Gorge itself, the river dropped less than 500 feet in 8 miles and permitted a 1.4 percent grade. Whether one was hauling ore out of the mountains or tons of supplies into them, such a modest gradient put smiles on the faces of construction engineers and locomotive engineers alike.

And even if it didn't, what other choices were there? North of the Royal Gorge, the grassy bowl of South Park was itself as high as Leadville. South of the gorge, the Sangre de Cristo Mountains formed a picket-fenced barrier until one reached La Veta Pass. The Denver and Rio Grande had managed to lay track across La Veta, but it was more than 100 miles south of the Arkansas Canyon and in the opposite direction from Leadville. All this fixed covetous eyes on the Royal Gorge.

There is little argument that William Jackson Palmer had his eyes on the gorge first. As early as his 1867 survey for the Kansas Pacific, Palmer considered the gorge a possible avenue west. Two years later, while Palmer was still in the employ of the Kansas Pacific, the general hired W. H. Greenwood to make a further survey of the entire Arkansas canyon and estimate construction costs. Even then, with Palmer's Denver and Rio Grande not yet a dream and the Atchison, Topeka and Santa Fe still struggling to get out of Topeka, Greenwood seems to have appreciated fully the secrecy that would envelope so many western railroad expansions.

"I will run a line through the cañon so that I can make a fair estimate of the cost of construction," Greenwood reported to Palmer. But first he was off to Raton Pass, Greenwood explained, "to look at that pass, but in reality to throw people out there off the track."[2]

After the Denver and Rio Grande was operational, Palmer scouted the Arkansas canyon himself in August 1871, while returning from a wider trip that included Raton Pass. Somewhere in the canyon, several of his party's mules rolled down a steep cliff. The animals emerged from the fall badly bruised but alive, and the experience reminded Palmer of the loss of his horse in the Verde canyon while on the Kansas Pacific survey.

"Our experience in the cañon was the most exciting and exhausting of any I have had since the Indian fight on the Verde in Arizona," Palmer wrote to his wife, Queen, from Cañon City. This time, it was only a battle with natural obstacles, but Palmer nonetheless described the canyon as "a fearful gorge."[3]

That same year, Denver and Rio Grande engineers J. A. McMurtrie and Ray Morley—the latter not yet working for the Santa Fe—staked a preliminary line through the gorge. During 1872 and 1873, they again inspected the canyon and rode the entire route from Cañon City to the Leadville area. But for all their activity in the field, Denver and Rio Grande officials did not comply with the provisions of the Right-of-Way Act after it became law in 1875. No one filed the required plat with the General Land Office to perfect the Rio Grande's priority claim to the Royal Gorge.

What Palmer and his associates did do was again run afoul of local sentiment. In the fall of 1872, the Denver and Rio Grande built 36 miles west from Pueblo to Labran (present-day Florence) to tap coal deposits. The railroad graded another 7 miles to the outskirts of Cañon City but did not lay rails, citing deteriorating economic conditions on the brink of the panic of 1873.

If that was indeed the case—construction throughout the West was sputtering to a halt—no one could fault the railroad. But Cañon City businessmen, who desperately wanted the railhead in their downtown, found it difficult to believe that the Denver and Rio Grande could grade 43 miles of roadbed from Pueblo, lay iron on 36 miles of it, and then profess poverty when it came to laying the remaining 7 miles of track. They looked around for the skunk.

The smell was coming from the county bond issues that Palmer and his associates routinely required as conditions for extending their road. Cañon City and surrounding Fremont County had in fact offered such an inducement as early as March 1871, if the Denver and Rio Grande would build directly from Colorado Springs to Cañon City instead of going to Pueblo.

At the time, Palmer refused the proffered $50,000 and headed for Pueblo, but two years later, with nothing but 7 miles of graded right-of-way separating his end of track from Cañon City, he demanded double that amount. The general insisted on $100,000 of bonds, claiming that the Denver and Rio Grande could easily secure Cañon City's business at Florence without the expense of the extension.

The despotic power of a railroad to make or break a town in those days is evidenced by the fact that Fremont County acquiesced to a long list of Palmer demands and voted $100,000 in bonds on May 21, 1873. In exchange, the Denver and Rio Grande promised to build to within three-quarters of a mile of Fourth and Main streets in downtown Cañon City within six months. But suddenly the county commissioners decided that despite the majority vote, there was not sufficient reason to take on the increased indebtedness.

A year passed while Florence enjoyed the economic boom of being a railhead. Cañon City merchants were forced to haul freight between their town and the end of track. Finally, the town of Cañon City—as opposed to surrounding Fremont County—voted $50,000 of town bonds, plus deeds to $50,000 of town real estate, if the Denver and Rio Grande would lay the remaining 7 miles of rail.

After this vote was taken in April 1874, the railroad promptly laid track from Florence. But instead of continuing into downtown Cañon City and being met with belated cheers, the Denver and Rio Grande built to precisely three-quarters of a mile from Fourth and Main streets—that point to which they were legally obligated by the bond issue—and not a single tie farther.

The result was predictable. The bond issue lands that the Denver and Rio Grande acquired near the new railhead increased in value faster than the downtown area, much to the chagrin of the town's established businessmen, who still had to haul passengers and freight some distance by wagon. Consequently, just as folks in Trinidad had looked to the Atchison, Topeka and Santa Fe as their savior after the Rio Grande's halt at El Moro, so too did the people of Cañon City search for another railroad. Since the Santa Fe was at Pueblo, they didn't have far to look.[4]

The Atchison, Topeka and Santa Fe had ample reasons of its own to build to the rescue. If the railroad's only interest had been in racing through Colorado for transcontinental destinations, it might have built from La Junta directly to Trinidad and over Raton Pass in 1875 instead of continuing up the Arkansas River to Pueblo. Now, in 1877, the Santa Fe eyed the Royal Gorge as a plausible route directly west. It led not only to Colorado's developing mining country but also toward Salt Lake City and a likely connection with the Big Four's Central Pacific.

Cañon City was doing a rush of business with Leadville even though the silver camp was still only on the cusp of its boom. With the enthusiastic blessing of Cañon City businessmen, the Santa Fe organized a subsidiary—the Cañon City and San Juan Railway Company—in February 1877. Its stated goal was to build to Leadville and the budding mining camps of Colorado's Western Slope.

The Santa Fe made the Cañon City and San Juan more than just another paper railroad when it quickly surveyed and staked the first 20 miles of the route through the Royal Gorge and up the Arkansas Canyon. The Santa Fe's surveyor, H. R. Holbrook, later testified that he had found old Rio Grande survey stakes in the gorge and in some places had in fact run his line fifty feet below them.

Nonetheless, the Santa Fe used Holbrook's survey to file the plat required by the Right-of-Way Act of 1875, and the General Land Office accepted it on June 22, 1877. Since there was enough room through this narrow canyon for only one railroad—and even then passage would require a famous "hanging bridge"—it appeared that the Santa Fe had won the day.[5]

By the end of the summer of 1877, the Leadville boom had broken wide open. Never mind the usual excitement of rich mining strikes; here, by some accounts, was the greatest El Dorado of them all. Negligent though Palmer may have been in adhering to the 1875 filing requirements, he certainly had never abandoned the gorge route, nor had he given up the promise of the Leadville trade. Now, mushrooming freighting receipts to and from the silver bonanza showed just how costly its loss would be to the Denver and Rio Grande.

Early in September 1877, Palmer was back in the Royal Gorge in person. Accompanied by J. A. McMurtrie, the general spent eight days making a thorough inspection of the main route to Leadville and adjacent routes to South Park, the Wet Mountains, and the San Luis Valley.

Afterward Palmer reported to Charles B. Lamborn, an old Fifteenth Pennsylvania Cavalry comrade who was then the Rio Grande's treasurer, that he was considering an alternative route that would eliminate the line through the gorge.

Even as he did so, however, Palmer gave Lamborn an exhaustive list of the benefits of the Royal Gorge route. He noted the "low gradient per mile, good water, freedom from snow, fertile lands, abundant timber, and rich mineral sources all the way to Leadville." The general also appreciated that the route's magnificent scenery might become a valuable tourist attraction. In Palmer's words, the Royal Gorge would bring the "Manitou frequenters and those from Denver" over the entire line from Denver to Leadville.

But the driving reason for Palmer's determination to seize the gorge seems to have been competition. With one line, Palmer saw the chance to block the Atchison, Topeka and Santa Fe on his southern flank and John Evans's Denver, South Park and Pacific to the north. Seize the corridor to Leadville, and tentacles could spread from that line as it raced through Tennessee Pass toward Salt Lake City.

"It is the shortest and cheapest single line," Palmer concluded, "which will at the same time tend to keep both the Atchison company and the Denver and South Park company from our territory; while certainly paying from the start." He suggested that the entire route could be built in winter just as readily as in summer and be completed in six months.[6]

As usual, Palmer was overly optimistic. Initial construction in the gorge by either the Rio Grande or the Santa Fe was delayed by winter weather and shortages of supplies and operating cash, as well as the uncertainty of what would transpire between the two roads at Raton Pass. William Barstow Strong's subsequent quick seizure of Raton for the Santa Fe rattled Palmer and was done amidst mounting evidence that the Denver and Rio Grande's standard gauge competitor would become far more aggressive. On March 23, 1878, the Rio Grande's traffic agent gave Palmer equally disturbing news about increasing ore shipments from the Harrison Reduction Works smelter at Leadville.

"Harrison goes east via the Santa Fe at the invitation of Mr. Strong," he reported. "They are determined to get his shipments of ore if possible. Mr. Strong is getting all the information he can with regard to that section [Cañon City to Leadville], and I believe intends to make a move in that direction."

When Rio Grande construction superintendent Robert F. Weitbrec asked chief engineer McMurtrie to join him in mid-April in yet another look at the Arkansas Canyon, McMurtrie told Palmer that he would rather not go. "All my movements are watched," he explained, "and should I go, I am afraid Atchison will know of it and take it that we mean to move in that direction and to stop us, jump into the Canon and commence work at once."

McMurtrie's fears were confirmed when he began to bring men off the futile efforts along Chicken Creek at Raton Pass. Santa Fe engineer A. A. Robinson telegraphed Strong that rather than merely an abandonment of Raton, McMurtrie's moves appeared to be a redeployment in force. Robinson surmised correctly that McMurtrie's destination was Cañon City. Strong replied at once and told his engineer to "see to it that we do not 'get left' in occupying the Grand Canyon."[7]

Palmer was indeed making his move. Ignoring the Santa Fe's filed plat, the general sent a telegram in cipher to McMurtrie that he should assemble a work crew and head for the gorge. Shortly after midnight on the morning of April 19, 1878, McMurtrie and about 150 men left El Moro bound for Pueblo on a heavy Denver and Rio Grande construction train that included carloads of mules and grading equipment. Robinson watched them go and immediately wired Ray Morley, who was at La Junta, to get to Cañon City first and once again beat the Rio Grande to the key portion of ground.

Morley commandeered a special Santa Fe train for the run from La Junta to Pueblo and later that morning boarded the regularly scheduled Rio Grande passenger train from Pueblo to Cañon City. Not surprisingly, the Rio Grande conductor recognized Morley as a rival. While McMurtrie and his crew chugged toward Cañon City with their construction train, the Rio Grande passenger train sat quietly at the Pueblo station. It did not depart on schedule, nor did it show any sign of departing at all. Finally, Morley realized that the Rio Grande was stalling to his detriment, and the Santa Fe engineer saddled his horse and hurriedly rode the 35 miles from Pueblo to Cañon City.

If the affair at Raton Pass has many conflicting versions, the battle for the Royal Gorge has it beat in spades. Partisans of the Santa Fe made Morley a hero and compared his Pueblo to Cañon City ride with Union general Phil Sheridan's famous dash from Winchester during the Civil War. Denver and Rio Grande partisans insisted that Morley had cruelly ridden his horse to death, a charge that was later met with considerable indignation by Morley's descendants, "as it suggested poor horsemanship on Grandfather's part."

Whatever the truth, Ray Morley arrived in Cañon City about noon on April 19, having passed the slow-moving construction train. Even though he was alone and seemingly outnumbered, Morley enlisted the assistance of Cañon City locals, who were all too willing to help the Santa Fe best the Rio Grande. Downtown merchants still smarting over the Rio Grande's halt on the outskirts donated tools, and every available man and boy in the city shouldered a shovel, gun, or pick and was ferried to the mouth of the gorge in a line of hacks and wagons.

Thirty minutes after Morley's arrival in Cañon City, McMurtrie's Rio Grande construction train came to a halt on the eastern edge of town. McMurtrie and his surveyors disembarked and fairly flew through town on a dead run, chaining the ground and setting survey stakes as fast as they could from the depot to the mouth of the gorge. But by then, Morley's hastily assembled forces were turning shovels of dirt and had managed to scrape at least one hundred feet of grade. For McMurtrie and his Rio Grande crew, it was a scene depressingly reminiscent of Raton Pass just six weeks before.

But this time, McMurtrie did not pause. Instead his party of surveyors rushed on, setting their stakes atop the Santa Fe's newly dug grade and creating considerable uncertainty over which railroad was the first to reach the point where the canyon narrowed and there was room for only one set of tracks.

Confusion ensued amidst volleys of threats from each side. Anxious workers kept looking over their shoulders toward Cañon City to see which side would be the first to receive reinforcements. Later that afternoon, another Rio Grande train rolled into Cañon City with one hundred more men for McMurtrie, but meanwhile, Morley had recruited additional Cañon City locals to the Santa Fe cause and dispatched them upriver to seize key points toward Leadville.[8]

By the next day, the lawyers got involved. The Cañon City directors of the Santa Fe's Cañon City and San Juan Railway subsidiary sought a preliminary injunction prohibiting the Denver and Rio Grande from further work in the gorge. Colorado district court judge John W. Henry was on vacation, so in his absence, Fremont County judge N. A. Bain ruled in favor of the local company and granted it. Writs were promptly served on McMurtrie and other Rio Grande officials, and, without abandoning any ground, they halted work about three o'clock on the afternoon of April 20.

The Denver and Rio Grande's attorneys immediately petitioned to move the case to federal court and out of what they deemed was the anti–Rio Grande atmosphere of Fremont County—self-induced by the Rio Grande though it may have been. But before the U.S. circuit court could issue any ruling, Judge Henry returned from vacation and held hearings to consider making the injunction permanent.

Initially Judge Henry enjoined both companies from further work. Later that same afternoon of April 27, he withdrew the injunction against the Santa Fe. But when Santa Fe workers attempted to return to the grade, they were met by armed Rio Grande guards and forced to turn back.

Meanwhile, part of the Rio Grande lawyers' argument in federal court was that the Cañon City and San Juan Railway was but a pawn of the Santa Fe—they were right about that—and that the Santa Fe itself had no standing because it was not chartered to do business in the state. It was one more twist in a complicated legal battle.

In the most simplistic terms, the Santa Fe appeared to hold a valid claim under federal law to the first 20 miles of right-of-way through the gorge and up the Arkansas canyon based on the plat that had been approved on June 22, 1877. The Denver and Rio Grande had also belatedly filed a plat to the gorge as well as the canyon beyond, but it had been approved subsequent to the Santa Fe's. This meant that while the Santa Fe had the priority claim through the critical 8-mile gorge and

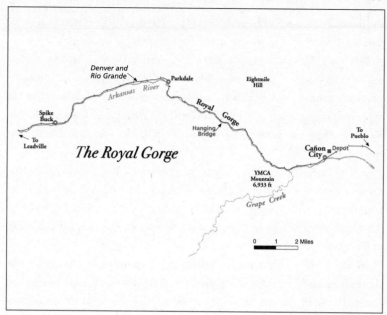

The Royal Gorge

west from Cañon City—a distance of 20 miles—the Rio Grande had a priority claim through the remainder of the Arkansas canyon.

Under the right-of-way law, an opposing company was not permitted to locate and build a parallel line until the company with the priority had completed its line. Consequently, during the testy summer of 1878, the Denver and Rio Grande had its tracks into Cañon City and controlled the Arkansas Canyon west of the Royal Gorge, but the Santa Fe held its 20 miles of ground in the middle between the mouth of the gorge and a point called Spike Buck.[9]

There is a widely circulated photo from that summer of Rio Grande engineer J. R. DeRemer's men at a hastily constructed breastwork of logs and dirt called "Fort DeRemer." This is often assumed to show Rio Grande men blocking the Santa Fe at the mouth of the gorge just outside Cañon City. Actually, the site is near Spike Buck, 20-some miles above Cañon City (between present-day Parkdale and the town of Texas Creek). DeRemer's men were intent on keeping the Santa Fe crews bottled up *inside* the gorge and prohibiting them from building farther up the Arkansas River. This photo may well have been staged as proof to the Santa Fe of the Rio Grande's resolve. There is no question that tempers were short and guns supplemented shovels on both sides.

From the McClure House hotel in Cañon City, Ray Morley took a moment to write to his beloved Ada. While "the war progresses in a satisfactory manner," he told her, "it has been prolonged further than we expected. It is a funny affair and is the death struggle of the D. & R. G., I think. They are moving heaven and earth, but we will whip them sooner or later."

Then Morley noted what was far too obvious: "The papers are beginning to get filled with stuff, the result of ponderous lying on both sides to influence public opinion." But he assured her, "do not, however be uneasy about me. I do not think there will be any serious fight outside of the courts."[10]

Morley was right. Despite history's shorthand of referring to the struggle as the Royal Gorge war, most of the battling *was* done in the courts between lawyers and not in the windswept canyons. Some secondary accounts say that men were killed in the field on both sides, but there is no proof of those claims.

Given the allegiances of the various newspapers and the frequently tongue-in-cheek journalism of the times, it is all the more difficult to separate fact from fiction. "John" Gallagher's moment in print is a case in point. Apparently, Gallagher was fired by the Santa Fe for some indiscretion, and a few days later he proved his volatility by becoming "very abusive and making violent threats" in the Santa Fe camp at Cañon City.

To quell Gallagher's outburst, a worker struck Gallagher on the head with an axe handle, "which fractured his skull." The *Colorado Weekly Chieftain* reported on page one both that Gallagher would not live through the night and that he was in fact dead.

But the following week, the *Chieftain* made a retraction—even if the newspaper put it on page four and had initially confused the man's first name: "Mr. James Gallagher, the man reported killed by Curly, showed up at the *Chieftain* office yesterday, one of the liveliest corpses we have seen for many a day. He has an ugly bump on his head, but will soon recover."[11]

Occasionally, misinformation was blamed on the telegraph lines that clicked in and out of Cañon City. "Yesterday where I said there were no marement [merriment] except in high wines," corrected one correspondent, "the telegraph made me say high winds. Today it has been whiskey straight on every side . . ."[12]

Indeed, if another story is to be believed, time wore heavily on the hands of the idle men holding the lines in the gorge, and they were not above a practical joke or two. Without saying which railroaders were the pranksters, the *Chieftain* reported that forty or fifty men dressed and painted as Indians "charged with a war whoop down one of the arroyos [gullies] on a party of tenderfeet, who were holding a point in the canon." The surprised workers beat a hasty retreat, and the *Chieftain* captured the tenor of sentiments on both sides by noting, "both sides, as usual, of course, claim the victory."[13]

Even during those periods when the courts permitted work on various sections of the right-of-way, the construction was not without controversy. Both railroads attempted to recruit manpower from as far away as the San Luis Valley and Denver. One grading firm was awarded contracts by both the Rio Grande and the Santa Fe. As a result, the company frequently shifted its crews from one line to the other. This may account for the reminiscences of some who worked in the canyon that "they worked for one railroad company in the day time and the other at night and drew pay from each one."[14]

As the summer dragged on, the question for the Denver and Rio Grande became whether there was a way that might bypass the gorge. Construction superintendent Robert F. Weitbrec came up with four possibilities—none of them good. The shortest and most logical ran up Grape Creek through Temple Canyon and circled back to the Arkansas River just above where it entered the gorge (the present-day Parkdale Bridge). This point was still within the Santa Fe's 20-mile plat, but Weitbrec thought that upstream from here, the canyon might accommodate two lines.

A second alternative climbed out of Grape Creek along the same route but went west and descended back to the Arkansas down Texas Creek, well upriver of the Santa Fe's domain. The other two alternatives followed Grape Creek upstream farther—no small feat given that this canyon has as many twists and turns as it has rattlesnakes. An area called "the Tights" forms what might be called a miniature Royal Gorge, and it would have required many bridges before these routes also returned to the Arkansas River near Texas Creek.[15]

If nothing else, the Denver and Rio Grande's quest to control alternate routes and all conceivable branch lines provided fodder for more lines of facetious journalism. When Palmer associates incorporated the Upper Arkansas, San Juan and Pacific Railroad Company in late May 1878 and listed routes up every major tributary of the upper Arkansas and then some, a correspondent to the *Chieftain*—possibly Cañon City's B. F. Rockafellow—proved a quick wit:

"This great continental, chain lightning railway, with forked adjuncts to every ranch and prospect hole in the southwest, will also extend from Salt Lake to the northwest passage, via the lava beds," the reporter teased. "From Ouray it will extend to Tampa Town and Stone's Hill, via the extinct Arizona diamond fields, also to Gulliverville and Munchausonville. They will hold at all hazards for fifty years, all of the known or suspected passes covered by said routes, after the manner of its illustrious prototype, the Denver and Rio Grande Railway."[16]

As Palmer and the Denver and Rio Grande pondered their options, William Barstow Strong and the Santa Fe ratcheted up their game. The traffic pooling agreement between the two roads along the Front Range was long since dead. As the resolution of the Royal Gorge right-of-way sat mired in the courts, the Santa Fe aggressively renewed its threat to parallel the Denver and Rio Grande's line from Pueblo to Denver with tracks of its own.

The Rio Grande had laid its narrow gauge tracks during a time of high costs in both construction and credit. Not only could the Santa Fe now build a competing line more cheaply and with less resulting indebtedness but also, as a standard gauge road, it could carry more tonnage at less cost.

Palmer confronted his bondholders with this threat, and the result was a humiliating defeat for the self-assured general. Rather than face economic ruin, the bondholders reluctantly leased the entire Denver and Rio Grande system to the Santa Fe in return for rather vague assurances that the combined roads would be operated as a unified system and that the Rio Grande's indebtedness would continue to be serviced. Wall Street investors appeared to like the arrangement, and Denver and Rio Grande bonds increased from 50 percent to 90 percent of par within a few weeks.[17]

Although the lease agreement was made on October 19, 1878, disagreements in the field ran deep. Palmer refused to turn over control of his road until the Santa Fe's Boston crowd of investors fulfilled certain financial guarantees. "The arrogant demand of possession before complying with the plain terms made by Strong has been repeated yesterday by Nickerson," Palmer groused. "I have declined of course point-blank."

Nickerson and Strong appear to have counted on their demand for possession and a mere *offer* to deposit security to secure the transfer, but Palmer would not be moved. "If they were to put up Boston itself now," he steamed on, "it would not avail. The actual provisions of the papers must be carried out or they lose the lease."

Sounding a little like Collis P. Huntington when the chips were down, Palmer asked his correspondent to keep his rant to himself, but he avowed as how "we may want to take up something else [besides railroading] now that this recent act has put things in a thoroughly antagonistic shape."

But also like Huntington, Palmer had railroading too deep in his blood to walk away. The Boston crowd soon provided the required bond guarantees, and the Denver and Rio Grande was finally turned over to Santa Fe control on December 14—with Palmer watching every move.[18]

This arrangement, however, did not halt the legal wrangles over the Royal Gorge right-of-way, and soon both railroads were also battling in the courts over the lease itself. The Rio Grande claimed that the Santa Fe's rate system adversely affected the Rio Grande's share of traffic and that the Santa Fe was operating the Rio Grande as if it were its own, purchasing new locomotives worth more than $100,000.

The Santa Fe also laid track through the gorge along the full 20 miles to which it had priority. Beyond that point near Spike Buck, its construction crews were still confronted by DeRemer's humble but effective fort because Palmer claimed that the lease to the Santa Fe did not include the Rio Grande's right-of-way upstream of the gorge. It looked as if it was going to be another long, hot summer of standoff. But then things got even wilder, and this time, Bat Masterson was indeed there.

Masterson received a telegram from officers of the Santa Fe asking him to recruit a posse from Dodge City and assist the railroad in defending its right-of-way through the gorge should the Rio Grande mount an attack. Just what authority a sheriff of a Kansas county had to lead armed men into a neighboring state and do the bidding of a private company is debatable. No one, however, doubted Bat's relationship with the Santa Fe.

Giving Masterson the benefit of the doubt, he may have been acting in his dual role as a deputy U.S. marshal and been determined to maintain order and the status quo pending further court action. The thirty-three men who joined Masterson on this excursion were not, however, concerned with legalities. As a boastful reminiscence later put it: " . . . where in the whole universe were there to be found fitter men for a desperate encounter of this kind. Dodge City bred such bold, reckless men, and it was their pride and delight to be called upon to do such work."[19]

DeRemer's Rio Grande forces were quick to recruit similar rowdies to their cause, and after Bat's little army arrived in Cañon City, it appeared that wild bedlam—if not open warfare—might break out between the two sides. But despite being the leader of what amounted to paid Santa Fe mercenaries, Masterson managed to keep an uneasy peace.

Tensions cooled in April 1879 after a U.S. Supreme Court ruling in favor of the Denver and Rio Grande, but there was still the nagging and uncertain matter of the Rio Grande's outright lease to the Santa Fe. While this matter was pending, Bat took his little army back to Dodge City to await further proceedings.

Early in June, in anticipation of an adverse decision on the lease, the Santa Fe sent out another call to Masterson, and he hurried back to Colorado with sixty men onboard a special train. Santa Fe reinforcements from Trinidad spread out along the Rio Grande line, and Bat assumed command of the critical Rio Grande depot and roundhouse at Pueblo.

On June 10, a Colorado state court friendly to the Denver and Rio Grande voided the Santa Fe lease and purported to return the railroad to Palmer's control. The Santa Fe was convinced that this ruling would be overturned on appeal, and William Barstow Strong gave orders to resist where possible. At six o'clock the next morning, Palmer and his troops successfully seized the Rio Grande's key points and took over most operations. One of the few Santa Fe holdouts was the depot and roundhouse in Pueblo, the latter of which by some accounts had by now been turned into a veritable fortress by Masterson and his compatriots.

Robert F. Weitbrec and J. A. McMurtrie of the Denver and Rio Grande conferred with Pueblo sheriff Henly R. Price to devise a plan of attack. Price was supposed to be the neutral legal authority serving the court order for Rio Grande possession. By one report, there was talk of commandeering the lone cannon from the state armory, but closer inspection determined that Masterson had already appropriated it for his own use.

McMurtrie was forced to assemble about fifty Rio Grande men in front of the Victoria Hotel and supply them with rifles and bayonets. At three o'clock that afternoon, this force marched to the depot and met Sheriff Price on the platform. A bystander was manhandled out of the way, and one of the armed Rio Grande men called out, "Come on now, let's take the telegraph office!"

There was a scuffle at the front door, and shots rang out. The door was quickly forced, and the attackers commenced to fire through the building, as the defenders sought escape out the back. There were conflicting reports whether the Santa Fe defenders returned fire, but one of Masterson's men, Harry Jenkins of Dodge City, was fatally shot in the back as he ran out the rear door. That left the roundhouse.

Unable to communicate with Santa Fe management, Masterson could not be sure of the exact state of the legal maneuverings. Weitbrec finally requested a parley with Bat and in the end proved persuasive. Regardless of the emotions on both sides, the current legal order required that the Santa Fe surrender its position, and Bat did so—much to the chagrin of "certain Dodge City folks, who . . . 'had been hoping that the home boys would be permitted to wipe the Denver & Rio Grande off the map.' " When the dust settled, Palmer's forces were in control of all points on their line, including the Pueblo roundhouse.[20]

Their victory was short lived, however, because the Santa Fe appeal to federal court on the lease bounced the Rio Grande back to Santa Fe control on July 16. A month later, the final shoe appeared to drop against Palmer's road when its bondholders forced the railroad into receivership.

For the remainder of the summer of 1879, the outlook for the Denver and Rio Grande appeared grim. But later that fall, the railroad's financial condition improved considerably when it received a sudden and sizeable investment in cash from an eastern investor who was no stranger to railroads. His name was Jay Gould, and he had already demonstrated a mastery of complicated deals. With an involvement in both the Union Pacific and the Kansas Pacific, Gould was keenly interested in railroad routes in the mountains of Colorado, particularly as they related to Leadville's silver riches.

Gould was to dabble in the affairs of both the Denver and Rio Grande and the Denver, South Park and Pacific, but his overriding concern was to keep William Barstow Strong and the Santa Fe out of Leadville. As long as the Rio Grande was leased to the Santa Fe, Strong held the upper hand.

One tactical move was for Gould to buy into John Evans's Denver, South Park and Pacific, which he did. Then he went to cash-strapped Palmer and bought a half interest in the Denver and Rio Grande, to cover all bases. Meanwhile, Gould arranged a traffic pool for Colorado business between his Union Pacific and the Santa Fe, "while he figured a way out of the stranglehold."

Gould encouraged Palmer and Evans to work together to build into Leadville from a point where the South Park's projected line out of Denver would intersect with the Rio Grande's claimed right-of-way upstream of the Royal Gorge—a right-of-way that Palmer defiantly continued to assert was not included in the lease to the Santa Fe.

But Gould was just beginning to flex his muscles among these railroads. The Santa Fe's threat to parallel the Denver and Rio Grande from Pueblo to Denver was a longstanding one. Now, for their own leverage, Gould and Palmer announced plans for a new railroad that would parallel the Santa Fe from connections with the Kansas Pacific deep in Kansas all the way to Pueblo. Strong and Santa Fe president Thomas Nickerson were not completely bluffed, but they had too much at stake to ignore the possibility that Gould might just pull it off, particularly in light of the increasingly favorable Denver and Rio Grande decisions that were slowly coming out of the U.S. Supreme Court.[21]

The Court breathed life back into the Denver and Rio Grande by ruling that the Right-of-Way Act of 1875 did not preempt the railroad's rights under its original 1872 right-of-way grant. The Court determined that the Rio Grande surveys of 1871 and 1872 were as complete as those made in 1877 by the Cañon City and San Juan on behalf of the Santa Fe. That fact followed by its occupancy of the route amidst the construction flurry of April 19, 1878—and despite a continuing debate whether Morley or McMurtrie had gotten to the critical ground first—was sufficient in the Court's view to give the Denver and Rio Grande the priority through the gorge.

This, of course, had been Palmer's contention all along. It was also his excuse for not complying initially with the Right-of-Way Act of 1875, although doing so would have saved him two years of delay, expense, and uncertainty.

The Supreme Court ruled further that the federal circuit court had been in error in enjoining the Denver and Rio Grande from construction and in allowing the Santa Fe's subsidiaries to proceed. But since the Santa Fe had incurred significant construction costs in good faith under the circuit court's ruling, the Supreme Court directed that the Rio Grande reimburse the Santa Fe for its construction costs throughout the gorge. These were to be determined by an independent commission.

This should have settled the matter. But now the Santa Fe went to the circuit court and alleged that there were no grounds for enforcing the Supreme Court's order to turn over the gorge because the Rio Grande had conveyed all its rights to the Santa Fe with its lease. Rather than immediately enforce the Supreme Court's decision, the circuit court chose to examine the Santa Fe's claims regarding the lease, including whether or not it had been intended to cover the Rio Grande's rights to the Leadville extension upstream from the gorge.

By the end of 1879, Denver and Rio Grande attorneys had an application for a writ of mandamus (a directive to a lower authority) before the Supreme Court asking it to order the circuit court to enforce the higher court's decision—in other words, require the Santa Fe to give up its gorge trackage to the Rio Grande. But when the Supreme Court ruled on this largely procedural matter on February 2, 1880, it denied the application on the grounds that because the lower court had exercised its judicial discretion with regard to the prior mandate, an *appeal*—not a writ of mandamus—was the proper remedy. It looked as if the legal posturing was going to drag on for yet another summer.[22]

Finally, it was the booming Leadville trade—and Jay Gould—that brought the leaders of both railroads to their economic senses. With considerable pressure from Gould, they sought a compromise. The legal morass of two years of court battles was resolved in a series of agreements between the Santa Fe and the Denver and Rio Grande and their various subsidiaries. Collectively, these came to be called the Treaty of Boston, because their terms were agreed upon in the boardrooms of the East and not the rocky canyons of the West. But significantly, their critical terms were first spelled out in a letter from Gould to the Santa Fe after he had conferred with Palmer's representatives, including Dr. Bell, "who happened to be in the City."

Essentially, the lease that had caused so much angst was declared null and void and all litigation terminated. The Santa Fe agreed not to build to Denver, Leadville, or the San Juan country, or any point west of the Rio Grande's lines for a period of ten years. In return, it was to receive half of the Rio Grande's business in and out of Leadville and southwestern Colorado and one-quarter of its Denver traffic. (In other words, ship east from Pueblo via the Santa Fe and not from Denver via the Kansas Pacific.)

The Rio Grande agreed not to build south of its existing railheads at El Moro, Colorado, or Española, New Mexico, on its San Luis Valley branch. Palmer's original goal of El Paso was extinguished, as was that of Santa Fe. And just to appease Jay Gould in his other ventures, the Rio Grande also promised that it would not build east to St. Louis. Meanwhile, Gould's stock in the Denver and Rio Grande went from $22 per share in the fall of 1879 to $75 in February 1880.

Finally, despite an appraisal by the court-appointed commission that the value of the Santa Fe's construction through the Royal Gorge was $566,216.35, based on A. A. Robinson's engineering records, the Denver and Rio Grande agreed to buy the 20 miles of line for $1.4 million. The components of the Treaty of Boston were signed as of March 27, 1880, and the first Denver and Rio Grande train ran through the Royal Gorge five days later. Its next major stop would be Leadville. Palmer's road celebrated its arrival in the booming silver capital on July 22, with a special carrying ex-president Ulysses S. Grant.[23]

The Denver and Rio Grande's payment for the Santa Fe's construction efforts in the Royal Gorge would soon become nothing but a number on accounting ledgers. In fact, time would quickly blur the history of which company had engineered the route through this difficult passage.

At the narrowest point in the gorge, Santa Fe engineers initially constructed a wooden-decked trestle that was supported by timber bents and piles of rock. This structure was in place when the first Santa Fe excursion ran into the gorge on May 7, 1879, but the train stopped just short of what reports called "the construction bridge."

Within weeks, a flash flood—or perhaps just the normal spring runoff—washed away the wooden structure. (Conspiracy theorists have speculated that this bridge's collapse was somehow related to the trouble between the two roads, but there is no evidence that anyone other than Mother Nature had a hand.)

Because the right-of-way at that point was still under court orders, the Santa Fe, through its Pueblo and Arkansas Valley subsidiary, petitioned the court for permission to replace the structure with what came to be called "the hanging bridge." Named for its construction and not some desperado act, the hanging bridge was supported in part by a rafter construction that spanned the river and was anchored on both sides to the canyon walls.

This structure passed from the Santa Fe to the Denver and Rio Grande under the Treaty of Boston along with the 20 miles of completed track. Over the years, as locomotive weights increased, the Rio Grande strengthened the bridge several times with elaborate masonry along the riverbed, and the crossbeams spanning the river became more a matter of decoration than strength.

But in the meantime, the Hanging Bridge had become a staple for tourism on the Royal Gorge route. The Denver and Rio Grande even listed a station on its timetables at the bottom of the gorge as Hanging Bridge. One of the most famous photographs of the structure shows President Theodore Roosevelt surveying the scene. Consequently, "no one in his right mind would have removed the useless supports, or admitted that the bridge did not truly hang." Some might argue that in terms of publicity value, the Denver and Rio Grande received far more than $1.4 million from the bridge over the years.

It came to be assumed that the Denver and Rio Grande was alone responsible for this engineering marvel. When the Rio Grande's J. R. DeRemer died about 1907, "the public press insisted on giving him the credit for designing and constructing the famous Hanging Bridge located in the still more famous Royal Gorge."

It was left to A. A. Robinson of the Santa Fe to set the record straight. "I was chief engineer of this construction," Robinson acknowledged in *Engineering News,* "and it is due to the late C. Schaler [*sic*] Smith of St. Louis to say that we visited the bridge site together and decided on the rafter plan of construction. . . . I engaged Mr. Smith to prepare the detailed plans from which the original bridge was constructed." History had almost forgotten that the Santa Fe had left a piece of its heritage in the bottom of the narrow gorge.[24]

In later years, the Denver and Rio Grande would be characterized as "Colorado's railroad" and closely identified with the Centennial State. William Jackson Palmer would be hailed as a builder of great cities. But this was far from true in the 1870s. Both Palmer and his railroad were looked at as outsiders in the towns he tried to bend to his purposes—Colorado City, Trinidad, and Cañon City among them.

If nothing else, the battle for the Royal Gorge showed how tenacious William Jackson Palmer could be when the stakes were all or nothing. Because at least for the Denver and Rio Grande, that is what the Royal Gorge war was about. If Palmer had not been successful—or had abandoned the field as quickly as he had at Raton—the main line west for the Santa Fe might have led to Leadville, over Tennessee Pass, and down the Colorado River bound for Salt Lake City. And the Denver and Rio Grande would have been choked off from the Leadville trade and left with only the marginal traffic of southwest Colorado.

"The contest for the Grand Canon," General Palmer reported to his board of directors, "was in reality a fight for the gateway, not to Leadville only, but to the far more important, because infinitely larger, mineral fields of the Gunnison country, the Blue and Eagle Rivers and Utah."[25]

For Thomas Nickerson and William Barstow Strong, the stakes had been high, but never about the Santa Fe's very corporate survival. In the end, the Atchison, Topeka and Santa Fe lost the battle for the Royal Gorge, but it remained to be seen whether or not it would lose the transcontinental war.

11

Handshake at Deming

As the Atchison, Topeka and Santa Fe turned away from the Royal Gorge and cast its fate toward a southerly route, the halt in construction that Collis P. Huntington's associates forced upon him after the bridge battle at Yuma had proven short lived. Money was still tight, the Big Four's corporate and individual debt still staggering, but there was too much at stake in the American Southwest to pause for very long.

There were whispers of silver bonanzas in the canyons of New Mexico. Countless boomtowns in the Colorado Rockies boasted of becoming another Leadville. In southeastern Arizona, a rowdy camp called Tombstone promised to rival Leadville in both silver and grit. All around, the West was getting smaller, with a steady influx of settlers and industries.

And draped across the map—as the Southern Pacific paused at Yuma, the Santa Fe crested Raton Pass, and the Texas and Pacific marshaled its forces in East Texas—there was still the prize to be won of a southern transcontinental rail connection. Sit out a hand, and you were likely to lose the game.

· · ·

While Huntington's partners held the Southern Pacific at Yuma, there was little doubt—in Huntington's mind, at least—that the railroad would eventually build eastward across the Arizona desert. The original compromise between Huntington and Tom Scott had been for Scott's Texas and Pacific Railroad to meet the Southern Pacific at Yuma. But where was Scott? For the moment, it appeared that despite its lucrative congressional land grant, the Texas and Pacific was mired in financing woes and construction delays while still near Fort Worth.

With perhaps too much bravado, Huntington unabashedly announced that if the Texas and Pacific was not up to the task, the Southern Pacific would gladly build along the 32nd parallel route *without* a government land grant or other subsidy. "We should not be asked to wait at the Colorado River indefinitely for an embarrassed and mismanaged connecting company to build 1,250 miles to give us connection," Huntington fumed to Congress, "when we are ready to construct right along and willing to provide the outlet to the East for ourselves without cost to the Government . . ."[1]

Charley Crocker didn't share Huntington's optimism, but as Yuma enjoyed its railhead boom, reports began to circulate that the Southern Pacific was amassing a large quantity of rails, ties, and rolling stock in preparation for just such a burst of construction. The fiery desert heat of the summer of 1878 led to increasingly wilder claims about the extent of these stockpiles. Finally, after one report of materiel on hand for 200 miles of rail and a 2-mile-long pile of some 500,000 ties, editor George Tyng of Yuma's *Arizona Sentinel* dubbed the entire story the "Southern Pacific Mirage."

Resorting to mangled poetry after Tyng himself had perhaps been a little touched by the sun, the editor began his verse by observing, "There were men, in brags most prolific, of their pushing the Southern Pacific," before concluding, "their yarns about ties were proven all lies, they swore they ne'er meditated such falsehoods or said it."[2]

By fall, Tyng was a member of the board of directors of the local Southern Pacific Railroad Company of Arizona after Huntington obtained the road's territorial charter. With this secured and Crocker still fretting about the money to be spent, the mirage of the Southern Pacific's advance eastward from Yuma became reality. Early in the morning darkness of October 10, 1878, while the desert was still cool, a locomotive pulled fifteen flatcars, each loaded with 250 redwood ties, across the Colorado River bridge into Yuma. More ties followed and then came flatcars loaded with rails.

It was a meticulously packaged operation. Each flatcar carried 44 steel rails 30 feet in length, 6 kegs of spikes, 88 steel connecting bars called fishplates, and 3 boxes of bolts—in all, weighing 23,000 pounds and being enough material to build 660 feet of track. By the time track-laying eastward began on November 18, twenty-car construction trains were arriving in Yuma every other day.[3]

Crocker's construction boss on this extension was James Harvey Stro-bridge, a hard-driving Yankee who had come to California with the gold rush. He had long ago proven his worth to Crocker on the Central Pacific when things had gotten tough in the Sierras. Showing his organizational skills, Strobridge flung a crew of graders 20 miles eastward to tackle the most difficult rockwork between Yuma and Tucson. Other crews laid track east from Yuma.

By the end of November, 7.5 miles of track had been spiked into place, and 1,300 men, including 1,100 Chinese laborers, were at work on the line. Editor Tyng commented that the Chinese "move dirt much more slowly than white men but as they have no pipes to fill and no political reforms to discuss, they manage to get in a fair day's work before night falls." As for motive power, if the "Santa Monica, No. 2" sounded a little out of place in the desert, this locomotive was a remnant of the Los Angeles and Independence Railroad that Huntington had gathered to his fold.[4]

As Southern Pacific surveyors moved eastward ahead of the graders, some of the survey stakes they set replaced older stakes driven by Texas and Pacific surveyors back in the days when Tom Scott was planning for San Diego to be the terminus of his road. At the time, no one on the Southern Pacific seemed to think that might cause a problem.

Having initially opposed the Yuma extension, Charley Crocker arrived on the scene in December and was quickly caught up in the excitement of the renewed construction. "It seemed like old times to meet 'Stro.' out there, and hear him order things around," Crocker reported to Huntington. Watching the construction across relatively flat country, Crocker enthused, "I do not think we have ever been able to build a railroad as cheaply as this is being built," and boasted that at thirty miles an hour, the cars rode as smoothly as they did on the New York Central.[5]

Initially, water for men, beasts, and machines had to be hauled everywhere. It was even more important than a reliable supply of rails and ties. Local sources were scarce and of dubious quality. Before deep wells were dug, Crocker complained that the alkali content created foam in the boilers of the steam locomotives.[6]

By April 1879, rails were spiked down all the way to the town of Gila Bend, and its stagecoach stop soon gave way to a depot. Eastward from there, the 19 miles to Maricopa Summit required a climb of almost 800 feet at a maximum grade of just over 1 percent. By April 29, the line was opened to the new town of Maricopa, which boomed as the railhead for the slightly older settlement (1868) of Phoenix to the north.

Already the Southern Pacific was in the business of developing Arizona's landscape and selling its scenery. A five-day special excursion for about two hundred people was operated from San Francisco at a round-trip fare of $40 to promote an auction of town lots. One writer promised, "There is hardly a sunrise, sunset, or midnight in this country that is not replete with either beauty or impressiveness."

Although there was initial confusion about which county the new town of Maricopa was located in, the railroad auctioned fifty-one lots at prices ranging from $25 to $1,000. Even Crocker was pleased by the results, reporting to Huntington, "We had a sale of town lots at Maricopa at auction, and sold a little over $10,000 worth, the *first pop,* so you will see that things are brightening up down that way. There is great talk of new mines being discovered all around, throughout the territory adjacent to the railroad."[7]

But now as a long straightaway stretched southeast toward Casa Grande, Strobridge and some of the same men who had tamed the snowy Sierras were faced with blistering heat—literally. Rails, plates, and tools left too long in the desert sun got so hot at midday that they burned on the hands of workers who touched them. Crocker fretted to Huntington about the approach of summer even as he pleaded with him to maintain a steady supply of rails.

Huntington could do nothing about the weather, of course, and there were days when he felt equally helpless about the railroad's orders for steel. By 1879, every major railroad in the United States and countless local lines were aggressively pushing construction on all fronts. Steel mills in the United States and as far away as Great Britain were taxed to their limits. Even as good—and forceful—a customer as Collis P. Huntington sometimes had to wait for promised deliveries.

Ties were also in short supply. Shipments of stout redwood ties from California flowed over the Southern Pacific, but they weren't coming fast enough. By the middle of May, 26 miles beyond Maricopa at Casa Grande, Crocker decided to stop construction and wait for cooler weather and more materiel.

"My idea of stopping the road," Crocker told Huntington, "was based on the fact that the reserve of ties on hand was pretty much exhausted" and the expectation of new deliveries "so irregular that we could not expect to continue the construction except at intervals." With the weather getting so hot, "the men could not work much longer to good advantage."

By then, Strobridge's crews had been at it for 139 working days and, as the *Arizona Sentinel* put it, "been constantly working at high pressure speed since November last, under the disadvantages of warm days, cold nights, scarcity of water and inhaling the dust of 182 miles now accomplished." So as Crocker stockpiled ties at Casa Grande, the town gathered in traffic from Tucson and points east, well aware that its future as a railhead would be short lived.[8]

Sixty-five miles south of Casa Grande, Tucson waited expectantly for the Southern Pacific. Unlike so many towns throughout southern Arizona and New Mexico—including Maricopa, Benson, Willcox, Lordsburg, and Deming—Tucson did not owe its existence to the coming of the railroad. A Papago Indian village stood on the site of Tucson when Jesuit priest Eusebio Kino visited the area in 1692. Franciscans followed, and, in 1775, a Spanish presidio was built there.

The 1848 Treaty of Guadalupe Hidalgo ending the Mexican-American War left Tucson in the Mexican province of Sonora. Five years later, it became American territory when the Gadsden Purchase secured the southern watershed of the Gila River and the 32nd parallel route, along which the Southern Pacific was now building.

Tucson had been on the route of John Butterfield's Overland Mail until the Civil War halted the line's operations, but the town thrived nonetheless. The 1880 census counted almost one in six of Arizona's non–Native American inhabitants—7,007 out of a territorial population of 40,400—as Tucson residents. The town was not only the largest by far in Arizona but also the largest between Los Angeles (11,183) and San Antonio (20,550).

Now with the railroad almost upon it, Tucson faced new growth and new issues. Some of the Chinese laborers furloughed for the summer at Casa Grande had already made their way into town. Conveniently overlooking the fact that the Americans themselves were relative newcomers to a historically Mexican town, Tucson's *Arizona Daily Star* bemoaned this influx.

"Hardly a stage arrives that does not bring one or more Chinamen to our city," the newspaper reported in early July 1879. With them came accoutrements. That same week, seven Chinese ladies of questionable virtue—the *Arizona Star* termed them "Celestial heroines"—arrived and "added to the number already here, make ten in all."

The *Arizona Star* found nothing but trouble with this new wave of immigration, but its afternoon competitor, the *Arizona Citizen,* struck at the core of the matter. "A good deal of the trouble about the Chinese," the paper noted wryly, "seems to grow out of their temperate habits, their determination to work for a living and their refusal to be bilked out of their wages."[9]

Meanwhile, there was railroad talk of all sorts. Some reports voiced fears that the Southern Pacific might bypass Tucson. Other rumors claimed that the railroad intended to build a new town complete with roundhouse and machine shops on the San Pedro River 40-some miles to the east and just that much closer to booming Tombstone. Tucson did its best to dissuade the Southern Pacific from either action and deeded the railroad a 100-foot-wide right-of-way through the northeast quadrant of town. It also vacated a strip for depot operations in addition to twelve city blocks for other facilities. To pay for these acquisitions, the town voted $10,000 in bonds by a resounding margin of 139 to 1 among white American males over twenty-one.

But rumors got so rife that they caused a rising tide of anti–Southern Pacific sentiment. This was reported to Huntington, who was focused on delivering rail shipments to Crocker and holding his transcontinental competitors at bay. He didn't need local dissension on his flanks. Perhaps remembering the trouble that William Jackson Palmer's land development tactics had caused the Denver and Rio Grande at Trinidad and Cañon City, Huntington had his managers assure Tucson residents that the Southern Pacific was indeed coming to town and had no major plans on the San Pedro.

About the same time, surveyors for the Atchison, Topeka and Santa Fe showed up in Tucson and stoked opposing rumors that not one but two railroads might soon be in town. The Santa Fe was exploring routes from Albuquerque southwest to Tombstone and Tucson with an eye toward further construction both west to California and south into Mexico. Despite the rugged terrain on a straight line between Tucson and Albuquerque, the Santa Fe engineer in charge hoped to find "a road of easy grade and reasonably cheap construction." If that happened, the *Arizona Star* predicted, it "will make Tucson without question . . . the Denver of Arizona."[10]

The survey work by the Santa Fe was reported to Charley Crocker. The man who had dug his feet in the most to hold Huntington at the Colorado River was once again urging Huntington to hasten an adequate supply of rails to the front. "I wish you would hurry up the steel," Crocker admonished, "as when we commence work in Arizona again, we do not want to be detained for lack of material." Huntington assured him, "I am doing all I can to get rails started but find it one of the most difficult things to do that I ever tried."[11]

By January 24, 1880, there was a sufficient supply of ties and rails at Casa Grande to commence work on the 65-mile extension to Tucson. But no sooner had Strobridge put his construction crews to work than a freak January snowstorm dumped eight inches of snow on Maricopa. Tucson had its first snow in years. The men who had found it too hot to work just months before now lost time because of slush and mud. Barely had the ground cleared when Strobridge reported more lost time because of Chinese New Year celebrations.

Once engaged, however, the work crews laid more than a mile of track a day. Three weeks later, well past the pointy spire of Picacho Peak and just 18 miles out of Tucson, Strobridge was forced to wire Huntington the result: "End of track Ariz. [February] 26. Out of steel."

Crocker grumbled about the added expense caused by the delay, but used the time to send grading crews east of Tucson to work on the approaches to the crossings of Cienega Creek and the San Pedro River.[12]

Crocker continued to fret, but enough rails arrived so that tracks were spiked down along the Southern Pacific right-of-way northeast of the Tucson town plaza on March 17, 1880. That afternoon a train "with No. 41 on the head end, followed by 2 water cars, 13 boxcars, 39 flatcars and 11 construction cars" was welcomed by a cheering crowd.

Three days later, Crocker and the usual dignitaries arrived for the official celebration. They steamed into town on a special train that was an hour early, and the shrill blast of their locomotive's whistle sent Tucson mayor R. N. Leatherwood and the local welcoming committee scurrying to the depot site.

Mayor Leatherwood had already sent numerous telegrams to a list of officials that stretched from the mayor of Yuma to President Rutherford B. Hayes. Also on the list, according to the *Arizona Daily Star,* was a telegram to Pope Leo XIII noting Tucson's long ties with the Catholic Church and informing his Holiness "that a railroad from San Francisco, California, now connects us with the Christian world."

As the story goes, this was a little too pompous for some Tucson residents, and one prankster fabricated a response from Rome that read: "His Holiness, the Pope, acknowledges with appreciation receipt of your telegram . . . but, for his own satisfaction would ask where in hell is Tucson?"[13]

Jokes aside, Tucson was well satisfied with its railroad. But Huntington and Crocker did not intend to pause there very long. No matter how speculative the Santa Fe's survey work around Tucson, there could be no denying that while the Southern Pacific was rushing eastward across Arizona, the Atchison, Topeka and Santa Fe had been building southward through New Mexico with equal determination. There might not be a Santa Fe locomotive steaming into Tucson any time soon, but that did not mean that the railroad did not have Arizona in its sights.

The first railroad car in New Mexico passed into the territory on December 7, 1878. That vehicle had indeed been an Atchison, Topeka and

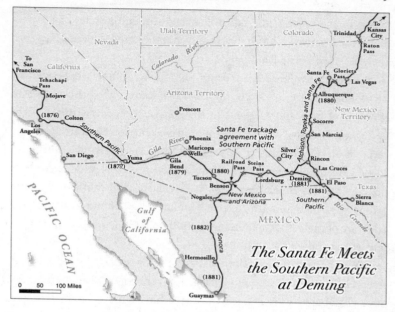

The Santa Fe Meets
the Southern Pacific
at Deming

Santa Fe *car* and not a *locomotive* because the train was being pushed *backward* over the temporary track across the Raton Pass switchbacks. Tentative though the clanging and clicking of those wheels were, in the next two and one-half years, the Santa Fe would build almost 1,000 miles of track in New Mexico.

Throughout the spring of 1879, Santa Fe crews under the supervision of A. A. Robinson graded south from Raton Pass, frequently in sight of the wagon ruts of the Mountain Branch of the Santa Fe Trail. The trail's old watering stop of Willow Springs became the town of Raton, New Mexico, and as the railroad built farther south, the new towns of Springer and Wagon Mound briefly flirted with the boom of being a railhead.

South of the oblong butte that gave Wagon Mound its name, the railroad grade passed near Fort Union and the point where the Mountain Branch and the Cimarron Cutoff of the Santa Fe Trail rejoined. By the Fourth of July, the rails had reached Las Vegas. Here the railroad was 50 miles due east of Santa Fe, but the southern slopes of the Sangre de Cristo Mountains forced it into a wide loop southward to get around them. In the process, the railroad snaked through a series of S curves along the headwaters of the Pecos River and crossed Glorieta Pass into the watershed of the Rio Grande.

Meanwhile, trains began using the Raton Tunnel in September 1879, and the elimination of the laborious Raton switchbacks sped up the flow of men and materiel to the construction front. But another event occurred that was much more important to the railroad's long-term vitality: the Atchison, Topeka and Santa Fe paid its first stock dividend. With construction rushing forward across New Mexico, here nonetheless was proof that Thomas Nickerson and William Barstow Strong were meticulous managers who knew how to run a railroad *and* take care of their stockholders. Such solid financial footing would be essential to winning battles yet to come.

From the summit of Glorieta Pass, the Santa Fe's line descended steep Galisteo Creek through Apache Canyon, where eastbound grades of 3 percent are still in place. At Galisteo Junction, soon to be renamed Lamy after the archbishop of Santa Fe, the main line streaked southwest to Bernalillo on the Rio Grande. But what about the railroad's long-sought goal of Santa Fe?

Ray Morley surveyed every inch of plausible grade between Raton Pass and the Rio Grande. He convinced A. A. Robinson—who in turn convinced William Barstow Strong—that Santa Fe, despite the town's prominence in their company's name, was not to be on the main line. It sat in too deep of a bowl and was surrounded by too many hills that demanded heavy grades. Building into Santa Fe simply wasn't conducive to through traffic. And truth be told, Santa Fe was no longer the economic magnet it had been for a half century on the Santa Fe Trail. The pull now was California and other points west.

Santa Fe town fathers were far from pleased, of course, but they promoted a local bond issue, and the railroad obliged them by building an 18-mile spur to bridge the gap between Lamy and a location just west of the town plaza. When the rails of the Atchison, Topeka and Santa Fe Railroad reached Santa Fe on February 9, 1880, an era ended.

No one cheered more loudly than a member of the Santa Fe's board of directors. A scant eleven years earlier, at a picnic celebrating the end of track at Wakarusa Creek just 7 miles out of Topeka, his talk of the railroad building to Santa Fe and the Pacific had been met with hoots of laughter. His name was Cyrus K. Holliday, and now it was his turn to hoot.

But there was other nostalgia as well. "Yesterday morning the last coach went out of Las Vegas for Santa Fe," the *Las Vegas Gazette* reported rather wistfully. "The officers were removed to Cañoncito . . . [and] we are sorry to see them go. The stage men and employees looked like they were leaving their earthly treasures."

What began in 1846 as "a mail every six months brought through under guard" had grown to daily stage service during what the paper called "halcyon days." As each new railhead was reached, the stage run was shortened until "gradually," the *Gazette* concluded, "the iron horse has been driven down the Santa Fe trail."[14]

But the way of the iron horse was hardly smooth. After the completion of the line to Lamy, engineer Jake Brown was taking a train up Apache Canyon when he noticed a train coming downgrade toward him at a high rate of speed. Brown reversed his locomotive in an attempt to get back to the siding at Lamy, but then watched in horror as the runaway train's crew gave up any hope of stopping and simply jumped from their posts.

The lone exception was the brave conductor, who made his way from the rear atop the swaying cars, frantically cranking brake wheels as he went. He made it to the cab of the locomotive just in time to bring the load to a halt and avoid a collision with Brown's train. Indeed, runaways on Glorieta Pass were so common that the *Las Vegas Daily Optic* expressed relief and no little surprise when an entire month went by without one.[15]

But others weren't so lucky. When Ed Stanley's eight-car freight train left Santa Fe one evening eastbound, the twenty-three-year-old conductor "was full of life—in unusually good spirits." It was a bitterly cold February night, and as the train climbed up the heavy grades east of town, Stanley graciously invited his brakemen down from the tops of the cars and into the relative warmth of the caboose.

Unfortunately, it was only Stanley's second trip on the run behind an engineer who was making his first run on the line. Not expecting any downgrades, Stanley was surprised when the train started to pick up speed beyond Glorieta Pass. The engineer was surprised too, and he whistled an anguished plea for brakes. Stanley and his brakemen scrambled to the top of the boxcars to answer the call. As a brakeman named Charley knelt to tighten the brake wheel on one car, Stanley ran past him and began to crank the wheel on the next car. Just then, the train bounced around a short curve. Stanley lost his balance and, despite a cry of "Oh, Charley!" to the nearby brakeman, he was hurled headlong from the car top.

The runaway train continued on about 3 miles before it could be brought to a stop and then slowly backed to the point of Stanley's fatal fall. "His dead body, considerably mangled, was picked up by friendly hands, placed in the caboose and brought to Las Vegas." The next day, a coroner's inquest found that "no blame attaches to any one" for the incident, but also acknowledged that the train "had gotten away from the engineer and brakemen and could not be controlled by them."[16]

That no blame was attached despite this acknowledgment was indicative of the relatively cheap value of human lives in those times *and* a recognition of the inherent danger of railroading. Accidents were part of the acceptable price of pushing the rails west and tying the nation together upon them. Ed Stanley was but one of thousands of ordinary trainmen who—for a few dollars a day—paid the price.

Such experiences gave rise to many songs, but among the most descriptive was a gospel hymn written about this time. Many a mountain railroader was laid to rest after his last run to the words of "Life Is Like a Mountain Railroad." It urged those who were of good faith to "watch the hills, the curves, and tunnels, never falter, never fail, keep your hand upon the throttle and your eye upon the rail." The men who operated the Santa Fe across Raton and Glorieta passes, the Rio Grande through the Rockies, or the Southern Pacific over the Tehachapi Loop never faltered.

The Santa Fe built down the Rio Grande and reached Albuquerque on April 15, 1880. There wasn't much celebration because the rail yards were located some distance from the old town. This was not from any fit of land speculation but rather to avoid the river bottom and pass through town as quickly as possible. By the end of summer, the Santa

Fe's tracks had been laid another 103 miles south to the little town of San Marcial.

Now the Santa Fe faced a tough decision about its ultimate objective. Due south down the Rio Grande lay El Paso. To the southwest—just as soon as the railroad could turn the corner of the Black and Mimbres mountains and skirt Cookes Peak—the 32nd parallel corridor ran west toward booming Tombstone, Tucson, and the oncoming Southern Pacific. Beyond lay California. But the Santa Fe was also interested in the ground farther south into Mexico.

The Santa Fe's "Boston crowd" of investors had organized the Sonora Railway Company along much the same route that Dr. Bell traveled during his side trip from Palmer's 1867 survey for the Kansas Pacific. Their investment anticipated significant Mexican mining revenues and a growing Pacific trade in and out of the Mexican port of Guaymas. But on the larger map of the Southwest, the proposed Sonora Railway was also seen as the perfect end run around the Southern Pacific should Huntington prove successful at blocking the way across Arizona.

During the spring and summer of 1880, Huntington lost no time in pushing the Southern Pacific eastward out of Tucson to counter the threat. Charley Crocker warned Huntington early on, however, not to expect rapid progress as the line dipped into the San Pedro Valley. "There is some quite heavy work, which at very best, will detain us from going on as fast as we have been accustomed to. After that, however, we can go to El Paso any time you want, if the steel is here, surely two miles a day, and if necessary, faster still! There will be no difficulty in reaching the boundary of Texas, by one year from today [April 22, 1880]."[17]

By now, the construction of a roundhouse, shops, and mushrooming yards overflowing with freight had convinced Tucson residents that they would not suffer greatly from whatever facilities the Southern Pacific built along its crossing of the San Pedro. But a town of some sort was inevitable at the San Pedro, and the Southern Pacific named it Benson after William B. Benson, a friend of Crocker's who had substantial mining interests throughout the West.

Train service into Benson began on June 22, 1880, and for much of the summer, it served as the railhead for construction farther east and stage and freighting service south to the windswept mesas and rocky arroyos near Tombstone. Among those tempted to try their hand in the stagecoach business was a recent arrival in Tombstone named Wyatt Earp. When existing lines offered too much competition, Earp turned to saloon keeping instead and was soon helping his brother, Virgil, with law enforcement chores.

East of Benson, the Southern Pacific encountered more of the tough ground that Crocker had warned Huntington about, as it climbed out of the San Pedro Valley and crested the northern end of the Dragoon Mountains. At an elevation of 4,613 feet, Dragoon Summit was the highest point on the Southern Pacific west of the Rio Grande—29 feet higher than its projected crossing of the Continental Divide in New Mexico.

East of Dragoon Summit, there was speedy construction across the smooth Sulphur Springs Valley, much of it a dry lake bed that made for a 20-mile straightaway. Along the way, the railroad named the town of Willcox for Major General Orlando Bolivar Willcox, who was then in command of the army's Department of Arizona. Willcox had earlier served in San Francisco and been in the chain of the "telegram war" over permission to cross the Fort Yuma bridge.

Northeast of Willcox, the railroad made a long curve north of the Dos Cabezas Mountains, two prominent rock towers that dominate the view for miles. The wide valley here was what Lieutenant John G. Parke called Railroad Pass on his 1853 survey. William Jackson Palmer's subsequent survey for the Kansas Pacific confirmed the value of the route, and now Huntington was taking full advantage of it.

By September 15, 1880, the Southern Pacific was officially opened to the old Butterfield stage station of San Simon, just inside the Arizona border. East of here, tough grades were encountered across Steins Pass astride the Peloncillo Mountains—a much more narrow gap than Railroad Pass. This section of railroad required a helper engine division, and it remains the heaviest grade—about 1.5 percent—on the Southern Pacific main line between Yuma and El Paso.[18]

In October, Atchison, Topeka and Santa Fe general manager William Barstow Strong, who was taking an increasingly active corporate role and would soon become the Santa Fe's president, met with Huntington in Boston to discuss the narrowing gap between the two roads.

By then, the Southern Pacific had reached a point 2 miles north of a feisty little silver mining town called Shakespeare. But, alas, Shakespeare was no Tombstone, and the railroad opted to build a new town and name it after Tucson merchant Charles H. Lord. Meanwhile, the Santa Fe had crossed the Rio Grande near San Marcial and built another 40 miles south. A gap of approximately 150 miles separated the two railheads.

Certainly Charley Crocker had his dander up about the advancing Santa Fe. The last thing that he wanted was for the Santa Fe to rush westward past the Southern Pacific at Lordsburg and parallel its new line across southern Arizona. Even if the Santa Fe merely crossed the Southern Pacific at some point bound for Mexico, it would siphon off some of the Tombstone trade. Tucson—both on its own and because of Tombstone—was booming and bringing the Southern Pacific handsome profits. "The earnings since we reached Tucson have been immense," Crocker reported.[19]

Consequently, Crocker urged Huntington to arrange for some meeting point with the Santa Fe. "If we don't make an arrangement," Crocker cautioned, "we will both make a great mistake." Huntington had El Paso and points farther east in his sights, and Crocker was concerned that the Big Four's wheeler-dealer wasn't giving this aggressive competitor on their flanks enough credit.

"I very much fear that you are underrating these men and do not give them credit for the energy and persistence which they are showing. They are the only ones that I have feared, or that I now fear," Crocker lectured Huntington. A week later, Crocker hoped that Huntington would "not get tired of my *eternal dinging* on this subject," but that did not keep him from asserting, "those people [the Santa Fe backers] have more power and money than you have given them credit for."[20]

Only reluctantly did Huntington—who had once given his own lecture to David Colton about trusting the staying power of Tom Scott—come to view Nickerson, Strong, and the Santa Fe's Boston crowd as comparable adversaries. "I did think last winter they would come to grief before this time," Huntington confessed to Crocker, "but they *seem* to be stronger now than then."

By "last winter," Huntington may have been referring to the Royal Gorge battle. But the Santa Fe had gotten a portion of Colorado's traffic east of Pueblo without the expense of new construction and had not let the fray divert it from larger goals. "Still," Huntington told Crocker—perhaps with some element of wishful thinking—"I cannot believe that any set of people that have been slashing around as they have, will ever make a perfect success, and I believe they will come to grief sooner or later."[21]

Huntington rarely underestimated a competitor, but he may have continued to do so with the Santa Fe when he finally sat down with William Barstow Strong in Boston. The two adversaries agreed that the Santa Fe could use Southern Pacific tracks between an undetermined point in southwestern New Mexico and Benson. In retrospect, it appears that Strong was willing to make this agreement on behalf of the Santa Fe because it meant a quick leap forward of approximately 175 miles toward its Sonora Railway subsidiary and the Mexican port of Guaymas. Strong also assumed that the Santa Fe would share in the Southern Pacific's east-west traffic.

For his part, Huntington seems to have thought that he had clearly gotten the better of Strong and had blunted further Santa Fe construction westward. "We agreed to this memorandum of contract," Huntington reported to Leland Stanford, "thinking it would give them [the Santa Fe] time to learn the whole situation of matters on that side, and that as soon as they did, they would hardly think of building through on the 35th parallel, or building the Guaymas road."[22]

Thinking that whatever point the two roads joined was destined to become a great railroad center, Stanford may have had a hand in suggesting that the junction be named after Charley Crocker's wife, Mary Ann Deming. Exactly where "Deming" would be located was still uncertain during November 1880, as the Southern Pacific built east from Lordsburg and the Santa Fe left the Rio Grande Valley at Rincon and struck southwest.

"Water, of course, will be the principal thing that will influence them in selecting the point," general superintendent A. N. Towne reported to Huntington. But that didn't stop the speculators from swarming. South of Cookes Peak and the old Butterfield Overland stage route, a tent city sprang up that was christened "New Chicago" in anticipation.

To finalize the meeting point, chief engineers George E. Gray of the Southern Pacific and A. A. Robinson of the Santa Fe met about 10 miles

east of the Rio Mimbres in mid-December. This point was a few miles
west of New Chicago, so its promoters simply packed up their tents and
moved the short distance to Deming. The Southern Pacific inaugurated
service into town at the same time.

Before long, the new town boasted "thirteen saloons, two groceries,
two Chinese laundries, one barber shop, one restaurant, one butcher
shop, and one cigar store." It was a typically rowdy railhead town.
"Deming morals," reported a visiting editor, "are not to be discussed in
a newspaper—till she has some."[23]

Whatever early Deming might have lacked, the Atchison, Topeka and
Santa Fe was eager to arrive there. In its 1880 annual report, the railroad reported that it had increased its total mileage about four hundred
miles during the year, "and we shall have reached before the annual
meeting the Southern Pacific Railroad at Deming, one hundred and
twenty-eight miles further. From this connection, we expect a large
business from California and the mining districts of Arizona."[24]

Indeed, when Santa Fe tracklayers reached Deming on March 8,
1881, William Barstow Strong and his associates had little reason to expect anything less. A silver spike was driven not only to join the two
lines but also to commemorate the completion of the country's second
transcontinental railroad.

Yes, it was true. Eleven years and ten months after the golden spike
ceremony at Promontory Summit, Utah, the Big Four had done it
again. A southern transcontinental line now stretched all the way from
San Francisco to Deming, New Mexico, via the Southern Pacific, and
from Deming to Kansas City, Missouri, via the Santa Fe. Cyrus K. Holliday's little road had grown into a key part of a transcontinental system. But few, including Collis P. Huntington, it turned out, paid much
attention to the accomplishment.

Among those who did notice, the *Boston Herald*—almost a hometown paper for the Santa Fe, given the large numbers of its Boston
investors—made a very prophetic observation. "The southern way will
without question be the favorite winter route to the Pacific," the paper
predicted. "Tourists for pleasure, who otherwise would like to make a
winter trip to California, together with invalids whose delicate lungs

have yearned for the balmy air of the Golden State, have shrunk from the hardships of the bleak journey across the snowy plains of the Union Pacific route, with its threatening delays from the furious storms that often block the way and bury the trains in their terrible drifts. But hereafter they may make the journey through the warm air and perpetual sunshine of New Mexico and Arizona direct to Southern California, the most perfect sanitarium on earth . . ."

Perhaps a bigger and even more prophetic pronouncement came from the *Railway Times* of London. "This month witnesses the opening of the new route to the Pacific, an event which is probably of as much significance in American railroad history as anything which has occurred in railroad construction since the opening of the first transcontinental line," the paper observed. It was to be of great value to general commerce, of course, but it "is also calculated to promote the development of a vast region of the Southwest and Pacific coast . . ."[25]

The Santa Fe's first through train from Kansas City to the Southern Pacific's connection at Deming departed late on the evening of March 17, 1881. Behind engine no. 85 was a consist (those cars making up the train) of eight cars: two express cars, a baggage car, three coaches, and two Pullman sleepers. Fares for the first run all the way from Kansas City to Los Angeles were advertised at $105 for first-class passengers and $47.50 for the lowest "emigrant" class—the latter the equivalent of about $1,000 in 2008 value.

But there was not to be a mad rush to California—at least not now and not over this Santa Fe–Southern Pacific route. There was a very good reason why Collis P. Huntington was not cheering his connection with the Santa Fe. He had his eye on developments in West Texas that he hoped would prove far more lucrative. He simply was not willing to share business into Southern California and Arizona when he could retain control of it via San Francisco.

To encourage the continuation of such roundabout, cross-country shipping, the Southern Pacific imposed excessive rates on all freight bound for Arizona and Southern California that originated on the Santa Fe. In response, the Santa Fe complained directly to Huntington, asserting, "the steps taken by the So. Pacific seem of the most unfriendly kind."

Particularly onerous was a prohibitory tariff from Tucson to Deming that "prevented all business from going east or from coming from the east." According to the Santa Fe, "a carload of beer coming from St. Louis to Tucson paid $400 to reach Deming, and had to pay $200 from Deming to Tucson." Within a week of the opening of the line to Deming, "the Santa Fe announced that no coast-bound freight would be accepted over the route."[26]

William Barstow Strong and his Boston cohorts were annoyed by this result, but they were far too experienced and far too seasoned businessmen to throw up their hands in despair. They were far from finished in the transcontinental sweepstakes, but for the moment, about all the Santa Fe got after arriving in Deming was a handshake.

12

West Across Texas

Having brushed off the Atchison, Topeka and Santa Fe at Deming, Collis P. Huntington and the Southern Pacific pushed eastward. At stake were connections with railroads that were rapidly building west across Texas. If Huntington could keep the supply of rails coming and his fidgety partners happy about construction costs, he hoped to meet these competitors as deep into Texas as possible.

Texas was no stranger to railroads. It had hardly declared its independence from Mexico when the Republic of Texas chartered the Texas Rail Road, Navigation, and Banking Company in December 1836. Its sweeping name and authority to construct railroads "from and to any such points . . . as selected" raised cries of monopoly, and no track was ever laid.

Prior to its admission as a state in 1845, the Republic of Texas granted three other railroad charters. All envisioned lines from various points near the Gulf Coast to the Brazos Valley, but, again, no rails were put down. The projected line from Harrisburg (on Buffalo Bayou, just east of Houston) to the Brazos, however, became the precursor to a succession of incorporations that by 1853—the year of the western railroad surveys—had constructed a 20-mile segment from Harrisburg to Stafford. This Buffalo Bayou, Brazos and Colorado Railway was the first operating railroad in Texas.

Other short lines soon followed, although railroad operations and new construction suffered during the Civil War, as they did throughout the South. Among those companies to survive the war with some momentum were the Houston and Texas Central Railway running generally north-south and the westward-bound Buffalo Bayou, Brazos and Colorado.

Building south from Missouri to tap the Texas cattle trade, the Missouri, Kansas and Texas Railway—the venerable Katy—reached Denison, Texas, on the Red River on December 24, 1872. When the Houston and Texas Central also reached Denison the following year, the spreading web of Texas railroads had its first connection to the nationwide rail network.

Meanwhile, the Buffalo Bayou, Brazos and Colorado reorganized as the Galveston, Harrisburg and San Antonio Railroad and built into San Antonio by February 1877. By then, its principal stockholder was Thomas A. Peirce, and locals commonly called the road "the Peirce line." The railroad itself, however, adopted the moniker the Sunset Route. By then, Tom Scott's Texas and Pacific had cobbled together some lines in East Texas and reached Fort Worth.

By the end of 1879—as the Southern Pacific was building across Arizona—there were 2,440 miles of railroads in Texas. Fewer than 100 miles, however, lay west of a line generally south from Denison through Fort Worth to San Antonio. East of that line, Texas was crisscrossed by tracks. West of that line, it was an entirely different matter. To understand the railroad moves into the emptiness of West Texas, it is necessary to backtrack a few years and review Thomas A. Scott's transcontinental exploits.[1]

By late 1870, the principal backers of the Union Pacific Railroad—among them brothers Oliver and Oakes Ames and Thomas Durant—had finally stretched their credit to the breaking point. Unable to meet their January 1871 interest payments, they approached J. Edgar Thom-

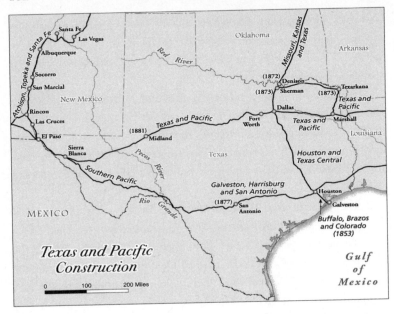

Texas and Pacific Construction

son and Thomas A. Scott for assistance. From their early westward expansion of the Pennsylvania Railroad to their postwar investment in the Kansas Pacific, Thomson and Scott had made no secret of their transcontinental interests. Despite their many other commitments, they found the lure of the Union Pacific impossible to resist.

When a myriad of financial moves were complete, Thomson, Scott, and two of their Pennsylvania Railroad cronies—budding steel magnate Andrew Carnegie and sleeping car innovator George Pullman—were on the Union Pacific's board of directors, and Scott had been elected to its presidency. This infusion of Pennsylvania Railroad capital and experience gave an immediate boost to Union Pacific stock and the creditworthiness of the railroad's bonds. The optimism, however, was fleeting.

The winter of 1871–72 struck with a particularly harsh vengeance and stranded Union Pacific trains from Wyoming across the Great Plains. For almost an entire month, the line sat silent. While Scott struggled to respond, Huntington fumed about the lack of through traffic to the Central Pacific and boasted that his men routinely operated across the Sierras through much worse. It is likely, however, that the Union Pacific's plight served to harden Huntington's resolve to control a more southerly transcontinental route on his own.

But more than blizzards soon overwhelmed Scott. Growing controversy over the Crédit Mobilier scandal, the Missouri River bridge project, and relationships with connecting lines demanded far more attention than Scott was able to give to the Union Pacific. He was simply spread too thin. Scott was "an able man," Oliver Ames conceded, "but he is so loaded with work that we have but very little of his service."

One action that Scott and his Pennsylvania group did take only served to infuriate the Union Pacific old-timers. Having bought in at low stock prices to rescue the road, the Pennsylvanians proved fleeting in their loyalties and were quick to sell at handsome profits. Carnegie even advised Oakes Ames to sell out above $30 per share, claiming the road "was not worth that." At the March 1872 shareholders meeting, Thomson, Scott, and Carnegie were not reelected to the board of directors.

Thus "the vaunted Pennsylvania connection," wrote historian Maury Klein, "departed as abruptly as it had come." The Union Pacific turned to Cornelius Vanderbilt's son-in-law Horace F. Clark as its new president. Clark had been running the Lake Shore and Michigan Southern Railroad, which linked Vanderbilt's New York Central with Chicago. Their alliance with the Union Pacific and a deal with the intervening Chicago and Northwestern Railroad threatened to unify a through line under one group's control from Utah to the East Coast. It also, of course, continued the historic New York Central–Pennsylvania Railroad rivalry well westward and—most important to the Texas railroad story—pushed the axis of Thomson and Scott's interests southward.

One is tempted to speculate what might have happened had Scott been able to manage the Union Pacific juggernaut as well as his other interests. In the end, his brief flirtation with the Union Pacific showed the extent of his insatiable railroad appetite and caused him to redouble his efforts with the Texas and Pacific.[2]

The man who stepped into Tom Scott's shoes as the chief financier of the Union Pacific was none other than Jay Gould. As it turned out, Gould, too, would come to have more than a passing interest in Texas railroads.

Jay Gould was born in 1836, in Roxbury, New York, in the western hollows of the Catskill Mountains. His given name was Jason, after one of his father's brothers. He was a sickly lad who followed five sisters into the family, and he grew slowly in body and mind. By his late teens, having been largely self-taught, young Jay worked as a surveyor and mapmaker and also published a 426-page history of surrounding Delaware County. Among his circle of friends was John Burroughs, who would achieve almost as much fame as a naturalist as Gould would as an entrepreneur.

Gould's first major business ventures were in leather tanneries. They were marked both with a steep learning curve that Gould readily climbed and by strained relations with his partners that gave Jay his first taste of protracted litigation. Unlike William Jackson Palmer, who was the same age, Gould eschewed service in the military during the Civil War and instead spent his time quietly and obscurely learning the ways of Wall Street.

Along the way, Gould practiced such secrecy in his business dealings that some contemporaries claimed it was proof of chicanery rather than calculating shrewdness. Even his closest advisors were frequently uninformed and oblivious to his plans. As one early business associate complained, "He never disclosed to his lawyers, or to anyone else except the particular ally chosen for the particular venture, what he was about to undertake—and never, to anyone, the full extent of what he had in mind."

But Gould would not operate below the public radar for very long. The event that made him anathema to those who detested the power of Wall Street involved the Erie Railroad. Squeezed between Vanderbilt's New York Central and Thomson's Pennsylvania Railroad, the Erie had been built to link New York City with the Great Lakes. By 1867, the road was being actively courted by both Vanderbilt and Boston interests who hoped to ally it with the Boston, Hartford and Erie Railroad.

When the complicated maneuverings of the 1867 annual meeting of the Erie Railroad were done, its board of directors included, among what the *Boston Herald* called "a batch of nobodies," a stockbroker named James Fisk, Jr.—so little known that some papers recorded his name as "Fiske" or "Fish"—and another listed simply as "J. Gould." Within a year, these two nobodies wrestled control of the Erie for themselves, and Gould assumed the presidency of his first railroad.

Gould and Fisk next turned to gold. Through a variety of agents, they quietly began amassing a large gold position and watched its price climb. On what came to be called Black Friday, September 24, 1869, Gould sold heavily in anticipation of the government putting $4 million of gold on the market. When that announcement was made midday, prices plummeted. Many investors blamed Gould and Fisk for the debacle. Gould was said to appear "quite depressed," but subsequent events suggest that his demeanor was simply a façade to mask huge profits made in the run-up.

"Gentleman Jim" Fisk came out of the attempted gold corner more flamboyant than ever. He was soon wallowing in a torrid love triangle that involved opera star Josie Mansfield and threatened to drag the secretive Gould through the mud with him. When Josie's other paramour shot Fisk dead on the steps of New York's Grand Central Hotel, Gould was suddenly without a partner, and he tried to return to a lower public profile.

But the Erie affair and the attempted gold corner—no matter what Gould's ultimate proceeds—were enough to mark Gould with disdain in many circles. The immediate result was that Gould was forced out of the presidency of the Erie, although not without a satisfactory settlement. Looking around for another venture—railroads were hard to ignore—Gould began investing in the Union Pacific. When Tom Scott left the Union Pacific in 1872 and his successor, Horace F. Clark, died suddenly about a year later, the Union Pacific faced another leadership vacuum into which Gould readily stepped.

Gould was elected to the Union Pacific's board in March 1874 and quickly took command of its finances. Some assumed—and others involved with the Union Pacific feared—that Gould would simply bull its stock, strip its resources, and then exit with huge profits. But while the Erie and gold-corner chapters of his life would forever color his reputation, Gould was to show considerable loyalty and staying power with the Union Pacific. And as for railroads, Jay Gould was just getting started.[3]

Jay Gould did not let his interest in the Union Pacific keep him from other railroad ventures. He invested in the Kansas Pacific and eventually engineered its absorption by the Union Pacific. He invested in the Denver and Rio Grande and the Denver, South Park and Pacific, and determined to profit from whatever company thrived. And he tied together several Midwest short lines into what would become the Missouri Pacific system and then aimed a line toward Texas. In June 1880, the Missouri Pacific leased the Katy, giving Gould a railhead at Denison, Texas, and putting Tom Scott's Texas and Pacific next in his sights.

Scott's interest in the struggling Texas and Pacific had long cast a huge shadow across southwestern transcontinental maneuvers. The panic of 1873 spawned the legend of Scott's vote to save the Texas and Pacific at all costs. But it was Oliver Ames's characterization of Scott as "so loaded with work" that may have said it best when it comes to evaluating his final transcontinental accomplishments.

Within two years of Scott's departure from the Union Pacific, J. Edgar Thomson, the patriarch of the unified railroad system and Scott's personal mentor, was dead at sixty-six. Scott was on his own. In addition to his many western ventures, he became the president of the Pennsylvania Railroad, a role he had managed unofficially as Thomson's health declined. At the time, the Pennsylvania Railroad was the largest corporation in the world, and it would seem to have been enough of a challenge for Scott.

But Scott was never satisfied with a regional role for the Pennsylvania any more than he was satisfied with being president of only one railroad. Try as Scott might, however—whether with his early efforts in Southern California to preempt the Big Four in their backyard or to wrestle a subsidy as well as a land grant from Congress to push the line west across Texas—he came up short with his transcontinental dreams.

"You know I never had much respect for Tom Scott's ability to *accomplish* any great undertaking," the Big Four's David Colton confessed to Huntington a year before Colton's own death. "He can give everybody a Pass, and get them to say he is a 'big Injun' and good fellow—but he is not the man to lay down a Hundred or Two Hundred Thousand Dollars Cash, to carry a scheme of his own."

According to Colton, Gould was a different sort: "the reverse of Scott; he is a one man power; consults no one, advises with no one, confides in no one, has no friends, wants none—is bold. Can always lay down Two or Three Hundred Thousand Dollars to accomplish his plans and *will* do it if he thinks it will pay."

Given that Colton had his own demons to fight—dubious financial dealings at the expense of the Big Four during the last year of his life being just one of them—one wonders if he was not overly harsh on Tom Scott or perhaps too quick to underestimate him. Huntington's own advice to Colton about Scott was more cautious. "You write that you think you have Scott beaten," Huntington ventured, "but allow me to suggest that you do not go to sleep while he is awake."[4]

Now, awake or asleep, Tom Scott was carrying an ever-increasing amount of debt. Because of Huntington's blocking maneuvers in Congress, Scott had never been able to wring a subsidy from Congress for the Texas and Pacific to go along with its land grants. He still needed to find funds for construction. By the time that Scott was seeking funds to build west from Fort Worth, one of his investors was Jay Gould.

Stretched thin as he was, Scott's staying power with the Texas and Pacific gradually ebbed, and Gould's power—as was his tendency—expanded to fill the void. By the spring of 1881, Scott had worn himself physically and emotionally to the breaking point. He approached Gould to cash out his remaining position in the Texas and Pacific. All too willingly, Gould acquired Scott's controlling interest in the line.

Four years earlier, when the Southern Pacific was barely across the Colorado River at Yuma, David Colton had accurately prophesied this result. "Disagreeable as the medicine is," Colton then advised Huntington, "it is better for us to have Gould buy Scott out, and get rid of him and all of these double contests, and then try to take from Gould the West End of the T. and P. Road."[5]

A month after he sold out to Gould, Thomas A. Scott was dead at fifty-seven. Supposedly, Huntington genuinely grieved at Scott's death because he had been "a mighty adversary." He died a wealthy man thanks to his Pennsylvania Railroad shares, but others would complete his transcontinental vision. Thus, it was Collis P. Huntington and Jay Gould who squared off in round two of the battle for the 32nd parallel route.[6]

· · ·

Even after Gould took over the Texas and Pacific, Huntington and the Southern Pacific appeared to have the edge in what was shaping up to be another race of construction. Certainly the Southern Pacific had the momentum. Having brushed off the Santa Fe after their meeting at Deming, the Southern Pacific rushed eastward toward El Paso, while the Santa Fe continued another line of its own straight down the Rio Grande.

But as the Southern Pacific and Santa Fe bore down on El Paso from slightly different directions, they were definitely focused on different destinations. For the Santa Fe, El Paso was a secondary gateway into Mexico; the railroad had no interest in building across West Texas. But for the Southern Pacific, El Paso and West Texas were essential to Huntington's goal of a southern transcontinental completely under his control. That, of course, brought him face to face with Jay Gould.

Gould, however, was not the only railroader with plans to build west across Texas. Thomas A. Peirce's Galveston, Harrisburg and San Antonio paused at San Antonio only because of the proverbial lack of funds, not any lack of ambition. Peirce, in fact, was quite eager to continue his line westward from San Antonio, but he sorely required additional capital. At some point, Peirce reached a secret agreement with Huntington that Huntington would provide him with capital in exchange for a share in Peirce's road.

Charley Crocker was among those who pushed Huntington to do so. Fearing rumors that Gould's Texas and Pacific was marshaling graders to occupy "our line down the cañon" east of El Paso, Crocker urged Huntington to take action and strike any alliance that would counter the Gould threat—even if that meant a belated handshake with the Santa Fe. "It seems to me," Crocker further counseled, "that if you cannot do anything with the Atchison and Topeka people, you had better at once conclude with Peirce."

Exactly when this Peirce-Huntington agreement was made is uncertain. But whenever the date and whatever the initial investment, it seems clear that Huntington allied himself early on with Peirce, thus hedging his bets for a route across Texas against whatever might transpire with Jay Gould. Much as Gould appears to have done with his purchase of Texas and Pacific stock, Huntington used this initial investment to exert an increasing influence over the Peirce line.[7]

But the first problem that Huntington faced as the Southern Pacific neared El Paso was that the railroad lacked the legal authority to operate in Texas. Given the past influence of Tom Scott with the Texas legislature, it had not granted the Southern Pacific a Texas charter, and with Gould now at the helm of the Texas and Pacific, it was unlikely that such authority would be granted any time soon.

With no authority to cross the Rio Grande and build into Texas, Huntington and Crocker nevertheless sang a refrain reminiscent of the bridge battle at Yuma. "I do not suppose," Crocker haughtily told Huntington early in 1881 as he eyed El Paso, "that anybody would interfere with our building it except the A.T. and S.F. people."[8]

As it turned out, both the Southern Pacific and the Santa Fe had to ask the War Department for permission to cross portions of Fort Bliss as the two roads neared El Paso. The Santa Fe graded right down the middle of the post's parade ground, while the Southern Pacific right-of-way passed behind the main buildings. "They really damage the Post," Crocker complained to Huntington, "whereas our line would not."

The Santa Fe line stayed on the east side of the river all the way from Las Cruces to El Paso. Coming from Deming, the Southern Pacific first had to cross the Rio Grande via a substantial bridge. "We crossed the bridge with the track yesterday, and Strobridge will pass through El Paso the latter part of this week," Crocker soon reported to Huntington. The first Southern Pacific train steamed into El Paso on May 19, 1881. The Santa Fe arrived in town three weeks later on June 11.[9]

The Southern Pacific did not intend to linger there for long. In typical fashion, Huntington quickly found a way around the lack of a Texas charter for the Southern Pacific. He was certainly not content to fund Peirce's expansion westward from San Antonio and then wait patiently at El Paso to see whether it or Gould's Texas and Pacific would arrive first.

So, by July 1881, the Southern Pacific took over a controlling interest in the Galveston, Harrisburg and San Antonio. The former Peirce line then contracted with the Southern Pacific's construction company to work out of El Paso on its behalf—which, of course, was really Collis P. Huntington's behalf. Using the same crews that had built across Arizona and New Mexico, these contractors hastily pushed the de facto Southern Pacific line southeast from El Paso along the Rio Grande.

Crocker was determined to control as much ground as possible. Looking to extend at least 100 miles within two months, the construction boss of the Big Four balked at any talk of a joint operating arrangement with the Texas and Pacific. The road "should be ours and controlled by us," he told Huntington. "I am afraid of any entangling alliances with that little fellow on Broadway [Gould]. If he should get any hitch on us, he would drive us to the wall any time he could."[10]

For his part, Gould was not convinced that Huntington would show any more loyalty to the Texas and Pacific than Huntington had toward the Santa Fe at Deming, and Gould, too, was determined to push the meeting point as far westward as possible. But as the Texas and Pacific built west at a mile a day, Gould discovered that he held a weapon far more potent than a-mile-a-day construction.

In its rush eastward, the Southern Pacific had built a portion of its line through southern Arizona and New Mexico on the right-of-way originally awarded to the Texas and Pacific by its congressional land grant. Gould visited his legal counsel and posed his question rather casually.

"If one man builds a house on the lot of another, without the consent of that other and especially against his protest, to whom does the house now belong?"

"It becomes annexed to the land and belongs to the landowner," the lawyer replied.

That was all Gould needed to know. He ordered a suit commenced against the Southern Pacific to claim that portion of track that Huntington had built over the Texas and Pacific land grant. For once, Huntington was caught off guard. If Gould won his case and also continued the Texas and Pacific westward to El Paso, not only would Huntington have to relinquish miles of track west of that point, but his new construction eastward from there would be paralleled by the Texas and Pacific through an area in which Crocker dismally noted, "there is no local business."[11]

Quoting the same Right-of-Way Act of 1875 that William Jackson Palmer had ignored to his detriment, Southern Pacific officials quickly countered that regardless of the Texas and Pacific land grant, a right-of-way through the public lands of the United States was available to any railroad duly organized under the laws of any state or territory. Despite the neatly sidestepped question of authority in Texas, the Southern Pacific had in fact organized legal subsidiaries to operate in both Arizona and New Mexico.

"I do not believe the Texas and Pacific can steal our road through New Mexico and Arizona," Crocker professed to Huntington. But if the uncertainty made him nervous, he had the Southern Pacific's usual answer: "we shall go right on building, regardless of negotiations."

For his part, Huntington thought that Gould was running a strong bluff. "My own opinion," he told Crocker, "is that this move to contest our rights west of the Rio Grande is got up as a basis to negotiate on our stopping at the Rio Grande . . ." But with characteristic bravado, Huntington added that he thought the threat would disappear once the Southern Pacific had laid a few hundred miles of track into Texas.[12]

For all the Big Four's own machinations, Crocker remained highly suspicious of Gould and told Huntington that he wanted "as little to do with him as possible." Referring to Gould, Crocker warned Huntington to "do more *watching* than 'praying,' when you come in contact with him."

When Huntington replied that Gould and his associates had been cordial with him despite the pending suit, Crocker growled back, "Their friendship is evidenced by the petitions which they filed . . . to steal what little road we have built in Texas. I assure you that I shall never go to sleep on their smiles . . ."[13]

Throughout October and November 1881, as the construction crews of the Southern Pacific and the Texas and Pacific raced toward each other across West Texas, Huntington and Gould carried on a delicate dance. "At our last meeting you were to prepare some suggestions concerning the basis of an arrangement," Gould wrote Huntington in a brief letter marked "Personal," adding, "I will be glad to confer with you any time."

Huntington, of course, was hardly anyone's dupe. But he also knew when to accomplish his objectives by making peace rather than by declaring war. Now there was too much at stake to risk losing a war. Gould, who had stared into just such a possibility of an annihilating war in Colorado the year before and forced the Treaty of Boston upon the belligerents, was also of a mind to secure his southern flanks with as little financial bloodshed as possible. *Compromise* was not a word that

Huntington and Gould used often, but here was a situation where it served both of them well.

On Thanksgiving Day 1881, Huntington and Gould met in New York and hammered out a railroad compromise more sweeping than the Treaty of Boston. The Texas and Pacific dropped its suit and transferred its right-of-way claims and land grants west of El Paso to the Southern Pacific. The two roads agreed to joint operations on the 90 miles of track that the Southern Pacific had by then built east of El Paso and an equal share of the earnings on through business from the Pacific coast.

The Texas and Pacific also promised never to build west of El Paso, and the Southern Pacific agreed not to parallel the Texas and Pacific east of El Paso or to build competing lines to the north or east of its line. Significantly, there was no mention of new construction to the *south* because Huntington had already covered his bases in that direction by controlling the Galveston, Harrisburg and San Antonio.

Despite his warnings, Crocker crowed that Huntington had gotten the best of the bargain, but it was to serve both moguls and their railroads well for almost fifty years. South of the new Southern Pacific–Texas and Pacific alliance, Huntington was free to continue his straight-line transcontinental eastward toward New Orleans. North of that line, Gould and Huntington momentarily joined as allies to keep the Atchison, Topeka and Santa Fe at bay. Paramount to Huntington's thinking was any strategy that would keep the Santa Fe dead-ended at Deming and prevent the construction of any railroad that would infringe on the Big Four's monopoly in California.[14]

There was, however, one benefit of the Gould-Huntington bargain that the Southern Pacific never received. When the railroad asked Congress for title to the original Texas and Pacific land grant west of El Paso, the legislators refused to approve the transfer. Officially, the stated reason was that the original grant did not provide for an assignment and that the Southern Pacific had built the line "not because of Congressional wishes but rather its own desires." More likely, the real reason was Huntington himself.

In the heat of the lengthy battles with Tom Scott over land grants and subsidies for the southern route, the Big Four's man in Washington had often boasted that the Southern Pacific didn't need federal assistance to build east from Yuma. Now, with the tide having turned against the largesse of land grants, Congress held Huntington to it. In 1885 Congress declared the western part of the Texas and Pacific land grant forfeit.[15]

Huntington fumed, but he had still gotten the best of the bargain. On December 1, 1881, 82 miles east of El Paso, the rails of Gould's Texas and Pacific and Huntington's Southern Pacific met at the high desert mountain town of Sierra Blanca. When the daughter of chief engineer General Grenville Dodge drove "an ordinary railroad spike" into a hole bored in the final tie, it completed what was ostensibly the nation's third (giving the Santa Fe the benefit of the doubt at Deming) transcontinental railroad.

There wasn't much hoopla, but rails now spanned the old oxbow route of John Butterfield's Overland Mail from St. Louis to San Francisco. "What should have been made a memorable occasion in the history of this city," the *Lone Star* of El Paso complained, "was, by some inexplicable lack of appreciation of its importance, allowed to pass without even a demonstration."[16]

For the Texas and Pacific, the junction at Sierra Blanca was the end of its line west. But the Southern Pacific veered southeast and continued toward its advancing Galveston, Harrisburg and San Antonio subsidiary. Huntington had needed no encouragement once past Yuma, but it was Leland Stanford who put their new goal into a few words.

In that pivotal year of 1881, the governor sent Huntington a map showing lines "such as will sooner or later need to be built." It might be of service, Stanford suggested, "in making the owners of other lines of railroad comprehend that, when our line is completed through to the Gulf of Mexico, we will have the shortest line for all the country west of the Rocky Mountains to tidewater on the Eastern Coast, and the cheapest route for all that section of country to Europe."[17]

There was one railroad, of course, with no intention of bending to such bravado.

13

Transcontinental at Last

The Atchison, Topeka and Santa Fe was one of the few western rail-roads with transcontinental ambitions that did not have the word *Pacific* in its name. That certainly did not mean, however, that the rail-road's transcontinental plans were any less determined or that they stopped in the middle of New Mexico. By 1881, the Atchison, Topeka and Santa Fe was advancing on the Pacific Ocean by three different fronts.

Admittedly, William Barstow Strong and the Santa Fe received little more than a handshake from Collis P. Huntington and the Southern Pacific at Deming, but Strong and his board of directors seem to have sensed well in advance that might be the case. They undertook the construction south from Albuquerque in part to protect the Santa Fe's southern flanks and to keep Jay Gould and/or Huntington from building north from El Paso.

The Santa Fe's second Pacific front was via the Sonora Railway to Guaymas, Mexico. But even though the Santa Fe built its own New Mexico and Arizona Railroad from Benson, Arizona, south to join the Sonora Railway at the Mexican border at Nogales, this route, too, was dependent on the dictates of the Southern Pacific because of the 174-mile joint trackage agreement between Deming and Benson.

What the Santa Fe needed—and what Strong had been patiently acquiring by bits and pieces—was a transcontinental route between the Mississippi and the Pacific completely under its own control. A key component was to come from assorted railroad ventures that traced their roots back to the fervent expansionism of Thomas Hart Benton.

Even before the Pacific Railroad surveys of 1853, Senator Benton had long championed a railway between St. Louis and San Francisco. What might lie in between was, Benton once told Congress, "a matter of detail." The most important thing to him was to set the termini of the route irrevocably in the two cities that hugged the 38th parallel. To that end, the Pacific Railroad Company of Missouri was incorporated in 1849, to build west from St. Louis.

It didn't get very far, and the trials and tragedies of John C. Frémont and John Gunnison while filling in the "detail" along the 38th parallel soon had Missourians pondering the more southerly 35th parallel route instead. St. Louis would still be the eastern terminal, but a south-west branch of the Pacific Railroad Company was projected to cut diagonally across the state to Springfield, which had long touted itself the logical railroad gateway to the 35th parallel route.

Amidst the land grant giveaway in the aftermath of the Civil War, Springfield got its opportunity. Benton was dead by then, but Frémont acquired control of the south-west branch—renamed the Southwest Pacific Railroad—and used the line's goal of Springfield to promote the new Atlantic and Pacific Railroad as the logical extension westward from there.[1]

With a lengthy list of incorporators that included J. Edgar Thomson and Thomas A. Scott, the Atlantic and Pacific Railroad Company was formed by an act of Congress on July 27, 1866. It was to run generally west from Springfield to a point on the Canadian River, then to Albuquerque, the headwaters of the Little Colorado River, and on to the Colorado River, "at such point as may be selected by said company for crossing; thence by the most practicable and eligible route to the Pacific."

There was no promise of the lucrative bond subsidies that had benefited the Union Pacific, but the Atlantic and Pacific land grant was generous—every alternate section to the extent of twenty alternate sections per mile on each side of the railroad line through the territories and ten alternate sections per mile on each side through any state. The Atlantic and Pacific was required to begin construction within two years, complete at least fifty miles per year, and finish its main line by July 4, 1878.

But there was one section in the enabling legislation that bespoke the hand of Collis P. Huntington. Despite authorizing the Atlantic and Pacific to proceed "by the most practicable and eligible route to the Pacific," section 18 provided that Huntington's Southern Pacific Railroad was "authorized to connect with the said Atlantic and Pacific Railroad . . . at such point, near the boundary line of the State of California, as they shall deem most suitable for a railroad line to San Francisco."[2]

Whether this provision merely afforded the Southern Pacific the *opportunity* to connect with the Atlantic and Pacific at the Colorado River or *prohibited* the Atlantic and Pacific from building beyond it into California would soon be a matter of heated debate.

The mercurial Frémont was soon off to other ventures, but by June 1871, the Atlantic and Pacific had consolidated with the Southwest Pacific as planned. It completed its line across Missouri through Springfield to the state line and continued into Indian Territory and a junction with the Missouri, Kansas and Texas Railroad (the Katy) at Vinita, Indian Territory.

Much as Tom Scott did to court San Diegans on behalf of the Texas and Pacific, a Missouri delegation traveled to San Francisco in 1872 to win friends and connections at the contemplated western end of the line. But Californians were of divided loyalties. Some favored Scott's Texas and Pacific enterprise; others wanted a line totally under Californian control; and, of course, the Big Four muddied the waters by opposing *any* railroad that might someday compete with the recently finished Central Pacific or the expanding Southern Pacific.

Meanwhile, the Atlantic and Pacific leased the original Pacific Railroad of Missouri that had finally made it from St. Louis to Kansas City, albeit by floating a staggering debt. This orphan of Benton's Pacific dreams would someday emerge as Jay Gould's vaunted Missouri Pacific, but in the mid-1870s, it floundered, and it took the Atlantic and Pacific down with it.

The Atlantic and Pacific went into receivership on November 3, 1875, but its directors and major shareholders quickly devised what became the ultimate coup. They formed a new corporation that would bid at foreclosure for the Atlantic and Pacific's franchise and land grant, while being free from the Atlantic and Pacific's debts.

On September 8, 1876, the Atlantic and Pacific went on the auction block on the east steps of the courthouse in St. Louis. Two days earlier, the soon-to-be Missouri Pacific had sold for $3 million. But this time the insiders were in control. When the auctioneer dropped his gavel, the Atlantic and Pacific Railroad—with its land grants potentially worth millions and millions of dollars—was sold for the paltry sum of $450,000 to the new corporation. "The new company is to be called the St. Louis & San Francisco Railway Company," the *Railroad Gazette* reported wryly, "because, perhaps, it has no terminus in either city."[3]

But the reality was that the St. Louis and San Francisco Railway now owned the Atlantic and Pacific franchise outright, and the parent company made plans to strike westward from its railhead at Vinita. When continuing uncertainty over its right-of-way and land grants across Indian reservations delayed that construction, the St. Louis and San Francisco bypassed Indian Territory and built westward into Kansas instead. Given its ultimate goal, the railroad replaced the old Atlantic and Pacific trademark of "the Vinita Route" with a new moniker. Henceforth, the St. Louis and San Francisco Railway would be known as "the Frisco Line."

The Frisco's immediate destination was Wichita, Kansas. While bypassed by the Atchison, Topeka and Santa Fe main line, Wichita had taken upon itself to build a 20-mile spur and ensure its future as a cattle town and commercial hub. Looking to become a rail center as well, Wichita encouraged the Frisco's advance by floating a county bond issue. But by the time the Frisco laid tracks into town, the Santa Fe main line stretched westward to Albuquerque. One look at the map told the story.

If the Frisco continued westward and paralleled the Santa Fe across southern Kansas, there would be fierce competition between the two roads. Regardless of how the Frisco's claims in Indian Territory were resolved, they were likely to be of dubious value. (Oil discoveries would change that, but not until much later.)

For its part, the Santa Fe was concerned about another competitor shadowing it across Kansas. It had long contended with just such com-

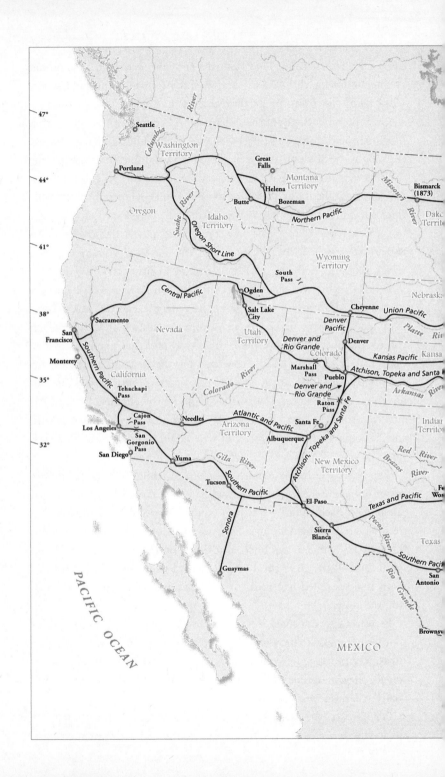

petition from the Kansas Pacific north of its line. Rather than competing with each other across the plains, perhaps there was a way that the
Frisco and the Santa Fe might work together and put their resources
into finishing the 35th parallel route west from Albuquerque instead of
knocking heads in Kansas.

It helped matters that the leaders of both railroads moved in the
same circles of Boston capitalists. Thomas Nickerson and his protégé
William Barstow Strong were already showing themselves to be patient
plodders focused on long-term results. The reborn Atlantic and Pacific
land grant was certainly of interest, but so too was another route by
which to challenge Collis P. Huntington's stranglehold on California.

Finally, both the Frisco and the Santa Fe were watching the increasingly large shadow that Jay Gould cast over *all* railroad ventures. Concerned about their own independence or Gould's role in a competitor,
the Frisco and the Santa Fe had additional reasons to be allies rather
than foes.

The 1879 annual report of the Atchison, Topeka and Santa Fe told
the results: "Another negotiation which required nearly six months to
complete, secures your Company an interest in the valuable franchise of
the Atlantic and Pacific Railroad which gives your road right of way
across Arizona and California to the Pacific Coast. Your Company,
jointly with the St. Louis and San Francisco Railway Company, will
build a new road from Albuquerque along the thirty-fifth parallel,
which in due time will form part of a transcontinental line."[4]

Formally ratified on January 31, 1880, this Tripartite Agreement
was in some respects more sweeping than the Treaty of Boston or even
the agreements between Huntington and Gould in Texas. Its triple nature came from the fact that the Santa Fe and the Frisco formed a jointly
owned subsidiary further preserving the fiction of the old Atlantic and
Pacific. Its stock, directors, costs of construction, and profits were to be
equally divided between the Santa Fe and the Frisco. This reborn Atlantic and Pacific Western Division was to build west from the Santa Fe
line at Albuquerque, claiming as it went the original Atlantic and Pacific land grant.

To fund this 600-mile expansion between Albuquerque and the Colorado River, the Santa Fe and the Frisco each agreed to raise $5 million
secured by a first mortgage of 6 percent thirty-year bonds to be guaran-

teed by both companies. All business to and from the Western Division was to pass over the Santa Fe from Albuquerque to Wichita—later changed to Halstead, Kansas, on the Santa Fe's main line. From that point east, all St. Louis business went via the Frisco and all Chicago-bound business continued over the Santa Fe to Kansas City.

The two roads further agreed that the Frisco or its St. Louis, Wichita and Western subsidiary would not build west from Wichita and that neither party would build new competing lines except by mutual consent and with joint ownership and cost.

Thomas Nickerson became president of the Atlantic and Pacific Western Division, while former Union general Edward F. Winslow became vice president to look after the Frisco's interests. It seemed a neat solution to everyone, although Wichita and surrounding Sedgwick County, having enticed the Frisco with a bond issue, now complained, "As a county we agreed to pay our money for the benefits to be derived from a direct competition and not for an extra track of a monopoly." Out of the ashes of previous 35th parallel failures, that is exactly what the Santa Fe was suddenly in the position to achieve.[5]

Not everyone, however, was keen on the idea of the Santa Fe building along the 35th parallel. Shortly after the initial battles at Raton Pass and the Royal Gorge, William Barstow Strong dispatched the steady A. A. Robinson west from Albuquerque to take a look. Robinson was not walking into the unknown but rather following the footsteps of Lieutenant Amiel Whipple's 1853 efforts and William Jackson Palmer's 1867 survey on behalf of the Kansas Pacific. But he wasn't impressed.

Robinson argued against the 35th parallel route west from Albuquerque because he believed that the depths of the Grand Canyon to the north precluded any trade or connecting lines in that direction. (Clearly, Robinson was not thinking about the *tourist* trade.) He urged instead that all efforts be directed to driving south down the Rio Grande to the 32nd parallel. But by the time the Santa Fe reached Deming, Huntington and the Southern Pacific had preempted that route.

Meanwhile, the Santa Fe surveyors who were momentarily cheered in Tucson in the summer of 1879 reported back that the territory between Albuquerque and Tucson was "hopeless" both for a suitable direct line and local traffic. That left Nickerson and Strong with Lieutenant

Whipple's preferred route along the 35th parallel. The fact that they seized on that route early in the game—regardless of Robinson's negative report—and made the deal with the Frisco is evidence that they were looking at the big picture of railroading in the American Southwest. Rather than taking the 35th parallel as a last resort, securing it early left Nickerson and Strong looking like rather shrewd railroaders after Huntington and Gould combined against them in the south.[6]

On paper, the railroad to be built west from Albuquerque would be known as the Atlantic and Pacific Western Division, but the men involved with its construction and later operation were definitely part of the greater Atchison, Topeka and Santa Fe organization. Barely was the ink dry on the Tripartite Agreement than A. A. Robinson—his doubts about the route put aside but not dismissed—sent survey crews west from Albuquerque in the summer of 1880 to pound stakes along a final alignment between there and the Colorado River.

George S. Van Law, a veteran of the Santa Fe's Raton and Royal Gorge battles, was in the lead party. It quickly became clear to him these preparations were "for the construction of a first class transcontinental railroad to do big business." Robinson's work specifications were very strict and called for light gradients and easy curves that in many cases "eased off at both ends."

But as Van Law and his party progressed west across northern Arizona, it also became clear that there was not much local business. Supposedly, they were following a semblance of an old trail, but Van Law found it a road "in name only." He never saw a man or wagon on it in an entire summer of work that at times was quite demanding. When the supply wagons were close, life was good, but when they failed to keep up with the advance or arrive at an agreed-upon rendezvous, hunger became a familiar companion. Breakfast one morning for Van Law's crew of nine consisted of two cans of tomatoes and one can of peaches. It was, he acknowledged, "a lot better than starving."

A few days later, after walking miles to start their work and running line for a half day, their lunch was only sugar and some bacon almost green with age and heat. But typical of the men who pushed these lines west, Van Law confessed, "we were a tough lot and nobody got sick."[7]

The Santa Fe was in a hurry, and construction crews quickly followed Van Law's markers west from near Albuquerque. The chosen junction point was Isleta, some 12 miles south of town, where the Santa Fe line down the Rio Grande crossed the river from east to west. The dust from the construction of that bridge and the Santa Fe's march toward Deming had settled only a few weeks. One would have been hard pressed to say which route was the main line. At the very least, the Santa Fe's frenzied construction on two fronts at once bespoke Nickerson's and Strong's transcontinental plans.

Certainly Robinson understood what was at stake. Not wanting a repeat of the conflict at Raton Pass, he sent a work crew 180 miles west of Albuquerque to seize and hold the staked right-of-way through Querino Canyon. Just west of the Arizona–New Mexico border, this 2-mile-long sandstone gap was wide enough for only a single set of tracks.

Robinson's caution was well founded, particularly after Charley Crocker himself showed up on Santa Fe turf in Albuquerque "on railroad business." Figuring that Crocker and Huntington were quite capable of being even more aggressive than General Palmer had been at Raton and the Royal Gorge, Robinson next directed that ties and rails be hauled by wagon to Querino Canyon well in advance of the railhead. Two and one-half miles of track were laid in the canyon during the summer of 1880 to hold the right-of-way. This section stood as a rather forlorn outpost while the end of track advanced toward it over the next year.[8]

When the first 50 miles of track were completed west of Isleta, the Santa Fe–Frisco–owned Atlantic and Pacific Western Division applied for the land grants due under the original 1866 Atlantic and Pacific charter. The legislation had mandated that the line be completed within ten years. Now, two years past that deadline, there was growing sentiment in Congress against land grants from the public domain.

But U.S. Attorney General Charles Devens, an appointee of President Hayes, ruled that the original act, while requiring completion in ten years, did not specifically provide for a forfeiture of the railroad's rights to such lands. They could be earned, Devens decided, by construction any time unless Congress wanted to intervene, take possession of the road, and complete it as a federal project, which clearly it did not.

So the Western Division received its first patents for land along the route.

By February 1881, 100 miles of track had been laid west from Isleta, and 80 were in operation. Crews kept on through the cold of the high-desert winter and reached Fort Wingate, now Gallup, New Mexico. Lewis Kingman, who located the line, was in charge of construction.

Most of Kingman's crews were Irish. Tracklayers and graders were paid $2.25 per day, and spikers and iron layers earned $2.50 per day—the latter equivalent to about $54 in 2008 dollars. Kingman also hired local Apaches and Navajos and later Mojaves from California as shovelers and day laborers.

Many of the Irish workers had built the Santa Fe or other roads across the plains, just as many of the Chinese working for Huntington in southern Arizona had labored through the Sierras. The simple economics of reaching the respective railheads dictated the labor pool—the Irish from the East and the Chinese from the West. Ethnic background meant little when it came to hoisting a fifty-two-pound rail, but that did not mean that there was no racism. "The directors of the 35th Parallel R.R.," a local Arizona newspaper declared, "certainly deserve much credit for employing none but white labor in building their great transcontinental railway from the Atlantic to the Pacific."

By April, the orphan track in Querino Canyon had been joined to the main line, and crews were building west across northern Arizona at the rate of a mile a day. "The whole country north of Prescott along the 35th parallel road," the *Weekly Arizona Miner* reported, "is alive with advance workmen, who are preparing the road bed of the Atlantic and Pacific Railroad, which is coming along from the East at break-neck rate. . . ."[9]

But up ahead, the flat tablelands of the Colorado Plateau held one of its many surprises. Twenty-six miles west of Winslow, the serpentine meanders of Cañon Diablo cut deep into the landscape. Its white and yellow limestone walls dropped 250 feet in blocky terraces to the intermittent stream coursing along its bottom. It was more than 500 feet across the chasm.

Stumbling upon the canyon in 1853, Lieutenant Whipple confessed his surprise and termed a descent to the "thread-like rill of water" far below to be "impossible." But he did conclude that "for a railroad it could be bridged and the banks would furnish plenty of stone for the purpose." Whipple and many other Arizona travelers bypassed the canyon by circling to the north, but the Atlantic and Pacific would take Whipple's advice and bridge it directly.

The rails of the Atlantic and Pacific reached the rim at Cañon Diablo on December 19, 1881. Having long anticipated this obstacle, the railroad had a rough and rowdy construction camp named Cañon Diablo going full blast near the east rim. Variously described as meaner than Tombstone and deadlier than Dodge City, the motley collection of windswept tents and rough buildings was home to 240 men working the bridge site and a bevy of prostitutes, gamblers, and barkeeps working the men.

John M. Price and Co. had the primary construction contract for the bridge crossing, and its first task was to blast and excavate platforms in the canyon walls and along the streambed to hold masonry pedestals for the support towers. In addition, one large stone abutment was constructed on each rim.

The Central Bridge Works of Buffalo, New York, prefabricated the bridge itself at a reported cost of $250,000. It was shipped to the site in pieces in some twenty railcars. Eleven separate spans—two of 100 feet in length, two of 30 feet, and seven of 40 feet—were fastened together and supported by ten sets of tower legs and the abutments on the rims. When completed, the narrow, spindly structure was 222 feet above the canyon floor and 560 feet long.

But as the final sections were put into place, they proved to be several feet short. Somehow, someone had measured incorrectly, or the excavation for the abutments on the rims had inadvertently widened the distance. Modifications were hurriedly made.

Meanwhile, grading crews leapfrogged ahead to work on the roadbed to the west. Finally, on July 1, 1882, the first train inched across the narrow structure under operating rules that required a maximum speed of four miles an hour, and the Cañon Diablo bridge was officially certified. At the time, it was easily the most impressive bridge structure on the combined Santa Fe–Atlantic and Pacific line between Kansas City and the Colorado River.[10]

During the construction pause at Cañon Diablo, the railhead halted at Winslow. A January 1882 visitor remarked, "the town at present

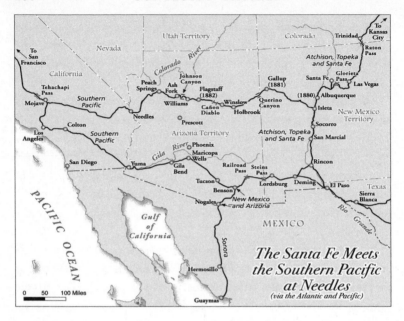

The Santa Fe Meets
the Southern Pacific
at Needles
(via the Atlantic and Pacific)

consists of a row of tents about one-fourth of a mile in extent." But that was to change quickly because Winslow was slated to become a division point on the line. Service buildings, yards, and a roundhouse were built in short order.

Of the major towns along the Atlantic and Pacific route through Arizona, all except Flagstaff and Williams were named for men somehow associated with the railroad. Edward Winslow was president of the Frisco and vice president of the Atlantic and Pacific; Lewis Kingman and H. R. Holbrook were surveyors and construction engineers (the town of Holbrook was originally called Horsehead Crossing); and Joseph Seligman was a prominent Frisco stockholder and financier.

The construction snafu at Cañon Diablo had also given Price and Co. time to complete a second major bridge just 5 miles to the west at Cañon Padre. Not quite as spectacular as the structure at Cañon Diablo, the bridge at Cañon Padre was only 230 feet long. Its measurements had been precise, and once track was laid across Cañon Diablo, tracklayers spiked their way across without a pause.

Up ahead at the base of the San Francisco Peaks was the booming lumber town of Flagstaff, already boasting one hundred houses. Across the dry mesas of northern Arizona, the San Francisco Peaks were a welcome oasis of green and a ready source of ponderosa pine for ties and lumber. The first train steamed into Flagstaff on August 1, 1882.[11]

All this construction was satisfying to the directors of the Atlantic and Pacific's parent organizations. As expected, local traffic along the expanding 35th parallel route was still weak, but westward lay the gateway to California. Expansion westward had become the mantra of William Barstow Strong, who became president of the Santa Fe in 1881, just as assuredly as it had been J. Edgar Thomson's charge on the Pennsylvania three decades earlier.

Strong recognized that "in the United States . . . the power of a Railroad to protect and increase its business depends upon its length, and the extent of the territory it can touch." Pausing at the Colorado River while westbound was really no more of an option for the Atlantic and Pacific than halting at the Colorado while eastbound had been for Huntington and the Southern Pacific several years earlier.

So, quite logically, Strong championed continued expansion westward into California. At their December 1881 Atlantic and Pacific board of directors meeting, the representatives of the Santa Fe and the Frisco jointly agreed to raise an additional $16.5 million. A small portion was to be used to extend the Vinita branch through Indian Territory, but the lion's share was to finance construction from the Colorado River crossing at Needles all the way to San Francisco.

A solicitation circular was distributed to this effect and met with initial success. Then, in February 1882, Strong and the Santa Fe were unexpectedly notified by their equal partner in the venture that the Frisco was not going to raise its one-half share. "Owing to changes going on in the ownership of the stock of the St. Louis and San Francisco Railroad Company," it was suspending all sales of the new issue of securities. It didn't take long to smell a rat. In fact, this time, from the Santa Fe's perspective, there were two rats, and they were acting in concert.[12]

Fresh from their agreement in West Texas, Collis P. Huntington and Jay Gould had decided that being allies wasn't so bad. The two titans momentarily found great commonality of purpose in joining forces to oppose the extension of the Santa Fe via the Atlantic and Pacific. Not only would the Santa Fe's 35th parallel line strike directly to Huntington's California border but also its eastern transcontinental traffic and the proposed Vinita expansion were threats to Gould's Texas and Pacific and his budding Missouri Pacific system.

From the New York banking firm of J. and W. Seligman and Company, of which Gould had been a client since the late 1860s, Huntington and Gould jointly bought a controlling interest in the stock of the Frisco. Apparently Huntington had taken to heart the advice his father is supposed to have given him: "Do not be afraid to do business with a rascal, only watch him; but avoid a fool . . ."

Controlling the Frisco, Huntington and Gould now owned half interest in the Atlantic and Pacific as well. The irony was that Joseph Seligman of Seligman and Company had championed the Santa Fe–Frisco alliance and expansion, but his recent death had given his brothers the opportunity to dispose of what they felt was an overly large investment in the 35th parallel route. Frisco president Edward Winslow balked at the sale, but the surviving Seligmans made it, at least in part because of past loyalties "to Gould as a client."[13]

This deft maneuver left Strong and his Santa Fe directors decidedly embarrassed. They had gone to great pains to promote the Atlantic and Pacific's construction and tout their strategic alliance with the Frisco. Suddenly, Santa Fe shareholders found themselves equal partners with Huntington and Gould in the Atlantic and Pacific, but partners with very different agendas.

When the Atlantic and Pacific's board of directors next convened, the newcomers—Collis Huntington, Leland Stanford, Jay Gould, and Gould's close associate, Russell Sage—sat down across the table from William Barstow Strong and the Santa Fe directors. The former group wanted to halt the Atlantic and Pacific at the Colorado River; the latter, to continue on to San Francisco as planned.

In public, Strong tried to put the best possible face on the new relationship. The Santa Fe president was quoted in the *New York Times* as saying that relations with Gould would be harmonious and that the new blood at the Frisco might even prove a positive advantage to his road. Offhandedly, Strong professed it "a matter of indifference to the Atchison who controls the San Francisco Road."

A week later, Strong received a letter written personally by Jay

Gould that left no doubt about who controlled the Frisco, as well as the immediate fate of the Atlantic and Pacific. "Mr. Huntington today informs me that he has decided to extend the Southern Pacific from Mohave to the Colorado River to connect with the Atlantic and Pacific," Gould wrote.

Gould claimed that "under other circumstances, I might think it desirable to extend the A & P to Mohave or even to San Francisco," but he saw no reason to "antagonize" the Southern Pacific when it was in "our interest to tie them up to our new line in the way suggested."

"My interests lie in working in harmony with both the Southern and the Atchison Companies," Gould told Strong, "and I think before any further steps are taken in issuing securities we should have a meeting and come to an equitable harmonious adjustment. . . ." Then Gould penned a much shorter note to Huntington: "Enclosed I hand you copy of letter written to Wm. Strong as per our conversation today." The rats were indeed working together.[14]

Strong's written response was equally cordial and, perhaps, equally disingenuous. "Your desire to secure harmony is appreciated," Strong replied to Gould, adding "that from the day you took charge of the Union Pacific Railroad to the present, whenever and wherever your interests and the interests of this Company have come in conflict, all differences have been arranged with a spirit of fairness."

Strong went on to delay the Huntington-Gould victory by pleading that he was "without official notice from the St. L. & S.F. that any change in the original plan is desired" and that he would refer Gould's letter to his board. But the outcome was as certain as the bold scrawl of Gould's handwriting.[15]

One New York financial paper—quite possibly encouraged in its perspective by the Santa Fe's investors—later went so far as to praise the Boston crowd's "sagacity and good sense" in not pursuing its own purchase of the Frisco before Gould and Huntington had done so.

While an independent line to the Pacific was "a pleasing idea," the *Commercial and Financial Chronicle* mused, it was far better "to discriminate and draw the line between ventures of a dubious or not very promising character and those offering a fair measure of success, that, is the true test . . ."[16]

But the ultimate test, as Strong well knew, was in reaching the Pacific. Strong and his Santa Fe directors, however, were quite willing to be patient in achieving that goal. They might have gotten into a cut-throat battle with Huntington and Gould that likely would have left the Santa Fe exhausted and still without a Pacific outlet. Instead Strong took a chapter from the Huntington-Gould agreement at Sierra Blanca. Why fight one's competitors if you could work with them to your own advantage?

When at the first opportunity Huntington formally proposed to the newly comprised Atlantic and Pacific board of directors that the Southern Pacific would meet the Atlantic and Pacific at Needles, Strong accepted the proposition without argument.

He concluded an agreement with Huntington and Gould that earmarked 25 percent of the Southern Pacific's gross revenues on through business over the Atlantic and Pacific to the payment of the interest on the latter's bonds, effectively helping to pay for the construction of the line. The two roads further agreed to expedite their construction and meet at Needles as soon as possible—the Southern Pacific extending a line eastward from Mojave and the Atlantic and Pacific completing its 35th parallel route west of Albuquerque.

In addition, the Atlantic and Pacific retained whatever rights it might have to build through California. But when Strong looked at the numbers, what was the rush? It had been projected to cost the Atlantic and Pacific at least $10 million to build from Needles to San Francisco. If, through its interest in the railroad, the Santa Fe could gain access to the entire Southern Pacific system without additional capital expense, the Atlantic and Pacific *and* the Santa Fe could save millions of dollars to use in improving their existing lines.

That is exactly what Strong set about doing throughout the remainder of 1882 and into 1883 as the two roads converged on Needles. Even Huntington had become envious of the financial condition of the Santa Fe. The railroad had "strong backers in Boston," Charley Crocker acknowledged to Huntington, "[who] do not seem to want for money." Part of the reason, of course, was that unlike many railroads, the Santa Fe was making money for its investors by means of steady but conservative expansion.

At the close of 1878—the year of the fight for Raton Pass and the opening blows in the Royal Gorge—the Atchison, Topeka and Santa Fe owned, leased, and operated 868 miles of track. It had net earnings of $2 million on gross earnings of $4 million. That left $2 million to service debt and reward shareholders with dividends. But just four years later, at the close of 1882—before completing the line to Needles— those numbers had more than tripled to 2,620 miles of track and net earnings of $6.5 million on gross earnings of $14.8 million.[17]

If nothing else, these numbers evidence the conservative financial leadership under Thomas Nickerson and William Barstow Strong that was to become a hallmark of the Santa Fe. Strong had big plans to increase those numbers much more, but for the moment in 1882, it served his long-term purposes to agree to meet Huntington at the Colorado River at Needles. After all, why do battle when one could achieve half the plum peacefully and ponder acquiring the other half at a later date?

So, the corporate shell of the Atlantic and Pacific Railroad, with the solid financial backing of both the Santa Fe and the Frisco, continued to build westward from Flagstaff in the summer of 1882. By September 1, the railhead had reached Williams—a bustling settlement named for mountain man and trapper "Old Bill" Williams. Land speculators anticipated the railroad's advance, and their optimism was rewarded when Williams was initially made a division point.

West of Williams, the terrain got tougher again. The line dropped 2,000 feet in elevation along a 3 percent grade to reach Ash Fork. The chief difficulty was in Johnson Canyon. Here workers were forced to blast two 150-foot cuts and a 328-foot tunnel through hardened lava flows.

It was dangerous work. On one hot summer day, two and one-half tons of powder were tamped into drill holes in preparation for the usual blast. Tamping with a copper or bronze rod was the correct procedure, but someone picked up an iron bar by mistake. It struck the hard rock with a spark that ignited the powder and caused a premature explosion. Six workers were killed and another three seriously injured. A young boy riding nearby in a mule cart became a seventh victim. The cart was totally demolished, but somehow the mule escaped unharmed.

J. T. Simms was the tunnel contractor, and he worked crews from

both ends. Once completed in the spring of 1882, the Johnson Canyon
Tunnel was a work of art. Because of loose rock, the tunnel was lined
with stonework retaining walls topped with sections of boilerplate that
arched across the roof.

The Santa Fe continued to use this tunnel until 1959. The fact that
it was the only tunnel on the Santa Fe line between Cajon Pass and
Raton Pass is a testament to the less mountainous terrain of the 35th
parallel route when compared to lines in the Rockies or Sierras. (The
Crookton Cutoff on the main line now bypasses this entire section of
Johnson Canyon and has reduced grades to about 1 percent.)

Once the Johnson Canyon Tunnel and two nearby viaducts across arroyos were ready for rails, the tracklayers quickly pushed westward to
Seligman, which eventually replaced Williams as the division point.
Beyond Seligman lay Chino Wash, a normally dry expanse of arroyos
that had the tendency to fill with raging flash floods when the rains of
July and August dumped moisture from the south onto the rocky terrain.

Construction crews had already learned the lesson of the infamous
summer monsoons of the Arizona desert the hard way. Flash floods and
high water destroyed portions of the Southern Pacific's new line across
Cienega Wash, east of Tucson, in the summer of 1880. The Atlantic and
Pacific experienced similar problems and was forced to rebuild sections
of roadbed around Holbrook the following year. Finally getting wise to
nature's vagaries, the Atlantic and Pacific opted to construct a 600-foot
iron viaduct across the usually dry flats of Chino Wash.

From there the line headed northwest to a more reliable and less tumultuous source of water. Near orchards that the Hualapai Indians cul-
tivated, Peach Springs gushed out a reliable supply. Crews constructed
a 50,000-gallon water tank there, and because of the reliability of water,
the little oasis became a place of importance to the railroad. Major side-
tracks and a six-bay roundhouse were also installed. Later, a generation
of Route 66 travelers found similar respite at Peach Springs.

By now it was March 1883, and Strong and his Santa Fe associates
were anxious to beat the Southern Pacific to Needles. Yes, they had
Huntington's word that he would meet them there and not build into
Arizona, but the Boston crowd well remembered the Southern Pacific's
charge into Yuma six years earlier. They urged their contractors onward,

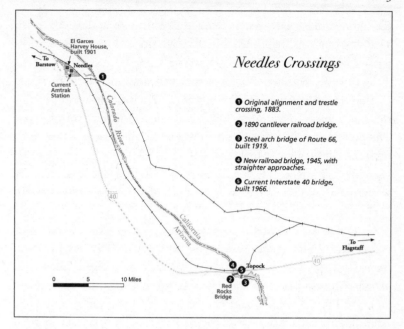

Needles Crossings

❶ *Original alignment and trestle crossing, 1883.*

❷ *1890 cantilever railroad bridge.*

❸ *Steel arch bridge of Route 66, built 1919.*

❹ *New railroad bridge, 1945, with straighter approaches.*

❺ *Current Interstate 40 bridge, built 1966.*

and crews put down from 2 to 2.5 miles of track per day. The line advanced so quickly that carpenters working on bridges were almost bowled out of the way as temporary shoo-fly tracks were thrown down on hastily piled debris around the permanent sites.

By the time the first train steamed into Kingman on March 27, 1883, the railhead had finally run itself out of rail. Tracklaying came to a halt for several weeks while more iron was rushed to the front. During the lull, all available carpenters were sent ahead to work on the Needles bridge. With them went 60-foot-long piles of fresh-cut pine from the San Francisco Peaks that were brought to Kingman by rail and then hauled by mule teams to the crossing site.[18]

Today the railroad and Interstate 40 cross the Colorado River within yards of each other about a dozen miles south of Needles at Topock, Arizona, where the river channel narrows. But in 1883, the surveyed line stayed on the east side of the river and ran north before crossing the river directly into what became the town of Needles.

Here the riverbed was very wide, with many braided channels. Long before the Colorado was harnessed by a succession of dams, spring floods—these caused by annual snowmelt high in the Rockies and not the summer monsoons—swept a muddy, brown torrent down the river. That's exactly what happened at the bridge site in June 1883 as workers attempted to erect a 1,700-foot trestle.

Meanwhile, Southern Pacific crews were pushing eastward across California's Mojave Desert. Truth be told, Huntington was in just as much of a hurry to reach the Colorado River at Needles as Strong was. The question of the Santa Fe extending into California appeared to be momentarily resolved, but Huntington was taking no chances. Huntington didn't intend to force his way across this bridge, but he certainly wasn't going to permit the Santa Fe much of a toehold on the western bank.

So, east from Mojave, the Southern Pacific crews raced at breakneck speed. Technically, it was Huntington and Stanford's Pacific Improvement Company doing the work, and its ranks were again filled with veteran Chinese laborers. The site of Barstow, California, was only an empty valley—a town would not be founded there until some years later. From there east to the Colorado River, the line snaked through 150 miles of desert mountain ranges, crested 2,770-foot Mountain Springs Summit, and descended to the Colorado at Needles.

The flurry of construction was at times as haphazard as that on the Atlantic and Pacific, but when the Southern Pacific laid rails into Needles, the Atlantic and Pacific crews were still struggling to complete the bridge. This time the agreed-upon boundary at the river would stand.

Finally, on August 3, 1883, Atlantic and Pacific tracklayers spiked rails across the long trestle and five days later joined those of the Southern Pacific. The 35th parallel route west from Albuquerque was complete, but more important, the Atchison, Topeka and Santa Fe had become a critical link in a transcontinental at last.

The line wasn't under one management, let alone one ownership, but it was now possible to travel by rail from St. Louis to San Francisco along a route generally free from the blizzards that routinely plagued the Union Pacific's route. By the fall of 1883, one could board a Pullman sleeper in St. Louis and travel west to Halstead on the Frisco, then continue to Albuquerque on the Santa Fe, to Needles on the Atlantic and Pacific, and finally arrive in San Francisco on the Southern Pacific.

The 574 miles between Albuquerque and Needles alone required twenty-four hours via what was unabashedly billed as "express service," but in time, the gentle grades, moderate climate, and beeline path of this southern route would make it the crux of America's greatest transcontinental line.[19]

At the time, William Barstow Strong and his backers did not pause to celebrate. No matter which way they looked—from Deming or from Needles—they were still hostage to the whims of Collis P. Huntington and the Southern Pacific. The Atchison, Topeka and Santa Fe had become a transcontinental link, but the battle for California remained to be fought.

14

Battling for California

aving long heard the boasts of a chorus of railroad promoters, San Diego waited with increasing frustration to be connected to America's growing railroad network. Tom Scott's promise of the Texas and Pacific steaming into town was long dead. Huntington's exit from the Los Angeles Basin at San Gorgonio Pass en route to Yuma with the Southern Pacific had been without so much as a glance in San Diego's direction. General Rosecrans had trumpeted his California Southern as San Diego's savior but then sold to the Big Four before laying a single rail. Still, there were plenty of San Diegans dreaming about railroads.

Remaining eager to attract a railroad at almost any cost, San Diego pledged six thousand acres of land and a mile of waterfront on San Diego Bay to any bona fide railroad venture. Local real estate developer Frank Kimball and his two brothers upped the ante by promising ten thousand additional acres and another mile of waterfront. Technically, the Kimballs were promoting their own interests at National City, a few miles south of Old Town San Diego, but *any* railroad would boost the prospects for both locations.

As this round of San Diego's railroad boosterism gained momentum, the town found willing allies 100 miles to the north. San Bernardino was nestled in the foothills of the San Bernardino Mountains near the canyon leading to Cajon Pass. Here was yet another town seething over its treatment by a particular railroad and eagerly looking to ally itself with a competitor.

The Southern Pacific had bypassed San Bernardino in favor of Colton—named for the Big Four's chief lieutenant—while en route to Yuma. The Big Four had also quashed the railroad dreams of Senator John P. Jones and the Los Angeles and Independence, but San Bernardino was still promoting the route over Cajon Pass. When railroad negotiations got serious again in San Diego in the fall of 1879, a committee of San Bernardino town fathers led by Fred T. Perris subscribed $40 to cover its travel expenses and made the pilgrimage south to lend its support.

This time, the railroad men meeting with local leaders were waving more than paper railroads. The interested parties proved to be none other than the same group of Boston investors who were so shrewdly backing the Atchison, Topeka and Santa Fe. The details took almost a year—during which time the Santa Fe resolved the Royal Gorge war and joined the Frisco in buying the Atlantic and Pacific.

Then in October 1880, the Boston crowd incorporated the California Southern Railroad Company—not to be confused with General Rosecrans's earlier paper venture—and joined forces with the locals. They announced plans to build north from National City, pass through San Bernardino, and meet the Atlantic and Pacific, well, somewhere.

There was no better example of the Boston crowd's commitment to Southern California and a western extension of its main line than the fact that Thomas Nickerson resigned the presidency of the Santa Fe to become president of the California Southern. As for Cajon Pass, no less an expert than the Santa Fe's Ray Morley took a look at the canyon leading to the Mojave Desert and reportedly proclaimed, "This is nothing; we can go through here easily enough."

Morley may have found the Cajon an easy passage, but his cost estimates for the line between National City and San Bernardino were another matter. Promoter Frank Kimball optimistically calculated construction costs for the 127-mile segment at $10,000 per mile; Morley's estimate was $15,000 per mile. In a subscription circular, Nickerson reported the number as $18,000 but then provided for $25,000 per mile just to be safe.[1]

Huntington and his cohorts were adamantly opposed, of course, to any railroad other than their own building through Cajon Pass or reaching out to San Diego via any route. Huntington did not begrudge San Diego a railroad, but he meant to provide one himself in his own good time. The alliance of the locals with the Boston crowd signaled a substantial raising of the stakes.

As was usually the case, feisty Charley Crocker was blunt in urging Huntington to pull no punches when it came to the Santa Fe. "You could knock their securities a good deal below par through the newspapers," he suggested to Huntington as the Santa Fe–financed California Southern gathered its forces.

Huntington no doubt appreciated his partner's sentiments, but he needed little reminder that a Santa Fe–controlled line across California to San Diego would likely result in steamship service between there and San Francisco. Such a system would compete head-on with the Big Four's Bay area monopoly.

If the Atlantic and Pacific or any other Santa Fe–backed venture could be held at the Colorado River or at least north of Cajon Pass, the California Southern—Boston dollars or not—would still be a line going nowhere except a connection with the Southern Pacific at Colton. Small wonder, then, that Crocker exhorted Huntington to "try and break them [the Boston crowd] down before they come into California."[2]

Construction on the California Southern started north from National City in June 1881. The route connected with adjacent San Diego and then charged up the coast to Oceanside, cut inland to Fallbrook, and wound up Temecula Canyon. Here the Santa Margarita River cut a rocky defile through the Coast Ranges that at first glance seemed to promise no passage for a railroad. But San Bernardino's Fred Perris, among the engineers surveying the route, was determined to keep the railroad bound for his town via as direct a route as possible. He ordered a line run along the canyon walls, above what a correspondent for *Harper's New Monthly* magazine described as "a brawling stream."

The local story handed down through the years is that one of the survey engineers—perhaps Perris or possibly chief engineer Joseph O. Osgood—asked an assistant to climb up and determine the high-water

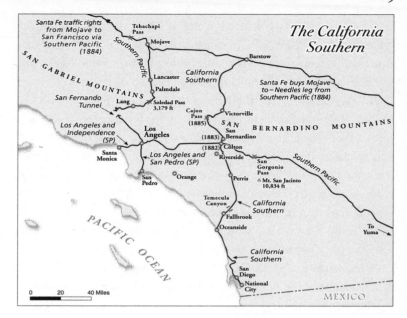

mark through the narrowest section of the gorge. More than halfway up
the cliff, the man found a cluster of pinecones. Since no pine trees grew
locally, the cones had clearly washed downstream from the higher
mountains, and their lofty presence indicated that the canyon was susceptible to extremely high flash floods. When this fact was reported to
the engineer, his response was a pompous "Nonsense," and he "proceeded to plot what he considered to be the natural flood level of the
canyon—some ten feet above the floor of the gorge." Time would tell
who was correct.[3]

Above Temecula Canyon lay the little town of Temecula, which had
its roots in vestiges of Spanish land grants. From there, easier ground
led north 40-some miles through a town named after Fred Perris and
then to Colton. In many places—particularly Temecula Canyon—
construction had been more difficult than expected, and President
Nickerson was greatly annoyed when he saw that costs were taking
every penny of $25,000 per mile and then some. Nickerson investi-
gated, but by then it was too late.

For once construction had been first-rate. In fact, supervised by chief
engineer Osgood, it had been too good. Osgood had spared no expense

and built a first-class railroad along a route that by one report "promised inadequate traffic to support the investment." Whether that pessimistic report—too good a railroad for too little traffic—held true would depend in part on the railroad's ultimate connections.[4]

On August 21, 1882, the rails of the California Southern reached Colton, where the Southern Pacific's main line lay across its path like a giant snake. The next step was to make a crossing of the Southern Pacific tracks by installing what in railroad parlance was called a "frog." This was a specially designed crisscross of rails that permitted one railroad to pass across the track of another without derailing. The railroad seeking the crossing was responsible for the cost of installing the frog, and it could not interfere with the normal operations of the first line. The first line, however, was required by law to permit the crossing.

What actually happened at Colton was far more bizarre. The Southern Pacific had been doing its best to retard the California Southern's northward construction through a variety of spurious writs and injunctions. These tactics continued at Colton when the Southern Pacific fenced off its tracks and denied the California Southern access to install its frog. The California Southern responded in kind and sought its own court order to force the Southern Pacific to permit the crossing. By the time this order was obtained—no small feat, considering the political influences of Huntington—almost a year had passed, and it was August of 1883.

California Southern engineer Fred Perris arranged for the construction of the Colton frog in the railroad's shops at National City. Southern Pacific informants learned of its location, and the local sheriff seized the frog on yet another trumped-up charge. The sheriff then posted men to guard what was in effect the physical key to the California Southern continuing north to join the Santa Fe main line.

Perris was furious but bided his time. Proving that vigilance is required most when all seems the quietest, the sheriff took a nap just long enough for Perris and a crew to retake the frog, load it on a flatcar, and hurry it north. But simply securing the frog and putting it into operation across the Southern Pacific line were two different matters.

The California Southern's onsite construction engineer at Colton, J. N. Victor, telegraphed the Southern Pacific's assistant superintendent at Los Angeles that all was in readiness to effect a crossing once the

Southern Pacific's overland mail had passed. But as Victor led his crew forward, a Southern Pacific locomotive, tender, and gondola appeared and began a major demonstration of moving back and forth at the contemplated point of intersection. Word spread through the California Southern workers that twenty to thirty armed men were crouched inside the gondola just itching for a fight—shades of the Bat Masterson rumors on Raton Pass.

When the locomotive finally stopped and stood hissing steam at the proposed intersection, the fire alarm at nearby San Bernardino rang loudly to summon reinforcements for the California Southern. An excited crowd quickly gathered and demanded that the track be cleared. Tensions were so high on both sides that Victor thought it advisable to have the court order requiring the frog's installation printed and served on each Southern Pacific employee.

The response was the time-honored "We don't know anything about it," and Victor had the order telegraphed to the sheriff of San Francisco to serve on the Southern Pacific's corporate officers. Victor subsequently reported to California Southern president Thomas Nickerson, "It will probably cost us one to three hundred dollars; but I thought it the best thing to do."

In the meantime, the local sheriff at Colton had organized an armed posse to enforce the court order and require the Southern Pacific track to be cleared whenever Victor gave the word. Victor, however, opted to be diplomatic. Because the California Southern had to use the Southern Pacific's turntable and track and was on its depot grounds, Victor thought it "advisable to work here peaceably if possible."

This approach resulted in begrudging overtures from the Southern Pacific crew. After some further posturing, all obstructions were removed, and both sides worked together to install the hotly contested frog that same afternoon. The Southern Pacific workers also agreed to release material for the California Southern extension to San Bernardino that had been held hostage in the Southern Pacific yards.[5]

With a truce called in the frog war, if not the greater corporate rivalry, the California Southern crossed the Southern Pacific line at Colton and laid tracks a few more miles into San Bernardino. It operated the first scheduled train into San Bernardino on September 13, 1883, just one month after the rails of the Southern Pacific and the Atlantic and Pacific joined at the Needles crossing of the Colorado River. This meant, of course, that there was still no access for the California Southern over Cajon Pass via *any* railroad, let alone a friendly one, and that left the California Southern at the mercy of the Southern Pacific, just as Huntington had planned.

"The Southern Pacific monopoly as completely ignores the existence of the 'California Southern R. R.' as though they had never heard of it," grumbled a San Diego merchant; "they refuse to receive or deliver freight to or from it in spite of the law to the contrary."

It didn't help matters that in the early 1880s, the city of San Diego was less than a quarter the size of Los Angeles. The 1880 census showed a similar disparity between the surrounding counties: 33,381 in Los Angeles County versus 8,018 in San Diego County. Without a line of its own into the San Diego area, the Southern Pacific was doing all that it could to maintain or increase that disparity in favor of Los Angeles. When newcomers "find out how much it costs to get *here*," the same San Diego merchant continued in despair, they "*stop* at Los Angeles."[6]

San Diego and the California Southern were not alone in their frustrations. The Atchison, Topeka and Santa Fe had long felt the hand of Huntington and the Southern Pacific—whether it was the brush-off handshake at Deming or the dilemma confronting the railroad at the Needles railhead of the Atlantic and Pacific. When one California newspaper learned that the Southern Pacific was building east from Mojave to confront this invader to the Golden State, it brashly predicted, "They [the Southern Pacific] are expected to gobble up the Atlantic and Pacific, scales, tails and fins."

But William Barstow Strong and the Santa Fe had already proven their staying power. In theory under the Tripartite Agreement, the Southern Pacific was supposed to send shipments eastward over the Atlantic and Pacific, and one-quarter of those revenues were to service the interest on the Atlantic and Pacific's bonds. It wasn't nearly that smooth in practice. With the Central Pacific to the north and the Southern Pacific to the south, Huntington could be very choosy about how much traffic he allowed to flow eastward to Needles for the Atlantic and Pacific.

In the Santa Fe's 1883 annual report, President Strong was forced to admit that while the company had completed another prosperous year, gross revenues remained on par with 1882. Despite the new connections with the Southern Pacific at Needles, Strong found himself reprising his report after joining the Southern Pacific at Deming: through traffic via the new connection had been very disappointing because Huntington was still directing the lion's share either north over the Central Pacific or south over the Southern Pacific.

What California traffic the 35th parallel line did see was fraught with delays, bungled bills of lading, and misplaced freight cars. Even when California shippers specified a routing via the Southern Pacific–Atlantic and Pacific–Santa Fe line, "freight often became lost or delayed rather mysteriously between Needles and San Francisco."[7]

Then disaster struck the newly completed California Southern. In December 1883 and January 1884, almost seven inches of rain fell at the Fallbrook weather station just downstream from normally arid Temecula Canyon. During February, rainfall of more than fifteen inches was recorded. The "brawling" Santa Margarita River through the gorge became a rising torrent. The man who found the pinecones had been right. The rushing water picked the track clean from its narrow perch and swept away bridges as if they were piles of kindling. San Diego learned the worst of the news on February 20, when passengers stranded by a rock slide near the southern end of the canyon walked into town.

To some, rebuilding the track in Temecula Canyon was a foregone conclusion. These included the Boston crowd, which footed the repair bill. To do otherwise would have abandoned their Southern California toehold and played right into Huntington's hand. By late summer 1884, about one thousand men were at work in the canyon putting the rails and bridges right back where they had been. Others weren't so sure about the decision. "Well," mused one old-timer, "I have lived here a great many years and I don't think you can ever put a railroad in that canyon which will stand."

The line was finally reopened to through traffic between San Diego and San Bernardino on January 6, 1885, and San Diego's ten-and-one-half-month isolation—after barely five months of rail service—was over.[8]

. . .

Meanwhile, the Atlantic and Pacific was hardly a road to nowhere, but given the freight situation along the Southern Pacific west of Needles, neither was it a paying concern. With the completion of a substantial and permanent bridge over the Colorado River at Needles in the summer of 1884, the Santa Fe faced one of those crossing-the-Rubicon moments that either make or break great corporations.

From whichever of its western termini the Santa Fe looked—Deming, Needles, or the Sonora Railway—the Southern Pacific in one manner or another acted as a sieve to filter its traffic and impact its rates. The Santa Fe could continue to operate as it was and attempt to extract some profit from the Atlantic and Pacific's massive though largely undeveloped land grants. But that was hardly in keeping with William Barstow Strong's mantra that a railroad must ever expand its markets and territories or die.

A second option for the Santa Fe was to abandon the Atlantic and Pacific line and retrench the railroad's core business on the plains and in the Midwest. That, too, was untenable for Strong, although one might speculate which result of this option Strong feared most: Huntington's taking advantage of the abandoned Atlantic and Pacific route and streaking into the Santa Fe's stronghold of New Mexico, or Cyrus K. Holliday's howl of indignation at abandoning the long-held Pacific dream. No, neither the status quo nor a retreat was an option to Strong. That left one other alternative: an all-out attack.

Leaving the Atlantic and Pacific as its unsteady subsidiary between Albuquerque and Needles, the Santa Fe proposed to strike west from Needles on its own and, if need be, parallel the entire route of the Southern Pacific for 600 miles from there to San Francisco. Huntington was far more concerned by this direct threat to San Francisco than he had been by the struggling efforts of the California Southern. But for once, the man whose partners had tried to rein him in at Yuma, had begged him not to throw out more branches, and had watched in awe as he juggled a myriad of complicated financings, was himself short of cash.

In part, this was because Huntington had great plans to join a number of eastern roads, including the Chesapeake and Ohio Railroad, to the Southern Pacific at New Orleans to make one single transcontinental line under his personal control. The complexities of Huntington's plan in the East were mind boggling, but the ramifications in the West were simple and beneficial to the Santa Fe.

Huntington was never one to fight unnecessary battles, particularly on multiple fronts. His need for cash became even more desperate after the country's financial markets suffered a sharp downturn. The result was that Huntington sat down with William Barstow Strong—just as he had years before with Tom Scott and later with Jay Gould—and hammered out another compromise.

First, the Atlantic and Pacific bought the recently completed 242-mile Southern Pacific line between Mojave and Needles for $30,000 per mile on what was technically an extended lease-purchase. This was almost the same as selling the line to the Santa Fe, but perhaps Huntington's ego required that he preserve the fiction of the Atlantic and Pacific as an independent. Huntington's own influence in the Atlantic and Pacific disappeared when he sold his shares in the Frisco about the same time as part of his marshaling of cash.

Second, Huntington granted what once would have been unthinkable. The Southern Pacific gave the Atlantic and Pacific trackage rights between Mojave and San Francisco Bay via its San Joaquin line over Tehachapi Pass for an annual rental of $1,200 per mile, if the Atlantic and Pacific chose to use it. It also offered terminal facilities in Oakland and San Francisco. Both of these provisions were acknowledged to be assignable to either the Santa Fe or the Frisco should it become successor to the Atlantic and Pacific—a likely prospect even then.

But what was Huntington getting out of this besides cash? The answer was even more cash. The Santa Fe and the Frisco agreed to purchase $3 million of Atlantic and Pacific bonds of dubious marketability that were held by the Southern Pacific. Huntington's Pacific Improvement Company had bought the bonds at 50 percent of par when it was constructing the Mojave-Needles line, and now Huntington was glad to cash them out for the same amount.[9]

The Huntington-Strong agreement became operational on October 1, 1884, and Atlantic and Pacific trains could steam across the bridge at Needles and climb across the ranges of the Mojave Desert to the Southern Pacific line at Mojave. That left an 80-some-mile section between the Atlantic and Pacific's Mojave line and the railhead of the California Southern at San Bernardino. In between lay Cajon Pass.

Ten years before, Huntington's surveyors had faced off here against the men of the Los Angeles and Independence. Now, with perhaps a sigh of the inevitable, the Southern Pacific did not contest the route, as Santa Fe surveyors worked upgrade from the Mojave flats and hacked a line through the piñons and junipers to Cajon's summit. Much of the grade on the southern side had already been staked in anticipation of the California Southern's extension from San Bernardino.

Once work crews repaired the flood damage in Temecula Canyon, they were dispatched north to Cajon Pass in January 1885. Many were veteran Chinese laborers; others were Mexican graders who had been working on the Santa Fe's Sonora Railroad. Work was slow, and the up-hill grade out of San Bernardino reached 2.2 percent. Here, too, the floods of the previous year had sent torrents of water down the canyon. Paying closer attention to the high water line this time, construction engineer Fred Perris moved the originally surveyed route to higher ground above normally dry Cajon Creek Wash.

By July 19, the right-of-way was graded as far as Cajon Station, about 5 miles from the 3,775-foot summit of the pass. Around what much later came to be called Sullivan's Curve and along Stein's Hill, the grade climbed at 3 percent. Just above Pine Lodge, the mouth of the tunnel that the Los Angeles and Independence had started in 1874 was choked with bushes and rockfall. Perris opted to avoid tunneling and instead dug out a series of deep cuts as the line climbed the final miles to the summit.

Meanwhile, another crew was working south from a little station called Waterman on what was now the Atlantic and Pacific's Mojave line. Westbound toward Cajon Pass, the grades were easier. The rails were joined on November 9, 1885, just below the summit on the south side, but the ensuing celebrations were not without another test of nature. Perris had moved the grade above the high-water line along Cajon Creek Wash, but he had failed to design culverts for the runoff streams that gushed down the smooth side canyons and pooled alongside the fills and embankments. The deep cuts posed a similar hazard and spewed mud onto the tracks before they were properly supported with a framework constructed from timber, or cribbed.

These problems were soon corrected and the obstacles overcome. In fact, the Santa Fe installed a modified version of the snowshed through some of the deeper cuts. Terraced hillsides were roofed over with wooden structures that angled outward from the center to channel runoff water to the ends of the cut and prevent it from falling directly onto the tracks.[10]

Even as this construction across Cajon Pass was completed late in 1885, William Barstow Strong had his share of critics among the normally loyal Boston press. Strong was criticized for having paid too much for the Mojave line. Some said that its very acquisition had been Huntington's cagey way of blunting the Santa Fe's drive to build an independent line to San Francisco. Still others found fault with Strong's rescue of the flooded California Southern. But in the battle for California—which was far from over—one name would in time seem prophetic. The little way station of Waterman, where the Cajon Pass route now cut south from the Mojave line, was renamed not Potter for Huntington's middle name, but Barstow in honor of Strong's.[11]

Meanwhile, San Diego waited expectantly for regular train service to commence. The *San Diego Union* could barely contain its enthusiasm: "San Diego is out in the highway of the world's activity to-day," an editorial proclaimed, "and needs to make haste to take her position in the onward march. It is an era of new ideas, new methods, new enterprises and new men. It is the day of the nimble dime rather than of the slow dollar. Old fogyism must go to the rear."

The first through train to the east pulled out of San Diego on November 16, 1885. The town paraded a little band for its send-off, but the real celebration was at San Bernardino. There the town turned out en masse to speed the train over Cajon Pass and cheer its place on what was at last a transcontinental line through California controlled by parties other than the Big Four.

Ten days later, the first through Pullman from Kansas City steamed into San Diego, and the *San Diego Union* predicted in far more tempered tones that the city would enjoy "a period of moderate expansion." What had happened to cool its ardor? The answer: stark economic reality.

Huntington, having lost his bid to hold the Santa Fe at Needles because of a need for cash, now sought to parry its further extension beyond the California Southern by granting it trackage rights into Los

Angeles. For the same annual rental terms that he had just extended for the line into San Francisco, Huntington gave the Santa Fe the right to operate trains on the 54-mile Southern Pacific line between Colton and downtown Los Angeles. Suddenly Santa Fe traffic descending Cajon Pass into San Bernardino could either proceed directly west to Los Angeles and its port of San Pedro or follow the California Southern line south to San Diego through tempestuous Temecula Canyon.[12]

San Diego was outraged even as it cheered the arrival of its first transcontinental train. Three days later, the first Santa Fe train operated over the Colton line into Los Angeles, which could now boast of not one but two transcontinental connections. It was a reminder that San Diego's own battle with its California neighbors was far from over, its own future far from resolved.

To the Santa Fe, San Diego had long been an important piece on the western chessboard, but the game itself was still San Francisco. With trackage rights down the San Joaquin Valley and now also into Los Angeles—and less than booming business in San Diego—the Santa Fe relegated the California Southern to a branch line, not the terminus of a great transcontinental system.

"San Diego should have anticipated from the very start," the *Los Angeles Times* lectured, "that this new overland system would make San Francisco its ultimate objective point." Recognizing its own town's secondary status, the *Times* freely admitted, "San Francisco is the Rome of the Pacific Coast: all roads lead to it."

And when it came to betting between Los Angeles and San Diego, the choice for the Santa Fe was equally clear. "It doesn't stand to reason," a Santa Fe official confessed somewhat apologetically, "that the road can afford to put those little merchants [in San Diego], who have only two or three straight carloads of through freight in a year, on the same footing with men here who have as much in a week . . . Los Angeles is our natural and inevitable western terminus."[13]

William Barstow Strong had his own take on the matter. It had, in fact, been purely economic. "Railroading is a business wherein progress is absolutely necessary," he told his shareholders. "A railroad cannot stand still. It must either get or give business; it must make new combinations, open new territory, and secure new traffic."[14]

If the battle for California was only about access into the state's markets, the Santa Fe had clearly won. But that did not mean that the war between the Southern Pacific and the Santa Fe was over. At the same time, on its eastern flank, the Santa Fe would have to face Jay Gould again.

15

——◆——

Gould Again

Throughout his business career, Jay Gould was simultaneously engaged on multiple fronts. To the casual observer, his actions all over the chessboard seemed erratic. To disgruntled opponents, Gould's propensity to anticipate, execute, and usually profit from seemingly unrelated moves was proof that he was an unscrupulous corporate raider in the worst sense of the term. Indeed, generations of business and railroad historians never mentioned Gould's name without the requisite adjective preceding it: infamous, nefarious, manipulative, and ruthless, to name a few of the kinder ones.

Thanks in large measure to the insightful investigative work of historian Maury Klein, Gould's reputation has undergone a reappraisal in recent years. Gould and his so-called "robber baron" contemporaries were no more one-dimensional than similar tycoons today. Certainly, in a choir that included Collis P. Huntington, William Jackson Palmer, and Thomas A. Scott, Gould hardly deserved to be singled out as "the supreme villain of his era."[1]

One might question Gould's movements, one might be envious of his successes, but on a one-to-one basis, even his adversaries admired his forthrightness. "I know there are many people who do not like him," his rival and occasional partner Collis P. Huntington remarked, but "I will say that I always found that he would do just as he agreed to do."

Similarly, the head of a commission investigating the affairs of the Union Pacific Railroad was obliged to admit, "I have always found, even to the most trivial detail, that Mr. Gould lived up to the whole nature of his obligations. Of course, he was always reticent and careful about what he promised, but that promise was invariably fulfilled."[2]

And General Grenville Dodge, who built the Union Pacific and whose reputation remained largely above cutthroat railroad shenanigans, worked with Gould for two decades without complaint. Dodge, who perhaps had his hand in more railroad construction in the West than anyone, said of Gould, for whom he built the Texas and Pacific and other legs of the Missouri Pacific system, "When we discussed any question and came to a conclusion and Mr. Gould said, 'General, we will go ahead,' or do this or that, no matter what it meant or into what difficulties we got, I never had doubts as to where Jay Gould would stand."[3]

Gould's reputation as somewhat of a loner may have come from the fact that he was leery of people wanting something from him. But that appears to have made him value his closest friends and family all the more. "I appreciate your friendship very highly," Gould confided to Silas Clark, his longtime business associate, "because I know it is the real stuff." As for his family, Gould was devoted to his quiet and shy wife, Helen, and their six children, particularly eldest son George and darling daughter Helen. Wall Street may have shuddered at Gould's approach, but underneath his receding hairline and jet-black beard, Gould's family knew him as a doting teddy bear.[4]

All this is not to say that Jay Gould was not a stickler for detail. Indeed, as will be seen some pages hence, Gould frequently held his opponents to the most minute points of a particular contract while using his multiple holdings to overlook its broader spirit. As the 1880s progressed, Gould's overriding goal became the consolidation of a major east-west transcontinental system under his independent control. He went about it with much the same imperial, entrepreneurial spirit as Collis P. Huntington.

This meant that the other railroads of the Southwest, chief among them the Atchison, Topeka and Santa Fe, were never quite sure where Gould would strike next. Just as the Santa Fe's entry into California did

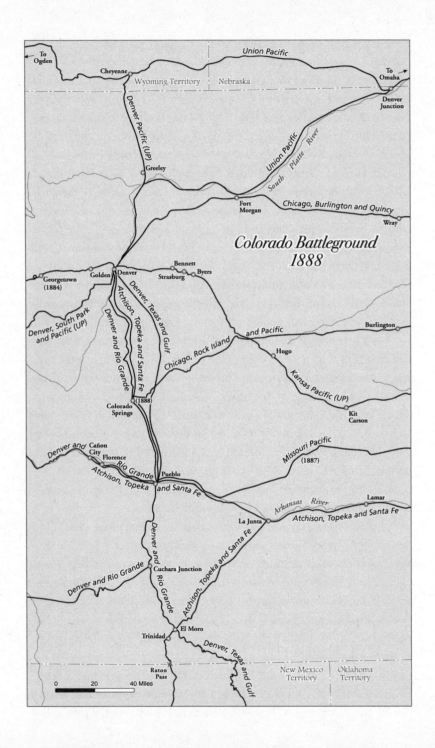

To
Ogden

Union Pacific

Cheyenne

To
Omaha

Wyoming Territory   Nebraska

Denver Junction

Denver Pacific (UP)

Greeley

Union Pacific

South Platte River

Fort
Morgan

Chicago, Burlington and Quincy

Wray

*Colorado Battleground
1888*

Georgetown
(1884)

Golden   Denver

Bennett

Strasburg   Byers

Burlington

Denver, South Park
and Pacific (UP)

Denver, Texas and Gulf

Atchison, Topeka and Santa Fe

Denver and Rio Grande

Chicago, Rock Island   and Pacific

Hugo

Kansas Pacific (UP)

Colorado
Springs

(1888)

Kit
Carson

Denver and   Cañon
City

Florence

Denver and
Rio Grande

Rio Grande

Atchison, Topeka

and Santa Fe

Pueblo

Missouri Pacific

(1887)

Arkansas   River

Lamar

La Junta

Atchison, Topeka and Santa Fe

Denver and Rio Grande

Denver and
Rio Grande

Cuchara Junction

Atchison, Topeka and Santa Fe

Trinidad   El Moro

Denver, Texas and Gulf

Raton
Pass

New Mexico
Territory

Oklahoma
Territory

0   20   40 Miles

The yards at Wyandotte, Kansas—soon to become Kansas City, Kansas; photographer Alexander Gardner, better known for his Civil War images, documented the advance of rails in a portfolio entitled "Across the Continent on the Union Pacific Railway, Eastern Division." (Kansas State Historical Society, Alexander Gardner photo)

The first major obstacle for the Union Pacific, Eastern Division—later the Kansas Pacific—was to bridge the Kaw (Kansas) River on the outskirts of Wyandotte, Kansas; all construction was by men or horsepower. (Kansas State Historical Society, Alexander Gardner photo)

Cyrus K. Holliday looked beyond Topeka and saw not only Santa Fe but also the Pacific. (Kansas State Historical Society)

This crew of Union Pacific, Eastern Division, section men rolled along on a handcar at Salina, Kansas, some 470 miles west of St. Louis. (Kansas State Historical Society, Alexander Gardner photo)

At an unknown location, this crew of Santa Fe workers looks like a pretty tough outfit; no matter how big the dreams of Holliday, Strong, or Ripley, these are the men who made them come true. (Kansas State Historical Society)

Atchison, Topeka and Santa Fe locomotive no. 5, a 4-4-0 American, waits at Topeka sometime after the large brick depot in the background was built about 1880. (Kansas Historical Society)

A Santa Fe construction train at the entrance to Mora Canyon, between Springer and Las Vegas, New Mexico; the line is being pushed south toward Glorieta Pass and Santa Fe. (J. R. Riddle, Palace of the Governors Photo Archives [NMHM/DCA], 038209)

Thomas A. Scott solidified the Pennsylvania Railroad but spread himself too thin out west. (Library of Congress, LC-USZ62-121283)

Collis P. Huntington became the insatiable railroad builder of the Big Four. (Library of Congress, LC-USZ62-63955)

John Evans was a businessman first, but much of his business was in railroads. (Denver Public Library, Western History Collection, Z-2873)

William Jackson Palmer won the battle for the Royal Gorge but lost the war for the Southwest. (Denver Public Library, Western History Collection, Z-310)

The Tehachapi Loop was William F. Hood's solution to climbing out of the San Joaquin Valley and into the high deserts around Mojave; his alignment remains in place and is among the busiest single-track railroad corridors in the country. (Library of Congress, from Lot 13476[H])

Tunnel no. 9 was the key to making the loop at Tehachapi; the track circled to the lower right and wound up on top of the lower track. (Library of Congress, from Lot 13476[H])

Atchison, Topeka and Santa Fe locomotive no. 137 at Glorieta Summit, October 1880; the Raton Tunnel was complete and the drive down the Rio Grande in full swing. (Ben Wittick, Palace of the Governors Photo Archives [NMHM/DCA], 015870)

The Southern Pacific's 1877 bridge across the Colorado River at Yuma from the swing span on the Arizona side; Huntington counted on the cheers of Arizonans to quiet the government's protests. (Library of Congress, LC-USZ62-49926)

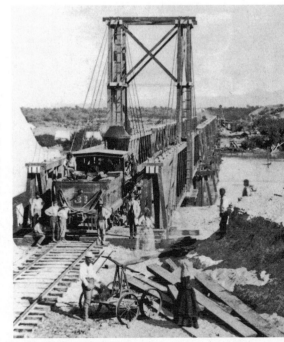

Santa Fe construction crews worked in the eastern end of the Royal Gorge while Denver and Rio Grande crews blocked their exit toward Leadville; this view looks east toward YMCA Mountain, beyond which Grape Creek flows into the Arkansas River. (Denver Public Library, Western History Collection, B. H. Gurnsey, Z-3369)

C. Shaler Smith of the Santa Fe produced the drawings and saw to the construction of the initial hanging bridge structure at the narrowest point in the Royal Gorge; the Denver and Rio Grande strengthened it over the years and long touted it as its own engineering marvel. (Colorado Historical Society, scan #20104180, W. H. Jackson Collection)

The Denver and Rio Grande's roundhouse at Salida, Colorado, was the cornerstone of its narrow gauge empire in Colorado; lines ran north up the Arkansas River to Leadville, west across Marshall Pass to Gunnison and Utah, and south over Poncha Pass to the San Luis Valley. (Denver Public Library, Western History Collection, Z-5735)

The Alpine Tunnel earned the Denver, South Park and Pacific a spot in railroad lore but cost the road its race west; no. 199 emerges from the west portal of the Alpine Tunnel en route to Gunnison. (Denver Public Library, Western History Collection, Z-52)

This spindly trestle, 560 feet long and 222 feet high, carried trains across Cañon Diablo west of Winslow, Arizona, from 1882 until 1947, albeit with some strengthening over the years. (Colorado Historical Society, scan #20101403, W. H. Jackson Collection)

With its centerpiece, the 300-foot-long high bridge, the Georgetown Loop was an impressive engineering achievement, even though its track went no farther west than another 4 miles; this was Jay Gould's last effort to build straight west from Denver. (Denver Public Library, Western History Collection, W. H. Jackson, WHJ-770)

William Barstow Strong pushed the Santa Fe through a decade of unbridled expansion. (Kansas State Historical Society)

Edward Payson Ripley took the Santa Fe from bankruptcy to the top of the heap. (Kansas State Historical Society)

A 4-6-0 ten-wheeler stops at Needles eastbound with two baggage cars and five coaches of the California Limited; the El Garces Harvey House at Needles was opened about 1901 and operated until 1948. (Kansas State Historical Society)

The only thing finer than Fred Harvey dining trackside was the elegance of a dinner in the dining car of the California Limited. (Kansas State Historical Society)

Nellie Bly captured the imagination of America with her round-the-world journey. (Library of Congress, LC-USZ62-75620)

The original crossing at Needles via a long, wooden trestle susceptible to floods was replaced by this cantilever bridge a few miles to the south at Topock in 1890; it served the Santa Fe until 1947, when it became the route of U.S. 66. (Colorado Historical Society, scan 20101516, W. H. Jackson Collection)

Jay Gould had his hand in many railroads but came up short in his transcontinental quest. (Library of Congress, LC-USZ62-104428)

George Gould tried to surpass his father in assembling a transcontinental empire. (Library of Congress, LC-USZ62-64445)

This great bridge across the Pecos River near its confluence with the Rio Grande was the key to the Southern Pacific's reaching across Texas to complete Huntington's Sunset Route from San Francisco to New Orleans. (Colorado Historical Society, scan 20103651, W. H. Jackson Collection)

Fred Harvey's tasty and affordable meals gave the Santa Fe a reliable advertising ace. (Kansas State Historical Society)

This Fred Harvey pass was good all along the Santa Fe and its associated lines; note that the number 2 in the date 1892 is printed upside down to make counterfeiting less likely. (Kansas State Historical Society)

The Harvey House at Syracuse, Kansas, just east of the Colorado-Kansas line, was originally a frame structure with only a lunch counter; it burned in 1906 and was eventually replaced by the Spanish-styled architecture of the Sequoyah Hotel. (Kansas State Historical Society)

If there was one thing besides elevation gain that made the Santa Fe route the ultimate winner in the Southwest transcontinental race, it was the lack of heavy snow; here the Colorado Midland, its one-time subsidiary, battles snow drifts on Hagerman Pass about 1900. (Colorado Historical Society, scan 20030238, Buckwalter Collection)

Famed railroad photographer Otto Perry caught the first run of the Super Chief westbound near La Junta, Colorado, on May 13, 1936, doing a reported seventy-five miles per hour; the blunt-nosed locomotive didn't last long but was the prototype for streamliners to come. (Denver Public Library, Western History Collection, Otto Perry, OP-211)

Two of Baldwin Locomotive Works's big and mighty 2-10-2 locomotives blast up the south side of Raton Pass near Lynn, New Mexico, in 1944, during the rush of World War II. (Colorado Historical Society, negative F-23, 160)

This photo combines two legends: the Moffat Tunnel that at long last gave Denver a rail connection straight west and the Vista Domes of the Denver and Rio Grande's vaunted California Zephyr. Even General Palmer had predicted that "someday they will call us slow old coaches." (Denver Public Library, Western History Collection, Z-5698)

The Chief, train no. 20, pounds upgrade near Raton, New Mexico, with engine no. 1790, a 2-8-8-2 in the lead as a helper, followed by road engine no. 3784, a 4-8-4 Northern; the date was June 16, 1945, and steam was enjoying its last heyday at the close of World War II. (Denver Public Library, Western History Collection, Otto Perry, OP-1351)

The Super Chief pauses at Albuquerque to refuel from tank cars in March 1943 at the height of World War II. (Library of Congress, Jack Delano, LC-USW3-020412-D)

not mean that its battles against Huntington and the Southern Pacific were over on the western end of its line, there would never be any rest from the continuing machinations of Jay Gould in the East. Gould's assault on the Santa Fe was complicated and multifaceted, but it generally occurred in three stages.

Initially, Gould negotiated with uneasy bondholders to acquire the Kansas Pacific. The Santa Fe had also been interested in the Kansas Pacific, but Gould outmaneuvered the Boston crowd. His leveraged purchase in 1879 and subsequent quick sale to the Union Pacific—a tactic he used frequently—"transformed a rival into a useful ally." Not only did this impact the Santa Fe across Kansas and into Colorado markets, but Gould and the Union Pacific were suddenly a powerful force within Colorado as well.[5]

The second major stage of Gould's expansion was the completion of the Texas and Pacific and its alliance with Gould's developing Missouri Pacific system. The result was that the Santa Fe was now shadowed across the plains by Gould lines—the Missouri Pacific to the north and the Texas and Pacific to the south—as well as the Union Pacific–Kansas Pacific system.

The third stage of Gould's western puzzle was his version of the "straight west from Denver" theme. After besting the Santa Fe in the Royal Gorge and reaching Leadville, William Jackson Palmer had built over Marshall Pass and beat his rival, John Evans and the Denver, South Park and Pacific, to Colorado's Western Slope. By 1883, Palmer had pushed the Denver and Rio Grande beyond Gunnison, through the depths of the Black Canyon, and on into Utah and a connection with the Union Pacific at Ogden. (Palmer interests had been building east from Ogden since 1881, and the rails were joined at Green River, Utah, on March 30, 1883.)

But the Denver and Rio Grande's finances were again in dire straits, and Palmer got into a dreadful battle with the road's outside investors over continued expansion. The general was finally forced to resign as president. He would, however, remain involved with the Utah portion of the line, the Rio Grande Western, and be a major competitor to any road building out of Colorado.

In this setting, Gould renewed his designs on the Rocky Mountain West. In just one example of his transcontinental reach, Gould con-

vinced the Union Pacific to acquire a derelict narrow gauge called the
Nevada Central that ran south from the Central Pacific into played-out
silver mining country. The line was never rejuvenated, but its purchase
showed Gould's willingness to throw himself into the terrain between
Palmer's westward advance and Huntington's California fiefdom and attempt to block the continued expansion of both.[6]

The best way for Gould to defeat Palmer, threaten Huntington's Southern Pacific, and strike a blow against the Santa Fe was to build straight
west from Denver. William H. Loveland's Colorado Central had never
made much progress in that direction, although not for lack of trying.
The aftermath of the panic of 1873 found the Colorado Central short of
cash and the Union Pacific reaching out to it—for the price of control,
of course. With plenty of grumbling in Colorado, but local opposition
useless in the face of eastern proxies, the Colorado Central's board of directors cast its lot with the Union Pacific. In 1875 it voted "that the
Colorado Central should be leased permanently to the Kansas Pacific,
which now meant the Union Pacific, which now meant Jay Gould."

With this infusion of capital, the Union Pacific supervised the completion of the Colorado Central line north to its main line west of
Cheyenne in 1877 and contemplated work on what was to be called its
Julesburg Cutoff across the northeastern corner of Colorado. Both of
these standard gauge lines were built with one eye toward Denver but
the other toward the mineral wealth of the mountains to the west. To
that end, the Colorado Central's narrow gauge rails were continued up
Clear Creek to Georgetown, yet another town with dreams of becoming
a silver queen.[7]

But the siren call to the Colorado Central—just as it was to the Rio
Grande, Santa Fe, and South Park roads—was Leadville and the San
Juan Mountains, as well as the long-awaited line straight west from
Denver. In 1878 Gould incorporated the Georgetown, Leadville and
San Juan Railroad. William Loveland was elected president—one of
Gould's usual tactics in nurturing local alliances—but there was no
doubt where the true power resided. Gould was in Colorado twice the
following summer and each time took a special from Golden to the end
of track at Georgetown to ponder the terrain beyond.

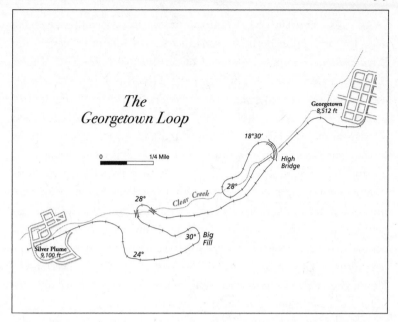

The Georgetown Loop

Only 2 miles separated Georgetown from the mining town of Silver Plume, but the elevation difference in that distance was 638 feet. To gain that amount of elevation in 2 mere miles required an average grade in excess of 6 percent, far beyond the capabilities of even the most powerful narrow gauge locomotive. To solve this problem, the Union Pacific's chief engineer, Jacob Blickensderfer, devised what came to be called the Georgetown Loop.

Immediately at the Georgetown station, Blickensderfer pushed the line above Georgetown on a series of rock retaining walls. Entering the narrow mouth of upper Clear Creek Canyon at a place called Devil's Gate, Blickensderfer surveyed the line to ascend Clear Creek, cross it, and then double-back on the opposite side of the creek, recrossing both the creek and the lower track via a spindly, high bridge.

Once across the bridge, which was to be built both on a grade and a curve, the line continued up the Clear Creek Valley and gained the additional elevation required to reach Silver Plume via an extensive cut and one large fill. The loop and its assorted curves stretched the distance between the two stations to 4.5 miles and reduced the maximum grade to 3.5 percent.[8]

As was so often the case in railroad surveys, it was one thing to stake out a line and quite another to construct it. The task of implementing Blickensderfer's proposed route fell to a man equal to the task. Robert Brewster Stanton was born in Woodville, Mississippi, in 1846. His father was a Presbyterian minister who became president of Miami University of Ohio. Young Robert graduated from Miami in 1871, and after a summer surveying the Atlantic and Pacific's tentative extension into Indian Territory, he determined to become a civil engineer.

Much later, Stanton wrote that John Wesley Powell's report of his Colorado River explorations through the Grand Canyon made an early impression on him and "created in me the first ambition of my engineering life . . . that I should some day throw a single span railway bridge across that chasm!" Stanton received a graduate degree in engineering from Miami, and by 1880, he was a division engineer on the Union Pacific, working for Jacob Blickensderfer, who had been his engineering mentor on the Atlantic and Pacific.[9]

Stanton spent much of 1881 re-surveying Blickensderfer's route and then supervised grading operations and the construction of the stonework for four main bridges. Spring floods washed out some of the grade in 1883, but tracklaying began, and by the end of September, it reached the abutment of the high bridge at Devil's Gate. Jay Gould was aboard the first special passenger train to the site. Given the relatively slow pace of construction and the reduced speeds that the line would require, Gould may have wondered whether he was building a main line west or a tourist attraction.

To be sure, the high bridge was a spectacular achievement. Four massive towers, each with four iron legs of riveted quarter-rounds 8 inches in diameter, rose to support eight 30-foot box girder sections. A 60-foot lattice girder completed the center span over Clear Creek. The bridge was 300 feet long and 75 feet above the lower track. It was built on a 2 percent grade, which in its length meant that the upgrade abutment was 6 feet higher than the downgrade one. Photographs of the bridge frequently failed to show that it and its approaches were also built on sharp curves.

All of this was completed by November 25, 1883, but when Robert Brewster Stanton inspected the structure, he refused to accept it. Not only did Stanton find some of the riveting defective but also, incredibly, the order of the support towers had been reversed. The towers at the higher, or upgrade, end of the bridge (toward Silver Plume) had been placed at the lower Georgetown end, causing the bridge to run suddenly downhill at a 2 percent grade rather than continuing the climb uphill. Who was to blame for the error was a matter of considerable debate.

"The bridge builders say this is not their fault," reported the *Georgetown Courier,* "but the fault of the railroad company, and hold that the company's officials gave them the wrong end to start." The defective riveting was also explained. First-class riveters were hard to come by, and "a number of men engaged for that purpose refused to work on the bridge when they arrived here and viewed the dangerous structure, not withstanding that high wages were offered. . . ."

That Gould was anxious to press ahead after three years of delay became obvious from the speed with which Stanton directed the remedial efforts. The entire structure was dismantled, the support towers exchanged and placed in their proper positions, and the faulty riveting redone. This was accomplished during the dead of winter.

After the anticipation, the *Georgetown Courier* took less than two column inches under a perfunctory "The Devil's Gate Bridge Completed" headline to advise: "'Tis done at last. The last stroke on one of the most wonderful viaducts ever constructed in the Rocky Mountains was made yesterday. The structure is now complete and ready for the ties." On March 11, 1884, the first locomotive steamed into Silver Plume and inaugurated more than fifty years of service over the Georgetown Loop. The following month, track was laid an additional 4 miles up Clear Creek to Graymont, present-day Bakerville.[10]

But what now of the lure of Leadville and a transcontinental line? Part of the answer lay in the geography west of Graymont. Piercing the Continental Divide in any realistic manner would require a tunnel far longer than the 1,400- to 1,600-foot bore first projected by Blickensderfer. But in the final analysis, Jay Gould's foray west of Georgetown ground to a halt at Graymont because there was no prize lucrative enough to summon the same caliber of engineering as the Georgetown Loop to surmount the Continental Divide.

By the time the Georgetown Loop was finally built, the Leadville trade had plateaued, and the town was tapped by the Union Pacific's

South Park line over Boreas Pass as well as the original Denver and Rio Grande line. The latter, in fact, would soon continue west from Leadville, over Tennessee Pass, and down the Colorado River toward Utah. Gould himself was spending less time with the Union Pacific— although he remained a shareholder—and concentrating more and more on his Missouri Pacific system. The reality of the situation west of Georgetown was that even as the Georgetown Loop was completed, the compelling reasons for its construction no longer existed.

So there was still no direct transcontinental link straight west from Denver. Only the Denver and Rio Grande had managed to pierce the inner Rockies, albeit by a circuitous route south from Denver. In the process, it had forced the axis of the Santa Fe south after the Royal Gorge battle. But it is ironic that the narrow gauge system William Jackson Palmer championed proved an albatross in the end. Its smaller size simply could not compete economically as freight volumes swelled. Worse, its narrow gauge was a major impediment to transcontinental traffic—switching from standard gauge cars to narrow gauge and then back again—between Pueblo and Utah. (A third rail was added in 1881 between Denver and Pueblo to accommodate both gauges on that section.)

South of the Colorado battleground, it was a different story. The Santa Fe had built a standard gauge line across generally easier terrain and linked Chicago and Los Angeles. The Denver and Rio Grande would persevere, but it would never be able to compete with the speed and high volume that the Santa Fe was able to push across Raton Pass. Perhaps the Santa Fe had won the battle of the Royal Gorge after all.

Meanwhile, as Jay Gould was entrenching his position in the midsection of the country with the Missouri Pacific, Collis P. Huntington completed his end run around Gould's southern flanks. Despite the Huntington-Gould agreement of 1881 at Sierra Blanca, Gould and the Texas and Pacific were not enjoying a boom in California trade via the Southern Pacific. The agreement had contemplated that El Paso to New Orleans traffic would pass over the Texas and Pacific via Fort Worth and Shreveport and then into the Crescent City. Huntington, of course, had other plans.

"Portions of the agreement originally made between Messrs. Gould and Huntington affecting the traffic between El Paso and New Orleans, were not complied with on the part of the Huntington system," the Texas and Pacific reported to shareholders. The reason was that after linking up with the Texas and Pacific at Sierra Blanca, Huntington pushed the Southern Pacific southeast across Texas toward San Antonio.

On January 12, 1883, outside a long tunnel near the confluence of the Pecos River and the Rio Grande, construction crews of the Southern Pacific met those of Huntington's ally, Thomas A. Peirce of the Galveston, Harrisburg and San Antonio. East of Galveston, Huntington and Peirce had acquired the Louisiana and Texas Railroad and Steamship Company, with rails into New Orleans. The company had long enjoyed a monopoly on the Texas-to-New Orleans trade as well as steamers on a water route between New Orleans and New York. The result was that by February 1883, one could ride Southern Pacific cars on the Sunset Route from San Francisco to New Orleans and continue on to New York City by steamer—all under the control of Collis P. Huntington.[11]

The Atchison, Topeka and Santa Fe did not stand by and idly watch this competition for the Gulf Coast. In many respects, William Barstow Strong was the antithesis of Huntington and Gould. Strong was not a grand-scale promoter or a wheeler-dealer. He did not personally invest—indeed, he did not have the personal financial capacity to invest—large amounts of capital.

Strong was subservient to his Boston crowd of investors. He was their manager, not a knight errant riding ahead of his partners like Huntington or a lone wolf prowling on his own like Gould. Strong was an able railroad operator, "bold and skillful in the acquisition of operating properties," as one of his contemporaries wrote, but discerning in his movements and methods.[12]

Under Strong's leadership, the Santa Fe continued many of the same conservative business principles that had been in evidence since the road started west across Kansas. Territory was crucial, Strong saw to that. The road had not hesitated to seize Raton Pass, contest the Royal Gorge, and claw its way into California. But the Santa Fe also paid particular attention to its operations: locomotive power, rolling stock, and

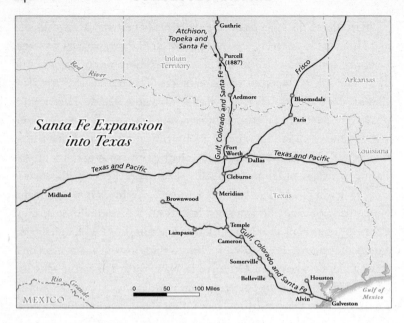

the condition of its roadbed and required facilities. What this meant was that while competitors continually battled its advance or nipped at its flanks, the Santa Fe strengthened its corporate core and was able to compete no matter where the battleground.

In 1886 Strong stabbed deep into Texas against the empires of both Gould and Huntington. Part of Cyrus K. Holliday's early vision for the Santa Fe had been that it would reach the Gulf of Mexico as well as the Pacific. As the Santa Fe built branch lines into Indian Territory, mostly reaching out to the cattle trade, its railheads advanced south from Arkansas City, Kansas, toward Purcell, Oklahoma, on the Canadian River and southwest from Kiowa, Kansas, bound for the Texas Panhandle. As Strong looked ahead across the vastness of Texas, he came up with a bold plan: Why build through the growing maze of Texas railroads if he could simply acquire a relatively straight, existing route to the gulf?

The likely candidate for acquisition was the Gulf, Colorado and Santa Fe Railway. The road had never been very profitable. To the north, it was beholden to Jay Gould for connections to the Katy, while Huntington's allies siphoned traffic off along the coast. Its purported main line had built west from Galveston past Temple to Brownwood. This was the natural direction to get the road to Colorado and the town of Santa Fe, but of greater interest to Strong were its branch lines running north to Fort Worth and Dallas.

Strong smelled a bargain in the making. For $8,000 per mile of Santa Fe stock, the Atchison, Topeka and Santa Fe acquired the Gulf, Colorado and Santa Fe's existing 625 miles of track, plus another 70 miles that was under construction. But then Strong showed his real strategic genius. Rather than merely buying the existing trackage, Strong contracted at the same price to buy an additional 300 miles of new track to be constructed by the Gulf, Colorado and Santa Fe within a year. There would be no worries about corporate entities, new surveys, or rights-of-way; the Santa Fe would simply use its purchase of the Gulf, Colorado and Santa Fe to finance that road's existing plans.

From the Gulf, Colorado and Santa Fe railheads at Fort Worth and Dallas, this new construction was to extend the arms of a Y and reach north to the Santa Fe's projected railhead at Purcell and the Santa Fe's allied Frisco railhead at Paris, Texas. When complete, Holliday and Strong's Santa Fe would have lines through to the gulf competing with Gould's Katy and the larger Missouri Pacific system, as well as challenging the Southern Pacific's dominance in southern Texas.

Building 300 miles of new track in one year was a major undertaking for the Gulf, Colorado and Santa Fe, but its construction crews proved themselves up to the task as they worked north toward Purcell. Meanwhile, the Santa Fe's Southern Kansas Railway subsidiary built south toward Purcell. Even though they were now allies, a race developed that proved good for worker morale as well as construction efficiency.

Walter Justin Sherman, the construction engineer of the Gulf, Colorado and Santa Fe, first promoted his own internal contest. He laid out enough materiel for more than a good day's work and told his crews that they could have the rest of the day off when that amount of track was laid. The hammers flew and the spikes clanged home, and inevitably the men finished a few minutes early—even though they had managed more than a normal day's work. Finishing early had its rewards, not the least of which was Sherman's daily whiskey ration: a dipper of liquor dispensed to each man.

Soon attention shifted to the oncoming Southern Kansas crews. Each team cheered its day's progress as rails converged on Purcell from north and south. When the junction at the town was finally reached on April 26, 1887, the Gulf, Colorado and Santa Fe won the race by hours or minutes, depending on who was telling the story. Of course, there wasn't much at Purcell at the time, and places such as Guthrie, Edmond, and Oklahoma City were no more than tiny railroad sidings. All that would change in only two years with the Oklahoma land rush and subsequent discoveries of oil and make Strong's push for the gulf look even more lucrative.[13]

So the reach of Gould's empire had been checked. Jay Gould and his son George would cast a huge shadow over American railroading for another two decades, but a combination of Colorado's mountains west of Denver and William Barstow Strong's expansion into Texas put limits on their transcontinental reach. Jay Gould would continue to exert enormous pressures in the Midwest, but it was the Atchison, Topeka and Santa Fe that reached beyond that region and expanded its system not only eastward to Chicago and westward to San Francisco but deeper into Mexico as well.

16

To the Halls
of Montezuma

One of the overlooked chapters of transcontinental railroading is the close relationship between the spreading American network of rails and American promotions for railroads in Mexico. Western railroad promoters saw little reason why the trade and mineral riches of the Southwest should stop at the U.S.-Mexican border. Mexico was an economic magnet just as Santa Fe had been a generation earlier, and the farther south one went, the shorter the distance to the Pacific.

Mexico's skepticism toward these overtures was based in part on its continuing resentment of the expansionism of President James K. Polk and the Mexican-American War. In the war's aftermath, some members of Polk's cabinet wanted to extract much more land from Mexico than the Treaty of Guadalupe Hidalgo granted—at least the next tier of provinces of Baja California, Sonora, Chihuahua, Coahuila, Nuevo León, and Tamaulipas. The Gadsden Purchase belatedly acquired enough of Sonora and Chihuahua to affirm American control of the 32nd parallel route, but that did not stop railroaders from looking farther south.

Another section of the Treaty of Guadalupe Hidalgo gave the United

States rights to a railway across the Isthmus of Tehuantepec *and* the right to intervene militarily to protect it. The Panama Canal ultimately superseded this railroad project, and the less-than-neighborly provision of the treaty was removed as part of the Good Neighbor Policy of the 1930s. Its original inclusion, however, demonstrates just how strongly some in the United States coveted Mexican routes and trade.

Mexico's first railroad venture was completed in 1873, thirty-six years, numerous false starts, and several civil wars after the first paper charter was granted. Named the Mexican Railway, it ran from Veracruz on the Gulf of Mexico and climbed 260 miles up steep grades into the bowl of Mexico City at more than 7,000 feet. The tenure of Benito Juárez as Mexico's president provided relative stability for the undertaking, and its construction instilled a sense of national pride after recent instabilities. It also encouraged American promoters to lobby the Mexican Congress for their own franchises.[1]

At the front of the charge—as he had not been at Chickamauga— was ex-general William S. Rosecrans. From 1868 to 1873, American railroading in Mexico was synonymous with his name. Initially U.S. ambassador to Mexico, Rosecrans discussed the Mexican Railway's progress with Juárez and became convinced that Mexican railroads were "a promising field for American capital." He enthusiastically advocated construction of American railroads to the U.S.-Mexican border and the extension of two or three lines into central Mexico. After his recall by President Grant—the two were never more than nominal allies, and Grant had in fact relieved Rosecrans after Chickamauga—Rosecrans remained committed to promoting American railroads in Mexico.[2]

His first effort was to appoint agents to petition the Mexican Congress for a concession for a Mexican version of a transcontinental line, running from Tampico or Tuxpan on the Gulf Coast, north of Mexico City, and westward to the general vicinity of Manzanillo on the Pacific Coast. Branch lines would connect south to Mexico City and north at least as far as Querétaro, perhaps all the way to the Rio Grande.

When an initial concession between Mexico City and Tuxpan was approved in December 1870 after lengthy debate, the only subsidy offered by the Mexican government was a grant of public lands. Unlike the United States, however, government ownership of lands in Mexico was fraught with uncertainty. The central government had lost control of any semblance of a public domain during various revolutions, and any attempt to reassert itself was likely to fuel renewed unrest.

Meanwhile, Rosecrans scoured the United States in search of capital to build the venture if more favorable terms could be negotiated. Among those he approached were many of his Civil War comrades, but he did not make much progress until J. Edgar Thomson suggested that Rosecrans contact William Jackson Palmer. Here was a strange turn of events. The major general who had commanded an army called upon a man seventeen years his junior who had been a young regimental commander assigned to Rosecrans's headquarters at Chickamauga.

Palmer and Rosecrans met in Denver on Thanksgiving Day 1871. The Tuxpan-to-Pacific line was not of much interest to Palmer, but he seized upon the second phase of a branch line north to Querétaro and ultimately to El Paso, which at that point Palmer intended to make the destination of his one-year-old Denver and Rio Grande.

In the spring of 1872, with the Rio Grande only recently arrived in Colorado Springs and still far from El Paso, Palmer made the first of many trips to Mexico. That Palmer chose to break away from his new Colorado enterprises is a testament to his long-range vision for the Rio Grande and the importance he placed on north-south traffic between the United States and Mexico.

Queen Palmer, who never enjoyed robust health, accompanied her husband as he chose to reconnoiter the western end of the proposed transcontinental line. Along with General Rosecrans, they landed at Manzanillo on the Pacific Coast, and while the gentlemen of the party rode horseback, Queen endured a jarring, monthlong coach ride to Mexico City. The journey provided Palmer firsthand evidence of Mexico's need for railroads, but it also gave him a taste of the country. On a subsequent reconnaissance north of Mexico City without Queen, he had an encounter with bandits and was grazed in the arm by one of their bullets.

But Palmer had already proven himself a steady field general who was not easily turned away. His bigger problem was that Rosecrans was having a difficult time winning suitable modifications of the franchise. Unrealistic time schedules, irrevocable performance bonds, uncertain terrain, and the lack of a cash subsidy all left the venture looking very risky. But one of the biggest problems was an argument over gauge.

The Mexican Railway had been built in standard gauge (1.435 meters), and while Palmer could recite his litany of reasons for the narrow gauge, many in Mexico were opposed to mixing gauges because of the problems it posed for a unified national system.

The Palmers left Mexico in May via Veracruz and sailed for New York, leaving Rosecrans to pursue the concessions. Part of their rush was personal. Queen was pregnant and would give birth to their first child, a daughter, later that fall at her father's home in Flushing, Queens. Palmer was in Colorado at the time attending to railroad and land business, but by December he was back in Mexico City checking on Rosecrans's progress.[3]

Juárez was dead by then and had been succeeded by Sebastián Lerdo de Tejada. The new president proved no friend of the narrow gauge, but complicating the negotiations further was the fact that Rosecrans and Palmer no longer had the field to themselves.

Their aggressive competitor was Edward Lee Plumb, another ex-diplomat and former chargé d'affaires of the American legation at Mexico City. Plumb represented a group of American investors backing a line reaching southward, the International Railroad of Texas. It not only proposed to build a main line from Laredo on the Rio Grande to San Blas on the Pacific, with the requisite branch to Mexico City, but to do so in standard gauge. Plumb was convinced that "Mr. Lerdo is taking a deep interest in our project."

On January 2, 1873, the day after Lerdo officially inaugurated the Mexican Railway between Veracruz and Mexico City, Palmer wrote Queen that despite Rosecrans's cheery optimism, Lerdo "is opposed to our gauge and wishes the old concession to die." While Rosecrans fancied himself the consummate and persuasive diplomat, Palmer was slowly coming to a different conclusion. "The General as usual has been constantly led on by his hopes," Palmer confessed to Queen. "Evidently we should have had someone here all along. If the good old Indian, Juárez, were still in office it would no doubt be very different."[4]

Palmer conducted his own round of lobbying but found it frustrating. "This business in Mexico is the most complicated and embarrassed that I have ever been connected with in the civil line," Palmer told Queen, before recounting that among his visitors had been the German minister to Mexico, who "wanted to know all about this Railway war, which is turning the Halls of the Montezumas upside down." Palmer claimed the German left "unreservedly for us and the 'Narrow Gauge,' " but the votes were with Lerdo and the Mexican Congress.[5]

Once more, Palmer left Mexico for a whirlwind of travel to Philadelphia, Colorado, and then back to Flushing for Queen's birthday before leaving again on April 10, 1873, for his third trip to Mexico within a year. This time the growing friction with Rosecrans boiled over. Finding that Rosecrans had done little but alienate Lerdo's government with reams of tactless correspondence, Palmer dressed down his former commander for his incompetence.

In a huff, Rosecrans offered his resignation, and Palmer called what may have been his bluff by immediately accepting it. "General Rosecrans, I am happy to say," Palmer reported to Queen, "left this morning for U.S.A. It is a great relief, as he appeared lately to have lost the power of correct judgment on men and things." His onetime lieutenant did not see Rosecrans off on the train to Veracruz.

Palmer tried to reverse the fortunes of the narrow gauge, but he soon realized that it was hopeless and returned to the United States. At the end of May 1873, the Mexican Congress finally cancelled Rosecrans's original concession and awarded a franchise to Plumb's International Railroad of Texas for a standard gauge line. Plumb's victory was short lived, however, as the panic of 1873 soon brought most railroad construction to a halt. Palmer turned his attention to saving his Colorado enterprises, but he was far from finished in Mexico.[6]

The panic of 1873 stalled rail prospects in Mexico, but it did not blind American promoters to potential there. Even before the Atchison, Topeka and Santa Fe arrived at Deming, William Barstow Strong was hedging his bets against Huntington's heavy-handed tactics. As early as November 1878, Strong dispatched the trusted Ray Morley to run a survey from Deming to Guaymas, Sonora, on the Gulf of California. It was part of Strong's multiple front against Huntington and the Southern Pacific. He intended to acquire a share of the California and Pacific trade no matter what stone walls Huntington erected on the Southern Pacific's main line west of Deming.

By now, Porfirio Díaz was president of Mexico. After running unsuccessfully in prior elections against both Juárez and Lerdo, Díaz used opposition to another four-year term for Lerdo as a rallying cry to come to power in 1876. While Díaz would stand by his own one-term pledge in 1880 and momentarily sit out a term, he would nonetheless be reelected in 1884 and preside over Mexico as its presidential strongman for another twenty-six years.

Díaz's terms of office were very significant to railroad construction in Mexico. After the short tenures and accompanying chaos of past governments, Díaz actively promoted a sense of national unity and relative economic stability. High on his priorities were settling Mexico's nagging foreign debts and encouraging renewed outside investment in Mexico's infrastructure. American railroads looking south were the immediate beneficiaries.

William Barstow Strong went to Mexico City in the fall of 1880 and negotiated with Díaz for a charter and subsidy for the proposed Sonora Railway between Deming and Guaymas. He won a ninety-nine-year concession and a promised cash subsidy equivalent to $11,270 per mile. To avoid lengthy shipments via Kansas City or meddling by the Southern Pacific with construction traffic over its line, Strong arranged for the rails and rolling stock for the Sonora Railway to be delivered to Guaymas. He also put Ray Morley in charge of building the line northward from there.

King William, the horse that Morley was supposed to have ridden to death in the race to the Royal Gorge, was with him. "William is looking as well as ever," Ray reported to Ada. "I took a ride over the work with him yesterday. He seemed to know me as well as ever and rather enjoyed my riding him again."

During 1881, Morley's construction progress convinced Huntington that the Santa Fe was serious about intruding upon, if not outright paralleling, portions of his southern line, and Huntington granted the Santa Fe trackage rights between Benson and Deming. That matter resolved, Strong incorporated the New Mexico and Arizona Railroad to bridge the 90-mile gap between Benson and Nogales on the U.S.-Mexican border.

A silver spike was driven at Nogales on October 25, 1882, to complete the 260-mile Sonora Railway section and open a continuous 1,700-mile Santa Fe line from Kansas City to Guaymas. At the time, it

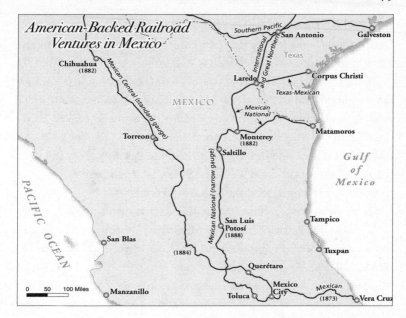

was the longest railroad segment in the world under one management, albeit with a portion dependent upon Southern Pacific tracks.

The Sonora Railway did not prove profitable for the Santa Fe—there wasn't enough internal Mexican trade to support it, and through traffic to the Pacific still gravitated to mighty San Francisco and not lowly Guaymas. Consequently, the line did little to counter or circumvent the head-on fights between the Santa Fe and Southern Pacific in California, although it would later figure in them as a bargaining chip.

But Strong's Boston crowd of backers was not persuaded against Mexico. In February 1880, two and one-half years before the completion of the Sonora Railway, they also incorporated the Mexican Central Railway to build from El Paso south to Mexico City along essentially the same route that had been initially sought by Rosecrans and Palmer. This intended route into Mexico figured heavily in the Santa Fe's plans when it split its main line south from Albuquerque at Rincon, New Mexico, and headed toward both Deming and El Paso.[7]

But the Santa Fe was not alone in its drive toward Mexico City. Despite his many ventures in Colorado, William Jackson Palmer was back in the hunt for a Mexican line. This time employing an agent defter than General Rosecrans had proven, Palmer secured a concession from Díaz to build a narrow gauge from Laredo south through Monterrey, Mexico, to Mexico City, a distance of 840 miles.

The southern half of Palmer's proposed Mexican National Railway ran roughly 75 miles east of the Mexican Central's survey, and Palmer received his concession just two days before the Santa Fe–backed Mexican Central started construction north from Mexico City. For a time, it looked as if there could be quite a race between Palmer's crews and their old nemesis from the Santa Fe, Ray Morley, who had been called upon to work as chief engineer of the Mexican Central.[8]

To no one's surprise, there was another well-known name in the contest. Jay Gould also had his hand in Mexico. In December 1880, Gould acquired control of the International Railroad, by then renamed the International and Great Northern, as part of his growing collection of Midwest railroads. Palmer had been counting on the International's railhead at Laredo as his gateway into Texas. Gould, in turn, wanted Palmer's Laredo–Mexico City concession outright. The general, who was fighting Gould in Colorado about that time, was not inclined to do business with him on either front.

So, in June 1881, Gould secured a concession from Díaz for yet a third Rio Grande to Mexico City line—this one to run southward from Eagle Pass, Texas. Palmer started construction south from Laredo on his planned route about the same time. Gould attempted to interest Boston investors in his Mexican route, but many of them were already involved with the Santa Fe's plan for the Mexican Central. Gould made plans to proceed on his own but found himself stretched a little thin given his other interests.[9]

Meanwhile, Palmer laid track east from Laredo to Corpus Christi, Texas, in an attempt to circumvent Gould's control of the International and Great Northern and pushed railheads forward at both ends of his line—south from Laredo and north from Mexico City. The Mexican Central was building between El Paso and Mexico City with equal determination.

The truly amazing thing about these Mexican railroad ventures by American promoters is that the most frenzied activity occurred concurrent with a similar burst of construction throughout the American West. The year 1881 was the high-water mark of western railroad construction. The Santa Fe reached Deming and hurried the Atlantic and Pacific west from Albuquerque; the Southern Pacific raced to Sierra Blanca and barely paused before continuing toward New Orleans; the Denver and Rio Grande surmounted Marshall Pass and clawed its way toward Utah; Gould was everywhere from the South Park at Leadville to the Texas and Pacific's own line to New Orleans.

It was no wonder that the *Denver Tribune* quoted Alexander Hunt of the Denver and Rio Grande as boasting that the railroad had more men on its payroll than the United States Army. Of the approximately thirty-two thousand total, three or four thousand were at work in New Mexico, five or six thousand in Colorado, three or four thousand in Utah, and nineteen thousand or so in Mexico.[10]

Palmer's Mexican National built south from Laredo and slowly climbed over comparatively easy ground to reach Monterrey in the foothills of the Sierra Madre Oriental by September 1882. The standard gauge rails of the Mexican Central made similar progress south from El Paso to Chihuahua. Construction out of the bowl of Mexico City was another matter.

The Mexican National climbed from an elevation of 7,700 feet at Mexico City to 10,000 feet at Salazar, 25 miles to the west, over 4 percent grades. For a time, it seemed as though Palmer's devotion to the narrow gauge was well founded and that Palmer was winning the race against Ray Morley and the Mexican Central.

But that was not to be. On January 3, 1883, about 200 miles south of Chihuahua, Morley was riding in a carriage with his engineering party as they arrived at their campsite. The driver's rifle was leaning against the front seat. Morley called the man's attention to it as unsafe and may have reached to take it from him. Somehow the rifle discharged, and the bullet struck Morley in the heart. He was dead at thirty-six.

One of Morley's prized possessions was a gold-plated Winchester rifle that William Barstow Strong had given him in appreciation of Morley's dogged ride from Pueblo to Cañon City to stake the Santa Fe's claim to the Royal Gorge. Many accounts say that this rifle was involved in the fatal accident and that Morley was showing it to an admirer. The Morley family history claims otherwise, and it seems unlikely that Morley would have had the trophy with him in the field.

Ada was in Chicago when she got the news and hurried to Cimarron for the funeral. She was left with three small children. The tributes flowed across the Santa Fe system and the Southwest. The American Society of Civil Engineers called Ray Morley "one of the most able and active of the men who have been identified with the great works of railroad extension in the Southwest, and probably none had the promise of a brighter future." The Kansas Pacific, Mule Shoe Curve, Raton Pass, the Royal Gorge, the 35th parallel west from Albuquerque, the line to Guaymas, and the Mexican Central—William Raymond Morley had left his mark on them all.

The Mexican Central went on without Ray Morley and completed its line between El Paso and Mexico City early in 1884. By then, the Mexican National had a gap of about 385 miles yet to be built. And the gap would remain for a long four years. Palmer and his associates had simply taken on too much debt, flung a network far too wide, and failed to account for the lack of local revenues along those sections that were completed. Palmer learned firsthand what one of Jay Gould's engineers had reported to Gould, "that so far as he could see, there was no business there for a railroad."[11]

Palmer suspended interest payments on the construction bonds and fought off receivership for three years until a foreclosure agreement in 1887 resulted in a new entity, the Mexican National Rail*road* Company. On September 29, 1888, the Mexican National Railroad was finally completed over the 840 miles between Laredo and Mexico City. Palmer remained on the board of directors until 1891, but by then the general had long refocused his main activities back in the mountains of Colorado.

The Mexican Central had better luck. Once again, the seasoned management, solid revenue stream, and deep pockets of the Atchison, Topeka and Santa Fe made the difference. With 1,224 miles of track between El Paso and Mexico City, the Santa Fe system could not compete with through passenger service between Chicago and the Mexican capital. (The Santa Fe–Mexican Central connections via El Paso took 128 hours versus a time of 88 hours from Chicago through St. Louis and Laredo on the Mexican National.) But even then, the real revenues were on the freight side, and as the growing Mexican economy slowly disproved the skepticism of Gould's engineer, the standard gauge rails of the Mexican Central began to haul more traffic more efficiently than the narrow gauge Mexican National. Compounding the problem of capacity was the difficulty of transferring freight to and from the standard gauge lines on the Texas border.

In the end, the Mexican National learned what Palmer was forced to come to grips with in the Colorado Rockies. On all but the most rugged of branch lines, narrow gauge for railroads in the United States and Mexico was an idea that came and went very quickly. The three-foot rails of the Mexican National lasted little more than twenty years. Between 1901 and 1903, its original track was torn up and relaid with standard gauge rails. About the same time, the Mexican government began to acquire substantial interests in both the Mexican National and the Mexican Central, and by 1908 the roads were among those merged into a new entity, the National Railways of Mexico.[12]

For the Atchison, Topeka and Santa Fe, the Mexican Central was never a big moneymaker, but it did extend the road's continental reach. Even without the Mexican Central, the Santa Fe by the mid-1880s could boast of three routes to the Pacific: the first via the Atlantic and Pacific across northern Arizona and Needles; the second west from Deming across the Colorado River at Yuma (albeit subject to the whims of the Southern Pacific); and the third, over the Sonora Railway to Guaymas. What one might do there except wait for an occasional ship was another matter.

The latter two routes made for good marketing copy in boasting of "three ways to the Pacific," but the reality was that the destiny of the Santa Fe was increasingly tied to its Atlantic and Pacific line via Needles into California. There was more of California to be had, and soon much of the country would be clamoring for a stake in it.

17

California for a Dollar

The next round in the continuing battle for California between the Atchison, Topeka and Santa Fe and the Southern Pacific was to be fought east of Kansas City, not west of Needles. The Santa Fe decided that access to Chicago via its own independent tracks was essential to its long-term growth and sustainability. Chicago had long been one of the great railroad centers of the country. By the mid-1880s, it was arguably the greatest of them all.

A complex web of lines spread out from Chicago's hub. Chicago marked the western ends of the great New York Central and Pennsylvania railroad systems. A tangle of regional roads ran from it to the Union Pacific at Council Bluffs, the Northern Pacific at St. Paul, and what would soon be James J. Hill's Great Northern system. South of Chicago, an array of lines led to Kansas City, St. Louis, and Memphis.

The Atchison, Topeka and Santa Fe built east from its roots and cut through the tangle of the Kansas City roads to secure a railhead on the Missouri River in 1874. Its uneasy partnership with the Frisco gained it access to St. Louis a few years later. As its attention was focused on the frenzied westward expansion of the early 1880s, the Santa Fe was content to rely on other roads for connections between Kansas City and Chicago. The Santa Fe carried the burgeoning cattle trade of the plains to these railroads at Kansas City, and they in turn provided the Santa Fe with freight flowing west. It was a mutually beneficial relationship.

These arrangements were disrupted, and William Barstow Strong and his Santa Fe investors made increasingly uneasy, when the Kansas City–Chicago roads began to construct their own lines west of Kansas City. The Santa Fe's initial public response was that it had no desire to build east of Kansas City because other roads adequately served it there. But as those same roads invaded the Santa Fe's territory, the farther west their railheads extended, the greater the threat became that they would capture the Santa Fe's business and haul it straight through to Chicago.[1]

Ostensibly, the Santa Fe and Jay Gould's developing Missouri Pacific system had an agreement not to build into each other's territory. But while the Missouri Pacific corporately adhered to the letter of the agreement, Gould's far-ranging personal investments permitted him to sidestep its spirit. One example of this was when the tiny St. Louis, Fort Scott, and Wichita Railroad fell under Gould's control. It threatened the Santa Fe's long-held dominance over southern Kansas by simultaneously pushing construction westward and making connections eastward to Gould's expanding system.

By the end of 1887, Gould's Missouri Pacific would complete its main line from Kansas City to Pueblo to tap the Colorado trade. This would be detrimental to the Santa Fe in the Colorado markets, but there was an even greater threat. Gould might well use his traffic alliance with the Denver and Rio Grande to forge a link for the Missouri Pacific through the Rockies to Huntington's Central Pacific at Ogden.

With Gould's encouragement, the Rio Grande slowly began to extend a third rail west from Pueblo along its narrow gauge tracks in anticipation of such standard gauge traffic. In return, Strong and the Santa Fe had little choice but to abandon their trackage agreement along the Rio Grande line between Denver and Pueblo—to which Palmer had added a third rail in 1881—and build the Santa Fe's long-threatened parallel line from Pueblo to Denver.

Even the Santa Fe's friendly rival, the Chicago, Burlington and Quincy Railroad, which had long been the Santa Fe's most favored connection between Kansas City and Chicago, made plans to build westward. Its first step was into Nebraska to challenge the Union Pacific, but it also contemplated a line across Kansas.

The Burlington's Kansas extension was not intended as a direct challenge to the Santa Fe, but rather was proposed because the Burlington's own vitality was threatened by the westward expansion of the Chicago, Rock Island and Pacific Railroad. The Rock Island Railroad was building west across Kansas and would eventually reach Colorado Springs and Denver, the latter via a trackage agreement over the Union Pacific's Kansas Pacific line.

In the face of this developing competition across the plains, the Santa Fe's long-term strategy looked obvious to President Strong. If the Santa Fe's competitors were building west so aggressively, the Santa Fe had little choice but to build east with equal determination to counter them.

As to the competition in the Chicago market, "the people along our whole system, above all other things," Strong rationalized, "want direct, rapid, and unobstructed communication with Chicago, with only one carrier to deal with in the entire transaction; and they will patronize the road which furnishes it."[2]

Once the Santa Fe made the decision to build independently from Kansas City to Chicago, there were three options. A. A. Robinson, now chief engineer of the Santa Fe, simply placed a ruler on the map and drew a straight line between the two cities. The object, after all, was a lifeline link between the western Santa Fe system and the hub of Chicago, not local traffic through an area already overdeveloped by competing roads.

A second option was to buy the Chicago and Alton Railway. This would have lengthened the distance between Kansas City and Chicago but also given the Santa Fe independent access to St. Louis. But the Alton thought rather highly of itself, and the Santa Fe's directors judged its reported $38 million asking price as highly inflated. That left a third option—essentially a variation on Robinson's straight ruler route.

From its name, the Chicago and St. Louis Railway sounded as if it

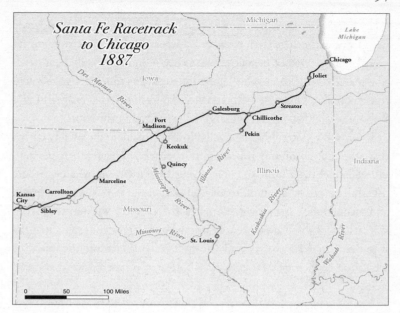

Santa Fe Racetrack to Chicago 1887

were a main artery between those two cities. In fact, the railroad's tracks had never extended farther south than Pekin, Illinois, about 150 miles from Chicago. The road was described as "two streaks of rust" and because it had only recently completed construction into Chicago, its terminal facilities were little more than a frame depot at Twenty-third Street, then well south of downtown. The road had been poorly built, with heavy grades and light rails, but it offered an established right-of-way over a portion of Robinson's planned route. And the price was right: $1.5 million.

The Santa Fe organized the requisite number of subsidiaries, including the Chicago, Santa Fe, and California Railway Company, which acquired the Chicago and St. Louis. Meanwhile, Robinson dispatched teams of surveyors to locate and acquire—as quietly as possible—the remainder of the proposed route.

By February 1887, all was in place. President Strong gave Robinson the order to proceed and have the line complete by the end of the year. Robinson soon had crews working all along the planned 450-mile Kansas City–Chicago route. How crowded the countryside was with competing roads was evidenced by no fewer than thirteen crossings of other lines that the Santa Fe was obliged to construct, some at grade with frogs and others with over- or underpasses. But these existing regional lines proved of benefit because they obligingly hauled construction materiel to a dozen points along the Santa Fe's route. This facilitated construction at multiple points rather than at only two railheads, and Robinson soon had seven thousand men engaged in the effort.

Robinson reportedly admonished his locators not to plan any curves that were not absolutely necessary. In their early development, eastern railroads had been built to connect existing towns via whatever route necessary. Later, western railroads built largely to the dictates of terrain and planned their own towns along the routes. Now without those considerations, Robinson laid out an uncannily straight route much of the way between Kansas City and Chicago, with the result that the line would be both a raceway and the shortest distance between the two hubs.

The two major exceptions to this course were at Fort Madison, Iowa, on the Mississippi River, and the town of Galesburg in upstate Illinois. Fort Madison outbid Keokuk, Iowa, as the crossing of the Mississippi, and this took the line northward into the sliver of southeastern Iowa between the Mississippi and Des Moines rivers. Galesburg was also north of Robinson's ruler line, but it offered twenty acres for a depot site and $100,000 as inducements. Once across the Illinois River at Chillicothe, Illinois, the line joined the right-of-way of the Chicago and St. Louis at Ancona, Illinois, and then ran along its grade that was relaid with heavier rails.[3]

Out west, the challenge had been steep mountain passes, narrow canyons, and deep arroyos, but across Missouri and Illinois, except for some stubborn glacial deposits, the main difficulty was bridging wide and unruly rivers. In addition to numerous side streams and creeks, five major river crossings presented themselves between Kansas City and Chicago. To overcome these obstacles, Robinson turned to Octave Chanute, a French-born engineer who was among the most-respected railway and bridge engineers of the day.[4] (Later, Chanute would become better known in another dimension as a mentor of Orville and Wilbur Wright.)

Despite bitter winter weather that delayed the completion of the Missouri River crossing for several months, Robinson closed the other gaps along the line with six hours to spare before Strong's year-end deadline, spiking down the last rail near Medill, Missouri, at six o'clock on December 31, 1887. A full schedule of revenue operations began the following spring.

By then, Strong had spared no expense in making certain that the passenger side of the Santa Fe's business would be second to none. The road took delivery of cars with vestibules—no longer would passengers have to step outside into the elements to pass from car to car—and electric lights powered by batteries charged by a central dynamo in the baggage car. And the cars were warmed by steam heat from the locomotive rather than sooty coal stoves. What better way to promote the railroad's freight business than to whisk bankers, businessmen, and stock growers between the two powerhouses of Kansas City and Chicago in thirteen hours and forty-five minutes of comfort?

Clearly, the old depot of the Chicago and St. Louis in Chicago's southern suburbs wouldn't do, so Strong spent millions of dollars to gain access to downtown Chicago. The railroad's passenger terminal was soon ensconced in Dearborn Station. Completed in 1885, Dearborn Station was operated by the Chicago and Western Indiana Railroad, essentially a cooperative providing five railroads, including the Wabash Railway, with Chicago access. The Santa Fe built its own tracks almost to the station and became the sixth member of the consortium.

But the Santa Fe would come to dominate the scene. Chicago's Dearborn Station, with its landmark clock tower and stable of crack Santa Fe passenger trains gathered around it, would come to symbolize both the Santa Fe's transcontinental reach and its reliable dominance.

Within three years, the other major chapter of the Santa Fe's eastern expansion would be written when the railroad finally acquired its struggling partner in the Atlantic and Pacific, the St. Louis and San Francisco Railway. The Frisco acquisition added 1,442 miles of track to the Santa Fe system, mostly in Kansas, Missouri, and Arkansas, but more important, it gave the Santa Fe independent access to St. Louis. The road's major presence in the three Midwest centers of America's railroad might—Kansas City, Chicago, and St. Louis—would serve the Santa Fe well as it completed its drive to the Pacific.[5]

. . .

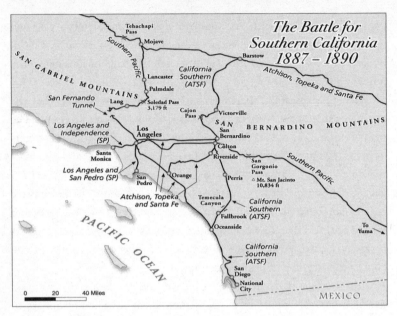

Even as the Atchison, Topeka and Santa Fe secured its own line to Chicago, reaching the Pacific and knocking down the Southern Pacific's iron fence around California remained paramount to the railroad's long-term strategy. As a result, the town of Los Angeles would be quiet no more. For its part, San Diego would fuss and never completely forgive the Santa Fe for seeming to abandon it.

The first shoe to drop for San Diegans was the news that William Barstow Strong and the Santa Fe had come to terms with Collis Huntington to operate over the Southern Pacific's tracks between Colton and Los Angeles. Much as he had done with the sale of the Southern Pacific's Mojave-to-Needles leg, Huntington hoped that by granting the Santa Fe access to Los Angeles, he might forestall its construction of parallel lines and further dissuade the road from building to the Southern Pacific's jugular at San Francisco and Oakland.

But Huntington had opened his door to California a crack at Needles, and Strong pushed it open farther and farther with every opportunity—the line to Mojave, the alliance with the California Southern over Cajon Pass, and the Southern Pacific trackage rights into Los Angeles. Now Strong wanted the California door flung wide open.

It was soon reported that the Santa Fe was aggressively courting San Bernardino and promising to move the railroad's maintenance shops there from San Diego. The Santa Fe offered $200,000 in capital improvements for a new depot, machine shops, and yard improvements if many of the same San Bernardino town fathers who had once hurried to San Diego to support the California Southern would donate an additional eighteen acres surrounding the existing depot site. When this form of persuasion was agreed to, the Santa Fe announced that San Bernardino would also become a division point.

To most knowledgeable observers, "division point" bespoke the obvious. For San Diegans, it was the final evidence that their dreams of a transcontinental terminus were to be divided—and less than equitably at that—with their northern competitor. The best that San Diego got from the deal was a promise from the Santa Fe to continue wharf improvements on San Diego Bay and to reduce some of the heavy grades on the California Southern between the city and Del Mar to facilitate cheaper and faster operations northward.[6]

Next came a battle over freight rates. Once again, Huntington—more because he was preoccupied with the eastern end of his transcontinental system and less because of any newfound generosity—appeared to extend an olive branch to the Santa Fe. Huntington had long been at the heart of various traffic pooling cartels. In 1885 he was instrumental in creating yet another, the Pacific Coast Association, which was to divide business between Chicago and St. Louis and the West Coast. While seven railroads, including the Santa Fe, were in the pool, the majority of transcontinental traffic went to the Southern Pacific.

Smaller roads, such as the Chicago, Burlington and Quincy and the Denver and Rio Grande, tried unsuccessfully to collect balances due them from the Southern Pacific under the pool's proportions and threatened withdrawal if they were not paid. But Strong and the Santa Fe—already sniffing about for an independent entry into Los Angeles—demanded past due balances *and* an increase in traffic share.

After a cantankerous February 1886 meeting in New York City, Huntington's representatives professed that they had done all they could "to keep peace, and even agreed to give the Atchison some of our earnings for the sake of peace, but it wanted more than it had earned or could earn." As Huntington's combative juices flowed, he huffed, "We have done all we propose to do, and I guess the Atchison will get tired of it before we are through." Meanwhile, the Southern Pacific continued to handle 70 percent to 75 percent of the east-west traffic.[7]

In response, Strong's biggest weapon against Huntington was the same strategy he was pursuing in the East by building an independent line into Chicago. Shrewdly, Strong looked for an opportunity to do the same into Los Angeles. It wasn't long before he found the perfect acquisition.

The Los Angeles and San Gabriel Valley Railroad was originally chartered in 1883 as a narrow gauge. It laid standard gauge rails instead, however, and eventually ran a line northeast to Pasadena, arriving there on September 11, 1885. Banking on developing agricultural markets, the Los Angeles and San Gabriel then continued eastward to Duarte for a total length of 31 miles.

None of this was particularly easy. Only begrudgingly did the Los Angeles city council grant the road a right-of-way into downtown, and the Southern Pacific extorted exorbitant freight rates to transport the new road's rails, locomotives, and equipment to its railhead. But the Los Angeles and San Gabriel's president was J. F. Crank, one of Southern California's earliest promoters and most determined businessmen.

Early in January 1887, Crank went east to New York in search of expansion capital. Scarcely had he arrived in New York City when Crank received an urgent invitation to visit Washington, DC, from Leland Stanford, who was then representing both the state of California and the greater Southern Pacific interests as a United States senator. Almost simultaneously, Crank received a similar invitation from William Barstow Strong to come to Boston and meet with the Santa Fe's board of directors. Crank was too prescient a businessman to doubt the topic both men wanted to discuss. The little Los Angeles and San Gabriel Valley Railroad was suddenly a pawn in a contest between two giants.

Having felt the heavy hand of the Southern Pacific in California firsthand, Crank eagerly accepted Strong's invitation and took the next train for Boston. His railroad's decision to build to standard gauge was about to pay huge dividends. Within an hour of meeting, Crank and Strong agreed to a "bargain" price for the short line. The exact dollars involved have not been documented, but whatever the amount, Strong was never afraid to spend money for strategic purposes. Crank's little road was a thriving business in its own right—an 1886 net profit of $46,381 on gross income of $95,318—but most important to Strong, its railhead at Duarte was just 40 miles west of San Bernardino, where the Santa Fe tracks emerged from Cajon Pass.

Strong immediately put construction crews to work to close the gap between San Bernardino and Duarte. Clearly showing that it had been planning ahead, the Santa Fe already owned the right-of-way for a telegraph line between the two towns that helped to speed construction. Less than five months later, on May 31, 1887, Los Angeles welcomed the first Santa Fe train to arrive in town over its own independent tracks. The result was a rate war with the Southern Pacific, the intensity of which even Huntington could not have predicted.[8]

The Southern Pacific's arrival in Los Angeles in 1876 had been welcome, but it did not unleash a huge Southern California boom. The population of Los Angeles took the decade from 1870 to 1880 merely to double to 11,183. During the same period, Denver mushroomed from 4,759 to 35,500, and San Francisco grew from 149,473 to 233,950.

Certainly there was no shortage of prospective settlers. Between 1860 and 1890, the population of the United States doubled from 31.5 million to 63 million people. One-third of the increase was fueled by immigration—mostly from European countries. The lack of immigrants to Southern California and its slow population growth stemmed in part from the cost of getting there. For starters, Huntington's Southern Pacific was not offering any cut-rate deals. Chicago to Los Angeles fares averaged about $130 in the early years—equivalent to about $3,000 in 2008.

Immigrants were lured first to the farm belt of the Midwest and later to the Pacific Northwest and even northern California. In some cases, the *Los Angeles Herald* was probably correct when it bemoaned that would-be newcomers "say they can purchase homes [elsewhere] for what it would cost them to get here."

There was also the issue of familiarity. European immigrants and East Coast transplants accustomed to winter weather, forested hills, and abundant water had to be sold on the potential of a different landscape.

"It seems almost impossible, by the exercise of any human powers of description," one Southern Pacific agent observed in 1884, "to bring them [potential immigrants] to a realization of the greater personal comfort, afforded by your equable and salubrious climate, and the additional productiveness and value that climate imparts to the soil on which it rests."[9]

But promoters kept singing the praises of warm weather and sunny skies, and after the Santa Fe arrived on the scene to give some rate competition, a new wave of visitors began to ride the rails into Southern California. Most weren't coming to stay, but they were the advance guard of a growing group of winter visitors. "Like birds of passage," one resident observed, "the whole flock took wing as soon as the almanac announced that spring had come, leaving only a few to conclude to settle."

Then in the spring of 1886, with the Santa Fe line complete over Cajon Pass, this seasonal exodus was balanced by a steady flow of incoming settlers throughout the summer. Once the Southern Pacific and the Santa Fe went to war over rates the following winter, the dam burst wide open.

At least one version of the "California for a dollar" story tells of a wild seesaw battle raging back and forth between the rate departments of the two railroads. First the Southern Pacific lowered its first-class ticket to $100. The Santa Fe announced fares for less than $100. As the price for fares between Chicago and California plummeted, each road shaved a few more dollars. Supposedly, on the morning of March 6, 1887, a furious exchange of telegrams found the Santa Fe down to $8 per ticket, to which the Southern Pacific responded with $6. By that afternoon, there were reports of rates as low as $1 per head.

Railroad accountants quickly brought their respective marketing departments to their economic senses. Fares promptly rebounded to $50 for first-class and $40 for second-class tickets, but the publicity accompanying the cry of $1 tickets to California had been heard. No more would the Midwest farmer, the newly arrived European immigrant, or the vacationer looking for a warmer climate think that they could not afford a passage westward.[10]

The result was that by the summer of 1887, the Southern Pacific and Santa Fe lines were both awash with huge numbers of passengers heading to California—many of whom put down roots and stayed. The flood of newcomers hurrying across the continent was reminiscent of the rush of the forty-niners. Only this time, instead of plodding along behind covered wagons pulled by oxen, these argonauts tossed their belongings into a freight car and rode across the country at twenty-five miles an hour in the comparative splendor of an immigrant-class coach.

Real estate prices in Southern California skyrocketed. Within a year, property transfers "increased from 6,000 to 14,000 and from $10 million to $28 million" in 1886 and then in 1887 reached 33,000 and $95 million. This boom would suffer a temporary bust two years later, but that would not stem the long-term trend. By 1890, the population of Los Angeles had quadrupled to more than 50,000 and a Santa Fe vice president predicted, "people will continue to come here until the whole country becomes one of the most densely populated sections of the United States."[11]

Seizing upon this boom, the Santa Fe was not content merely to terminate in downtown Los Angeles. Strong undertook just the sort of local network expansion that Huntington had feared. Separate companies built these lines, but they had one thing in common: They all answered to the dictates of the Santa Fe.

Under the moniker of the San Bernardino and San Diego Railroad, the Santa Fe built a second independent line from San Bernardino into Los Angeles via the town of Riverside and Orange County. Running through the gap between the Chino Hills and the Santa Ana Mountains, this 70-mile leg opened in August 1888.

That same year, what came to be called "the Surf Line" was extended south along the coast to Oceanside and Del Mar and on into San Diego. This was part of the Santa Fe's plan to mollify San Diegans, but more important to the railroad's operations, this leg bypassed the original California Southern route through flood-prone Temecula Canyon. The town of Temecula withered as a result, and when another flood swept down the Santa Margarita in 1891, the original California Southern tracks were not rebuilt.

The Santa Fe also reached out from downtown Los Angeles to the coast. Branch lines were built south to Redondo Beach to gain access to a harbor and west to Santa Monica to compete with the Southern Pacific's ownership of Senator Jones's original Los Angeles and Independence. Both of these lines quickly became popular tourist routes to serve the developing ocean-side resorts, and their success was a portent of what the overall tourist trade would soon become to the Santa Fe.

Having reached Los Angeles and broken down the Southern Pacific's fence around California, the Atchison, Topeka and Santa Fe was poised for the next chapter of its expansion. To be sure, there would be some rough spots in the tracks up ahead, but the proven leadership of Thomas Nickerson and William Barstow Strong had laid a solid financial and geographic foundation that would serve it well come what may.

In the last annual report he authored for the company, that of 1888, Strong wrote: "The history of Western railroad construction for the past quarter of a century has demonstrated that successful results can only be attained by occupying territory promptly, and often in advance of actual business necessity. This was the policy of the Atchison Company from the first," Strong insisted. "It led the way. It built, not upon assured returns of profit, but upon a faith which time has abundantly vindicated—that the great Western and South-western regions of the country were rich in possibilities and that the company which first occupied the territory would reap the first and greatest rewards."[12]

At the end of 1888, the Atchison, Topeka and Santa Fe owned, operated, or controlled 7,706 miles of railroad—much of it in first-class condition. The little railroad that first steamed out of Topeka had become a corporate powerhouse in America's transcontinental sweepstakes. About the only thing that hadn't changed since it laid its first rails in 1869 was that Cyrus K. Holliday was still on its board of directors. "Santa Fe," Holliday had once rhapsodized, dreaming of a destination. Soon that dream would become the reality of "Santa Fe all the way."

Inaugurated in 1892, the California Limited became the first of the Santa Fe's crack passenger trains between Chicago and Los Angeles; here engine no. 53, a 4-6-0 ten-wheeler, waits with its consist at La Grande Station in Los Angeles. *(Colorado Historical Society, scan 20104180, W. H. Jackson Collection)*

Part Three

—◆—

Santa Fe All the Way

(1889–1909)

An American cowboy is coming east on a special train faster than any cowpuncher ever rode before; how much shall I break the transcontinental record?

—WALTER "DEATH VALLEY SCOTTY" SCOTT TO
PRESIDENT THEODORE ROOSEVELT, 1905

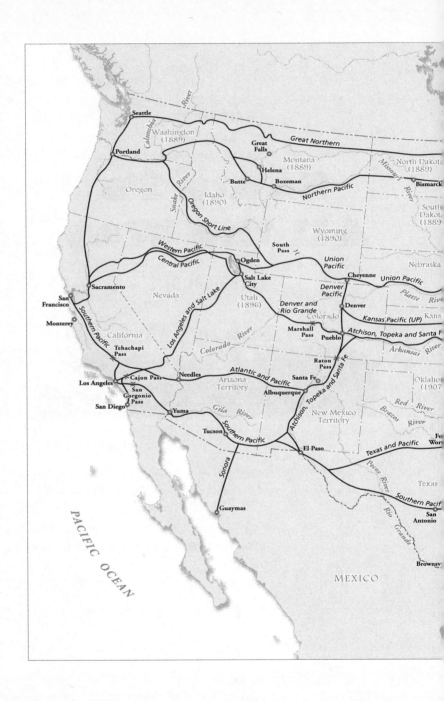

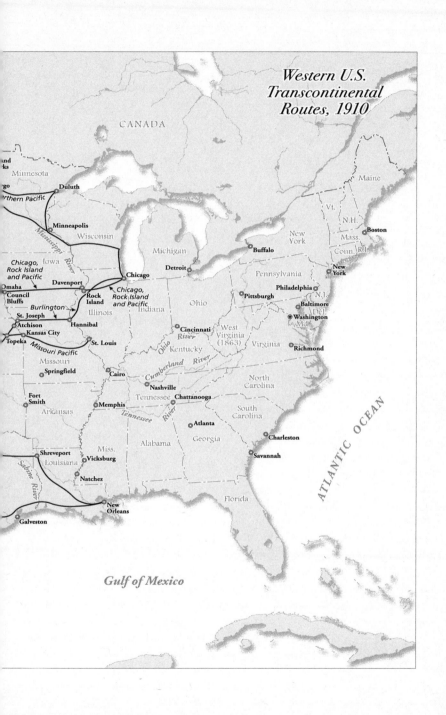

Western U.S. Transcontinental Routes, 1910

CANADA

Minnesota

and
ks

Duluth

go

rthern Pacific

Mississippi River

Minneapolis

Wisconsin

Michigan

Iowa

Chicago,
Rock Island
and Pacific

Omaha

Davenport

Chicago

Detroit

Buffalo

New
York

Maine

Vt.

N.H.

Mass.

Conn. R.I.

Boston

Council
Bluffs

Burlington

St. Joseph

Atchison

Kansas City

Topeka

Missouri Pacific

Rock
Island

Chicago,
Rock Island
and Pacific

Hannibal

Illinois

Indiana

St. Louis

Ohio

Ohio River

Cincinnati
River

West
Virginia
(1863)

Kentucky

Pittsburgh

Philadelphia

N.J.

Washington
Md.

Del.

Baltimore

New
York

Pennsylvania

Virginia

Richmond

Missouri

Springfield

Cairo

Cumberland River

Nashville

Fort
Smith

Arkansas

Memphis

Tennessee River

Chattanooga

Tennessee

North
Carolina

South
Carolina

Atlanta

Alabama

Georgia

Charleston

Shreveport

Sabine River

Louisiana

Vicksburg

Miss.

Natchez

Savannah

ATLANTIC OCEAN

New
Orleans

Florida

Galveston

Gulf of Mexico

18

Making the Markets

The southwestern railroads flung their tracks across generally wide-open spaces. Land grant sales in Kansas, mining revenues from Colorado, and transcontinental traffic across Arizona and New Mexico helped to pay some of the bills, but in many cases the railroads had to make their own markets. It was rarely easy.

When Frisco president Edward Winslow expressed interest in buying a 50,000-acre ranch out of the Atlantic and Pacific land grant in northern Arizona in an effort to spur land sales, Winslow's wife and some friends made an inspection tour. A bumpy wagon ride across stark terrain and a sudden storm were enough to elicit a spousal veto. "Her impressions of the country," the railroad's land agent reported, "are not highly favorable."[1]

But there were others who looked at the landscape with a different eye. William Jackson Palmer had pushed the merits of Colorado's climate and scenery since his first love letters to Queen before the founding of Colorado Springs. After the Rio Grande reached Ogden, tourism through the mountains of Colorado became big business on the narrow gauge road. The awesome scenery of the Royal Gorge, Marshall Pass, and the Black Canyon of the Gunnison prompted the Rio Grande to adopt the marketing slogan "Scenic Line of America."

But why stop there? In 1884 Shadrach K. Hooper, general passenger and ticket agent of the Rio Grande, went one step further and changed the slogan to read "Scenic Line of the World," taking as its symbol the spire of Curecanti Needle in the depths of the Black Canyon. Advertisements made it clear that whether one was traveling "for business" or "for health and pleasure," the mountain scenery "of this line is unequaled in variety and grandeur by that of any other railway on either hemisphere. . . ."[2]

But the Denver and Rio Grande did not have a monopoly on scenery. Jay Gould's attempt to build straight west from Denver had not been successful, but that did not keep hordes of sightseers from flocking to the Georgetown Loop. Scarcely had Robert Brewster Stanton ensured its proper completion when famed western photographer William Henry Jackson arrived on the scene in a private car provided by the railroad. Jackson staged four trains at various locations around the loop and produced a promotional series of photographs for the Union Pacific.

Excursions westward from Denver around the loop and to the end of track at Graymont became a staple for many Colorado visitors. The story is told that when one sophisticated Victorian lady apologized to her Denver hostess for arriving in a sooty condition after just such an excursion, the hostess brushed off her guest's embarrassment by assuring her, "Never mind, my dear. We have all been around the Loop."[3]

And although it was comparatively short lived, the Denver, South Park and Pacific, along with its Union Pacific–controlled successors, also had a star attraction in the Alpine Tunnel. Not only did the line traverse "some of the finest scenery on the continent," but also the South Park could boast that it crossed the "highest point reached by rail in North America." One Union Pacific brochure from 1886 told of its glories: "It is something to know that the world cannot duplicate this ride—this audacity of engineering; man has always before stopped short of this extreme."[4]

The Atchison, Topeka and Santa Fe approached its marketing slightly differently. In time, the railroad would come to promote the grandeur of the Grand Canyon, the glories of sunsets setting the desert sky ablaze, and a close affinity to the historical cultures of the Southwest. But from the beginning—and overriding all these later themes—the Santa Fe focused on access and speed.

Within three years of the Santa Fe's arrival at Deming in 1881, its advertisements were boasting of "Three Lines to the Pacific." First and foremost, according to the Santa Fe, was its "Great Needles Route" via Albuquerque, over the Atlantic and Pacific to Needles, and the Southern Pacific on to San Francisco. The second route—again at the mercy of the Southern Pacific—was "the Los Angeles Route" west from Deming to the rider's choice of Los Angeles, San Diego, or San Francisco. Finally, the third route touted connections from the Santa Fe spur at Pueblo, over the Denver and Rio Grande to Ogden, and westward on the Central Pacific to San Francisco.[5]

By the end of the 1880s, the Santa Fe's aggressive expansion had rid itself of much of its reliance on the Southern Pacific, to say nothing of reaching Chicago's Dearborn Station. With independent control of its own roadbed from Chicago all the way to Los Angeles came not only an ability to promote transcontinental access but also ever-greater speed.

In September 1889, William Barstow Strong, who had been the mainstay of the Santa Fe's expansion for a decade, was forced to resign the railroad's presidency. Strong was a casualty of an increasingly bitter power struggle between the road's old-line Boston crowd and a new group of financiers centered in New York City. The conflict was a prelude to a period of financial unrest, but Strong's successor, Allen Manvel, was to make one lasting contribution to the road.

A native New Yorker who came to the Santa Fe with more than thirty years in railroading, Manvel decreed that something significant had to be done to herald the completion of the Santa Fe's Chicago–Los Angeles main line. The result was the California Limited, a passenger train that would operate between these two cornerstones of the American economy for more than a half century.

Manvel instructed his equipment managers to special order five first-class all-Pullman trains. Each consisted of six cars: (1) a combination baggage, club, and parlor car; (2) a dining car; (3) a through compartment car to Los Angeles; (4) a Chicago–San Francisco compartment and drawing-room sleeper car; (5) a Chicago–San Diego compartment and drawing-room sleeper; and (6) a combination sleeper and observation car with a small parlor and a covered observation platform at the rear of the train. (The San Francisco and San Diego cars were switched onto other trains at Mojave and Los Angeles, respectively, and sent on to their destinations without disturbing their occupants.)

The first westbound California Limited departed Dearborn Station at nine-thirty on the night of November 27, 1892. Designated train no. 3, by the next afternoon it was in Kansas City. Then westward the train roared across Kansas, eastern Colorado, and the grades of Raton Pass. By the evening of day two, the Limited was beyond Albuquerque and crossing the Colorado River at Needles. By nine in the morning on the third day, the train pulled into the station in downtown Los Angeles, after 2,265 miles and two and one-half days en route.

Sister trains were soon running in both directions on what was commonly advertised as the fastest service between the two cities. Over the years, the equipment and motive power of the California Limited changed with the times, and eventually it was relegated to second-class status by more glamorous successors, but at its inception and for years thereafter, the California Limited set the standard for transcontinental travel.[6]

In the race for transcontinental dominance, the Atchison, Topeka and Santa Fe was to have one not-so-secret weapon that had nothing to do with land grants, fast trains, low fares, or scenery. Well, maybe a different kind of scenery on a male-dominated frontier.

Early western railroad food was very grim pickings. The choices were few, the freshness of the serving never in doubt—it simply wasn't—and the sanitary conditions decidedly suspect. In the business of getting from one place to another, food, it seemed, was an afterthought.

Passengers poured off a train as it wheezed to a stop at a food station and then swarmed around a so-called lunch counter, frequently competing with an even larger swarm of flies. Those who managed to find a seat and attempt civil dining were routinely interrupted midway through the fare by a whistle signaling an imminent departure.

Another option was to procure a box lunch from the station or a sandwich from the "butcher boy" who roamed the cars. On tepid summer afternoons on the plains of Kansas, these were best consumed straight off the hoof or not at all. Egg salad was definitely not recommended. Even the Santa Fe's employee lunchroom in the main depot at Topeka was to be avoided.

All this began to change in 1876, when an impeccably dressed man called on the local Santa Fe manager in Topeka and expressed interest in leasing the Topeka depot's lunch counter. His name was Frederick Henry Harvey. Born in London in 1835, Harvey immigrated to the United States at the age of fifteen and found his first job as a busboy in a New York City café. He soon left for greater rewards and eventually became the western freight agent for the Chicago, Burlington and Quincy.

Harvey's work for the Burlington required extensive travel, and he was forced to endure the physical as well as the gastronomic discomforts of the road. After those experiences, he was only too happy to return home to his wife and growing brood of children, where he always found a safe haven of good cooking and a clean bed.

In 1875 Harvey made his first attempt to refine traveling conditions. He formed a partnership to operate restaurants on the Kansas Pacific at the division points of Wallace, Kansas, and Hugo, Colorado. But Harvey's absences working for the Burlington and a disagreement with his partner over the appropriate standards to be maintained soon terminated the venture. Harvey suggested his idea of standards to the Burlington, but its managers weren't interested. Food simply was not deemed important to selling railroad tickets.

So Fred Harvey went to the Santa Fe with the same idea: a clean eating space, prompt and courteous service, reliably good food, and a reasonable price. How could one go wrong? The Santa Fe agreed. Soon the Topeka operation was booming, and early in 1878, Harvey opened his second restaurant and some adjacent sleeping rooms at Florence, Kansas. Thereafter, he resigned his job with the Burlington and became a full-time restaurateur, opening a third restaurant in Lakin, Kansas, near the Colorado border, in 1879. After that, the westward march of Fred Harvey establishments was almost as steady as the advance of the Santa Fe's rails.

The Fred Harvey–Santa Fe partnership proved unique. Done in the early years on the basis of a handshake, the agreements usually gave the railroad the responsibility for real estate and capital improvements, while Harvey was responsible for furnishings and kitchen equipment.

The railroad also proved accommodating in transporting produce, dairy items, and fresh meat to Harvey facilities along the line, as well as providing coal, ice, and water.

These early operations were housed in relatively crude buildings, but they all promised and delivered the same high quality of food and service. Among the Fred Harvey innovations that a tired and hungry traveler could count on were fresh-baked pies cut into four—not six—pieces; spring water for coffee hauled in by tank car, not pumped from alkali-laden wells; and farm-fresh produce shipped by rail or purchased directly from local farmers.

Seeing the impact that Fred Harvey's operations had on its passengers—not to mention its train crews, who also flocked to eat there—the Santa Fe quickly decided that well-fed passengers made for happy passengers, and happy passengers were good for business. There was an affinity between food and railroads after all. So Fred Harvey and the Santa Fe worked together to bring food service to a new level of efficiency.

Conductors went through the coaches prior to a food stop and asked how many passengers planned to visit the lunch counter or the dining room. The tally was telegraphed ahead, so that when the train stopped, everything was ready. And Harvey's prompt service meant no more wolfing down half a steak as one's train started to roll out of the station. With prior planning and civil service, a twenty-minute food stop could seem like a far longer respite from the clanging and swaying of the coaches.

One anecdote says much about the special standards that Fred Harvey demanded. While conducting an inspection of one of his kitchens, Harvey heard a commotion in the dining room. He immediately asked what the problem was, and the steward replied, "Oh, that man is an out-and-out crank. No one can please him." Of the first point, Harvey readily agreed. "Of course he is a crank," but, Harvey went on, "we must please him. It is our business to please cranks, for anyone can please a gentleman."[7]

So popular did Harvey Houses become that for a short time Harvey tried to limit service to railroad travelers and not serve locals. Recognizing a good thing, locals rebelled, and Harvey Houses went on to become the social and cultural center of some of these small towns. Then, of course, there were the Harvey girls.

In the early years of the Santa Fe's expansion across Kansas, there was a saying that there were "no ladies west of Dodge City; no women west of Albuquerque." Fred Harvey changed that and saw to it that in an era when the morals of single women on the frontier were immediately suspect, his Harvey girls were all respectable ladies.

They came from varied, lower- to middle-class backgrounds, some escaping factory jobs, others leaving the farm, more than a few seeking adventure as much as a regular paycheck. What they found was Fred Harvey's rigid code of recruitment, training, dress, and living arrangements.

All prospective Harvey girls were carefully recruited and indoctrinated into the Fred Harvey way of doing things. They wore simple but immaculate uniforms of black and white, the predominance of the color indicating whether they worked the lunch counter or the more refined dining room. Living arrangements were in Harvey-run dormitories, two girls to a room, under the watchful eye of a housemother or chaperone. Heaven help the Harvey girl who was caught sneaking back into her room after curfew.

In truth, twelve- or fourteen-hour shifts were not uncommon, and as one trainload of passengers disappeared down the tracks, there was plenty to do in preparation for the next load. As one Harvey girl reminisced, "We didn't have *time* to do all the bad things people claimed we were doing!"

But in a West where the male-to-female ratio was still heavily tilted toward the former, Harvey girls frequently were accorded celebrity status. Many a cowboy, railroader, or traveling salesman professed his love for his waitress somewhere between his first cup of coffee and dessert. Some Harvey girls rose in the ranks and worked for the company for decades. Others served their initial six- or nine-month contract and accepted one of these proposals.

Sometimes it seemed as if Fred Harvey was in the matrimony business as much as food service. Many Harvey girls married locals and became a part of growing communities from Hutchison to Santa Fe to Barstow. By one account, "they used to say that the Harvey employment agent guaranteed the girls a fireman on a six-months' contract, or an engineer on a one-year contract."[8]

Two other Harvey institutions bear notice. The first was the coat rule. Fred Harvey carried his penchant for civility and proper form to a dress code for his patrons. All were welcome at the lunch counter no matter their attire, but in the dining room, gentlemen were required to wear a jacket at all times. Sensitive to his frontier customers, however, Harvey graciously provided an ample selection of dark alpaca coats that one could borrow and don for the occasion. Few, if any, gentlemen objected, and that little touch of class elevated the Harvey dining experience all the more. It became part of why it was so often said that Fred Harvey civilized the West.

Another Harvey institution was the cup code. As customers were seated, a waitress would ensure that the first course of fruit or salad was on the table or served immediately and then would take drink orders, arranging the patron's cup so that the drink server would know immediately what to pour. There were variations over the years, but "a cup turned upside down meant hot tea; a cup right side up in the saucer meant coffee; upside down and tilted against the saucer, iced tea; upside down and away from the saucer, milk." The cup code was another example of Fred Harvey's ever-efficient system.[9]

The Fred Harvey–Santa Fe partnership was so successful that the railroad did not begin dining car operations on its trains until the completion of its Kansas City-to-Chicago leg in 1888. Even then, there were no dining cars west of Kansas City until the California Limited began service in 1892. And, of course, Fred Harvey operated those dining cars, and "Meals by Fred Harvey" became an important part of the Santa Fe's advertising slogans.

By the time that the Santa Fe completed its full reach from Chicago to Los Angeles, the Harvey system of restaurants had evolved to include a growing number of adjacent lodging facilities. These were a far cry from the rudimentary beds Harvey first installed at Florence, Kansas, in 1878. Harvey Houses opened in Las Vegas, New Mexico, in 1882; Newton and Hutchison, Kansas, La Junta, Colorado, and Lamy and Albuquerque, New Mexico, in 1883; and Winslow and Williams, Arizona, and Needles and Barstow, California, in 1887. In later years, many of these facilities would be replaced by grander destination structures, such as Albuquerque's Alvarado, Barstow's Casa del Desierto, and Winslow's La Posada.

No matter what the competition, Fred Harvey gave the Santa Fe a leg up by serving scrumptious, reliable meals at reasonable prices and, along the way, creating the western legend of Harvey girls. It was no wonder that the veteran observer of Americana, William Allen White of Emporia, Kansas, wryly noted that Fred Harvey "had more friends west of the Mississippi than William McKinley."[10]

Fortified by Fred Harvey meals, the Santa Fe's growing reputation for speed and efficiency was further enhanced when the railroad whisked a young reporter named Nellie Bly from San Francisco to Chicago in a breathtaking sixty-nine hours. Bly's excursion was not the most famous high-speed run on the Santa Fe, but it was a good indication of things to come.

Born Elizabeth Jane Cochran, Nellie Bly acquired her pseudonym when she went to work for the *Pittsburgh Dispatch* in 1885 at the age of twenty-one. A no-nonsense series on working girls gained her local notoriety, but one day in the spring of 1887, Bly failed to show up for work, leaving only a cursory note: "I am off for New York. Look out for me."

New York City was awash with newspapers, but Bly decided that she wanted to work for the *New York World,* a rising star that Joseph Pulitzer had recently purchased from among the business holdings of Jay Gould. Her first major series was an exposé on New York's insane asylums, for which Bly posed as unbalanced and had herself committed. Afterward, Bly attracted ever-increasing national attention as she combined her role as a serious investigative reporter with newspaper-selling publicity stunts.

By Nellie's account, she came up with the idea to better the round-the-world record of Jules Verne's fiction. In the fifteen years since the publication of *Around the World in Eighty Days,* no one had tried to equal let alone beat the mark established by the fictitious Phineas Fogg. At first Bly's editors brushed off the suggestion—at least as to her role in it. A single female traveling alone would, after all, require a chaperone.

When told that the *World* might send a man on the assignment instead, Bly's reply was short and to the point. "Start the man," she retorted, "and I'll start the same day for some other newspaper and beat him." By then, her reputation was such that her editors had no doubt that she would do just that. The *World* momentarily backed off the project, but when competitors threatened to do the stunt, Bly was hastily summoned and told to be ready to depart in just four days.

At 9:40 a.m. on the morning of Thursday, November 14, 1889, Nellie Bly—traveling solo but hardly as an innocent—departed the Hoboken, New Jersey, pier on board the steamer *Augusta Victoria,* and the clock began to tick. Seasickness proved an immediate challenge, but Nellie had plenty of time to get over it.

Bly's route took her from New York to London, then France, Italy, Egypt, and Ceylon. The *World* made the most of her journey and ran a guessing game for its readers to submit predictions of the exact time down to the second that it would take her to circumnavigate the globe. Among the prizes was a trip to Europe.

Meanwhile, Bly fretted about her delayed departure from Ceylon and eventually reached Singapore and Hong Kong. On January 7, 1890, fifty-five days into her journey, she sailed eastward from Yokohama, Japan, on board the *Oceanic.* When storms slowed her progress, the captain rang up for more steam, and an obliging engineer scrawled a new motto on the ship's turbines: "For Nellie Bly, we'll win or die. January 20, 1890."

As the *Oceanic* neared the West Coast, the *World* dispatched a team of publicists, advertising agents, and general-purpose promoters to blanket her proposed route across the United States and sing the praises of Nellie Bly and the *New York World.* "On the line out to this point," reported one contingent from a snowy Ogden, Utah, "the name of *The World*'s globe-girdler is as familiar as President Harrison's and more familiar than the names of many of his Cabinet."

By now, Nellie had more competition than the clock. John Brisben Walker's *Cosmopolitan* magazine had put a rival in the field and sent its star reporter, Elizabeth Bisland, westward at the same time as Nellie sailed east. Nellie was blissfully ignorant of this competition for most of her journey, but now it seemed as if the race to New York from opposite ends of the globe would be quite close.

Nellie's arrival in San Francisco with Miss Bisland's exact whereabouts unknown argued for a quick transcontinental run due east on the Central Pacific and then across the plains on the Union Pacific. But snow in Ogden was just part of the problem. Record snowfalls in the Sierras had recently dumped foot upon foot of new snow and stalled trains for more than fifty hours. After covering 21,000 miles in sixty-eight days, it appeared that Nellie Bly's final 3,000 miles across the good old USA might jeopardize her record pace.

With proponents of the southern transcontinental routes no doubt chortling over their morning coffee, the *World* avoided the Central Pacific–Union Pacific route. Instead Nellie Bly boarded a special train that was soon speeding south on Southern Pacific tracks bound for Mojave and the western terminus of the Santa Fe's Atlantic and Pacific leg. For once, the Southern Pacific and the Santa Fe appeared to cooperate fully. (The last thing Collis P. Huntington wanted at this point was a hail of criticism that somehow America's favorite traveler was stuck in a snowdrift or rerouted to Deming.)

From Mojave, the Bly special sped eastward through the California desert, across the Colorado River at Needles, and past Flagstaff and the San Francisco Peaks. If one report is true, Bly's train roared across a bridge that was under repair near Gallup without slowing. The startled workmen heard the train coming, but at fifty miles an hour, there was no time to flag it down.

Between Albuquerque and Kansas City, even though it was forced to climb Raton Pass, Nellie's train established a speed record of forty-six miles an hour for the 918 miles. Almost two thousand people waited to see her as she passed through Topeka. Next came the perfect test for the speedway that A. A. Robinson had recently built between Kansas City and Chicago.

Reaching Dearborn Station, Bly was feted by the Chicago Press Club at an early morning reception before she made the transfer to the tracks of the Pennsylvania Railroad for the run into New York. The following afternoon, Saturday, January 25, 1890, Nellie Bly stepped off the train in Jersey City, having circled the globe in 72 days, 6 hours, 11 minutes, and 14 seconds, at an average speed of 22.47 miles per hour.[11]

Nellie Bly's fame was secure, but she would never again be quite the celebrity that she was during the last few days of her cross-country sprint. As for the Atchison, Topeka and Santa Fe, its role in Nellie's blitz was just a small indication of things to come. Whatever else can be said of Nellie Bly's adventure, this much was certain: The world was getting smaller, and the Santa Fe's developing southern transcontinental speedway had a hand in it.

19

---◆---

Canyon Dreams
and Schemes

The blank spots on the map of the West were filling up. In 1889, as the Santa Fe was preparing to whisk Nellie Bly across the continent, the Denver and Rio Grande pushed its Tennessee Pass line westward down the Colorado River to Rifle, Colorado. Save for a link through the San Luis Valley built the following year, this 27-mile extension was the last narrow gauge construction the Denver and Rio Grande undertook on a main line. The remaining 62 miles between Rifle and the railroad's existing narrow gauge tracks at Grand Junction were laid as standard gauge in 1890.

That same year, the Denver and Rio Grande added a third rail to its line from Salida, Colorado, to Leadville and converted the remainder of its track from Leadville over Tennessee Pass to Rifle to standard gauge. The result by November 1890 was that Grand Junction was served by both the Rio Grande's original narrow gauge line over Marshall Pass and its new standard gauge line over Tennessee Pass. West of Grand Junction, William Jackson Palmer's Rio Grande Western was making a similar conversion to standard gauge all the way to Ogden. The dream of a line straight west from Denver still had not been achieved, but Colorado was not yet out of the transcontinental contest.[1]

All this railroad attention directed toward Grand Junction was enough to give certain people pause. Admittedly, the logical gateways through the Rockies and across the Colorado Plateau were bustling with tracks, but there was one major passage to which little attention had yet been paid.

Early in 1889, a real estate speculator named Frank M. Brown fixed on a dream to build a railroad along the snow-free water grade of the Colorado River all the way to California—through the Grand Canyon. Such a line would be a pipeline between the immense coal deposits on Colorado's Western Slope and energy-starved Southern California, which in the days before hydroelectric power and oil and natural gas production was importing coal from as far away as Australia and British Columbia. For additional revenue, the route's scenery was apt to rival if not surpass the Denver and Rio Grande's Scenic Line of the World. The logical starting point for such a line was Grand Junction.

On March 25, 1889, Brown and an assortment of business partners incorporated the Denver, Colorado Canyon, and Pacific Railroad Company. Brown wasted no time in hiring a mining engineer, Frank C. Kendrick, and an assistant for him, Thomas Rigney, and hurrying with them to Grand Junction by Denver and Rio Grande train. Arriving there at a quarter to four in the morning on March 28, Brown nonetheless immediately led an impromptu procession down to the banks of the Colorado River.

There Brown thrust a survey stake in the mud and for the benefit of several newspaper reporters proceeded to give Kendrick and Rigney grandiose instructions for their survey of the westward route of the Denver, Colorado Canyon, and Pacific: straight down the Colorado River through the Grand Canyon. This media event complete, Brown caught a train back east and prepared to lure investors with the news that he already had a survey crew in the field. Kendrick and Rigney loaded supplies into a fifteen-foot dory christened the *Black Betty* and pushed off downstream.

In that spring of 1889, the recorded history of the Grand Canyon was still sparse. When Lieutenant Amiel W. Whipple surveyed west from Albuquerque along the 35th parallel in 1853, he kept well south of the canyon and never considered introducing railroad tracks into its depths. William Jackson Palmer, while on his 1867 Kansas Pacific survey, speculated about bridging the gorge, but did so without any first-hand knowledge.

Some of the unknown changed in 1869. That spring Major John Wesley Powell left the Union Pacific tracks at Green River, Wyoming, and floated the Green and Colorado rivers through Flaming Gorge and the canyons of Lodore, Cataract, Glen, Marble, and the Grand. Powell returned for a second trip during 1871–72, and by the time his maps and journals were published, he had filled in one of the remaining blanks on the map of the West. The major did not, however, say anything encouraging about railroads following his route. Indeed, twenty years later, no one had.

Kendrick and Rigney floated the Colorado downstream to its confluence with the Green and then surveyed up that river to the Rio Grande Western tracks at Green River, Utah. When they reported to Brown in mid-May 1889, Brown was busy organizing the next phase of the trip. Rigney agreed to join him, but Kendrick opted out, confiding to his diary, "I have given up going back, as I think a man's place is near home and those he loves . . . even if he does not make so much money or gain as much glory." As it turned out, money and glory would both soon be in short supply.[2]

Brown led a diverse party of sixteen others back to Green River, Utah, by train. There were six surveyors, including photographer Franklin Nims; five boatmen, including Rigney; two would-be investors traveling as Brown's guests; two cooks; and the newly appointed chief engineer of the Denver, Colorado Canyon, and Pacific. This was none other than Robert Brewster Stanton, who had already proven with the Georgetown Loop that he was not one to shrink from an engineering challenge no matter how seemingly insurmountable it first appeared.

The veteran *Black Betty*—now renamed the *Brown Betty*—was joined by a flotilla of five fifteen-foot boats specially commissioned by Brown and built out of light wood with narrow beams, rounded bottoms, and

pointed bows and sterns. They all eased down the Green to its confluence with the Colorado and then poured into the boulder-strewn mill-
race of Cataract Canyon. The result was disaster.

The narrow, round-bottomed boats behaved like easily rolled kayaks,
but with open decks. The *Brown Betty* fared little better and soon
jammed under a boulder and stuck fast. Precious supplies, including
much food, were swept away, and soon survival became paramount to
surveying. Frank Brown saw his railroad dreams fading and opted to
strike downstream for the placer mining camps in Glen Canyon and
then quit the river.

Stalwart Stanton, who, like John Wesley Powell, could neither row
nor swim well because of a childhood injury to one arm, thought otherwise and resolved to stay behind with one boat and four companions to
continue the survey. Brown and the others pushed on to seek help. By
the time that Stanton's party emerged from lower Cataract Canyon and
paddled into the placid waters and cottonwood-studded beaches of
Glen Canyon, a little bit of food and talk about gold, cattle, and timber
had rekindled Brown's speculative appetite. Forget Cataract Canyon,
Brown told Stanton. His railroad could reach Glen Canyon directly
from the north and be making money from this booming paradise even
before its tracks entered the Grand Canyon.

Reinvigorated, Brown headed downriver with Stanton on the Colorado's lazy, muddy current through Glen Canyon. At Lees Ferry, Arizona, Warren Johnson, a Mormon operating the ferry there, wished
them luck without knowing just how much he was to see of Stanton in
the next year.

On July 9, 1889, three kayaklike boats splashed through the riffle at
the mouth of the Paria River just below the ferry and headed into Marble Canyon. They portaged the rapids at Badger Creek and started to do
the same at Soap Creek a few miles farther downstream. But evening
was upon them, and before the Soap Creek portage was complete, they
set up camp for the night beside its ominous roar. In the morning,
Brown and boatman Harry McDonald decided that Soap Creek rapid's
tail waves could be run without further portaging, and so they put their
boat in and pushed off.

Almost immediately Brown doubted the wisdom of the decision and
ordered McDonald to pull for shore. But as the round-bottomed boat

swung into a powerful eddy at the foot of the rapid, the opposing current rolled it over like a breaching whale. McDonald swam clear, but Brown was nowhere to be found. For all the gear he had packed, life jackets were not included. When the capsized boat was recovered 1.5 miles downstream, there was still no sign of Brown, and his body was never found.

Few would have blamed Stanton if he had simply walked out of the canyon and back to Lees Ferry, but he did not. Despite Brown's death—or perhaps because of it—Stanton was more determined than ever to complete the survey. Five days later and 14 miles deeper into Marble Canyon, the tipsy boats caused another accident. Peter Hansbrough and one of Stanton's servants rolled a boat after it was pinned against a cliff. Both drowned.

Now even Stanton had his doubts, but not, it appears, about the railroad route itself. He led the remaining men up South Canyon to Kanab, Utah, paid them off with funds borrowed from the local Mormon bishop—Brown had been carrying the expedition's cash—and then headed for Denver to plead his case with the directors of the Denver, Colorado Canyon, and Pacific.[3]

The directors were increasingly skeptical and very reluctant in their allocation of meager funds, but five months later Stanton was back on the river. After Christmas dinner at Lees Ferry with Warren Johnson and his family, his party once again floated downstream into Marble Canyon in newly built, flat-bottomed boats. Each man now wore a cork life jacket, but this time disaster struck on the canyon walls.

On New Year's Day 1890, just below the rapids that had claimed Frank Brown, Franklin Nims fell twenty feet from a rock while taking a photograph, breaking his jaw and one leg and rendering himself unconscious with a concussion. While Stanton returned to Lees Ferry to ask Warren Johnson for help, the rest of the party laboriously hauled the injured Nims up to the canyon rim. Mercifully, Nims remained unconscious for most of the bone-jarring trip.

Stanton and Johnson met them with a wagon, took Nims to the ferry, and arranged with some passing Mormons to transport him to the Santa Fe railroad station at Winslow, some 185 miles to the south. Nims arrived there on January 21, battered but miraculously alive. Later, Nims wrote bitterly that the fledgling railroad company had "cut my salary off January 1, 1890, the day of the accident" and failed to pay any of his expenses.[4]

Once again, Stanton returned to the river. Downstream from where they had cached their boats, the party came across Peter Hansbrough's remains near what is now called Hansbrough Point. It was a grisly find made recognizable only by the remaining shreds of his clothing. More trials awaited them at the mouth of the Little Colorado, where a surprise winter flood swept down the aquamarine stream and tossed their boats about like driftwood.

Whatever Stanton now thought of a railroad route through the Grand Canyon, there was evidence that other railroads were making it easier to reach the canyon. Since its completion through Arizona in 1883, the Santa Fe had accommodated prospectors and even a few tourists in reaching the South Rim from the general vicinity of Williams. Below the mouth of the Little Colorado, Stanton's party encountered a trail built by prospector Seth Tanner that dropped down from the rim near Desert View. John Hance had built a similar trail down from near Moran Point.

Soon Stanton's flotilla was in the Inner Gorge, and there was little option but to continue. The next escape was at Diamond Creek, still 127 miles ahead. In between were raging rapids, including the foaming melee of Lava Falls, which was carefully portaged. Finally, the boats pulled into the mouth of Diamond Creek with their exhausted occupants.

Could a railroad negotiate what they had just come through? Stanton was optimistic, but now what mattered most was that there was a railroad close by. A 23-mile hike up Diamond Creek and Peach Springs Canyon led to the Santa Fe stop at Peach Springs. They made the hike, replenished supplies, and—reluctant to quit—returned to the river.

Late in February 1890, they ran Separation Canyon, where Stanton was thrown from his boat for the first time. Even this dunking couldn't diminish his awe. It must have been a particularly grueling undertaking, yet Stanton wrote repeatedly of the canyon's beauties. It was, he noted, "a living, moving being, ever changing in form and color."[5]

By April 9, the surveyors were safely at Fort Mojave near Needles, feasting on roast beef. Two weeks later they reached the river's mouth on the Gulf of California. Backtracking to Yuma, Stanton hopped on the Southern Pacific and headed east. False starts and tragedies aside, in roughly a year he had accomplished a remarkable feat of surveying and documented the canyon route with reams of engineering calculations, construction estimates, and twenty-two hundred photographs—all to prove that the dream was feasible. Despite this, Stanton met with a cool reception, in part because recent oil discoveries in California were reducing the market for Utah and Colorado coal.

John Wesley Powell, the one man who might have best appreciated Stanton's achievement, turned a cold shoulder, perhaps out of jealousy that anyone else might dare to travel "his" canyon. Stanton went to see "the Major" in Washington in 1892, but he recorded in his diary that "not one word did he express of compliment at my final success—but rather sneered at any value in my work."[6]

A year later, Stanton shared a podium with Powell at an irrigation conference in Los Angeles. Under a banner proclaiming, "Irrigation: Science, Not Chance," Powell nostalgically recalled his 1869 trip. Stanton hoped to link his railroad venture with the growing irrigation movement, but he took Powell to task for focusing on past glories rather than future potentials. Powell was not dreaming big enough, said Stanton. With Thomas Edison's assistance, Stanton proposed to construct a dam in the Grand Canyon complete with a dynamo to generate electricity with which to power a railroad. "When your great irrigation empire is completed," Stanton told the assembled delegates, mining and railroading would provide "the foundation to stand on."[7]

As it turned out, not a single foot of track was ever laid on the Denver, Colorado Canyon, and Pacific. Palmer's Rio Grande Western and the Atchison, Topeka and Santa Fe would be the only railroads to cross the Colorado Plateau near it, although in time the Santa Fe would bring tourists to within a few yards of the South Rim.

Robert Brewster Stanton, however, could never shake the pull of the river. In 1897 he returned to Glen Canyon with a plan to extract the fine gold that had stymied earlier placer operations. Backed by eastern capital, Stanton assembled a giant gold dredge about 4 miles above the mouth of Bullfrog Creek. The 46-bucket, 105-foot-long dredge was shipped piecemeal and hauled in wagons from the Rio Grande Western at Green River. The fine gold proved elusive even to this monster, however, and submerged sandbars and river silt further impeded progress.

Stanton's first cleanup of $30.15 in gold—after more than a $100,000 investment—was indicative of things to come. Stanton finally abandoned the dredge in 1901 in mid-river, where it sat until entombed by the rising waters of Lake Powell.[8]

About the same time as Robert Brewster Stanton was laboring through the depths of the Grand Canyon in pursuit of railroad dreams, a band of unsavory characters was descending on nearby Cañon Diablo in pursuit of a far less noble scheme. Train robberies in the West were part of the price of pushing steel rails across great expanses of territory. Many were bungled attempts that made off with little of value, but they caused quite a sensation nonetheless.

Train robbers had harassed the Atchison, Topeka and Santa Fe since its early days on the plains of Kansas. Bat Masterson's dogged pursuit of Dave Rudabaugh's gang outside Dodge City in 1878 set the precedent that the company would vigorously pursue and prosecute such mischief. That was to be the case across New Mexico and Arizona on both the Santa Fe and the Southern Pacific.

Between 1875 and 1890, there were ninety-nine successful stagecoach robberies in Arizona Territory alone. By the late 1880s, these numbers were in decline, and a spate of train robberies began. The reason for the switch was the proverbial "because that's where the money is," as stage traffic declined and railroads became the transport of choice for money, mail, and other valuables.

The first train robbery in Arizona occurred on the Southern Pacific line east of Tucson on the night of April 27, 1887. Using a red lantern to signal the engineer to halt, the outlaws made off with about $3,200, although the Wells Fargo agent managed to hide another $3,500 in gold in the express car's stove. Later that summer, the same train with the same Wells Fargo agent on board was held up about a mile east of the first robbery site. The Southern Pacific was hit a third time when two men boarded a train near Steins Pass on the Arizona–New Mexico border and made off with about $700.

The Santa Fe's Atlantic and Pacific line between Albuquerque and Needles was also the target of attacks. On September 16, 1887, five masked men built a bonfire on the tracks near Navajo Springs, east of

Holbrook, and as the train chugged to a halt, they were bold enough to fire shots at the crew before taking a small safe from the express car. An abortive attempt on another train occurred a year later west of Flagstaff when three robbers uncoupled the locomotive and one car and ordered the fireman to pull a mile down the track. Too late, they realized that they had captured the baggage car and not the sought-after Wells Fargo express car.

Despite gunfire in at least two of these robberies, no one was injured. But the increasing brazenness of train robbers—six bandits killed two men and seriously wounded two others in a holdup south of Nogales in Mexico during this same period—convinced the Arizona Territorial Legislature to pass a bill making train robbery a capital offense punishable by death. Three weeks later, on March 20, 1889, three—or as time would tell, probably four masked men—boarded an eastbound Santa Fe passenger train as it paused at the station at Cañon Diablo.

By all accounts, the initial act was a relatively low-key affair. The robbers demanded that the Wells Fargo agent empty the safe, which he did, although the luck of the draw made for a take of only about $1,000—less than normally carried. No one was hurt, and apparently the passengers were blissfully unaware of the act. The desperadoes then rode off in a snowstorm and left fresh tracks in about three inches of snow. Enter the newly elected sheriff of Yavapai County, William O'Neill.

"Bucky" O'Neill, so nicknamed for his early ability to stay on wild broncos, became the centerpiece in a dogged pursuit. O'Neill, a Wells Fargo special agent, and two deputies from Flagstaff went east by train and arrived at Cañon Diablo two days after the robbery. Some criticized O'Neill for dawdling, but he patiently trailed the outlaws north to Lees Ferry, where they had gotten the drop on Warren Johnson and forced him to ferry them across the river. That there were four outlaws at this point seemed certain.

O'Neill and his posse trailed the quartet across southern Utah and all the way to a densely wooded canyon near Beaver in the southwest corner of the territory. By one account—and they vary greatly—some forty shots were fired in a frantic gun battle before the four surrendered.

Separated from the county seat at Prescott by some 300 miles and the obstacle of the Grand Canyon, O'Neill chose to take his prisoners to

Ogden and then by train east on the Union Pacific to Denver. From there, they went south on the Santa Fe to Trinidad en route back to Flagstaff and eventually Prescott. Somewhere near Raton Pass, however, one of the prisoners, J. J. Smith, loosened his leg shackles and jumped out a window.

The train ground to a halt, but Smith was not to be found. Two deputies got off and combed the nearby mountains for him while O'Neill and the third deputy took the remaining three prisoners on to Prescott without further incident. By the evening of April 15, almost a month after the robbery, three of the train robbers were secure in O'Neill's jail. Their mood turned increasingly somber as it became clear that sentiment favored making them the first example under the recently enacted capital crime statute.

Faced with the death penalty, the trio quickly agreed to a plea bargain whereby they would plead guilty to a robbery charge in exchange for dropping the *train* robbery indictment. This they did, and by the end of July, they began serving twenty-five-year sentences at the territorial prison in Yuma—from which they could hear the daily whistles of the nearby Southern Pacific locomotives.

But what about J. J. Smith? He had been indicted along with the others but was not captured until some weeks later in Texas after an exchange of gunfire that left him with a bullet in his left thigh. O'Neill arrived on the scene, and Smith was extradited back to Prescott in time for the October court term.

Common sense suggested that Smith would simply follow his partners and avoid the noose by pleading guilty to the lesser charge and hoping that the judge would overlook his escape. Instead Smith chose to plead not guilty to everything and stand trial. Robert Brown, the defense attorney who had engineered the original plea bargain, became his aggressive representative.

After some procedural smoke screens, Brown attempted to create doubt as to whether the Wells Fargo agent on the night of the robbery had seen three men or four. And even if there had been four, could the agent be certain that under their masks one of them was Smith? For a time, it looked as if Smith's imprisoned friends might be transported from Yuma to testify. Brown first objected that their testimony for the prosecution might be biased in exchange for a reduction of their sentences, but then the prosecution itself decided not to put them on the stand after they appeared ready to swear that Smith had not been involved with the robbery. Despite attorney Brown's efforts, Smith was found guilty of the simple robbery charge and sentenced to join his cohorts in Yuma for a thirty-year sentence. But that is not quite the end of the story.

Four years later, suffering from consumption, like a majority of his Yuma cellmates, Smith petitioned the territorial governor for clemency. He claimed to have fallen innocently in with the other three near Lees Ferry and escaped at Raton out of fear for his life. His role in two gun battles and evidence of Wells Fargo money on him when he was captured were quietly ignored. These facts aside, Smith's petition was granted, and he was released from Yuma, having served less than four years of his sentence.[9]

Bucky O'Neill's dogged pursuit of these train robbers made him a celebrity in Arizona. He served three terms as sheriff and was elected mayor of Prescott. But his enduring fame came with Theodore Roosevelt and his Rough Riders in Cuba during the Spanish-American War. Ignoring the pleas of his men that he seek cover, O'Neill strolled the lines in front of Kettle Hill. The Spanish bullet had not been made that could kill him, O'Neill boasted. A moment later, he fell dead with one through his head.

After the affair at Cañon Diablo, train robberies in Arizona decreased—perhaps in part because of the threat of capital punishment. But that did not stop two rough-cut characters from attempting to wreck a Santa Fe passenger train near the Johnson Canyon tunnel in 1893. An alert watchman thwarted their plans, and a posse from Flagstaff shot them dead on the banks of the Verde River several days later.

Four years later, three robbers held up a westbound passenger train at Peach Springs and ransacked the express car. Express agents shot one robber dead on the rear vestibule of the car, but the other two led lawmen on a wild chase that ended deep in the Grand Canyon near the mouth of Diamond Creek. When the ringleader, Jim Parker, was finally hung in June 1898, his last words—sincere or not—were reportedly, "All this hullabaloo has sure taught me a lesson."[10]

There would be a few more train robberies in the Southwest—one of the last occurred on Marshall Pass in 1902—but they would be seen as rather fleeting and transitional events. Nothing else had stopped the railroads from their headlong expansion across half a continent, and a few outlaws with six-shooters could not do so. But just as the panic of 1873 had stalled most construction in the early years, there was to be an event that would bring all railroads to their knees. The boom could not last forever.

20

The Boom Goes Bust

In the spring of 1893, America paused to celebrate a generation of wild expansion. All eyes focused on the World's Columbian Exposition, which opened to the public on May 1 in Chicago. Over the course of the summer, millions of people visited the sprawling six-hundred-acre site to gawk at the latest wonders of industrial technology and social entertainment. Out of the exposition came such staples of American culture as Shredded Wheat cereal, Aunt Jemima syrup, Juicy Fruit gum, and the Ferris wheel.

Railroads throughout the country offered reduced fares and sponsored special excursions to Chicago to entice America's middle class to take what for many was a journey of a lifetime. Those visitors returned home to tell of carbonated sodas and a piece of meat between two slices of bread that was being called a "hamburger." But whether from San Francisco, St. Louis, and Pittsburgh or small towns such as Keokuk, Winslow, and Pierre, most completed their journey to the fair with a realization that America had grown both smaller and larger.

Geographically, thanks to America's railroads, there were no longer major barriers to transcontinental travel. Demographically, a nation divided after the Civil War had picked itself up and followed the railroads west to swell the population of California and every whistle-stop, hamlet, and town in between. America's next step would be that of a world leader.

But as the Chicago exposition wound down and closed that fall, all was not well. After a period of tremendous economic growth, the world's economy was strangled by an overdue contraction. Business failures in the United States and abroad led to tightened credit and caused a run on gold deposits in banks. When this collapse of a worldwide boom fell on America's railroads, it landed particularly hard because for a wild quarter of a century, they had led the boom with an insatiable building spree.

In the decade of the 1870s, the United States built 39,712 miles of new track, reaching an aggregate of 93,292 miles by 1880. In the next decade, that number almost doubled to 166,703 miles. This amazing increase of 73,000 miles of additional track during the 1880s was equivalent to the construction of four of the original Sacramento-to-Omaha transcontinental lines every year.[1]

Build west, J. Edgar Thomson had said. Build west, William Barstow Strong had said. Build everywhere, Collis P. Huntington had said. But when the major transcontinental lines were completed, the railroads continued to lay tracks to every mining camp, grain silo, cattle pen, and crossroads on the map. America was overbuilt with railroads, and consequently, America's railroads—even that paragon of corporate conservatism, the Atchison, Topeka and Santa Fe—were awash with debt.

Like America's overall economic woes, the Atchison, Topeka and Santa Fe's own crisis had been a long time in coming. Crop failures in the railroad's financial breadbasket of the Midwest started the downslide. In Kansas alone, wheat production fell from 48 million bushels in 1884 to barely 10 million in 1887; the corn crop also plummeted, from 191 million bushels in 1884 to 76 million three years later. These declines drastically cut freight revenues outbound from Kansas; furthermore, the resulting downturn in local economies meant that fewer goods and building supplies were being shipped into the state.

What freight traffic remained came under increasing competition from the Santa Fe's growing rivals across the plains, including Jay Gould's Missouri Pacific. Previously, such rivalries frequently led to traffic pools that had the effect of fixing rates above a floor of profitability. But in 1887, a reform-minded Congress passed the Interstate Commerce Act.

This new law prohibited pooling agreements and regulated how rates were adjusted, requiring, among other things, formal notices of future changes. The general national result was lower freight rates, but any reduction of revenues impacted railroads already highly leveraged by the construction surge. From 1887 to 1888, the Santa Fe's average freight rate per ton per mile fell from 1.347 to 1.258 cents, a significant 9 percent decrease.

Another national trend to impact the Santa Fe was the march of organized labor. In March 1888, the Brotherhood of Locomotive Engineers struck the Chicago, Burlington and Quincy over wages and working conditions. A ten-month struggle ensued that became particularly bitter when scabs operated trains under armed guards. While some Santa Fe engineers walked off in support for the brotherhood, the railroad avoided major interruptions because its record as an employer was relatively progressive. The Santa Fe negotiated major labor contracts in 1890 and 1892 and kept its trains running, but the resulting higher wages were yet another impact on the railroad's bottom line.

Finally, during this same time, construction activity on the Kansas City-to-Chicago extension as well as the push into California was at its peak. From January 1886 to October 1888, the Santa Fe laid 2,776 miles of track, and that didn't include the purchase and new construction of the Gulf, Colorado and Santa Fe. This additional trackage meant a staggering increase in the railroad's bonded indebtedness.[2]

Taken alone, any of these troubles—crop failures, rate regulation, labor strife, and construction costs—would likely not have been sufficient to cripple the Santa Fe, but taken together, they became a death-blow when played out against the backdrop of the panic of 1893.

Not surprisingly, the Santa Fe's floating debt began to climb as an early indicator of brewing trouble. Never a good sign in any business, floating debt is the short-term, unsecured obligations of a company. If it spirals out of control, it quickly impacts a company's ability to pay stock dividends and the interest on its bonds.

Shareholders squawked when dividends were cut—which the Santa

Fe did in 1888 from 1.75 percent to 1.5 percent—but failure to pay bond interest usually made foreclosure by bondholders and a forced receivership inevitable. It was this slippery slope of finance that forced the resignation of President William Barstow Strong and led to the emergence of a New York–based circle of Santa Fe investors.

While the financial details were mind numbing, the Santa Fe embarked on a complicated plan of restructuring. The centerpiece was a $100 million second mortgage that was supposed to retire $80 million in income bonds and leave $20 million of ready cash both to harness the floating debt and to provide a cushion for future operations. (Mortgage bonds paid a fixed rate regardless of corporate circumstances; income bonds, while yielding higher, paid interest only if the company was making money.)

At the start of what would become the worst year, William Barstow Strong's successor, Allen Manvel, died on February 24, 1893, in San Diego. Manvel would be remembered most for inaugurating the California Limited. In his place, the board of directors chose a young vice president, J. W. Reinhart, who enjoyed a growing reputation as the financial whiz behind the recent refinancing.

Many had assumed that the top job would go to A. A. Robinson, long Strong's right-hand man and, since 1888, the Santa Fe's general manager. But Robinson was passed over, and with some bitterness he resigned shortly afterward to become president of the Mexican Central. This was another signal that the influence of the old Boston crowd was waning and that the New Yorkers were ascendant.

Quite reassuringly, new president Reinhart announced in June 1893 that the floating debts of the railroads the Santa Fe had been acquiring had been consolidated on its balance sheet and that they were "amply and satisfactorily secured" and would be eliminated "when the financial atmosphere brightens."

But the financial atmosphere did not brighten. Instead it got increasingly worse. By October 1893, the Santa Fe sought to defer payment on its 1888 6 percent mortgage bonds for five years, promising the holders that both principal and interest at 6 percent would then be payable in gold. But in a hint of panic, the railroad also promised a cash commission of 5 percent if holders would hurry up and assent to the extension by October 25.

Meanwhile, President Reinhart gave the entire situation the kiss of death by glibly announcing that the finances of the company "are in such condition that no uneasiness need be felt" and that "the earnings of the Santa Fe properties, notwithstanding the general depression, are largely in excess of fixed charges." The bears smelled blood, and Atchison, Topeka and Santa Fe stock fell, further compounding the problem.

Reinhart scurried to Europe to find funds to meet the railroad's January 1894 interest obligations, even though a tight credit market had spread across that continent as well. He returned proclaiming that his mission had been "a success in every respect," but no foreign financing was forthcoming. A week later, on December 23, 1893, the Santa Fe and its Frisco subsidiary were forced into receivership upon the complaints of two New York banks.

Even then, Reinhart tried to put the best possible light on the situation. He acknowledged that the collapse of "pending negotiations for financial relief has caused temporary embarrassment to the companies" and would prevent the January payments of all obligations. But Reinhart also claimed that the Santa Fe system as a whole, which now accounted for 9,345 miles of railroad including the Frisco, "is amply able even under the present adverse condition to earn a safe balance above its fixed charges" if relieved from the albatross of its floating debt.[3]

This latter assertion was a testament to the powerhouse that the Santa Fe was on the verge of becoming, but things would get much worse before they got better. Six months into the Santa Fe's receivership, an audit report claimed that the railroad had overstated its income by more than $7 million during the preceding four years. A major portion of the problem stemmed from rebates to shippers that had been booked into a suspense account as assets rather than being expensed against their related earnings.

Reinhart sought to defend the overall numbers, but closer scrutiny showed that certain entries had been forwarded to company bookkeepers in Topeka from his East Coast office that either had "no foundation in fact" or were related to off-balance-sheet transactions or valuations. A day after his reply to the auditor, J. W. Reinhart tendered his resignations as president of the Santa Fe system and one of its court-appointed receivers. He was later indicted on charges of having given rebates to shippers that were in violation of the Interstate Commerce Act in the first place.

By the time the final audit report was issued in November 1894, the overstatement of the Santa Fe's income had grown to more than $10 million. But the thorough examination of the books validated Reinhart's bravado about its future earnings capacity. The Santa Fe had become top-heavy by assuming the floating debt of a round of acquisitions, but for the year ending June 30, 1894, it had generated $6 million in earnings. This suggested that if a reorganization could be accomplished, there was a sufficient income stream to secure long-term debt.[4]

In order to satisfy both secured bondholders and stockholders, any reorganization had "to rid the company of its floating debt," reduce fixed charges, and "provide fresh capital for needed improvements." It was a tall order, and various schemes were put forth by different constituencies during 1894 and early 1895.

The final plan adopted by the receivers called for the foreclosure of the general mortgage placed on the road in 1888 and its subsequent sale to representatives of the new lenders. They would in turn organize a new company. In the process, the railroad's floating debt was rolled into long-term debt or securities, and enough capital was left to fund needed repairs and improvements.

On December 12, 1895, a new corporation was formed with the nearly identical name of the Atchison, Topeka and Santa Fe *Railway* Company. Cyrus K. Holliday became a member of its board of directors, just as he had been for the old company since 1860. He was also given the rather perfunctory title of president of the original Atchison, Topeka and Santa Fe *Railroad* Company as it wound up its affairs.[5]

Such receiverships and reorganizations were certainly not unique to the Santa Fe. Sixty-five American railroads went into receivership during 1893 alone. This made a total of 123 roads then under court control and represented about 19 percent of the railroad mileage in the country. Among them were the Union Pacific and the Northern Pacific.[6]

But as new energy slowly returned to America's railroads, there was one titanic name missing. Jay Gould was dead. His last few years were a debilitating struggle with tuberculosis, and he died on December 2,

1892, at fifty-six. Among the many mourners at his funeral was Collis P. Huntington, himself beginning to show signs of declining health.

The mantle of the Gould empire fell upon Jay's oldest son, George, not quite twenty-nine. George would never share his father's innate sense of business strategy, but he had studied dutifully at his side for more than a decade and had taken an increasingly central role as Jay's health failed.

Charged with preserving the Gould empire, George set out to accomplish what for all of Jay's thrusts and parries the elder Gould had never been able to complete: a transcontinental railroad system under his own control. As George Gould looked to his cornerstone property of the Missouri Pacific to spearhead this effort, the Atchison, Topeka and Santa Fe cast about for a new leader not only to counter this threat but also to take the road into the next century.

In the Santa Fe's first fifty years, four men stood out: Cyrus K. Holliday, the progenitor of the dream and a member of its board for forty years; William Barstow Strong, who overcame all obstacles to make the Santa Fe a transcontinental system; A. A. Robinson, the steady engineer who turned Holliday's vision and Strong's strategic moves into track on the ground; and Edward Payson Ripley, the man who led the road out of the panic of 1893. During a quarter century at the helm of the Santa Fe, Ripley was to rely less on flash and more on substance to make the road an operational model of speed, comfort, and reliability.

Edward Payson Ripley was born in Dorchester, Massachusetts, in 1845. His father was a merchant, and young Ripley's first work was in a wholesale dry goods store in Boston. In 1868 he went to work for J. Edgar Thomson's Pennsylvania Railroad as part of its specialty fast freight line. Two years later, he entered into a long career with the Chicago, Burlington and Quincy Railroad. Ripley worked his way up from clerk to New England agent for the line and then in 1878 became general freight agent for the road out of the company's headquarters in Chicago.

In 1887 the Burlington made Ripley its traffic manager and soon thereafter its general manager. By this time, he was married with four children and happily ensconced in Chicago's Riverside area, being a member of the elite Chicago Club. But in August 1890, Ripley resigned from the Burlington and took a job with the Chicago, Milwaukee and St. Paul Railway as a vice president in charge of traffic operations. Here he stayed until tapped by the Santa Fe's board of directors to lead the reorganized company out of the wilderness.

Central to Ripley's success would be his understanding of the operating side of the railroad business and his belief that railroads could be run for the public good and still make a profit. He firmly "believed in the good old doctrine that railroads are common carriers, and he would devote his entire energies and those of his subordinates strictly to the railroad business. Convinced that the only business of a railroad is to sell transportation, he would make the Atchison a great and efficient transportation company. . . ."[7]

Following the drive of the company westward, the Santa Fe's board had already decided to close its venerable Boston headquarters and relocate to Chicago, leaving only a financial staff in New York. This suited Ripley perfectly, as he could maintain his family's status in Chicago and be just that much closer to the operations of his railroad. Indeed, Los Angeles was now only two and one-half days from Dearborn Station on the California Limited.

Upon assuming the Santa Fe presidency on December 12, 1895, Ripley immediately faced many challenges. Some were related to the dismal national economy; others were more internal to the Santa Fe's own operations. Two issues weighed particularly heavy on his mind. The first was the Atlantic and Pacific line from Albuquerque to Needles. Despite its strategic importance, this segment had never been a paying concern. Several growth spurts notwithstanding, through traffic between the heartland and California did not generate reliable revenues. The general condition of the line was poor, and in many places it needed to be rebuilt with heavier rails and lesser grades.

The Needles-to-Mojave extension of this route that was leased from the Southern Pacific was not in any better shape. Financially, it cost $436,266 a year in lease payments alone. Some of Ripley's critics suggested that the entire Albuquerque-to-Mojave line should be abandoned and that the Santa Fe should retrench its core system across the plains. This move would leave the hard-won routes in Southern California as orphans, but perhaps they could be sold to the Southern Pacific.

Ripley's other albatross was the Santa Fe's Sonora Railway, linking its trackage rights over the Southern Pacific at Benson, Arizona, with

Guaymas, Mexico. The road's construction had seemed like a good idea in the early 1880s, but it developed neither as an effective end-around competition to the Southern Pacific nor as a promising transcontinental link. Northern Mexico was too economically depressed and likely to remain so.

Ripley looked at the map of the Santa Fe system and pondered a solution. Others could attend to the myriad of financial and legal matters. What Ripley cared about most was operating trains. He simply could not fathom severing the Atlantic and Pacific connection to California. Stubbornly, he remained adamant that in time California would boom far beyond the recent spurts and that the 35th parallel corridor would resound with transcontinental traffic.

Ripley contemplated a plan to save the Santa Fe's link to California, while at the same time trim costs and eliminate liabilities. To bring this about, he went to the Southern Pacific and proposed a handshake far different from the one Collis P. Huntington had extended to William Barstow Strong at Deming years before.

The Southern Pacific was now irrevocably ensconced along the 32nd parallel from Yuma to New Orleans. South of that line, the Sonora Railway was a liability to the Santa Fe and clearly belonged in the Southern Pacific's orbit. On the other hand, the Mojave–Needles leg of the Southern Pacific had become a 240-mile stub that led nowhere except to the Santa Fe's lease payments. By handy coincidence, the value of both lines and their relative condition was about the same.

Ripley proposed a trade, and the Southern Pacific agreed. The attorneys would not get done clearing titles and completing the transaction for some years, but beginning in 1897, the Southern Pacific took over operations on the Sonora Railway, and the Santa Fe assumed full responsibility for the Mojave–Needles leg. This meant that Ripley could throw all his corporate energies into what was now clearly the Santa Fe's main line.

A final uncertainty was removed about the same time when Atlantic and Pacific bondholders foreclosed. Ripley cobbled together a plan whereby the Santa Fe purchased the bonds in default for a combination of new Santa Fe bonds and preferred stock. The result was that the Atchison, Topeka and Santa Fe owned the 564 miles of Atlantic and Pacific line between Needles and Albuquerque outright and was finally the sole owner of its entire length of track between Los Angeles and Chicago.[8]

Edward Payson Ripley's shareholders were impressed but not quite ready to cheer. What he had to do next was produce a winning revenue stream. Ripley firmly believed that the best way for the Atchison, Topeka and Santa Fe to regain profitability was to invest aggressively in its existing infrastructure. Consequently, he directed a massive program to upgrade, replace, or rebuild the Santa Fe's main arteries, rolling stock, and maintenance facilities.

In 1898 alone, 11.25 miles of wooden bridges were replaced with steel or earthen fills, 489 miles of track were ballasted, and 767 miles of heavier rails were laid. New machine shops, depots, and roundhouses were built or expanded, and almost every station between Chicago and El Paso was given a fresh coat of paint.

Most significant for the future, the expensive and laborious process of double tracking—adding a second set of tracks to the right-of-way to facilitate trains running in both directions at once—began in earnest. Twenty-five miles of double track was added between Florence and Emporia, Kansas. Thousands of miles remained to be done between Los Angeles and Chicago, but this was the start toward a double-tracked transcontinental speedway.

Meanwhile, operating revenues climbed from $28.8 million in 1895 to $46.2 million in 1900. A roster of 1,136 locomotives shuttled almost 30,000 passenger, freight, and service cars around a Santa Fe network of almost 7,500 miles of lines owned, controlled, or allied by the company. Ripley's emphasis on operating efficiencies and debt consolidation converted an annual $4.4 million deficit in 1895 to a $9.7 million surplus for shareholders in 1900. Perhaps the most impressive fact is that Ripley engineered this rebuilding turnaround without incurring additional long-term debt or resorting to floating debt; he did it all out of current earnings.[9]

During this time of rebuilding, Ripley undertook one major expansion to complete Cyrus K. Holliday's transcontinental vision. It had taken

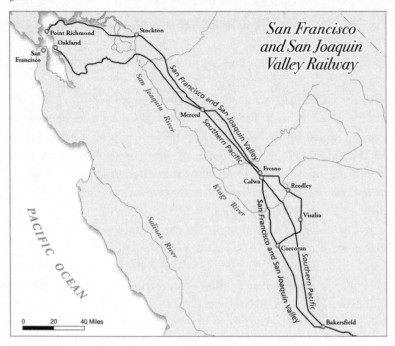

the Santa Fe the better part of two decades to break the grip that Huntington's Southern Pacific held over Southern California—from San
Diego's vote against Tom Scott and the Texas and Pacific in 1872, until
the Santa Fe secured its own independent tracks into downtown Los
Angeles in 1887. In 1898 Ripley took the final step and announced that
the Santa Fe would acquire its own independent tracks from Mojave
into San Francisco.

As in the case of the California Southern, the Santa Fe received considerable assistance in this endeavor from an existing road that had
begun to challenge the Southern Pacific's Bay Area market share. As
early as 1893, the San Francisco Traffic Association—composed of merchants, farmers, and local shippers—determined not to remain at the
mercy of Southern Pacific rates, and it made plans to build an independent line from San Francisco Bay to a connection with the Santa Fe at
Mojave.

The year 1893 was not a good one for new railroad construction, and
in order to save money, an initial plan was devised to employ ferries between the San Francisco–Oakland waterfront and Stockton and to build

only 230 miles of railroad from there to Bakersfield, California. But even this effort proved daunting.

Despite widespread motivation to challenge the Southern Pacific, the economic hangover from the panic of 1893 and a fear that the Southern Pacific would simply bull its way into the ownership of any competing venture stalled early progress. Then a major player appeared in the person of Claus Spreckels, a sugar-refining tycoon with substantial interests in the San Joaquin Valley.

When a meeting of the San Francisco Chamber of Commerce reported only half of the venture's $350,000 initial goal had been subscribed—not enough for even 10 miles of track—Spreckels challenged the group to dream bigger. Within two weeks, fueled by Spreckels's personal pledge of $500,000, subscriptions had grown to $2 million. Among the supporters were Spreckels's two sons, Adolph and John, who pledged $100,000 each. (John's own railroad interests would later include the San Diego and Arizona Railway leading directly east from San Diego to Yuma.)

With the initial logjam broken, stock subscriptions poured in from the rank and file of the San Joaquin Valley. The *San Francisco Examiner* reported that these amounts were evidence that the new road would be "largely built and owned by people of modest circumstances" and not controlled by the monopolistic railroad powers that Frank Norris would soon write about in his novel *The Octopus*.

Promptly dubbed "the People's Railroad," the San Francisco and San Joaquin Valley was chartered on February 25, 1895, and began laying track south from Stockton that summer. By October of the following year, the line was complete between Stockton and Fresno, and a special excursion train named "the Emancipator" ran to inaugurate the service that many valley residents hoped would emancipate them from the yoke of the Southern Pacific.[10]

Over the next two years, the railroad built another 110 miles from Fresno to Bakersfield and completed an eastern loop to Visalia. But while revenues were promising, it could not hope to meet operating expenses and retire the construction debt. Up ahead, a 68-mile gap over Tehachapi Pass remained between Bakersfield and the Santa Fe terminus at Mojave.

Claus Spreckels convinced the San Joaquin Valley's board of directors that the time had come to make a deal with the Santa Fe for an outright purchase of the existing line. Fortunately for them, Edward Payson Ripley agreed. The Santa Fe board of directors authorized the purchase of the San Francisco and San Joaquin Valley for $2,462,300 in December 1898 and got the local investors off the hook. But this still did not close the Bakersfield-Mojave gap or solve the inefficiencies of the Stockton-to-Bay Area ferryboats.

The first bottleneck was Tehachapi Pass. Even if Ripley had wanted to challenge the Southern Pacific there, his engineers soon confirmed that there was simply no room to build a second line—loop or no loop. The end result was that the Santa Fe negotiated a lease from the Southern Pacific of the Tehachapi Pass segment that allowed it to operate its own trains on equal priority over the line. A century later, this agreement is still in place, and the Tehachapi Loop is among the busiest single-track sections of railroad in the United States.

The second bottleneck—ferry service between Stockton and San Francisco—was no easier, but much of it would eventually be eliminated with independent tracks. After the Santa Fe's purchase of the San Francisco and San Joaquin Valley, Ripley retained its principal engineer, William Benson Storey, to work in that direction. Despite Storey's gloomy report on the physical obstacles along the 77-mile Stockton-to-Point Richmond route—"the coast range would be pierced by a long tunnel near Martinez, the tule swamps would require considerable dredging and three drawbridges, and the land at Point Richmond needed massive earth and rock fills before port facilities could be built"—the work went forward.

It was difficult construction with water everywhere, from saturated hillsides that made tunneling and cuts problematic, to swamps and tidelands that required long viaducts and high fills. And once the terminal facilities were complete in Point Richmond, there was still the crossing of the bay and construction of similar port facilities in San Francisco just south of the present-day Oakland Bay Bridge.

The flagship of the Santa Fe's fleet of ferries was the double-ended side-wheeler *San Pablo*. With the Santa Fe's cross logo emblazoned on her single smokestack, the *San Pablo* was a common sight on the bay for some thirty years. Fred Harvey meals were served on the crossing, just as they were on any other Santa Fe Railway conveyance.

On July 6, 1900, Santa Fe passengers departed San Francisco, crossed the bay, boarded a train at Point Richmond, and rode cross-country all the way to Chicago on Atchison, Topeka and Santa Fe rails. This was the final realization of Cyrus K. Holliday's transcontinental dream. The colonel almost lived to see it.

Over the years, he had never been shy about demanding credit for the birth of the railroad. Recently, when an obituary of a Kansas pioneer mentioned the deceased's founding role in the Santa Fe, Holliday had been quick to tell William Barstow Strong, "the same thing has occurred for the last fifteen or twenty years, whenever any prominent citizen of Atchison has died. They were all founders of the Santa Fe Railroad, wrote or inspired its charter, etc. [but] it was the 'inspiration' of an hour, and of my own, and . . . I wrote every word and every syllable. . . ."[11]

Now, as of March 29, Holliday himself was also dead. But in many respects, not only had the Santa Fe fulfilled his transcontinental dream but it had also made good the boast that young William Jackson Palmer had made to the Big Four back in 1867: They alone would not control the West's transcontinental destinies.

21

Still West from Denver

As the Atchison, Topeka and Santa Fe clawed its way back from the panic of 1893 and its own overindulgences, one thing had not changed on the map of the American West. There was still no direct rail link through Colorado's mountains straight west from Denver.

Despite its loss of the Royal Gorge, the Santa Fe never completely gave up the idea of a line through Colorado's mountains. The road's independent line from Pueblo north to Denver was completed in 1887. That same year, a standard gauge upstart led by mining man J. J. Hagerman entered the Colorado fray.

Hagerman's Colorado Midland Railroad built west from Colorado Springs, across South Park to Buena Vista, and then crossed the Continental Divide via a tunnel under Hagerman Pass west of Leadville. From the pass, a tortuous crossing at best, the line descended into the Roaring Fork Valley with a branch to Aspen, which was then enjoying a silver rush long before any boom from its silvery snows.

But there the Colorado Midland faltered. The best the road could do was connect with the Denver and Rio Grande near Glenwood Springs—a connection it might have made at Leadville or Buena Vista some 100 miles of mountain railroading and one backbreaking pass earlier.

Nonetheless, the Santa Fe was interested. From its inception, the Midland had a friendly relationship with the Santa Fe, receiving approximately three-quarters of its westbound passengers and freight from connections with the eastern road. For its part, the Santa Fe viewed the Midland as an excellent feeder into its system. The odd man out proved to be the Denver and Rio Grande. It feared a standard gauge Santa Fe–Colorado Midland connection to the Rio Grande Western at Grand Junction even as the Denver and Rio Grande was converting its circuitous Royal Gorge line over Tennessee Pass to standard gauge.

Consequently, in 1890 the Denver and Rio Grande crowd in Denver led by banker David Moffat approached Hagerman about buying the Midland outright. But somewhere along the line, Moffat and his associates raised the hackles of Hagerman, an independent Midwesterner who'd come west for his health. Well aware of the eastern capital that controlled most western railroads, Hagerman growled, "I do not suppose there are 500 shares of Rio Grande stock owned in Colorado, but to hear the officers here talk, you would suppose they owned it all."

The Denver and Rio Grande sent its chairman to London to arrange financing for the purchase of the Midland, but the day before he arrived, Hagerman closed a sale to the Santa Fe. Four million dollars was a hefty price to pay, but the Santa Fe considered it necessary to protect its northern flanks and promote a connection in Utah with the Union Pacific. The Santa Fe's ultimate goal, of course, was a point of entry into northern California, and if nothing else, its acquisition of the Midland proved that the Santa Fe had not forgiven the Rio Grande for past rivalries.

For his part, Hagerman was elated with the deal. Not only did he receive his investment in the Midland back at a tidy profit, but "it enables me with one grand whack," Hagerman wrote, "to get even with [Moffat's Denver] combination, and pay them and their followers back for all the sneers, belittlement and other dirt they have heaped on me for the last four years."

The result for the Santa Fe was not so rosy. In the six years from 1890 through 1895, the operations of the Colorado Midland cost the Santa Fe a $2.25 million loss. In the end, the debt of the Colorado Midland purchase became one of the millstones that pulled the Santa Fe into bankruptcy after the panic of 1893. What the Santa Fe's brief ownership of the Colorado Midland proved, however, was that the Santa Fe was still concerned about railroad developments on the Sacramento–Salt Lake–Denver axis.

The Colorado Midland emerged from receivership as a separate entity once again. It would linger on the Colorado scene, even building a longer, lower tunnel under Hagerman Pass, but the geography of its mountainous route simply wasn't conducive to a transcontinental haul. Meanwhile, the standard gauging of the Denver and Rio Grande main line was complete, and that railroad was teaming up with a much more formidable ally than the Midland.[1]

Not surprisingly, the Denver and Rio Grande's new ally proved to be George Gould. In the beginning, Gould's Missouri Pacific system was content to cooperate with the Denver and Rio Grande via mutually beneficial traffic agreements. But in 1900, with the economic calamities of the past decade receding and George Gould's confidence in his own powers rising, the Missouri Pacific began to buy Denver and Rio Grande stock. Young Gould's desire to surpass his dad's empire was only part of the reason.

Despite the fact that Colorado had the largest population of the Rocky Mountain states, a varied economy of mines, farming, and cattle, and a well-developed system of local railroads, Denver was still forced to ship westbound goods north to the Union Pacific at Cheyenne or south to Pueblo on the Denver and Rio Grande's roundabout Royal Gorge route. Denver had transcontinental connections, but the Mile High City was not even close to being on a transcontinental main line.

Four hundred air miles to the west, Salt Lake City was singing much the same refrain. It had connections to the Union Pacific at Ogden and was served by the Rio Grande Western–Denver and Rio Grande line to the southeast, but it too did not sit squarely on a transcontinental main line. The idea of a direct rail link between these two cities that was also a main line transcontinental quickened the pulses of conservative businessmen and rank speculators alike.

The map of the West was indeed filling up, but here was an enticing void. "Such another opportunity for railroad builders is not to be found anywhere in the United States," the *Denver Republican* proclaimed under the headline "An Empire Without a Railroad."[2]

The first step in this last great Rocky Mountain railroad play was for George Gould to acquire control of the Denver and Rio Grande. But no sooner had Gould and the Missouri Pacific begun to buy into the Denver and Rio Grande aggressively than an event akin to Jay Gould's passing occurred. It might be said that the other shoe dropped. Collis P. Huntington died at the age of seventy-eight on August 14, 1900. He was the last surviving member of the Big Four, and into his hands over half a lifetime had been gathered control of arguably the most powerful transportation empire in the country.

Barely was Huntington cold than E. H. Harriman, a New York financier and architect of a resurgent Union Pacific, made an attempt to buy the Central Pacific segment of the original transcontinental from Huntington's estate. The only thing diminutive about Harriman was his stature. His banking background belied the fact that he had been quietly accumulating railroad expertise since joining the board of a little road in upstate New York.

In fact, as a Wall Street financier in an era when railroad stocks dominated the market, Harriman had little choice but to learn the railroad business. The myriad of financial details came to him easily enough, but, like the Santa Fe's Edward Payson Ripley, Harriman also readily embraced the operational aspects, correctly appreciating that poorly maintained roadbeds, underpowered locomotives, and dilapidated rolling stock all suppressed the bottom line.

After brokering Illinois Central Railroad bonds and subsequently joining its board of directors, Harriman became the Illinois Central's vice president in 1887. Here Harriman realized another aspect of his maturing persona: He simply wasn't cut out to be *vice* president of anything. He left the operational role but remained on the Illinois Central's board of directors as chairman of its finance committee, astutely guiding the road largely unscathed through the panic of 1893. Finally, it was time to look west.

As the Union Pacific emerged from its 1893-induced receivership, Harriman bulled his way onto the reborn road's executive committee and quickly became its chairman. His first major task was to make a

tour of the Union Pacific system. He found it in better physical condition than many on Wall Street assumed, and he moved aggressively to
increase its capacity and efficiency. The one weak link in his reborn
Union Pacific vision was the Central Pacific's portion of the first
transcontinental that was still owned by Huntington.

After Huntington died and Harriman's initial efforts failed to purchase the Central Pacific between Ogden and San Francisco from Huntington's estate, Harriman and his Union Pacific supporters began to
buy the stock of its parent, the Southern Pacific. By the time they were
done, not only did Harriman control the Central Pacific but Huntington's entire Southern Pacific system as well. It was no overstatement for
Harriman to assert, "We have bought not only a railroad, but an empire."[3]

Throughout these negotiations, George Gould continued to buy
Denver and Rio Grande stock and refrained from any direct role—for or
against—in Harriman's machinations for the Southern Pacific. Gould
could not have been unaware, however, that whatever the result, it was
likely to impact the Missouri Pacific and the Denver and Rio Grande at
the vaunted Ogden gateway to the Union Pacific system.

So while Harriman bought his empire, George Gould focused on the
Denver and Rio Grande, which in turn was trying to buy William Jackson Palmer's Rio Grande Western between Grand Junction and Ogden.
Palmer had clung to this line tenaciously after his ouster from the Denver and Rio Grande and continued to run a first-class railroad. Despite
many offers, Palmer and his associates knew that they had a strategi-
cally located property that was increasing in value. It was useless to negotiate with Palmer, one Denver and Rio Grande executive complained,
because at each negotiation he "advanced the price at which they were
willing to sell. . . ."

Now, with George Gould sitting on the board of the Denver and Rio
Grande and about to become its chairman, the capital and the timing
came together to consummate the purchase of the Rio Grande Western
for $15 million. Palmer's personal take appears to have amounted to
about $1 million. For the general, this transaction marked the end of an
active railroad career begun more than forty years before at the elbow of
J. Edgar Thomson.

Palmer's personal heartbreak appears to have been his marriage to

Queen. The ardor between them in the heady days of dreaming about their own little railroad cooled as the demands of Palmer's far-flung enterprises disrupted Queen's vision of tranquil family life with three daughters. Queen blamed a heart condition on her desire to give up life at altitude in Colorado and to live with the girls first in New York City and then England. Palmer visited once or twice a year, combining family time with financial meetings. When Queen did in fact succumb to heart failure at the comparatively young age of forty-four, the general rushed to her side but arrived too late.

There is a well-circulated story that Palmer, having made an ample fortune from real estate, coal, and other ventures, shared the largesse from his Rio Grande Western sale with his employees. At many levels, he had been as shrewd and calculating as any of his contemporaries, but this act of kindness underscored that since his days at the helm of the Fifteenth Pennsylvania Cavalry, Palmer had taken a keen interest in the welfare of those under him.[4]

For George Gould, the Rio Grande Western purchase was simply another piece in the puzzle of the western expansion of his Missouri Pacific system. His next step was to complete his control of the Denver and Rio Grande. As Harriman was then wrapping up his purchase of the entire Southern Pacific system, Gould went to him and suggested that if Harriman did not want the entire Huntington network, Gould would be quite willing to buy the southern pieces of it—principally the Los Angeles–Tucson–El Paso–Houston main line of the Southern Pacific. (Gould, of course, continued to control the Texas and Pacific as far as the Southern Pacific connection at Sierra Blanca, and the Southern Pacific line would have given him a distinct advantage against the Santa Fe with both transcontinental and Gulf Coast traffic.)

When Harriman declined the offer, "Gould asked for a half interest in the purchase," claiming that such a joint venture would "exemplify the community of interest spirit" that Harriman had been promoting among the western roads.

Such public relations talk designed to lull one's opponents was one thing, but with the "empire" securely in his hands, Harriman was not about to share it. A half interest was not possible, Harriman told a suddenly ruffled Gould, but Gould would be more than welcome to become a director of the Southern Pacific.

Shortly thereafter, Gould's control of the enlarged Denver and Rio Grande became public knowledge as he stepped into its chairmanship. Learning this news, Harriman reportedly remarked to Gould—perhaps with a sly grin—"You bought that, I suppose, for both interests: Union Pacific and your own."

When Gould replied with a curt no, Harriman nonetheless suggested that he would like to have a half interest in the road. Showing that he was at least capable of flashes of his father's intellect, George Gould replied, "That cannot be arranged, but I would like you to serve on the Rio Grande board."[5]

This exchange, however anecdotal, nonetheless characterizes the next round of battle. Gould could almost hear the bang as Harriman slammed the California door shut. With the northern and southern access to California via the Central Pacific and Southern Pacific controlled by Harriman—and no love lost between the Missouri Pacific and the Santa Fe that controlled the third California door—Gould was still stuck, as the Denver and Rio Grande had long been, at Ogden. If Gould's Missouri Pacific–Denver and Rio Grande system was to enjoy trade west of Ogden, it was going to have to lay its own tracks to California.

George Gould set about it with considerable stealth. During 1902 he quietly dispatched teams of surveyors to find a route through the Sierra Nevada preferable to the Central Pacific's original line over Donner Pass. The easy winner was 5,218-foot Beckwourth Pass, discovered in 1850 by mountain man Jim Beckwourth and some 2,000 feet lower than Donner. Once across the pass, the route dropped down California's Feather River Canyon and into the Sacramento Valley.

By March 1903, enough of the right-of-way was under Gould's control that he incorporated the Western Pacific Railway. But Gould's history with the line was not to be a happy one. Construction began from both the Oakland and Salt Lake ends early in 1906. While the low elevation of Beckwourth Pass and water grade of the Feather River Canyon were assets, Gould's bondholders stipulated that the line have a maximum grade of 1 percent. That was admirable from an operational standpoint, but it lengthened the route and made for some circuitous swings.[6]

Where the line crossed the existing Central Pacific–Southern Pacific

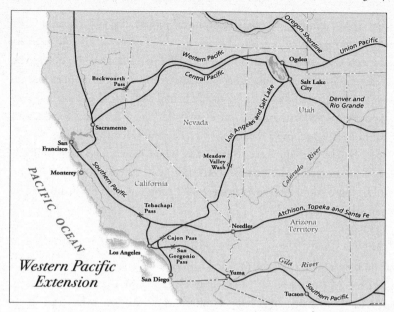

Western Pacific Extension

grade, the Western Pacific had to foot the expense of grade crossings because the other line had been there first. Then there were some forty-one steel bridges and forty-four tunnels. When the road was completed late in 1909, it was 927 miles from Oakland to Salt Lake City, 150 miles longer than the original Central Pacific, albeit over more gradual grades.

By then, George Gould's attempt to surpass his father as a railroad tycoon had come to ruin. He overreached his Midwest power base, locked horns with E. H. Harriman to his detriment, and, in the end, became a financial casualty of the panic of 1907. Perhaps the *Wall Street Journal* best summed up the difference between the younger Gould and Harriman. "The policies, ambitions, and apparent destinies of these two magnates are identical . . ." the *Journal* concluded, but "Mr. Gould is swayed by incidental circumstances, while Mr. Harriman's vocation in life is to triumph over incidental circumstances."

Not only had the Western Pacific been expensive to build, but also its eastern connection to the Missouri Pacific still led over the mountainous and circuitous route of the Denver and Rio Grande from Salt Lake to Pueblo. Even east of Pueblo, the Missouri Pacific "still had light fifty-six-pound rail, dirt ballast, short passing tracks, and a host of other shortcomings."[7]

Compared to Harriman's Union Pacific main line to the north, the Western Pacific was only a second-class competitor. But there was an even sharper contrast to the south. Thanks to Edward Payson Ripley's determined investments in infrastructure, the Atchison, Topeka and Santa Fe had become a model of efficiency and reliability. It was not yet the biggest and the best, but Colonel Holliday's road was well ensconced among America's railroads as a Wall Street blue chip. On no other route could one travel from Los Angeles to Chicago with such ease and speed.

The final chapter to control the California–Salt Lake–Denver axis was written in Colorado. While George Gould built the Western Pacific, David Moffat—the Denver banker who had so infuriated J. J. Hagerman—announced that he would build the long-sought standard gauge straight west from Denver. Past history spawned many skeptics, but Moffat's Denver, Northwestern and Pacific Railway promised to shorten the distance between Denver and Salt Lake City via the Denver and Rio Grande from 735 to 525 miles.

The Denver and Rio Grande bristled at this incursion into its territory, but it was hamstrung by the financial weight of Gould's Western Pacific expansion. The Rio Grande had difficulty maintaining its own operations and simply was in no position to challenge Moffat. As a retired William Jackson Palmer wryly wrote, "As to the D. and R. G.— if it has an engine that doesn't leak, I am not aware of it."

Palmer, like so many of his contemporaries, was approaching the end of the line. In the fall of 1906, he fell from his horse while riding on the grounds of his beloved Glen Eyrie estate west of Colorado Springs. He spent his last two and one-half years incapacitated from a broken neck. But even that injury could not keep the general from grandly entertaining 280 veterans of his old Fifteenth Pennsylvania Cavalry regiment for one last reunion. Many of them were loyal comrades from his railroad wars as well.

Without Palmer or the Denver and Rio Grande to oppose him corporately, Moffat built west from Denver, but his railroad was challenged physically by the heights of the Continental Divide at 11,680-foot Rollins Pass. (The railroad also called it Corona Pass.) Steep grades, winter snows, and howling winds made operations costly and sometimes impossible. Once across the pass, the Denver, Northwestern and Pacific made it only as far as sparsely populated Craig in northwest Colorado.

By then, David Moffat was also dead, having died in 1911 after spending $14 million on the "straight west" dream. Civic leaders in Denver rallied to the cause and, after the better part of two decades of wrangling, secured bonds to construct a 6.2-mile tunnel that avoided the climb over Rollins Pass. The Moffat Tunnel was finally completed in 1927.

Having gone through its share of receiverships, the reorganized Denver and Rio Grande Western acquired the remnants of Moffat's system and then completed the 38-mile Dotsero Cutoff between Moffat's road and its own Tennessee Pass main line. The Denver and Rio Grande was thus able to link the two systems and use the Moffat Tunnel to reduce its mileage between Denver and Grand Junction. Only in that way did Denver finally—after more than fifty years—get its long-sought line straight west.[8]

22

---·---

Top of the Heap

As the map of the American West was filled in, the Atchison, Topeka and Santa Fe Railway patiently yet firmly continued its growth. In the summer of 1902, Edward Payson Ripley cast an expansionist eye southeast from Phoenix toward the Southern Pacific line at Benson. He also looked north from the Santa Fe's new terminal at Oakland into the timberlands of northern California. E. H. Harriman and the Union Pacific were not pleased by the challenge on either front. If the Santa Fe kept expanding, it might connect to its Deming stub or parallel the Southern Pacific all the way north to Portland, Oregon.

In Arizona, the Santa Fe and the Southern Pacific had long acted in relative harmony. The Southern Pacific held sway across the southern part of the territory, and the Santa Fe did likewise in the north. In between, the sleepy little town of Phoenix didn't attract much attention, although the Southern Pacific had promoted a branch from its main line at Maricopa by 1887 and gone to some lengths to discourage other competitors.

In the northern part of the territory, scarcely had the Santa Fe–backed Atlantic and Pacific built west from Flagstaff than town fathers from the territorial capital of Prescott lobbied for a branch extension south to their town. When the Atlantic and Pacific showed no in-clination to undertake the route, local interests incorporated the narrow gauge Prescott and Arizona Central Railway and built between Prescott and the main line at Seligman in 1887. The terrain was tough, the road's equipment second rate, and the service anything but regular.

Consequently, in 1889, the Santa Fe looked to the feasibility of a 57-mile standard gauge route from the main line at Ash Fork to Prescott that would also serve nearby copper mines and could logically be ex-tended to Phoenix. Named the Santa Fe, Prescott and Phoenix Rail-road, this Santa Fe ally opened to Prescott in 1893 and continued to Phoenix by 1895. It was nicknamed the "Pea Vine" route because of its tight spirals and curves. According to one oft-told joke, a locomotive engineer could pass his tobacco plug to the rear brakeman on the hair-pin curves.

After Ripley acquired the Pea Vine line outright for the Santa Fe in 1901, he immediately ordered major track and grade improvements along the route. By then, what concerned E. H. Harriman were Ripley's intentions southeast of Phoenix.[1]

Ripley was backing another local line called the Phoenix and Eastern Railroad. It ran southeast from Phoenix up the Gila River and proposed continuing up the San Pedro River to the Southern Pacific main line at Benson. On the surface, it seemed like a rather innocuous threat to the Southern Pacific.

But in an era when many western railroads were contemplating cut-offs to shorten their original lines, Harriman was toying with a South-ern Pacific cutoff between Lordsburg and Yuma that would run along the Gila River, put Phoenix on the main line, and save both mileage and heavy grades. Tucson didn't think much of the idea, of course, but Harriman saw it as his prerogative.

Harriman also saw southern Arizona as a Southern Pacific fiefdom and strenuously objected to the Santa Fe's incursion. The threat wasn't so much a Santa Fe–backed connection at Benson, but rather the line continuing up the Gila and connecting with the Santa Fe stub that had ended so ingloriously at Deming in 1881. This would cut through the heart of southeastern Arizona and flirt with the copper mines at Clifton and Morenci.

In December 1903, Phoenix and Eastern grading crews building east crossed to the north bank of the Gila just west of Kelvin. This move gave every appearance that rather than following the San Pedro upstream to Benson, the Santa Fe–backed effort was intent on pushing straight through the Gila Canyon toward Deming. Harriman saw red. He immediately dispatched his own survey crews to contest the narrow canyon where Phoenix and Eastern surveyors were already pounding stakes beneath rocky walls that in some places towered hundreds of feet above the river.

Once again, opposing forces fought for a strategic passage. Rival surveyors rushed competing lines that overlapped each other almost every step of the way. Grading crews close behind added to the frenzy by blasting rock onto each other's staked line. And journalists filled their columns with descriptions reminiscent of the Royal Gorge war.[2]

Meanwhile, northern California was no less hotly contested, if without quite the drama of the Gila Canyon. When Ripley attempted to acquire the California and Northwestern Railroad in the summer of 1902, Harriman beat him to it. Harriman considered any Santa Fe expansion north of San Francisco to be in the same vein as the Phoenix maneuver. In no uncertain terms, Harriman told the Santa Fe that he was adamantly opposed to it. Ripley acquired the little Eel River and Eureka Railroad instead and showed no sign of backing down.

Harriman focused again on the Arizona situation and repeated his demand that the Santa Fe sell him the Phoenix and Eastern and abandon its route. Ripley once again carefully studied the map of the West. The truth of the matter was that the Gila Canyon was a tortuous route. With serpentine meanders and tight passages, it was never going to be a major speedway. But perhaps Ripley could use Harriman's angst about it to leverage the Santa Fe's more strategic goals. Ripley shrewdly replied to Harriman that the Santa Fe would drop its expansion up the Gila River, but only as part of a broader settlement of competing interests in northern California.

Initially, Harriman scoffed at the offer, but after considerable negotiation, he agreed to a compromise. It provided for the Southern Pacific and Santa Fe to own the competing lines in northern California jointly. In return, Harriman got the Phoenix and Eastern and the lion's share of the press.

But if there is any opinion as to who won and who lost this fight, it

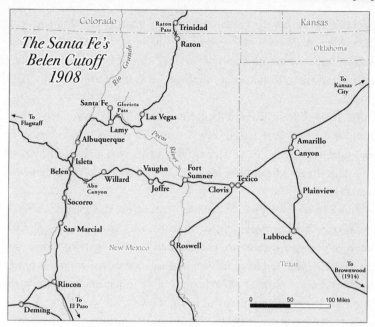

The Santa Fe's
Belen Cutoff
1908

should be noted that the Southern Pacific main line never pierced the Gila Canyon. It continues to run on generally its original route between Lordsburg and Yuma. The Santa Fe, on the other hand, enjoyed future growth in the Pacific Northwest, and connections there eventually helped to facilitate the road's merger with the Burlington Northern Railroad in 1995.[3]

The Ripley team undertook another strategic decision during this time without trouble from competitors. Despite the Santa Fe's integrated system, there was still one section in the Los Angeles-to-Chicago corridor that posed a major operational bottleneck. The steep grades of Raton Pass limited the size of trains, required costly helper engine operations, and slowed through operations on the single track. Conditions weren't much better climbing out of the Rio Grande Valley over Glorieta Pass.

William Jackson Palmer had recognized the problem as early as his 1867 survey for the Kansas Pacific. Palmer's alternative had been to avoid the Raton Mountains and roughly follow the main branch of the

Santa Fe Trail from the headwaters of the Cimarron River to Las Vegas, New Mexico. Even if this Cimarron line was "not adopted at first," Palmer had written presciently in 1867, "it must be built eventually, to economize the transportation of *through* passenger and freight traffic" [his italics].

By 1902, Edward Payson Ripley had agreed and determined to build a cutoff for east-west freight operations that would bypass *both* Raton and Glorieta passes. To do so required a line well south of Raton and smack in the middle of New Mexico, but this was to have numerous advantages.

Santa Fe was never on the railroad's main line, and the town's branch traffic consisted increasingly of destination passengers. Even Albuquerque was not a large freight market. Bypassing both towns with transcontinental freight traffic would speed operations at no loss to local markets. So the railroad looked south of Albuquerque for a route that offered low grades and plenty of straightaways.

Surveyors took to the field in the spring of 1902 and soon pinpointed Abo Canyon, about 50 miles south of Albuquerque, as the low-angle gateway from the Rio Grande Valley to the broad expanses of eastern New Mexico. Engineers picked Belen on the Albuquerque-to-El Paso line as the jumping-off point. In a short time, Belen would become the busiest railroad junction in New Mexico.

The new cutoff ran southeast from Belen, up Abo Canyon, and topped out at 6,535 feet at a station named Mountainair. This was only 1,100 feet lower than the elevation at the Raton Tunnel, but the difference in grades was startling. The maximum gradient at Raton Pass was 184.8 feet per mile. The new Belen Cutoff had a maximum gradient of 66 feet per mile in Abo Canyon and half that along the rest of the route as it ran east to Vaughn, Fort Sumner, and Clovis.

Just inside the Texas border at Texico, the strategic genius of this tactical effort to reduce costs showed itself. Northeast from tiny Texico, the Santa Fe built on to Amarillo and its Southern Kansas Railway subsidiary. This, of course, led straight to the Santa Fe's Kansas main line. The roadbed and tracks of the Southern Kansas were quickly rebuilt to handle the increased volume of traffic.

When the construction dust settled, the mileage over Raton Pass versus Abo Canyon was almost identical, but the gradients made all the difference. The California Limited and later passenger trains usually still operated over Raton Pass, providing service to Las Vegas, Santa Fe, and Albuquerque, but if the question was heavy freight for transcontinental service, the route led through Abo Canyon and over the Belen Cutoff.

The Belen Cutoff became operational on July 1, 1908. But even before its completion, the Santa Fe undertook surveys on the second leg of its strategic Y at Texico. This leg led southeast through Lubbock to hook up with the old Gulf, Colorado and Santa Fe. By the time it was completed in 1914, the Atchison, Topeka and Santa Fe had finally rid itself of the coolness of the handshake that it had received from the Southern Pacific at Deming in 1881.

The new direct route of the Gulf, Colorado and Santa Fe across Texas, over the Belen cutoff, and west to California cut the distance over the Santa Fe from Galveston to San Francisco from 2,666 miles to 2,192 miles and to Los Angeles from 2,355 to 1,881 miles. Regardless of the strengths of the Southern Pacific, the Santa Fe had made itself a key player not only in the California-to-Chicago markets, but in the California-to-Gulf Coast markets as well.[4]

At the macro level, it was Edward Payson Ripley's strategic expansions and his determined focus on solid infrastructure, rolling stock, and personnel that pushed the Atchison, Topeka and Santa Fe to the top of the heap. But beneath this corporate saga, there are two stories that underscore what the railroad came to mean to the American Southwest.

As Fred Harvey's Harvey Houses made the transition from overnight stay to destination resort, scenic locales and cultural enclaves along the Santa Fe's main line became increasingly popular and figured prominently in the railroad's marketing plans. These locations included the mountain air and mineral springs of Las Vegas, New Mexico; the special allure of Santa Fe; and the respite of California's sun and surf.

But none could match the grandeur and breathtaking majesty of the Grand Canyon. While railroad tracks would never wind through the canyon's serpentine length, here at one of the scenic wonders of the world, the Santa Fe Railway, the Fred Harvey Company, and a diminutive but determined woman would join forces to tie the Santa Fe inexorably to the landscape it traversed.

Mary Elizabeth Jane Colter was born in Pittsburgh to Irish parents in 1869. Her father operated millinery and furniture businesses, and the family's moves took them to Texas and Colorado before they settled in St. Paul in 1880. Mary showed early signs of being a gifted artist, and she begged her father to attend an art school. Her dream was realized at the California School of Design—later named the San Francisco Art Institute—and she graduated with a four-year degree in art and design as well as her teaching credentials.

During her academic program, Colter also apprenticed in a local architect's office. At the time, there were only about eleven thousand architects in the United States, and California did not even have a licensing requirement. Women in the profession were rare, and after graduation in 1892, Colter returned to St. Paul and began a fifteen-year career teaching art. But there were to be interludes.

On a return visit to San Francisco, Colter found one of her friends working at a Fred Harvey establishment. She happened to strike up a conversation with the manager and expressed an interest in working for the company as it expanded its operations to include gift shops and newsstands. Nothing came of the encounter immediately, but it is a testament to the Harvey system of scouting out talent that the manager reported Colter's name and her credentials up the Harvey chain of command.

By 1902, the Fred Harvey Company—absent its founder, who had died the preceding year—was completing one of the jewels of its budding system: the Alvarado Hotel in Albuquerque. Surrounded by quiet courtyards, sweeping lawns, and brick pathways, the hotel boasted seventy-five guest rooms, pleasant parlors, and spacious dining rooms to be run to the very best of Fred Harvey standards. The Alvarado was connected to the Santa Fe depot by a two-hundred-foot arcade, and the stucco exterior of both structures resembled the historical Spanish mission architecture of the Southwest rather than the European influences of so many recent buildings.

As part of its plan to emphasize the cultures of the Southwest, the Fred Harvey Company proposed to build an "Indian building" along the arcade adjacent to the Alvarado. It would both showcase Native American artifacts and provide a sales outlet for contemporary arts and crafts. What the company needed to perfect the plan was "a decorator who knew Indian things and had imagination." When Mary Colter received a lengthy telegram asking if she was the right person, she hurried to Albuquerque and began a forty-year association with both the Fred Harvey Company and the Atchison, Topeka and Santa Fe.

The importance of Mary Jane Colter's initial contribution at the Alvarado to Southwest architecture cannot be overstated. As an advertisement for the hotel boasted that summer, the Alvarado was "the first building in New Mexico to revive the Spanish tradition and thereby make the whole Southwest history-conscious." Colter's role was to provide the vehicle—part museum, part shop—to make that culture readily accessible to the thousands upon thousands of passengers who passed through the region on the Santa Fe's trains.

When her assignment at the Alvarado was complete, Colter returned to St. Paul to continue teaching, but two years later, the Fred Harvey Company summoned her to the rim of the Grand Canyon to undertake a bigger venture. In 1901 the Santa Fe had acquired an old mining railroad and extended its tracks from a copper mine at Anita to the South Rim. It was only 65 miles from Williams on the Santa Fe's main line to the canyon, and easier access meant more visitors.

The Fred Harvey Company quickly determined that more visitors required overnight accommodations, so the architect of the Alvarado, Charles F. Whittlesey of Chicago, was engaged to design the fabled El Tovar Hotel near the railroad's terminus. For some reason, despite his experience at Albuquerque, Whittlesey chose to design El Tovar in the chalet style of the great resort hotels of Europe. But Mary Colter was commissioned to design the adjacent "Indian building," to be called Hopi House, and all subsequent structures on the rim would follow her architectural lead.

Designed after a traditional Hopi dwelling, Hopi House again combined a museum for Native American rugs, baskets, and other artifacts, with a sales area for contemporary crafts. Hopi and Navajo artisans frequently worked on site to make jewelry, baskets, blankets, and other sales items. Both Hopi House and El Tovar opened to rave reviews in 1905.

Among early visitors was artist Thomas Moran, who came at the request of the Fred Harvey Company and produced a series of landscapes that captured the special beauty and sweeping magnitude of the canyon. Moran's works did much to publicize the Grand Canyon, and that was good for business, selling both Santa Fe passenger tickets and Fred Harvey meals and beds.

Once again, Mary Colter returned to St. Paul to teach, but finally Fred Harvey hired her full-time as an architect and designer to oversee the company's expanding facilities. Technically, she worked for Fred Harvey, but a portion of her salary was paid by the Santa Fe under the continuing arrangement that Mr. Harvey had first proposed to the railroad in 1876: Fred Harvey operated the restaurants and hotels and owned the furnishings, but the Santa Fe owned the buildings and land.

Colter's first full-time project was the interior decoration of the El Ortiz at Lamy, New Mexico. By Harvey House standards, El Ortiz was small—fewer than ten rooms—but it was the perfect gateway to Santa Fe. No less a western authority than Owen Wister, author of *The Virginian*, described El Ortiz as a temptation "to give up all plans and stay a week for the pleasure of living and resting in such a place."

Then it was back to the Grand Canyon to design Hermit's Rest. The Fred Harvey Company had constructed a road for tours west along the South Rim and needed a place for shelter, refreshments, and, of course, the requisite souvenirs. With its haphazard stonework, a stout bear trap out front, a huge stone fireplace, and a crude interior, the building indeed looked like the den of a hermit—exactly what Colter intended.

Hermit's Rest and the Lookout Studio on the rim just west of El Tovar were both completed in 1914. After the interruption of World War I, Grand Canyon National Park was established in 1919, and Mary Jane Colter went on to design the facilities at Phantom Ranch, the Watchtower at Desert View, and Bright Angel Lodge. Before her career was complete, Colter's influence would be felt up and down the Santa Fe line, from the interior of La Fonda at Santa Fe to La Posada at Winslow, Arizona, for which she was both architect and decorator.

"Her buildings," wrote biographer Virginia Grattan, "fit their setting because they grew out of the history of the land. They belonged." And because the Santa Fe also embraced this history with its train names, décor, and advertising, it too belonged. Perhaps no other railroad became as closely associated with the landscape it traversed as did the Santa Fe across the American Southwest.[5]

But if there was no doubt that the Santa Fe belonged to the land it served, could it truly deliver the goods? It needed a public relations exclamation point, and it got one. In early July 1905, a showboating cowboy with the moniker "Death Valley Scotty" swaggered into the Santa Fe's Los Angeles depot and flashed a roll of bills. Chicago, fast as can be done, he ordered.

It quickly became a publicity stunt—indeed, Scotty appears to have intended it that way from the start—but the fact that the Santa Fe obliged was proof that it had emerged at the top of the heap as America's greatest transcontinental line. Soon the jingle "Santa Fe All the Way" would become more than a marketing slogan and attest to the railroad's transcontinental racetrack.

Walter Edward Scott was one of those people who, through a mix of charm, humor, and congenial deception, surrounded himself with a veil of mystery that confounds any attempt to tell his story. Part of the problem is that Scotty himself was one of the biggest storytellers of them all.

He was born in Kentucky in 1872. His father was a harness-horse trainer and breeder, and young Scott developed an early ease with horses and mules. As early as 1884, he left home for the West to join older brothers who were working as cowboys. Reports have Scott working as a water boy on the California-Nevada boundary survey and as a helper on the famed twenty-mule teams of the Harmony Borax Works in Death Valley.

About 1890, Buffalo Bill Cody hired Scott for his Wild West Show. Somewhere along the line, Scotty—by then, no one was calling him Walter—took on the moniker Death Valley Scotty. He worked the show for twelve seasons before quitting after a reported dispute with Cody. In the interim, it's likely that Scott used at least some of his off-seasons to return periodically to Death Valley. He also seems to have spent two winters working in gold mines near Cripple Creek, Colorado.

By the time Scott left Cody's Wild West Show in 1902, one of the last chapters of the American mining frontier was being played out in and around his old stomping grounds. The Nevada towns of Tonopah, Goldfield, and Rhyolite all hoped to rival Leadville or Tombstone, not with silver but with gold, and no one was at all certain what riches might lie hidden in Death Valley's rocky ravines.

First and foremost, Scott was a promoter. He flashed two souvenir nuggets that his wife, Ella, had gotten from a Colorado gold mine and spun a story of riches hidden in a location in Death Valley known only to him. He then parlayed this tale into a grubstake from a New York banker named Julian Gerard.

Scott alternated his time between Los Angeles and Death Valley but did not develop his purported mining property. Instead he lived the life of a high roller and spent Gerard's cash as his own, all the while asserting that his newfound wealth came from his fabulous, hidden mine. This charade went on for the better part of two years before Scott approached a Chicago businessman for a similar grubstake.

Aside from sharing 1872 as their birth year, Albert M. Johnson was the polar opposite of Walter Scott. Born in Oberlin, Ohio, Johnson was the son of a wealthy banker and businessman. He graduated from Cornell University in 1895 with a civil engineering degree and married a Cornell classmate, Bessilyn "Bessie" Penniman, the following year. Johnson worked for his father in the family businesses until a tragic railroad accident on a Denver and Rio Grande train near Salida, Colorado, in December 1899 killed his father and left Johnson with a spinal injury that caused him chronic back pain and some paralysis the rest of his life.

In 1902 Johnson and his father's former business partner, Edward A. Shedd, bought the National Life Insurance Company of Chicago at foreclosure. Johnson eventually increased his holdings to 90 percent of the ownership. Sometime in 1904, Johnson met either a man fronting for Scott or Scott himself and heard the now well-worn tale of Scott's Death Valley riches.

Having made a considerable profit from a lead-zinc mine in Missouri, Johnson was willing to take a chance on Scotty. But given their future relationship, it must also be speculated that something clicked between the two men. The following year, probably with funds provided by Johnson, and quite likely in an attempt to impress Johnson with the success of his Death Valley venture, Walter Scott swaggered into the Los Angeles office of the Atchison, Topeka and Santa Fe and made his simple but profound request: "Chicago, fast as you can do it."[6]

Supposedly, Scott suggested that his goal was a time of forty-six hours. If so, that was a full day faster than the schedule of the California Limited and twelve hours faster than the existing Los Angeles-to-Chicago record. That eastbound record over the Santa Fe was held by a special train called the Peacock Special that made the run in fifty-seven hours and fifty-six minutes in March 1900, carrying the vice president of the Carnegie Steel and Iron Company, Alexander R. Peacock, on his way to Pittsburgh for an urgent board meeting.

Later there would be ample speculation whether Scott was just plain crazy, whether he had indeed peeled off $5,500 in big bills to pay for the excursion, or whether the Santa Fe was somehow involved as a coconspirator in a publicity stunt. Certainly the railroad gave its all for the run.

What is fact is that on the afternoon of Sunday, July 9, 1905, Walter and Ella Scott arrived at La Grande Station in Los Angeles and stepped aboard a train that would quickly come to be called "the Scott Special," or with the hyperbole of hindsight, "the Coyote Special." Engine no. 442 was to start the journey and pull a consist of one baggage car, one dining car, and one standard Pullman, the Muskegon.

Eastbound to San Bernardino the special roared, pausing only long enough to pick up a helper for the climb over Cajon Pass. At the summit, "the helper engine was uncoupled on the fly and, while the speed of the train never slackened for an instant," the helper engine raced ahead and darted onto a siding. The switch to the main line was then closed, and the oncoming special sped past without so much as a hint of slowing.

East of Cajon, Scott's special flashed downgrade to Barstow at more than a mile a minute. The problem here, Frank Holman, a reporter on the train recalled, "was not how fast we could run, but how fast we dared to run." Reportedly, the distance between mileposts 44 and 43 went by in 39 seconds—96 miles per hour.

At Barstow came the first change of crews and locomotives. Then it was on to the Colorado River at Needles and a Sunday evening arrival just six hours and seventeen minutes after leaving Los Angeles. After another crew and locomotive change—there would be nineteen engines and engineers used in all—the special roared across the river on the steel cantilever bridge south of Needles that had replaced the early wooden structure opposite town.

Dinner was served in the dining car—to Fred Harvey standards, of course—despite the rocketing motion of the train. By the time the newspapers got ahold of the story, the menu was reported to have featured a "Caviare Sandwich à la Death Valley" and a juicy, two-inch-thick "Porterhouse Steak à la Coyote."

Meanwhile, northern Arizona flew by outside the windows as the train climbed up and down the heavy grades below the San Francisco Peaks and rushed on eastward in the darkness across Cañon Diablo, past Gallup, and on into Albuquerque. North of Albuquerque at Lamy another helper was put on for the climb over Glorieta Pass. Even across Glorieta and Raton, the Scott special averaged just over forty-six miles per hour—quite a record, considering the tough mountain railroading involved.

By the time the train raced into La Junta, Colorado, the mountains were behind it, and up ahead the Santa Fe's raceway across the plains of Kansas and into the heartland urged even greater speeds. From Dodge City, Scotty sent President Theodore Roosevelt a telegram: "An American cowboy is coming East on a special train faster than any cowpuncher ever rode before; how much shall I break transcontinental record?"

East of Dodge City, a continuing succession of men and equipment sped the Coyote Special through the darkness of a second night. Josiah Gossard, a Santa Fe veteran with twenty years' experience as a road engineer, took the throttle for the run between Emporia and Argentine, just short of Kansas City. Notwithstanding four slow orders, Gossard covered 124 miles in 130 minutes, the fastest time yet recorded between those two points.

Shortly before eight in the morning on Tuesday, the train thundered across the big steel bridge across the Mississippi, just south of Fort Madison, Iowa, and charged down A. A. Robinson's straightaway toward Chicago. The 105 miles between the river and Chillicothe flew by in 101 minutes. One report claimed that the special bore down on Dearborn Station doing 60 miles an hour.

At six minutes before noon on Tuesday, July 11, 1905, Death Valley Scotty's special came to a halt outside the station. The train had covered 2,265 miles in just 44 hours and 54 minutes—an average, including all delays, of 50.4 miles per hour.

It's hard to say who was more elated—Scotty or the Santa Fe's public relations department. Scott no doubt called on Albert Johnson, but the Santa Fe had a story that it would tell up and down the line and across the country. The special had been given the right-of-way across the country—even the vaunted California Limited was sidetracked for it—but otherwise, no extraordinary provisions had been made. The run was completed with regular equipment and standard crews.

"I'm buying speed" was the pithy quote attributed to Scott, but the Santa Fe copywriters put a good deal more spin on it. "The value of a whirlwind run," the Santa Fe rationalized, "lies in the fact that such spurts thoroughly put to test the track, the engines, and the operating force. They demonstrate to the world of travel that the regular hurry-up schedule can be easily maintained the year round; that the track is solid and dependable; that the engines are powerful and swift; also that the men on and behind the engines and along the track are keen of eye, clear-brained, and quick to act."[7]

A few years after this publicity stunt, Albert Johnson finally decided that he should visit Death Valley and see firsthand how Walter Scott had been spending his money. What he discovered surprised him. There was no sign of a gold mine, of course, but Johnson found himself invigorated by the dry heat and stark beauty of Death Valley. He returned again and again and spent weeks on end poking around its canyons with Scott. He "loves a good time and is a high roller," Johnson admitted of Scotty, but, said Johnson, Scott was "absolutely reliable, and I don't know of any man in the world that I would rather go on a camping trip with than Scott."

By the 1920s, Death Valley Scotty was a national legend, and Scotty's Castle, a huge estate of Moorish architecture, was taking shape in Grapevine Canyon, fueled by Scotty's lost mine stories and in truth financed by Johnson's millions. Did Johnson care? "Scott repays me in laughs," Johnson is reported to have said.[8]

Johnson's wife, Bessie, was killed in an automobile crash in Death Valley in 1943. Johnson passed away in 1948. Death Valley Scotty told tales of his secret mine until his end on January 5, 1954. Scott is buried on a hill above the castle that Albert Johnson graciously let him call his. It later became part of Death Valley National Park.

The 1905 ride of the Scott special was a flash in the pan of railroad hype and hoopla, but it called undeniable attention to the railroad system that Colonel Holliday's little line had become. Santa Fe mileage had grown from 6,444 miles in 1897 to 9,527 in 1906—an increase of nearly 48 percent. Gross earnings during this same period had climbed from $30 million to $81 million, resulting in a net income of $18 million in 1906 as opposed to zero nine years earlier.

But Edward Payson Ripley was far from finished. In his annual report for 1906—echoing the refrain of William Barstow Strong that a company could not afford not to build—Ripley announced that despite recent expansions and acquisitions, it would be necessary to continue such an expansionist policy for an indefinite period of time. "The country served by the System is growing so rapidly that a large amount of additional equipment and of other facilities for the transaction of business must be provided."[9]

Ripley might have added that the country served by the Santa Fe was in fact growing so fast *because* of the railroad and that the Santa Fe continued to fuel that growth with ever-increasing capacity, branch lines, and land grant sales. Thanks in no small measure to the railroad's advance, the territory that President James K. Polk had wrested from Mexico sixty-some years before had become an integral part of the burgeoning United States. In 1846 the wagon master's cry had been "On to Santa Fe!" Cyrus K. Holliday and his associates pushed their railroad to Santa Fe and then beyond. In doing so, they inexorably changed the landscape the rails traversed.

In 1870 the Atchison, Topeka and Santa Fe was not yet one-third of the way across Kansas. But between then and 1910, the population of the states and territories its main lines served—Kansas, Colorado, New Mexico, Arizona, California, Oklahoma, and Texas—increased 5.7 times, more than twice the national average.

Those seven states and territories, encompassing one-third of the continental area of the United States, grew from populations of 1.9 million in 1870 to 10.9 million in 1910. This surge was perhaps most visible in the U.S. House of Representatives, where new apportionments and statehoods increased the region's representation from nine congressmen in 1870 to fifty-one in 1910—a westward trend of population and political power that has continued into the twenty-first century.

Colorado became a state in 1876. Oklahoma, spurred by a land rush and oil discoveries, followed in 1907. By 1912, the territories of Arizona and New Mexico would round out the lower forty-eight states. And along the way, the towns served by the Santa Fe became the commercial hubs and political centers of a region where before there had largely been wild prairies, sweeping deserts, and quiet countryside.

With Santa Fe connections, Los Angeles and San Diego in California, Phoenix in Arizona, and Albuquerque and Las Cruces in New Mexico grew to prominence. The Santa Fe paced the Denver and Rio Grande along Colorado's Front Range and boosted Denver, Colorado Springs, and Pueblo.

Along with the venerable Katy, the Santa Fe stocked the Oklahoma boom and brought competition to Dallas, Fort Worth, and Houston. More than anything else, it was the passenger prestige and freight tonnage of the Santa Fe that solidified Kansas City as the western gateway to the Southwest. Perhaps most important, the Atchison, Topeka and Santa Fe tied together East and West along the most direct transcontinental route between the Midwest and the Pacific Coast.

Some would later say that Ripley had worked a "virtual miracle"—not just on the Main Streets of so many towns in the Southwest but on Wall Street as well. Ripley's fiscal conservatism and calculated expansion had made the Santa Fe a "blue chip" investment. Meanwhile, his investment in the physical plant continued, including the double-tracking of the main line from Chicago to Newton, Kansas, by 1911.[10]

The road was "winning its right," one contemporary financial writer noted, to be called "the Pennsylvania of the West." In case there was any doubt exactly what that meant, the writer spelled it out: "The Pennsylvania policy is not one of parsimonious dividends, nor of shrinking from heavy capital expenses. It is one of liberal maintenance, aggressive expansion, and the free issue of stocks and bonds." No doubt, J. Edgar Thomson smiled in his grave at that.[11]

When Edward Payson Ripley relinquished the presidency of the Atchison, Topeka and Santa Fe on January 1, 1920, "the road had become universally recognized as one of the best physically and soundest financially, in the world, besides having established an enviable reputation for the character of service rendered." It had indeed reached the top of the heap.[12]

23

Dueling Streamliners

There is, of course, one more story that must be told. Any account of the Atchison, Topeka and Santa Fe would not be complete without it. By 1909, the transcontinental routes had been built, empires won and lost, but the American West was still a contested battleground. Increasingly, the objective would become transcontinental speed, and the high visibility weapons would be sleek, new streamliners racing between California and Chicago.

Edward Payson Ripley first responded to calls for increased passenger speed and service by inaugurating the Santa Fe's de-Luxe between Chicago and Los Angeles in December 1911. Powered by a steam locomotive pulling heavy steel cars, the de-Luxe made the trip once a week in just over sixty hours. Its nine o'clock morning arrival in Los Angeles bettered the schedule of the California Limited by five and one-half hours and, according to one advertisement, "saves a business day."

The only stops the de-Luxe made for passenger boarding were at Kansas City and Williams, Arizona, the latter for Grand Canyon traffic.

A limit of sixty passengers per trip could take advantage of service that the railroad boasted was "extra fine, extra fast, extra fare." At last, the West had a train that could rival the New York Central's famed 20th Century Limited or the Pennsylvania Railroad's stalwart Broadway Limited.[1]

World War I came along all too quickly and was not a very pleasant time for American railroads. In 1918 President Woodrow Wilson assumed federal control of the railroads in order to consolidate routes and make rolling stock available to the war effort. The de-Luxe was one of the casualties. The one bright spot was the growing reliability with which the nation's rail network moved men and materiel around the country. In many respects, it was a test for a far greater effort less than a generation later.

As America raced into the Roaring Twenties, the Santa Fe reintroduced the de-Luxe under a new name destined for railroad stardom. The road relied on its ties with southwestern Native American culture to name the train the "Chief." Still powered by steam, the Chief was made up of eight Pullman cars. Naturally, these included a Fred Harvey dining car, because, as the original brochure for the Chief asserted, "California, the Santa Fe Railway and the Fred Harvey cuisine have been inseparable in the minds of travelers for over forty years."

Perhaps the biggest change was that the Chief operated daily and began its inaugural run with twin consists that left Chicago and Los Angeles simultaneously on November 14, 1926. There were a few additional passenger stops—including Ash Fork, Arizona, for connections to Phoenix—but the Chief shaved minutes off the timetable of the de-Luxe and arrived in Los Angeles in just under sixty hours.[2]

Yet another boom went bust in 1929, but America's passenger trains responded with a new level of sophistication and innovation. The Santa Fe's rival Chicago, Burlington and Quincy debuted a silver rocket of a train that it called the Zephyr. Streamlined to slice through the air and reduce drag, the train was also "streamlined" by the use of lighter stainless steel. The three-car Zephyr consisted of a diesel power car with railway post office; a center car with a baggage-express compartment, buffet area, and twenty coach seats; and a rear observation-lounge car with fifty-two seats.

The Burlington sent the new streamliner on a five-week publicity tour of the Northeast and then let it kick up its heels on a run from

Denver to Chicago. On May 26, 1934, the Zephyr left Denver's Union Station and fairly flew across the plains to arrive in Chicago thirteen hours and five minutes later at an average speed of 77.6 miles per hour. An estimated half million Midwesterners lined the Burlington's tracks to watch, and for a nation still staggered by the Great Depression, it was a very futuristic and optimistic sight.[3]

Not to be outdone, the Union Pacific competed with the Burlington's Zephyr by introducing a streamliner of its own. Marketed under the slogan "Tomorrow's Train Today," its canary yellow paint with golden brown trim became distinctive Union Pacific colors. Officially, the bright yellow was chosen for safety reasons because it "can be seen for a greater distance than any other color," but there was little doubt that the Union Pacific wanted everyone to know *which* train was coming. By the summer of 1936, the Union Pacific was running City of San Francisco and City of Los Angeles streamliners between Chicago and those cities in a record time of thirty-nine hours and forty-five minutes.[4]

Then it was the Santa Fe's turn. On May 12, 1936, in direct response to the challenge of the Union Pacific's "City" streamliners, the Santa Fe started its first Super Chief west from Dearborn Station in Chicago. The consist was standard Pullmans without a stainless-steel car in the line, but the motive power was twin 1,800-horsepower diesels that had routinely hit 150 miles per hour during their trials. These early diesels were shaped like boxcars with a straight front end, but the Super Chief matched the Union Pacific's time to Los Angeles to the minute.

By April 1937, the Super Chief was all streamlined with a silvery nine-car consist of mail car, mail-baggage car, four sleepers, lounge, diner, and sleeper-observation car that carried 104 passengers in style. The following year, the Santa Fe took delivery of its first E-type diesels with their hawkish nose and distinctive Indian warbonnet colors and paint scheme.

By 1939, the Santa Fe was running a fleet of streamliners between Chicago and Los Angeles. The all-Pullman Super Chief set the standard and operated twice weekly. The original Chief continued to operate daily as an all-Pullman train but without quite the speed or fanfare of its younger sibling. And to cater to the cost-conscious traveler who still wanted speed, the all-chair coaches of El Capitan carried 188 passengers on a twice-weekly schedule that matched the speed of the Super Chief.

Why did the Santa Fe's Super Chief eclipse the Union Pacific's City of Los Angeles in fact and lore even though the competing trains had identical time schedules? In three words: marketing, service, and mystique. The Santa Fe promoted the splendor of traversing the American Southwest in unparalleled style. The Fred Harvey Company catered to every need with five-star meals and gracious hospitality. And thanks to those two things, the train became the train to be seen on for a generation.

One Santa Fe advertisement from the period said it all. It showed a glamorous movie star walking toward a gaggle of reporters next to the rounded end of a stainless-steel observation car complete with Super Chief drumhead. "She came in on the Super Chief," read the caption. Indeed, for anyone traveling between the West Coast and America's heartland, the phrase "just got in on the Super" quickly became the boast that set one above the crowd.[5]

With this Depression-era emphasis on speed, there was to be one more battle for California. This time, the Santa Fe and the Southern Pacific would go head to head for the San Francisco–Los Angeles corridor. The Southern Pacific had long monopolized this market because its Pacific Coast line was the shortest rail distance between the two cities. It was here that the dashing Coast Daylight whisked passengers in comfort approaching that of the Super Chief. And while Santa Fe partisans were quick to take exception, many rail travelers stared at the Daylight's red, orange, and black paint scheme and pronounced it simply the most beautiful train in the world.

For the Santa Fe to compete in this market, it had to shorten its roundabout route over Cajon Pass to Barstow, back over Tehachapi Pass to Bakersfield, and then down the San Joaquin Valley to Oakland. Even then, a ferry was required to reach downtown San Francisco. The Santa Fe studied the problem and found an unwitting ally. The California Highway Department was improving the road system between Los Angeles and Bakersfield via Tejon Pass, which later became the route of Interstate 5. The Santa Fe took advantage of this and inaugurated a combination rail-bus service.

A traveler left Los Angeles by bus, arrived in Bakersfield, boarded the streamlined Golden Gate, and then settled in for a 313-mile sprint to Oakland. From there, another fleet of air-conditioned buses completed the journey to downtown San Francisco via the recently completed Bay Bridge. Not only was this service cheaper than the rail-only or bus-only options—$6 compared to $9.47 on the Southern Pacific and $6.75 on the buses of Pacific Greyhound—but it beat the Southern Pacific's all-rail time by ten minutes. Suddenly the Santa Fe was the fastest way between California's twin hubs.[6]

The prewar glory days of streamliners were destined to be short lived. After December 7, 1941, the demands of a two-ocean global war tested America's railroads to the limit. The Santa Fe continued to operate the Chiefs and El Capitan, but the schedule for the Chicago–Los Angeles speedway was increased by two hours because of the tremendous volume of troop trains on the line.

All along the Santa Fe main line, Fred Harvey establishments worked overtime to feed the large numbers of men and women moving about the country for the war effort. For many young draftees away from home for the first time, Fred Harvey meals provided a brief respite and memories of a mother's kitchen. (Sixty years later, the author's father was still talking about the pheasant sandwich he had been served "somewhere in Montana" while en route from Cleveland to Fort Lewis, Washington, in 1944.)

But it was freight that proved the worth of the Santa Fe's California-to-Chicago main line. With much of the route double-tracked, freight ton-miles (a ton of freight moved one mile) almost doubled between 1941 and 1942. The critical 82-mile Cajon Pass leg shared with the Union Pacific between San Bernardino and Barstow routinely handled twenty to thirty freight trains a day. Tehachapi Pass saw similar traffic, but perhaps nowhere was the Santa Fe busier than on its "surf line" between Los Angeles and San Diego. Both cities, past rivalries momentarily put aside, boomed as major military centers and embarkation ports. On one day alone in 1942, the Santa Fe moved almost five thousand people between the two places.

The biggest operational change for the Santa Fe during this time was that World War II proved the worth of the diesel locomotive and hastened the end of steam. The first diesel freight locomotive was delivered to the Santa Fe for road tests in February 1938. Comprising four units generating 5,400 horsepower, the locomotive pulled sixty-six loaded freight cars from Kansas City to Los Angeles. "Bypassing water stops, crossing passes without helpers, and moving at a high rate of speed," its performance encouraged the Santa Fe to place the first order for freight diesels by any railroad in the United States.

There was soon little doubt that steam locomotives—majestic and thunderous though they were—had seen their glory years. Only the enormous demands of World War II gave them a temporary reprieve. Steam locomotives belched black smoke and worked alongside their diesel upstarts, but by the end of the war, it was clear that diesels had prevailed over steam by every measure of efficiency, moving 100-car trains 500 miles without a stop and often running 10,000 miles per month. During this intense period of national mobilization, revenue train-miles on the Santa Fe jumped from 40.9 million in 1938 to 70.7 million in 1945. Steam couldn't have done it alone.[7]

After World War II had been fought and won, "the greatest generation" raced homeward to embrace a new level of prosperity and mobility. Everyone wanted a new automobile, but America's railroads also responded with family travel advertisements and a renewed commitment to streamliners.

The Super Chief once again became a mainstay of the traveling elite. It even had a role in numerous movies and books, including Frederic Wakeman's early postwar novel *The Hucksters.* Racy for its time, *The Hucksters* entwined the glitz and glamour of high-powered advertising agencies with a torrid bicoastal love affair. Few things were certain, but in one paragraph Wakeman captured what the Santa Fe's prize train had come to mean to a war-weary world.

"One thing about the Chief," Wakeman wrote, "east or westbound, it never changes. That's what a man likes about this extra-fare, extra exclusive, super-deluxe commuter special that makes Toots Shor's handy to Romanoff's, that connects Sunset Boulevard with Wall Street. The Chief never changes. A man can depend on the Chief. It's one of the few enduring values left in this unstable old world."[8]

Robert R. Young took the hucksterism of Wakeman's novel to the extreme in 1946 when he launched a public crusade for coast-to-coast Pullman car service. Young was the freewheeling president of the Chesapeake and Ohio Railroad, and some joked that his initials really stood for "RailRoad" Young.

Young firmly believed that the railroad industry was not doing enough to plan for the postwar years, particularly new competition from airlines. Young waged a contest to control the Pullman Company, which effectively ruled the nation's passenger service because it dictated where and when its cars were assigned. This frequently meant that passengers changing railroads for transcontinental travel through the mid-continent hubs of Chicago, St. Louis, and New Orleans were forced to change Pullman cars even if it was the middle of the night. Young decreed there was a better way.

The most famous salvo of his campaign was an advertisement placed in national newspapers that proclaimed, "A Hog Can Cross the Country Without Changing Trains—But YOU Can't!" It showed a totally satisfied pig standing at the door of a boxcar smoking a cigar while a distraught family labeled "John Q. Traveler" looked on in disbelief.[9]

Young's "hog ad" got repeated national attention, and while he ultimately failed to control Pullman, the company made it easier to ticket coast-to-coast service. Accordingly, the Santa Fe teamed up with both the Pennsylvania Railroad and the New York Central to hook through cars from the Broadway Limited and the 20th Century Limited onto the Chief for delivery to Los Angeles and back.

Coast-to-coast cars made publicity, but at the core of the postwar rail travel boom in the West was an innovation sparked by a ride taken during the last days of the war. Cyrus R. Osborn, the head of the General Motors Electromotive Division, happened to be in the cab of a Denver and Rio Grande diesel as it was passing through the depths of Colorado's spectacular Glenwood Canyon.

"A lot of people would pay $500 for this fireman's seat from Chicago to San Francisco if they knew what they could see from it," Osborn remarked to the engineer. "Why wouldn't it be possible," he mused, "to build some sort of glass covered room in the roof of a car so passengers could get this kind of a view?" Later that week, Osborn sketched out a rough design for a series of vista dome observation cars.[10]

Streamliners pulling sleek, stainless-steel vista domes set the stage for one last round of railroad rivalry in the American Southwest. Once again, the competition between California and Chicago focused on the Denver and Rio Grande, the Union Pacific, and the Atchison, Topeka and Santa Fe.

Despite competition to the north and south, the Denver and Rio Grande teamed up with the Burlington east of Denver and the Western Pacific west of Ogden. The three roads ordered six identical train sets and launched the California Zephyr between Chicago and Oakland in March 1949. Billed "the most talked-about train in America," its service was impeccable and Rocky Mountain trout the specialty of the dining car.[11]

The Union Pacific made a strong postwar run at both the California Zephyr and the Santa Fe's competition after it put the City of Los Angeles and the City of San Francisco into daily service in 1947. The City streamliners soon became "Domeliners," with the introduction of the only domed dining cars ever put into operation.[12]

Throughout these years, the Super Chief was still the train to be seen on and the train to beat. It reverted to its prewar schedule of thirty-nine hours and forty-five minutes on June 2, 1946, and never looked back. By 1948, the Santa Fe was operating both the Super Chief and El Capitan on a daily schedule on that timetable. Onboard the Super Chief, there was almost unparalleled postwar luxury, from the sweeping vistas viewed from the Pleasure Dome lounge to the private dining of the Turquoise Room. Advertisements hailed the dome as "the top of the Super, next to the stars."

Romance, both with one's companion and with the landscape the train traversed, remained a huge selling point. Southwest-style advertisements continued to be a Santa Fe staple, including one of the most famous, a full-color, full-page painting by Hernando Villa of the *Meeting of the Chiefs*—one a Native American on horseback and the other a warbonnet-painted locomotive racing across the Southwest.[13]

Just as it had before the war, Santa Fe management encouraged close ties to Hollywood's booming motion picture industry. The Super Chief made a special stop in Pasadena to allow Hollywood names to board or disembark without the crush of the Los Angeles Union Passenger Terminal. This didn't keep the press from covering the event—usually with the star's concurrence, as he or she now was the acknowledged celebrity of the smaller Pasadena station.

Over the years, the Super Chief's high-profile passengers included Humphrey Bogart and Lauren Bacall, Desi Arnaz and Lucille Ball, and Richard Burton and Elizabeth Taylor. The train also carried Ronald Reagan in his Hollywood days and, later, former presidents Harry Truman and Dwight Eisenhower.

But people remained only a small portion of the Santa Fe's overall load. When Santa Fe management now thought of speed, it was not only the Super Chief, but also its core Los Angeles-to-Chicago freight service. With continued upgrades to roadbed and equipment, freight times decreased to the point that the road introduced the Super C, a hotshot freight that bettered the Super Chief schedule and moved long trains of piggyback truck trailers and containers between Los Angeles and Chicago on a schedule of thirty-four and one-half hours.

As the Sunbelt of Southern California, Arizona, and Texas boomed during the 1950s, the Santa Fe grew right along with it. In the summer of 1955, the longest stretch of new track to be laid in the United States in twenty years—some 49 miles—was built from the Santa Fe's Chicago-to-Galveston line at Fort Worth directly east to Dallas, eliminating the original roundabout route. That same year, the Atchison, Topeka and Santa Fe system grew to 13,073 miles and was ranked as the country's longest railroad.[14]

The polished sophistication of the Super Chief firmly embedded the Santa Fe in the psyche of the American traveling public. But it was the heavy freight traffic between California and the Midwest during World War II and afterward that confirmed the Santa Fe's continuing dominance at the top of the heap of America's transcontinental railroads. Not only had the railroad become a key transcontinental connection, but mushrooming trade with Japan, China, and the Pacific Rim made it a vital land bridge in the growing global economy as well.

From a dream on the Kansas prairie, through the fights for strategic gateways, two world wars, and the booms and busts of economic cycles, the Atchison, Topeka and Santa Fe had proven its staying power and inexorably entwined itself with the American Southwest. Wherever one was bound, it was indeed possible to ride Santa Fe all the way.

Afterword

American Railroads in the Twenty-first Century

On the morning of Saturday, January 12, 1957, the Santa Fe's vaunted Super Chief and stalwart El Capitan left Dearborn Station in Chicago westbound as usual. But there was one major difference. They were no longer two separate trains but a combined consist. Due to declining passenger traffic, the Santa Fe had consolidated the schedules of its two crack streamliners into one train. Its published schedule was still thirty-nine and three-quarters hours, but as the nation looked ahead toward new frontiers, this suddenly seemed terribly slow.

Overhead, new Boeing 707 jets were beginning to whisk Hollywood stars as well as ordinary folks across what was once a contested empire in less than five hours. On that raw winter's day, few paused to notice that the moment marked the beginning of the end for the nation's premier transcontinental passenger trains.

Within a few years, the entire American railroad system was in chaos and disrepair. The once-proud streamliners of the Santa Fe, Union Pacific, and other roads had been ingloriously swept into Amtrak, which in its early form often seemed more of a graveyard caretaker than a public conveyance. The bankruptcy of the vaunted Penn Central merger was taken as gospel that bigger was not always better and that bigger certainly did not ensure profitability.

Out west, the successors to Harriman's Union Pacific, Huntington's Southern Pacific, and Colonel Holliday's Santa Fe hung on to their freight business and pondered their fate. The Denver and Rio Grande Western proved that it still had a feisty streak by opting out of Amtrak and operating the Zephyr on its own between Denver and Salt Lake City.

The eventual demise of the Zephyr in 1983 came with more bad news for the Denver and Rio Grande Western. The Union Pacific acquired the Rio Grande's friendly competition at both ends of its system: the Missouri Pacific to the east and the Western Pacific to the west, and left General Palmer's legacy rather isolated.

Then an event that would have been unthinkable to Collis P. Huntington and William Barstow Strong occurred. In 1984 the Southern Pacific and the Atchison, Topeka and Santa Fe attempted to merge. The Interstate Commerce Commission (ICC) denied the union as monopolistic two years later, but a trend had been set. Bigger might indeed be better. (The ICC itself would be phased out in 1995.)

Meanwhile, in 1985, a Denver oil tycoon, Philip Anschutz, acquired the struggling Denver and Rio Grande Western. Three years later, the direction of Anschutz's thinking was revealed when his Rio Grande holding company also acquired the Southern Pacific as it staggered out of its attempted merger with the Santa Fe.

Faced with this combined competition in the Southwest and the Union Pacific's growing network across the nation's midsection, the Santa Fe went shopping for another partner. Colonel Holliday's road found it in the Burlington Northern, and the merger of the two roads into the Burlington Northern Santa Fe was finalized in 1995. The western railroad merger mania was completed the following year when Philip Anschutz sold the combined Southern Pacific–Denver and Rio Grande Western system to the Union Pacific.

The immediate casualty of this consolidation of the West's railroads into two corporate giants was the Royal Gorge route through the Rockies. The Union Pacific chose to run most of its freight through Wyoming and relegate the Moffat Tunnel line to regional coal trains and the Amtrak route of the reborn California Zephyr. The line through

the Royal Gorge and over Tennessee Pass that the Rio Grande and Santa
Fe had fought over so hard saw its last train in 1997.

These titanic railroad mergers—a situation that occurred in the East
as well with the emergence of the Norfolk Southern and CSX
behemoths—left rail fans and historians mourning a disappearing past.
But nostalgia for logos, paint schemes, and train names aside, the first
decade of the twenty-first century has been incredibly good for railroads.

Energy demands for coal, cross-country container shipments, just-in-
time deliveries, and the strains of higher fuel prices and growing air
congestion have all given railroads greater market share. Even Amtrak
has become an increasingly pleasant way to travel. And just when it
seemed that the days of railroad empire builders like Huntington,
Palmer, Strong, and Ripley were a thing of the past, financial guru Warren Buffett and Berkshire Hathaway made a bullish bet on America's
rails by acquiring the Burlington Northern Santa Fe in 2010.

Railroads, it seems, still have a very important role to play in American commerce. Nowhere is that more obvious than in the American
Southwest. Drive I-40 across Arizona and New Mexico, and you are
rarely out of sight of a Burlington Northern Santa Fe freight hurrying
west or east. The Los Angeles-to-Chicago corridor that was so fiercely
contested for more than a quarter century remains one of the most heavily traveled rail routes in North America; and the railroad that first led
the way west from Topeka toward Santa Fe continues to lead America
into the future.

Acknowledgments

———◆———

This book rests on my research in special collections and personal papers, but I would be remiss if I did not thank the historians who have traveled the grade ahead of me. Their works are gratefully acknowledged in the bibliography, but from that list I must single out: Maury Klein for his exhaustive history of the Union Pacific and his insightful biographies of Jay Gould and E. H. Harriman; Richard Saunders, Jr., for his authoritative two-volume study of American railroads in the twentieth century; and Keith L. Bryant, Jr., for his landmark history of the Atchison, Topeka and Santa Fe.

Colorado—historically and as a research location—was at the center of much of this story. The Colorado Historical Society houses the William Jackson Palmer, John Evans, and Denver and Rio Grande collections. The Western History Department of the Denver Public Library, in addition to superb newspaper and photograph collections, holds a microfilm set of the Collis P. Huntington Papers. And I always appreciate the respite of the Penrose Library of the University of Denver, as well as the special collections of the University of Colorado.

Like the Santa Fe, the Kansas Historical Society is at the top of the heap, and I particularly appreciate the assistance there of Nancy Sherbert and Lisa Keys. Thanks, as well, to Sally King, the curator of the art and photo archives of the Burlington Northern Santa Fe, and to Al Dunton of Centennial Galleries, Fort Collins, Colorado.

Of course, the places where railroad history and realism come together best are the railroad museums. In particular, my thanks go to the Colorado Railroad Museum, the Arizona Railway Museum, the California State Railroad Museum, the Orange Empire Railway Museum, the Southern Arizona Transportation Museum, and the Pacific Southwest Railway Museum (San Diego).

Once again, I thank the skill and patience of David Lambert for making legible maps from my scratches. I also appreciate the research assistance of Greg W. Stoehr at the University of Arizona and the Arizona Historical Society libraries, Monica Wisler at the San Diego Public Library, and Shea Houlihan at the University of Texas El Paso Library. I am particularly grateful to James E. Fell, Jr., and Lyndon J. Lampert, both accomplished writers and historians, for their critical reviews and insights. Courtney Turco deserves high praise for doing numerous tasks exceedingly well.

It would be difficult to find a more knowledgeable railroad enthusiast and historian than my highly esteemed agent, Alexander C. Hoyt. He is simply the best. My deep thanks go to Alex at many levels.

As always, I have enjoyed my research in the field: chasing trains across the Southwest, riding the rails with Marlene, and exploring abandoned grades from Marshall Pass to Alpine Tunnel with my friends Anne and Omar Richardson.

Notes

CHAPTER 1: LINES UPON THE MAP

1. Oscar Osburn Winther, *The Transportation Frontier: 1865–1890* (New York: Holt, Rinehart and Winston, 1964), pp. 48–49; *Butterfield Overland Mail—The Pinery*, Guadalupe Mountains National Park brochure, 1988; Lyle H. Wright and Josephine M. Bynum, eds., *The Butterfield Overland Mail* (San Marino, Calif.: Huntington Library, 1942), pp. 72–76.

2. W. H. Emory, *Notes on a Military Reconnaissance from Fort Leavenworth, in Missouri, to San Diego, in California, Including Parts of the Arkansas, Del Norte, and Gila Rivers,* 30th Cong., 1st sess., H.R. Ex. Doc. 41, pp. 35–36.

3. *"The consequences of such"*: William H. Goetzmann, *Army Exploration in the American West, 1803–1863* (Lincoln: University of Nebraska Press, 1979), p. 209. Colonel Abert should not be confused with his son, Lieutenant James W. Abert, who served in New Mexico in 1846.

4. Goetzmann, *Army Exploration*, p. 263.

5. Goetzmann, *Army Exploration*, pp. 218–19, 265.

6. *Congressional Globe*, 32nd Cong., 2nd sess., vol. 26 (March 2, 1853), p. 841.

7. Goetzmann, *Army Exploration*, p. 262.

8. Calculating grade requires basic trigonometry. The rise (or fall) of a line over its particular run (distance) is expressed as a percentage. A vertical rise in elevation of 52.8 feet over a horizontal distance of 1 mile equals a grade of 1 percent—quite gentle (52.8 divided by 5,280 equals .01, or 1 percent). A rise of 211 feet over 1 mile makes for a grade of 4 percent—quite steep in railroad terms.

9. *Reports of the Explorations and Surveys, to Ascertain the Most Practicable and Economical Route for a Railroad from the Mississippi River to the Pacific Ocean,* 33rd Cong., 2nd sess., H.R. Ex. Doc. 91 (hereinafter *Pacific Railroad Reports;* note the reports are individually paginated, although they may be combined in one volume), vol. 1, p. iv.

10. Goetzmann, *Army Exploration,* p. 305.

11. Jefferson Davis, "Introduction," *Pacific Railroad Reports,* vol. 1, p. 12.

12. Philip Henry Overmeyer, "George B. McClellan and the Pacific Northwest," *Pacific Northwest Quarterly* 32 (1941): 48–60.

13. Isaac I. Stevens, *Narrative and Final Report of Explorations for a Route for a Pacific Railroad near the Forty-seventh and Forty-ninth Parallels of North Latitude from St. Paul to Puget Sound, Pacific Railroad Reports,* vol. 12, p. 331.

14. Goetzmann, *Army Exploration,* p. 283.

15. For an account, see Howard Stansbury, *An Exploration to the Valley of the Great Salt Lake of Utah* (Philadelphia: Lippincott, Grambo & Co., 1852).

16. E. G. Beckwith, *Report of Explorations for a Route for the Pacific Railroad, by Capt. J. W. Gunnison, Topographical Engineers, near the 38th and 39th Parallels of North Latitude, from the Mouth of the Kansas River, Mo., to the Sevier Lake, in the Great Basin, Pacific Railroad Reports,* vol. 2, p. 85.

17. Beckwith, *Report, Pacific Railroad Reports,* vol. 2, pp. 56, 70.

18. Benton was so obsessed with the 38th parallel corridor that he financed two private expeditions along it that same year. Edward Fitzgerald Beale, who had just been appointed Indian agent for California and Nevada under Benton's patronage, led one party. Lest Gunnison's official report prove negative, Benton hedged his bets by dispatching an eastern reporter named Gwin Harris Heap along with Beale as his press agent. Frémont led the other private excursion, although having apparently learned nothing from his 1848 trip, he again entered the mountains late in the season and achieved little more than following on Gunnison's heels (Goetzmann, *Army Exploration,* p. 284).

19. A. W. Whipple, *Report of Explorations for a Railway Route near the Thirty-fifth Parallel of North Latitude from the Mississippi River to the Pacific Ocean, Pacific Railroad Reports,* vol. 3, p. 132; cost estimates in *Report of Captain A. A. Humphreys, Top. Engineers, upon the Progress of the Pacific Railroad Explorations and Surveys,* 34th Cong., 1st sess., Senate Ex. Doc. 1, pt. 2, p. 94.

20. John G. Parke, *Report of Explorations for That Portion of a Railroad Route, Near the Thirty-second Parallel of North Latitude, Lying Between Dona Ana, on the Rio Grande, and Pimas Villages, on the Gila, Pacific Railroad Reports,* vol. 2, pp. 4, 18–19.

21. John Pope, *Report of Exploration of a Route for the Pacific Railroad, near the Thirty-second Parallel of North Latitude, from the Red River to the Rio Grande, Pacific Railroad Reports,* vol. 2, p. 56.

22. Pope, *Report, Pacific Railroad Reports,* vol. 2, pp. 35, 49–50.

23. *Congressional Globe,* 35th Cong., 2nd sess., pt. 1 (December 14, 1858), p. 73.

CHAPTER 2: LEARNING THE RAILS

1. "*Nothing stops us*": William Jackson Palmer Collection, Stephen H. Hart Library, Colorado Historical Society, Denver (hereinafter Palmer Collection), Box 8, File Folder (FF) 641 (Palmer to Isaac Clothier, June 23, 1853).

2. *"spending the time"*: John S. Fisher, *A Builder of the West: The Life of General William Jackson Palmer* (Caldwell, Idaho: The Caxton Printers, 1939), p. 40; salary in Palmer Collection, Box 3, FF 223 (Palmer daily pocket diary, June 1, 1857).

3. "John Edgar Thomson," *Dictionary of American Biography*, vol. 18 (New York: Charles Scribner's Sons, 1943), p. 486; Albro Martin, *Railroads Triumphant: The Growth, Rejection, and Rebirth of a Vital American Force* (New York: Oxford University Press, 1992), pp. 260–61; James A. Ward, *J. Edgar Thomson: Master of the Pennsylvania* (Westport, Conn.: Greenwood Press, 1980), pp. 25, 42.

4. Ward, *Thomson*, pp. 70, 78, 80, 90; Timothy Jacobs, *The History of the Pennsylvania Railroad* (Greenwich, Conn.: Bonanza Books, 1988), pp. 21, 24–25.

5. *"Quick-witted, dapper"*: Ward, *Thomson*, p. 95–96; *"the best investment"*: Martin, *Railroads Triumphant*, pp. 263–64; see also Scott biography at www.texaspacificrailway .org/history and "Re-assessing Tom Scott, the 'Railroad Prince,' " a paper given for the Mid-America Conference on History, Furman University, September 16, 1995, by T. Lloyd Benson and Trina Rossman.

6. *"You Pennsylvania people"*: Lela Barnes, ed., "Letters of Cyrus Kurtz Holliday, 1854–1859," *Kansas Historical Quarterly* 6 (August 1937): 249 (Holliday to Mary Holliday, December 31, 1854); Holliday biographical information from Keith L. Bryant, Jr., *History of the Atchison, Topeka and Santa Fe Railway* (New York: Macmillan Publishing Co., 1974), pp. 4–9; L. L. Waters, *Steel Trails to Santa Fe* (Lawrence: University of Kansas Press, 1950), pp. 24–29.

7. This account of Huntington's early years is from David Lavender, *The Great Persuader* (New York: Doubleday, 1970), specifically, *"a fine trip,"* p. 39. In December 1887, when the Frémonts moved from New York to Los Angeles for his health, they were nearly destitute after numerous fortunes made and lost. Collis P. Huntington, then at the height of his railroad powers, gave them free passage. Pride initially forced Frémont to reject the offer, but Huntington was quick with a magnanimous reply: "You forget," he told the old explorer, "our road goes over your buried campfires and climbs many a grade you jogged over on a mule; I think we rather owe you this." Tom Chaffin, *Pathfinder: John Charles Frémont and the Course of American Empire* (New York: Hill and Wang, 2002), pp. 3–4.

8. *Thirteenth Annual Report of the Board of Directors of the Pennsylvania Rail Road Company*, pp. 20–21; quoted in Brit Allan Storey, "William Jackson Palmer: A Biography," unpublished PhD dissertation, University of Kentucky, 1968, p. 38.

9. Palmer Collection, Box 9, FF 696 (Palmer to John and Matilda Palmer, September 10, 1859).

10. Palmer Collection, Box 4, FF 243 (draft letter, Thomson to Gov. Hon. Alex Stevens [*sic*], Ga, undated; back has "Manuscript of letter to Hon. Jno. C. Kunkel relative to Pacific Railroad May 20, 1858." In another hand: "proposed but never sent J. Edgar Thomson").

11. Palmer Collection, Box 4, FF 250 (Ellet to Palmer, March 19, 1860).

12. Palmer Collection, Box 7, FF 496 (Palmer to Lamborn, March 6, 1861).

CHAPTER 3: AN INTERRUPTION OF WAR

1. *The War of the Rebellion: A Compilation of the Official Records of the Union and Confederate Armies*, Series 1, vol. 2, p. 596, hereinafter cited as *Official Records* (Thomson to Cameron, April 23, 1861).

2. *Official Records,* Series 1, vol. 2, p. 596 (Thomson to Cameron, April 23, 1861).

3. Palmer Collection, Box 2, FF 78 (Scott to Palmer, May 8, 1861).

4. Fisher, *A Builder of the West,* p. 75.

5. Palmer Collection, Box 3, FF 184 (Palmer to Jackson, April 10, 1862).

6. David Haward Bain, *Empire Express: Building the First Transcontinental Railroad* (New York: Penguin Books, 1999), p. 110.

7. Bain, *Empire Express,* pp. 106–8.

8. Lavender, *The Great Persuader,* pp. 97–98; Bain, *Empire Express,* p. 110.

9. Bain, *Empire Express,* pp. 112–14.

10. Bain, *Empire Express,* pp. 115–16; *U.S. Statutes at Large,* 37th Cong., 2nd sess., chap. 120 (1862), pp. 492–95; for an analysis of the traditional "drawn the elephant" quote, see Lavender, *The Great Persuader,* pp. 113, 391n5.

11. Robert C. Black III, *The Railroads of the Confederacy* (Chapel Hill: University of North Carolina Press, 1952), pp. 185–91.

12. John Bowers, *Chickamauga and Chattanooga: The Battles That Doomed the Confederacy* (New York: Avon Books, 1995), pp. 136–38, 153.

13. *"the most monstrous and flagrant":* Congressman E. B. Washburne of Illinois comments in *Congressional Globe,* 40th Cong., 2nd sess. (March 26, 1868), p. 2136.

14. *U.S. Statutes at Large,* 38th Cong., 1st sess., chap. 216 (1864), pp. 358, 360.

15. *"How dare you":* Bain, *Empire Express,* p. 179; see also Lavender, *The Great Persuader,* pp. 152–53, and *U.S. Statutes at Large,* 38th Cong., 1st sess., chap. 216 (1864), p. 363.

16. *Official Records,* Series 1, vol. 49, pt. 2, pp. 488–89 (Thomas to Stoneman, April 27, 1865); *Official Records,* Series 1, vol. 49, pt. 1, p. 548 (*Report of Bvt. Brig. Gen. William J. Palmer, May 6, 1865*).

17. *Official Records,* Series 1, vol. 49, pt. 1, pp. 550–54 (*Reports of Bvt. Brig. Gen. William J. Palmer, May 1865*); *"General Wilson held":* Charles H. Kirk, ed., *History of the Fifteenth Pennsylvania Volunteer Cavalry* (Philadelphia: Society of the Fifteenth Pennsylvania Cavalry, 1906), p. 517.

18. Palmer Collection, Box 3, FF 194 (Palmer to Jackson, June 23, 1865).

19. Samuel Bowles, *Across the Continent: A Summer's Journey to the Rocky Mountains, the Mormons, and the Pacific States, with Speaker Colfax* (Springfield, Mass.: Samuel Bowles & Company, 1865), *"It was a magnificent":* p. 18, *"I believe":* p. 412.

20. John Hoyt Williams, *A Great & Shining Road* (New York: Times Books, 1988), p. 72.

CHAPTER 4: TRANSCONTINENTAL BY ANY NAME

1. Troop numbers in *Official Records,* Series 3, vol. 5, p. 494 (Stanton to the president, November 22, 1865); *"Can you meet me":* Storey, "William Jackson Palmer: A Biography," p. 142 (Scott to Palmer, July 26, 1865, telegram); Palmer Collection, Box 9, FF 690 (Palmer to Jackson, August 7, 1865).

2. Maury Klein, *Union Pacific: The Birth of a Railroad, 1862–1893* (New York: Doubleday, 1987), pp. 27–28, 36–37; Bain, *Empire Express,* pp. 162, 168; Charles N. Glaab, *Kansas City and the Railroads* (Madison: State Historical Society of Wisconsin, 1962), pp. 112–13, 117–21, 231–32, specifically, *"the biggest swindle yet,"* p. 121. For a version more favorable to Hallett, see Alan W. Farley, "Samuel Hallett and the Union

Pacific Railway Company in Kansas," *Kansas Historical Quarterly,* 25, no. 1 (Spring 1959): 1–16.

3. *"Scott drove a pretty hard bargain"* and *"Young men without money"*: Palmer Collection, Box 9, FF 690 (Palmer to Jackson, August 25, 1865); Lavender, *The Great Persuader,* pp. 173–74, 214; Klein, *Union Pacific, Birth,* pp. 79–80; *U.S. Statutes at Large,* 39th Cong., 1st sess., chap. 159 (1866), pp. 79–80.

4. George Anderson, *General William J. Palmer: A Decade of Colorado Railroad Building, 1870–1880* (Colorado Springs: Colorado College Publication, 1936), pp. 14–15; Kansas Pacific construction dates and mileages in Palmer Collection, Box 4, FF 287 (*Report of the Condition and Progress of the Union Pacific Railway, E.D., for the year ending September 30, 1867*); UP reaching 100th meridian in Bain, *Empire Express,* p. 290; UP construction mileage in Lavender, *The Great Persuader,* p. 175.

5. Palmer Collection, Box 8, FF 606 (Thomson to Perry, March 20, 1867). Palmer gave one version of the change in route from the Republican River to the Smoky Hill on September 21, 1867, during an address to citizens of New Mexico while surveying the line's continuation. The "political reasons" for the line's original northward bent had vanished with the end of the war, he said, and "an *independent trunk line* through to the Pacific, on a latitude free from those wintry obstacles" was thought best. In Palmer Collection, Box 4, FF 287 ("Address of William Jackson Palmer Delivered Before a Meeting of Citizens of New Mexico, at Santa Fe, September 21, 1867").

6. William J. Palmer, *Report of Surveys Across the Continent, in 1867–68, on the Thirty-fifth and Thirty-second Parallels, for a Route Extending the Kansas Pacific Railway to the Pacific Ocean at San Francisco and San Diego* (Philadelphia: W. B. Selheimer, printer, 1869), specifically, "to ascertain the best" p. 3, "dry and inferior country," p. 13; *"by far the best"*: William A. Bell, *New Tracks in North America: A Journal of Travel and Adventure Whilst Engaged in the Survey for a Southern Railroad to the Pacific Ocean in 1867–1868* (London: Chapman and Hall, 1870), pp. 94–95. Bell was an Englishman and doctor by training, who signed on as the expedition's photographer because that was the only vacancy. He spent a frantic couple of weeks learning to use the expedition's photographic equipment.

7. *"General Palmer held"*: Bell, *New Tracks,* p. 152; *"the decided preference"*: ibid., pp. 245–46.

8. Bell, *New Tracks,* pp. 254–55, 286–88; *"information as to"*: p. 327; *"they seemed to me,"* p. 367; *"radiating from the coast inland,"* p. 371.

9. Bell, *New Tracks:* "A very small place," p. 315; *"an excellent bridging point,"* p. 319; pp. 320–21.

10. Bell, *New Tracks,* pp. 405, 411–20, specifically, *"This country belongs,"* p. 413, "The grades up to this," p. 420.

11. *"If the Grand Canyon"* and *"The innumerable side cañons"*: Palmer, *Report of Surveys,* p. 47; Bell, *New Tracks,* pp. 424–25; Donald Worster, *A River Running West: The Life of John Wesley Powell* (New York: Oxford University Press, 2001), pp. 133, 299.

12. *"We can never get"*: Storey, "William Jackson Palmer," p. 179, quoting Palmer to John D. Perry, September 17, 1867; *"I, of course"*: Bain, *Empire Express,* p. 457, quoting E. B. Crocker to Huntington, January 20, 1868; Bell, *New Tracks,* pp. 17, 455, 470.

13. *"practicable and good"*: Palmer, *Report of Surveys,* p. 181; *"The results along"*: ibid., pp. 5–6; *"the Government should"*: ibid., p. 192.

14. *"would not think of it"* and *"would only be a small"*: Collis P. Huntington Papers, *1856–1901,* microfilm edition in Western History Department, Denver Public Library, Denver (hereinafter cited as *Huntington Papers*), Series 4, Reel 2 (Huntington to E. B. Crocker, March 13, 1868); *"Their proposition was"* and *"very sharp"* and *"said if I would"*: ibid. (Huntington to E. B. Crocker, March 21, 1868); *"agree to what we want"*: ibid. (Huntington to Hopkins, March 31, 1868).

15. *"Since General Palmer's return"* and *"I could do nothing"*: *Huntington Papers,* Series 4, Reel 2 (Huntington to Hopkins, April 13, 1868); New York meeting in ibid. (Huntington to Hopkins, April 17, 1868); *"I think we have got"*: ibid. (Huntington to E. B. Crocker, April 21, 1868).

CHAPTER 5: THE SANTA FE JOINS THE FRAY

1. *U.S. Statutes at Large,* 37th Cong., 3rd sess., chap. 98 (1863), pp. 772–74. Technically, this congressional legislation conditionally granted the lands to the State of Kansas, which accepted them on February 9, 1864, and in turn passed them on to the Santa Fe and the Leavenworth, Lawrence, and Fort Gibson Railroad and Telegraph Company, with the same conditions. The latter road was to build from Leavenworth to Indian Territory.

2. Bryant, *Atchison, Topeka and Santa Fe,* pp. 12–13; *"The child is born"*: *Kansas State Record* (Topeka), October 7, 1868.

3. William E. Treadway, *Cyrus K. Holliday: A Documentary Biography* (Topeka: Kansas State Historical Society, 1979), p. 214 (quoting Holliday to Mary Holliday, August 30, 1873).

4. Bryant, *Atchison, Topeka and Santa Fe,* pp. 15, 17–18; *"old earth slowly careened"*: Joseph W. Snell and Don W. Wilson, "The Birth of the Atchison, Topeka and Santa Fe Railroad," *Kansas Historical Quarterly* 34, no. 2 (Summer 1968): 135, quoting *Osage Chronicle,* September 18, 1869.

5. Bryant, *Atchison, Topeka and Santa Fe,* pp. 21–24.

6. *Kansas Daily Commonwealth* (Topeka), April 27, 1872.

7. Joseph W. Snell and Don W. Wilson, "The Birth of the Atchison, Topeka and Santa Fe Railroad—Concluded," *Kansas Historical Quarterly* 35, no. 3 (Fall 1968): 332–37; *"an enterprising railroad town"*: *Kansas Daily Commonwealth* (Topeka), May 30, 1871; *"It must be borne"*: *Emporia News,* August 25, 1871.

8. Bryant, *Atchison, Topeka and Santa Fe,* pp. 26–29; *"This beats anything"*: *Kansas Daily Commonwealth* (Topeka), July 16, 1872; tie boom in Snell and Wilson, "The Birth of the Atchison, Topeka and Santa Fe Railroad—Concluded," p. 348, quoting the *Hutchinson News,* July 18, 1872.

9. Snell and Wilson, "The Birth of the Atchison, Topeka and Santa Fe Railroad—Concluded," pp. 351–52.

10. Bat Masterson is one of those characters whose myth transcends the facts, but perhaps his most solid biographer is Robert K. DeArment, *Bat Masterson: The Man and the Legend* (Norman: University of Oklahoma Press, 1979), from which this account of Bat's Dodge City days is taken, specifically, the grading contract, pp. 19–21; *"led the*

way" and *"considered a man,"* pp. 32–33; *"offering one-hundred-dollar"* and the train robbers hunt, pp. 87–95. For Ed's death, see pp. 97–108.

11. Bryant, *Atchison, Topeka and Santa Fe,* pp. 29–31; " *'State Line City' "*: Snell and Wilson, "The Birth of the Atchison, Topeka and Santa Fe Railroad—Concluded," p. 352, quoting *Hutchinson News,* December 12, 1872; *"We send you greeting"*: *Hutchinson News,* January 2, 1873.

12. *"The road cannot"*: *Kansas Daily Commonwealth* (Topeka), December 29, 1872.

CHAPTER 6: STRAIGHT WEST FROM DENVER

1. The principal biography of John Evans is Harry E. Kelsey, Jr., *Frontier Capitalist: The Life of John Evans* (Denver: State Historical Society of Colorado and Pruett Publishing, 1969). Railroads were not the only thing that Evans was interested in building. He was instrumental in founding both Northwestern University and the University of Denver. He ran for Congress in 1854 and campaigned for Lincoln in 1860, which put him in line for a political appointment. He declined the governorship of Washington Territory as too far removed from his Chicago interests but accepted the governorship of Colorado Territory.

2. *"Whether famine reigns"*: *Rocky Mountain News,* May 24, 1862.

3. S. D. Mock, "Colorado and the Surveys for a Pacific Railroad," *Colorado Magazine,* vol. 17, no. 2 (March 1940): 56–57.

4. Instructions to John Pierce, John Evans Collection, Stephen H. Hart Library, Colorado Historical Society, Denver, Box 7, File Folder (FF) 78 (Evans to Pierce, February 24, 1866), hereinafter cited as Evans Collection by box and file folder number. *"The richness of the country"*: Evans Collection, Box 7, FF 78 (Pierce to Evans, February 25, 1866); Mock, "Colorado and the Surveys," pp. 60–61, and Kelsey, *Frontier Capitalist,* pp. 127, 170–72.

5. S. D. Mock, "The Financing of Early Colorado Railroads," *Colorado Magazine* 18, no. 6 (November 1941): 202–3; Kelsey, *Frontier Capitalist,* pp. 173–74.

6. *"I am very busy"*: Evans Collection, Box 2, FF 17 (Evans to Margaret Evans, July 5, 1868); Kelsey, *Frontier Capitalist,* pp. 174–75; Mock, "Financing of Early Colorado Railroads," pp. 204–205; *U.S. Statutes at Large,* 40th Cong., 3rd sess., chap. 127 (1869), p. 324; Klein, *Union Pacific: Birth,* pp. 344–45.

7. Kelsey, *Frontier Capitalist,* pp. 176–79; Mock, "Financing of Early Colorado Railroads," pp. 205–6; Palmer Collection, Box 9, FF 304 (Certificate of Interest in Assignment, July 1869); Elmer O. Davis, *The First Five Years of the Railroad Era in Colorado* (Golden, Colo.: Sage Books, 1948), pp. 38, 90–91; *"Everybody and wife"*: *Colorado Tribune* (Denver), June 18, 1870.

8. *"Our long agony"*: Palmer Collection, Box 9, FF 701 (Palmer to Queen Mellen, July 2, 1869); *"Poor Sheridan!"*: Palmer Collection, Box 9, FF 706 (Palmer to Queen Mellen, February 13, 1870); *"brisk and lively"* and *"the water about town"*: *Rocky Mountain News* (Weekly), April 27, 1870.

9. *"the business men"*: Davis, *First Five Years,* p. 72; tie advertisement in Anderson, *Palmer,* pp. 32–34; construction schedule and Indian raids in Davis, *First Five Years,* pp. 70, 74, 76, 78, 94–95; *"fighting along our line"*: Palmer Collection, Box 9, FF 707 (Palmer to Queen Mellen, May 15, 1870).

10. *Rocky Mountain News* (Weekly), August 17, 1870.

11. *"In the name"*: Palmer Collection, Box 7, FF 552 (telegram, Perry to Palmer, August 16, 1870); *"The coach has given"*: *Rocky Mountain News,* August 19, 1870; *"the only road"*: *Rocky Mountain News* (Weekly), April 27, 1870.

12. Davis, *First Five Years,* pp. 107–8; see also an inserted supplement in Davis entitled "Completion Dates for the First Trans-continental Railway."

13. Kelsey, *Frontier Capitalist,* pp. 180–81. William H. Loveland, who was intent on making the town of Golden, about 15 miles west of Denver, Colorado's commercial hub, incorporated the Colorado Central and grabbed control of Clear Creek Canyon, leading from Golden to the mining districts of Central City and Black Hawk. Loveland also flirted with the Union Pacific for support of a Golden-Cheyenne connection. When this was not forthcoming, the Colorado Central built down Clear Creek from Golden to connect with the Denver Pacific–Kansas Pacific rail junction just northeast of what remains Denver Union Station.

14. *addressing him as "General"*: Palmer Collection, Box 9, FF 700 (Palmer to Queen Mellen, April 16, 1869); *"a little railroad"*: Palmer Collection, Box 9, FF 706 (Palmer to Queen Mellen, January 17, 1870); *"laid the smallest"* and *"but not near enough"*: Palmer Collection, Box 9, FF 706 (Palmer to Queen Mellen, February 4, 1870).

15. *"run from the Missouri"*: U.S. *Statutes at Large,* 37th Cong., 2nd sess., chap. 120 (July 1, 1862), p. 495; U.S. *Statutes at Large,* 37th Cong., 3rd sess., chap 112 (March 3, 1863), p. 807; Bain, *Empire Express,* pp. 131–32.

16. Anderson, *William J. Palmer,* pp. 54–57; *"how fine it would be"*: Palmer Collection, Box 9, FF 706 (Palmer to Queen Mellen, January 17, 1870). A key difference in construction costs between the gauges was in rails. Early narrow gauge rails weighed thirty pounds per yard compared to fifty-six pounds for standard gauge.

17. U.S. *Statutes at Large,* 42nd Cong., 2nd sess., chap. 354 (1872), p. 339; Davis, *First Five Years,* pp. 152, 163; Tivis E. Wilkins, *Colorado Railroads* (Boulder, Colo.: Pruett, 1974), pp. 7, 11. The Rio Grande was built largely without federal subsidies or major land grants. After construction began, Congress ratified the railroad's territorial charter and granted it a right-of-way 200 feet wide through the public domain. It also gave it the same right to condemn private land with appropriate due process that was given to the other Pacific roads under the 1862 act. Finally, the railroad got the privilege of taking timber, stone, and earth from public lands adjacent to the right-of-way and 20 acres of land every 10 miles for station and yard purposes.

CHAPTER 7: "WHY IS IT WE HAVE SO MANY BITTER ENEMIES?"

1. Oscar Lewis, *The Big Four: The Story of Huntington, Stanford, Hopkins, and Crocker, and of the Building of the Central Pacific* (New York: Alfred A. Knopf, 1938), p. 211.

2. Stuart Daggett, *Chapters on the History of the Southern Pacific* (1922; rpr., New York: Augustus M. Kelley, 1966), pp. 120, 122; Atlantic and Pacific Railroad Company incorporation at U.S. *Statutes at Large,* 39th Cong., 1st sess., chap. 278 (1866), pp. 292–99. The San Jose-to-Gilroy extension was technically undertaken by the Santa Clara and Pajaro Valley Railroad Company, just one of many instances where controlling interests, for a variety of reasons, incorporated what were in essence subsidiary companies.

3. Lavender, *The Great Persuader,* pp. 122, 164, 178, 186.

4. *"I notice that you"*: *Huntington Papers,* Series 4, Reel 2 (Huntington to Hopkins, April 14, 1868).

5. Cerinda W. Evans, *Collis Potter Huntington,* vol. 1 (Newport News, Va.: Mariners' Museum, 1954), pp. 239–40.

6. Daggett, *Southern Pacific,* pp. 122–23.

7. Lavender, *The Great Persuader,* pp. 265–66.

8. Lavender, *The Great Persuader,* pp. 283, 413n2.

9. Lavender, *The Great Persuader,* pp. 284–85; Daggett, *Southern Pacific,* p. 125; see also Lewis B. Lesley, "A Southern Transcontinental Railroad into California: Texas and Pacific Versus Southern Pacific, 1865–1885," *Pacific Historical Review* 5, no. 1 (1936): 55; *"from a point at"*: *U.S. Statutes at Large,* 41st Cong., 3rd sess., chap. 122 (1871), p. 579; Texas Pacific name change at *U.S. Statutes at Large,* 42nd Cong., 2nd sess., chap. 132 (1872), p. 59.

10. Robert M. Fogelson, *The Fragmented Metropolis: Los Angeles, 1850–1930* (Cambridge, Mass.: Harvard University Press, 1967), pp. 52–56; Lavender, *The Great Persuader,* pp. 289–91; Los Angeles and San Pedro dates and census, Daggett, *Southern Pacific,* p. 127.

11. *"where the money"*: *Huntington Papers,* Series 4, Reel 2 (Huntington to Hopkins, April 3, 1872). For all his expenditures in pursuit of railroad empires, Huntington stayed quite frugal personally in these lean years, supposedly saying later in life, "Young man, you can't follow me through life by the quarters I have dropped" (Lewis, *The Big Four,* p. 213).

12. *"It is possible"*: *Huntington Papers,* Series 4, Reel 3 (Huntington to Hopkins, October 29, 1872); New York meeting with Scott in ibid. (Huntington to Hopkins, November 30, 1872); *"I thought it would"*: ibid.. (Huntington to Hopkins, December 13, 1872); *"I have been out to see"*: ibid. (Huntington to Hopkins, December 3, 1872); floating debt analysis in Julius Grodinsky, *Transcontinental Railway Strategy, 1869–1893* (Philadelphia: University of Pennsylvania Press, 1962), pp. 50–51.

13. Scott's offer of $16 million and *"while I think the property"*: *Huntington Papers,* Series 4, Reel 3 (Huntington to Hopkins, January 17, 1873); *"sell anything that"* and *"I am doing all"*: ibid. (Huntington to Hopkins, February 15, 1873).

14. *"made up my mind"*: *Huntington Papers,* Series 4, Reel 3 (Huntington to Stanford, February 28, 1873); *"I have never seen"*: ibid. (Huntington to Hopkins, March 8, 1873); *"You know that"*: ibid. (Huntington to Hopkins, March 10, 1873).

15. *"It looks a little"* and *"If we do not trade"*: *Huntington Papers,* Series 4, Reel 3 (Huntington to Hopkins, March 11, 1873); *"been out today"* and *"he cannot do anything"*: ibid. (Huntington to Hopkins, March 26, 1873). Hopkins and Stanford were also negotiating for a sale of Southern Pacific and/or Central Pacific interests to a group of San Francisco investors fronted by Alfred A. Cohen. Hopkins speculated that Cohen might be working with Scott; see, for example, ibid. (Hopkins to Huntington, February 4, 1873).

16. *"Why is it"*: *Huntington Papers,* Series 2, Reel 5 (Huntington to Hopkins, February 20, 1873); *"these hellhounds"*: ibid. (Huntington to Hopkins, March 3, 1873); *"the truth, but nothing more"*: ibid. (Huntington to Hopkins, February 27, 1873); testimony gen-

erally and destruction of records in Lavender, *The Great Persuader,* pp. 291–93. Whether it was correct to say that the Big Four operation involved three, four, or five men depended on the dates. Charles Crocker and his brother, Judge E. B. Crocker, sold many of their interests to the other three in 1871 for $900,000 each. When Charles confronted Huntington in the fall of 1873 for his second installment and learned the dire straits the associates were in, he promptly returned his down payment and rejoined the operations. Huntington wasn't pleased to divide the pie again but needed the money. By then, the judge was incapacitated from a stroke; he died in 1875.

17. *"the* remote *cause"*: Treadway, *Cyrus K. Holliday,* p. 215 (quoting Holliday to Mary Holliday, September 20, 1873); for an economic analysis of the panic of 1873, see Rendigs Fels, "American Business Cycles, 1865–79," *American Economic Review* 41, no. 3 (June 1951): 325–49.

18. Grodinsky, *Transcontinental Railway Strategy,* p. 45.

19. $14,000 payment and *"I would not"*: *Huntington Papers,* Series 4, Reel 3 (Huntington to Hopkins, October 29, 1873).

CHAPTER 8: SHOWDOWN AT YUMA

1. Neill C. Wilson and Frank J. Taylor, *Southern Pacific: The Roaring Story of a Fighting Railroad* (New York: McGraw-Hill Book Company, 1952), p. 57; *"The figures are large"*: *Huntington Papers,* Series 4, Reel 3 (Huntington to Hopkins, November 24, 1873).

2. Daggett, *Southern Pacific,* p. 126. Changing the Southern Pacific route created a long and complicated land dispute. Out of the confusion of the priority of railroad land grants versus homesteads acquired from the public domain would come the infamous Mussel Slough land feud, popularized by Frank Norris in his novel *The Octopus.* The San Joaquin Valley branch was opened to Goshen in August 1872. The continuing Southern Pacific tracks reached another 40 miles south to Delano, California, on July 14, 1873.

3. Lavender, *The Great Persuader,* pp. 304–5.

4. John R. Signor, *Tehachapi: Southern Pacific–Santa Fe* (San Marino, Calif.: Golden West Books, 1983), pp. 15–18, 56–57, 80–81. An eighteenth tunnel was built in 1885 just outside of Caliente. It was "daylighted" (collapsed and made into a cut) after major flooding in 1983.

5. *"Join hands with"* and *"We are camped"*: Wilson and Taylor, *Southern Pacific,* pp. 61–62; see also Paul R. Spitzzeri, "The Road to Independence: The Los Angeles and Independence Railroad and the Conception of a City," *Southern California Quarterly* 83, no. 1 (Spring 2001): 23–58.

6. Signor, *Tehachapi,* pp. 18–19, specifically, *"time dragged heavily"* and *"have not only lived"*; time schedule, Evans, *Huntington,* p. 249.

7. *"Scott is making"*: *Huntington Papers,* Series 2, Reel 5 (Huntington to Colton, March 22, 1876); Lavender, *The Great Persuader,* pp. 309–10; *"We must split"*: Grodinsky, *Transcontinental Railway Strategy,* p. 64, quoting Colton to Huntington, May 22, 1876.

8. Authorization to prevent waste in *Huntington Papers,* Series 4, Reel 3 (McCrary to

McDowell, September 6, 1877); *"So far as going"*: ibid. (Crocker to Huntington, September 25, 1877); Lavender, *The Great Persuader,* pp. 318–19, 322.

9. Bridge specifications in David F. Myrick, *Railroads of Arizona,* vol. 1, *The Southern Roads* (Berkeley, Calif.: Howell-North Books, 1975), p. 22; *"Bridge Across Colorado"*: *Huntington Papers,* Series 1, Reel 13 (telegram, Crocker to Huntington, September 30, 1877); *"one officer, twelve soldiers"*: ibid., Series 4, Reel 3 (telegram, Crocker to Huntington, October 2, 1877); Lavender, *The Great Persuader,* pp. 323–24.

10. *"By the completion"* and *"By prohibiting"*: *Huntington Papers,* Series 4, Reel 3 (Safford et al. to McCreary [sic], October 1, 1877); *"an outrage to be put"*: ibid. (Crocker to Huntington, October 5, 1877).

11. *"Stanford and Company"*: San Francisco *Daily Alta California,* October 7, 1877; *"I do not believe"*: Lavender, *The Great Persuader,* p. 323, quoting Colton to Huntington, late September 1877.

12. Huntington's account of his conversation with President Hayes is in *Huntington Papers,* Series 2, Reel 6 (Huntington to Colton, October 10, 1877).

13. *"taking all things"*: *Huntington Papers,* Series 4, Reel 3 (Crocker to Huntington, September 1, 1877); *"I notice what you say"*: ibid., Series 1, Reel 14 (Crocker to Huntington, January 30, 1878); Hopkins's refusal at Lavender, *The Great Persuader,* p. 324.

14. Lavender, *The Great Persuader,* p. 326; Lewis, *The Big Four,* p. 139.

CHAPTER 9: IMPASSE AT RATON

1. Waters, *Steel Trails,* pp. 51–53. The Santa Fe's eastward extension began in December 1868 when the irrepressible Cyrus K. Holliday secured a Kansas charter for the Lawrence and Topeka Railway to run eastward from Topeka. No construction took place until 1872, when a summer's work quickly depleted all funds. The next year, the Lawrence and Topeka contracted with a new company, the Kansas Midland Railroad, to complete the line, but even then, rails did not reach Lawrence—only halfway from Topeka to Kansas City—until the summer of 1874.

Meanwhile, an even greater patchwork of interests was building between Lawrence and the Missouri River with the intent of *bypassing* Kansas City. (The reason for this is best explained by the venture's name: *St. Louis,* Lawrence, and Denver Railroad.) The Kansas Midland began to use a portion of this line and then secured trackage rights over yet another road to reach Kansas City via a circuitous route.

Finally, the Kansas City, Lawrence, and Topeka Railroad, which had originally been incorporated only in Missouri to build from Kansas City to the state line, was induced to build farther west and hook up directly with the Kansas Midland. With this construction under way, the Kansas Midland and the original Lawrence and Topeka merged to become the Kansas City, Topeka, and Western Railroad Company, which was then promptly leased to the Santa Fe.

While this corporate confusion might seem in hindsight as make-work for lawyers, it was really the result of the state charter, local town support, and general financing issues that confronted all railroads in that era. The important point is that out of this piecemeal construction, the Atchison, Topeka and Santa Fe acquired control over its own direct line into Kansas City.

2. Anderson, *William J. Palmer,* pp. 75–76, 86–87; Grodinsky, *Transcontinental Railway*

Strategy, pp. 90–91; Klein, *Union Pacific: Birth,* pp. 349, 395–96, specifically, "crumbling beneath the pressures," p. 395; for an expression of Palmer's land speculation, see Palmer Collection, Box 9, FF 716 (Palmer to Queen Palmer, October 12, 1874), in which he acknowledges, "There will probably be the same sort of fight [at El Moro] that we had with Colorado City."

3. Wilkins, *Colorado Railroads,* pp. 11–21. The Kansas Pacific, via its Arkansas Valley Railroad subsidiary, built from Kit Carson 56 miles south to Las Animas on the Arkansas River in 1873 before funds dried up. The Kansas Pacific managed another 24 miles up the Arkansas River in 1875, most of it close alongside the Santa Fe's tracks. It halted construction at the mouth of Timpas Creek, just west of La Junta, stopped operating trains on its Arkansas Valley line in 1877, and started dismantling the track the following year. This 80-mile section was the first major abandonment in Colorado and would remain the state's largest for more than forty years.

4. Waters, *Steel Trails,* p. 114 (Nickerson), p. 54 (Strong). Strong was to have his own right-hand man in these endeavors. A. A. Robinson, seven years younger than Strong, was another son of Vermont. He moved to Wisconsin after his father's death and clerked in his stepfather's store. When his stepfather became ill and closed the store, Robinson supported the family by farming, saving enough to enroll at the University of Michigan. He received an undergraduate degree in 1869 and a master of science in 1871. By then, Robinson was on the payroll of the Santa Fe and on his way to becoming its chief engineer. Little did Robinson know that during his long tenure with the railroad, he would supervise the construction of an incredible 5,000 miles of track (pp. 45–46).

5. *"cocky and resolute"* and *"believed in a future life"*: George S. Van Law, *Four Years on Santa Fe Railroad Surveys, 1878 to 1882,* p. 1, unpublished manuscript, Atchison, Topeka and Santa Fe Railroad Collection, Box 1, File Folder (FF) 1A, Stephen H. Hart Library, Colorado Historical Society, Denver (hereinafter Santa Fe Collection); *An Act Granting to Railroads the Right of Way Through the Public Lands of the United States, U.S. Statutes at Large,* 18, Pt. 3, 43rd Cong., 2nd sess., chap. 152, pp. 482–83; *"It is understood"*: William A. Bell Collection, Box 6, File Folder (FF) "Telegrams from Dr. Bell's Files, 1875–1876" (Palmer to Bell, cable to London, March 25, 1876), Stephen H. Hart Library, Colorado Historical Society, Denver (hereinafter Bell Collection).

6. Norman Cleaveland (with George Fitzpatrick), *The Morleys—Young Upstarts on the Southwest Frontier* (Albuquerque: Calvin Horn Publisher, 1971), pp. 40–41, 49–50, 57, 63, 68, 160–61; *"he was no"* and *"he asked no,"* p. 214.

7. *"Of course we have no"* and *"it is predicted"*: *Colorado Weekly Chieftain* (Pueblo), February 21, 1878; *"The air is full"* and *"as railroad companies do not"*: ibid., February 28, 1878.

8. Waters, *Steel Trails,* pp. 54, 98–100; Bryant, *Atchison, Topeka and Santa Fe,* pp. 43–45; for a local account and *"at three of the most,"* see *Colorado Weekly Chieftain,* March 7, 1878. Confusion over Bat Masterson's role at Raton Pass may stem from the fact that he later served as city marshal of Trinidad. Whatever deficiencies Palmer found with Trinchera Pass were refuted a scant ten years later when the Denver, Texas and Fort Worth Railroad built a standard gauge line across it in the process of completing Denver's first continuous rail link to the Gulf of Mexico.

9. Bryant, *Atchison, Topeka and Santa Fe,* pp. 45–46; Robert M. Ormes, *Railroads and the*

Rockies: A Record of Lines in and near Colorado (Denver: Sage Books, 1963), p. 78; *Denver Daily Tribune,* December 1, 1878. The tunnel's final dimensions were 2,011 feet long, 14.5 feet wide, and 19 feet high.

10. *"devote all of their resources":* Colorado Weekly Chieftain, March 7, 1878; *"to play a game":* Robert G. Athearn, *Rebel of the Rockies: The Denver and Rio Grande Western Railroad* (New Haven, Conn.: Yale University Press, 1962), p. 56; advice on impasse in McMurtrie to Palmer, April 14, 1878, and *"cutthroat policy,"* McMurtrie to Palmer, April 1, 1881, McMurtrie Letter Book, quoted in Athearn, *Rebel of the Rockies,* p. 56.

CHAPTER 10: BATTLE ROYAL FOR THE GORGE

1. As early as 1878, the U.S. Supreme Court used the name "Royal Gorge" in the case of *Denver and Rio Grande Railway Co. v. C. T. Alling, et al.* It is the common usage today and distinguishes the steepest 8-mile section of *gorge* from the longer Arkansas River *canyon,* of which it is a part.

2. *"I will run a line"* and *"to look at that pass":* Palmer Collection, Box 4, FF 461 (Greenwood to Palmer, February 8, 1869).

3. *"Our experience"* and *"a fearful gorge":* Palmer Collection, Box 9, FF 708 (Palmer to Queen Palmer, August 24, 1871).

4. Anderson, *William J. Palmer,* pp. 69–70, 134–36. The Denver and Rio Grande had already employed a two-step financing approach with Pueblo County. In step one, the county voted $100,000 in bonds if the railroad would build its depot within a mile of the courthouse in Pueblo. In step two, another $50,000 in bonds carried the tracks into the downtown area.

5. Anderson, *William J. Palmer,* pp. 87–88.

6. Anderson, *William J. Palmer,* pp. 88–90, specifically, *"low gradient per mile"* and *"Manitou frequenters,"* p. 89, and *"It is the shortest,"* p. 90.

7. *"Harrison goes east":* Anderson, *William J. Palmer,* p. 91; *"All my movements":* McMurtrie to Palmer, April 14, 1878, McMurtrie Letter Book, quoted in Athearn, *Rebel of the Rockies,* pp. 56–57; *"see to it that":* Waters, *Steel Trails,* p. 106.

8. This account of the first day's activities of the Royal Gorge war is based on articles in the *Colorado Weekly Chieftain,* April 25, 1878. The principal one was entitled "Catching Weasels Asleep. Or How Morley Outflanked McMurtrie. Bronchos vs. Iron Horses." The Pueblo paper was generally opposed to the Rio Grande, and its stories had a strong Santa Fe slant. The *Chieftain's* Cañon City correspondent, B. F. Rockafellow, was a resident of Cañon City and one of the organizers of the Cañon City and San Juan Railway. While Anderson did not document his source, he wrote in *William J. Palmer* (p. 95) that Rockafellow later admitted that he embellished the more colorful articles "to tickle the public fancy." Morley's grandson recounted the horsemanship quote in Cleaveland, *The Morleys,* p. 172. Sheridan's dash refers to the general's wild, twenty-mile ride from a leisurely staff breakfast in Winchester, Virginia, to stem a Union rout at the 1864 Battle of Cedar Creek; Thomas Buchanan Read wrote a poem about the event, "Sheridan's Ride," that was a staple of recitation for northern schoolchildren after the war.

9. Anderson, *William J. Palmer,* pp. 93–95.

10. Cleaveland, *The Morleys,* pp. 175–76. (Ray Morley to Ada Morley, May 6, 1878). Un-

fortunately, Ray Morley's personal diaries and many business papers and family letters were destroyed in the great Berkeley fire of 1923 while in possession of one of his daughters. Since he was well known as a careful observer and unbiased reporter, it would be of great historical value to have his additional insights.

11. *"very abusive and making"* and *"which fractured his skull"*: *Colorado Weekly Chieftain,* May 9, 1878; *"Mr. James Gallagher"*: *Colorado Weekly Chieftain,* May 16, 1878.

12. *Colorado Weekly Chieftain,* May 9, 1878.

13. *Colorado Weekly Chieftain,* May 16, 1878.

14. Anderson, *William Jackson Palmer,* p. 101.

15. Cornelius W. Hauck and Robert W. Richardson, eds., "The Santa Fe's D&RG War No. 2," *Colorado Rail Annual* (Golden, Colo.: Colorado Railroad Museum, 1965), 4–5. Three years later, the Denver and Rio Grande constructed a narrow gauge line up Grape Creek to reach Westcliffe and access promising silver camps in the Wet Mountain Valley. The line washed out in 1889 and was not rebuilt. Instead, in 1901 the Rio Grande completed a standard gauge line to Westcliffe from Texas Creek. It was abandoned in 1937.

16. *Colorado Weekly Chieftain,* June 13, 1878.

17. "Indenture between the Denver & Rio Grande Railway Company and the Atchison, Topeka & Santa Fe Railroad Company, October 1878," Denver and Rio Grande Western Railroad Collection, Box 30, File Folder (FF) 1284, Stephen H. Hart Library, Colorado Historical Society, Denver (hereinafter Denver and Rio Grande Collection); bond prices reported in Waters, *Steel Trails,* p. 122.

18. *"The arrogant demand"* and *"If they were to"* and *"we may want to take"*: Denver and Rio Grande Collection, Box 23, FF 1083 (Palmer to Dodge, December 4, 1878); for one expression of Palmer worrying about the Santa Fe's compliance with the lease and required audit of funds, see ibid. (Palmer to Strong, January 19, 1879).

19. Equipment purchase in Hauck and Richardson, "The Santa Fe's D&RG War No. 2," p. 7; *"where in the whole universe"*: DeArment, *Bat Masterson,* pp. 149–51.

20. *"Come on, now"*: *Colorado Weekly Chieftain,* June 19, 1879; *"certain Dodge City folks"*: DeArment, *Bat Masterson,* pp. 151–53. The *Chieftain* account does not mention Masterson by name, once again suggesting that his role in these railroad wars grew with his later reputation.

21. *"while he figured a way"*: Maury Klein, *The Life and Legend of Jay Gould* (Baltimore: Johns Hopkins University Press, 1986), p. 228; see also p. 243 for the threat to parallel the Santa Fe in Kansas; Gould's Rio Grande stock purchase at Denver and Rio Grande Collection, Box 22, FF 1033 (Gould et al., agreement, September 8, 1879).

22. Anderson, *William J. Palmer,* pp. 107–116. The court cases involved the Santa Fe's Pueblo and Arkansas Valley subsidiary, which had absorbed the Cañon City and San Juan.

23. Gould letter and *"who happened to be"*: Bell Collection, Box 1, FF 22 (Gould to Nickerson, December 17, 1879); Palmer Collection, Box 5, FF 320 (agreement between Atchison, Topeka and Santa Fe Railroad Company, et al., and the Denver & Rio Grande Railway Company, March 27, 1880); commission appraisal in Anderson, *William J. Palmer,* p. 113; Gould's Rio Grande stock quotes in Klein, *Jay Gould,* p. 243. Palmer responded to Bell's meeting with Gould, "Any peace that stops A.T. &

S.F. at South Pueblo and gives us Leadville & San Juan, and prevents coal and coke competition to westward, will put D&RG on stock dividend paying basis. . . ." Bell Collection, Box 1, FF 22 (Palmer to Bell, December 18, 1879).

24. Robert A. Le Massena, "The Royal Gorge," *Denver Westerners Monthly Roundup* 21, no. 11 (November 1965): 7, 14–16, specifically, *"no one in his right"* and *"the public press insisted,"* p. 15, and *"I was chief engineer,"* p. 16.

25. *Report of the Board of Directors to the Stockholders of the Denver and Rio Grande Railway Company, 1880,* pp. 12–13, Denver and Rio Grande Collection, Box 15, FF 506. Palmer's fight with the Santa Fe primed him for his next battle: a race against John Evans's Denver, South Park and Pacific for Colorado's Western Slope and a transcontinental connection with the Central Pacific at Ogden. As Evans learned during the Denver Pacific fight and Palmer experienced firsthand during the Royal Gorge war, railroading, like politics, sometimes made for strange bedfellows. This was particularly true when one of the parties in the room was Jay Gould after he'd bought into both the Rio Grande and the South Park.

As Gould negotiated with the Santa Fe to resolve the Royal Gorge war, he forced a joint operating agreement on Palmer and Evans. Once released from the gorge, the Denver and Rio Grande would build to Leadville, but the South Park was to have equal trackage rights on the last 30 miles from Buena Vista north. In exchange, the South Park would give the Rio Grande the same trackage rights along its planned line from Buena Vista west across the Continental Divide and into the Gunnison country.

But with the Royal Gorge battle resolved, Palmer began counting shares and reasserting himself as the decision maker of the Denver and Rio Grande. When Gould got wind of this, he wrote Evans in frustration: "As I understood the contract, the D&RG were not to build an *independent* line into the Gunnison country [because] such a line would sooner or later get the two companies into a collision." Gould reminded Evans that the joint operating agreement contemplated that the two roads be consolidated and he urged Evans, "the sooner this is done the better" (Evans Collection, Box 7, FF 82 [Gould to Evans, July 5, 1880]).

A review of the agreement showed that while the Rio Grande had in fact been granted rights over a South Park line to Gunnison, there was no prohibition on the Rio Grande building its own line despite the general understanding that it would not. Whether this contractual lapse was Gould's fault or that of his attorneys made little difference as Palmer champed at the bit to head west independent of the South Park. The general knew that if he did so, it would mean a rate war with the South Park and quite probably the wrath of the Union Pacific system over which Gould held considerable sway. But if Palmer could acquire controlling interest in the South Park, the move would rid the Rio Grande of Union Pacific influence in the central Rockies.

So, Evans—at Gould's urging—and Palmer—for his own interests—sat down to haggle. Reportedly, Palmer first offered Evans a straight stock trade: one share of Rio Grande stock for one share of South Park. Having achieved somewhat of a rebirth thanks to Gould's investment, Rio Grande stock was then trading between $60 and $70 a share. South Park stock was not on the market because after Gould bought about 25 percent, Evans and his Denver cronies shrewdly put their remaining shares into a trust, with instructions that it be voted or sold as a block. They did not intend to be minority shareholders; it was all or nothing.

Meanwhile, thanks to the rush to Leadville, the Denver, South Park and Pacific was having a banner year. Its Denver investors thought that its stock was worth at least par—$100 a share. Palmer countered with a $700,000 cash sweetener above the Rio Grande stock, but wanted nine-month terms. When Evans discussed this with Gould in his role as a South Park shareholder who would have to consent as to his quarter interest, Gould "offered to purchase the South Park himself at $90 per share, and, as an added inducement, offered to let Evans remain as president." When Evans asked why he should still be president after the transaction, Gould tipped his hand. "I thought you might like to remain as president and be identified with the Union Pacific." That, of course, was exactly what Palmer feared the most.

Evans responded to Gould as he had to Palmer, holding out for par. Just to be certain that he fully understood Evans's position, Gould asked Evans to make an all-cash proposal. "We will take cash par for our railroad stock," the governor wired back on behalf of his Denver group. Done, answered Gould, "Your offer is accepted."

Evans and his associates reaped substantial profits, and Jay Gould became the sole owner of the Denver, South Park and Pacific. By one count, Evans's personal take was almost $800,000. Gould made money too, because he sold his shares at par two months later to the Union Pacific, recovering what he had paid the Denver group and making more than a half million dollars on the quarter stake he had held previously. What Gould's interest in the Rio Grande was at this time is uncertain, but it seems probable that by the 1881 annual meeting, Palmer had rounded up enough support to outvote him, and Gould subsequently sold his minority position. By then, the Denver and Rio Grande and the Denver, South Park and Pacific were racing each other for the Gunnison country.

The Denver and Rio Grande chose to build over the comparatively gentle grades of 10,846-foot Marshall Pass. The South Park committed to Chalk Creek and crossing the divide via what would be called the Alpine Tunnel. The Rio Grande crested the summit of Marshall Pass and then laid tracks another 45 miles into Gunnison, reaching the town on August 6, 1881. Palmer did not pause to celebrate, but rapidly continued his main line westward toward Utah. The South Park finally arrived in Gunnison in September 1882. The Alpine Tunnel reserved a spot in railroad lore for the line, but it cost the railroad dearly in construction costs, in a year's delay in reaching Gunnison, and in lives and materiel as the years went by. For the Denver, South Park and Pacific, Gunnison proved the end of the line—the demise of its transcontinental efforts.

Various versions exist for Gould's role in the Denver and Rio Grande, Palmer's decision to build independently to the Gunnison country, and Gould's purchase of control of the South Park. The most reasoned and best researched may be Kelsey, *Frontier Capitalist*, pp. 187–93, 316–17n, which is based on correspondence between Gould and Evans; other interpretations, along with Gould's profit on the South Park sale, can be found at Klein, *Union Pacific, Birth*, pp. 431–32, and Klein, *Jay Gould*, p. 257.

CHAPTER 11: HANDSHAKE AT DEMING

1. Evans, *Huntington,* vol. 1, p. 258.
2. Myrick, *Railroads of Arizona, Southern Roads,* p. 32.
3. *Arizona Weekly Citizen,* November 2, 1878; Myrick, *Railroads of Arizona, Southern Roads,* p. 33.
4. *"move dirt much more":* Arizona Sentinel, December 7, 1878; Myrick, *Railroads of Arizona, Southern Roads,* pp. 34–36.
5. *"It seemed like old times": Huntington Papers,* Series 1, Reel 16 (Crocker to Huntington, December 10, 1878); *"I do not think":* ibid., Series 4, Reel 3 (Crocker to Huntington, February 7, 1879).
6. *Huntington Papers,* Series 4, Reel 3 (Crocker to Huntington, February 7, 1879).
7. Myrick, *Railroads of Arizona, Southern Roads,* p. 40; *"There is hardly": San Francisco Bulletin,* April 1, 1879; auction results in *Arizona Sentinel,* May 17, 1879; *"We had a sale": Huntington Papers,* Series 1, Reel 17 (Crocker to Huntington, May 17, 1879). Once down the east side of the Maricopas, the railroad began a long, continuous 5-mile curve of ten minutes (about one-sixth of 1 degree) and by some accounts the longest continuous railroad curve in the world.
8. *"My idea of stopping"* and *"the men could not work": Huntington Papers,* Series 1, Reel 17 (Crocker to Huntington, May 17, 1879); *"been constantly working": Arizona Sentinel,* May 24, 1879; stockpiling ties in Myrick, *Railroads of Arizona, Southern Roads,* p. 42.
9. Census figures from Myrick, *Railroads of Arizona, Southern Roads,* p. 46; *"Hardly a stage": Arizona Daily Star,* July 9, 1879; *"A good deal of the trouble": Arizona Daily Star,* July 20, 1879.
10. David Devine, *Slavery, Scandal, and Steel Rails: The 1854 Gadsden Purchase and the Building of the Second Transcontinental Railroad Across Arizona and New Mexico Twenty-five Years Later* (New York: iUniverse, 2004), pp. 159–60, 164; bond election results in *Arizona Daily Citizen,* June 21, 1879; *"a road of easy grade": Arizona Daily Star,* September 30, 1879; *"will make Tucson": Arizona Daily Star,* October 7, 1879.
11. *"I wish you would": Huntington Papers,* Series 1, Reel 18 (Crocker to Huntington, September 16, 1879); *"I am doing all I can":* ibid., Series 2, Reel 6 (Huntington to Crocker, November 3, 1879).
12. Myrick, *Railroads of Arizona, Southern Roads,* p. 50.
13. Myrick, *Railroads of Arizona, Southern Roads,* pp. 50–51, 54; *"that a railroad": Arizona Daily Star,* March 19, 1880; *"His Holiness, the Pope":* Myrick, *Railroads of Arizona, Southern Roads,* p. 54.
14. David F. Myrick, *New Mexico's Railroads: A Historical Survey* (Albuquerque: University of New Mexico Press, 1993), pp. 4–5, 7; first Santa Fe dividend in Glenn D. Bradley, *The Story of the Santa Fe* (Palmdale, Calif.: Omni Publications, 1995), p. 138; Santa Fe town issues and Wakarusa picnic in Bryant, *Atchison, Topeka and Santa Fe,* pp. 1–2, 60–63; *"Yesterday morning": Las Vegas Gazette,* about January 20, 1880, quoted in Bradley, *Santa Fe,* p. 137.
15. James H. Ducker, *Men of the Steel Rails: Workers on the Atchison, Topeka & Santa Fe Railroad, 1869–1900* (Lincoln: University of Nebraska Press, 1983), p. 8.
16. *Las Vegas Daily Optic,* February 20, 1880.

17. *"There is some quite"*: *Huntington Papers,* Series 1, Reel 19 (Crocker to Huntington, April 22, 1880).

18. Myrick, *Railroads of Arizona, Southern Roads,* pp. 57–61; Orlando Bolivar Willcox at www.arlingtoncemetery.net/owillcox.htm, downloaded October 10, 2007. By coincidence, both Willcox and John G. Parke ended their Civil War service as generals in the same corps of the Army of the Potomac.

19. For fears of Santa Fe impacting Southern Pacific traffic around Tucson, see *Huntington Papers,* Series 1, Reel 19 (Crocker to Huntington, March 24, 1880); *"The earnings since we"*: *Huntington Papers,* Series 1, Reel 19 (Crocker to Huntington, April 19, 1880); naming Lordsburg for Charles H. Lord is recounted in Devine, *Slavery, Scandal, and Steel Rails,* p. 193, but some claim that the town was named for a Delbert Lord, who was somehow associated with the Southern Pacific.

20. *"If we don't make"*: *Huntington Papers,* Series 1, Reel 20 (Crocker to Huntington, July 20, 1880); *"I very much fear"*: ibid. (Crocker to Huntington, June 24, 1880); *"not get tired"* and *"those people [the Santa Fe backers] have"*: ibid. (Crocker to Huntington, July 2, 1880).

21. *"I did think"* and *"Still . . . I cannot believe"*: *Huntington Papers,* Series 2, Reel 6 (Huntington to Crocker, July 2, 1880).

22. Trackage agreement in Bradley, *Santa Fe,* pp. 152–53; *"We agreed to this"*: *Huntington Papers,* Series 2, Reel 6 (Huntington to Stanford, October 9, 1880).

23. Stanford suggests Deming name and *"Water, of course"*: Devine, *Slavery, Scandal, and Steel Rails,* p. 193, quoting Towne to Huntington, November 19, 1880; *"thirteen saloons"*: Devine, *Slavery, Scandal, and Steel Rails,* p. 195; *"Deming morals"*: C. M. Chase, *The Editor's Run in New Mexico and Colorado* (Fort Davis, Tex.: Frontier Book Company, 1968), p. 127.

24. *Annual Report of the Board of Directors of the Atchison, Topeka and Santa Fe Railroad Co. to the Stockholders for the Year Ending December 31, 1880,* Santa Fe Collection, Box 1, FF 30, p. 6.

25. *"The southern way"* and *"Tourists for pleasure"*: *Boston Herald* quote reprinted in *Arizona Daily Citizen,* December 2, 1880; *"This month witnesses"*: *Railway Times,* March 26, 1881, p. 283.

26. Arrival in Deming, first trains, and *"the Santa Fe announced"*: Bryant, *Atchison, Topeka and Santa Fe,* pp. 79–80; fares from Devine, *Slavery, Scandal, and Steel Rails,* p. 196; relative values adjusted for CPI from www.measuringworth.com/uscompare, downloaded November 23, 2009; *"the steps taken"* and *"prevented all business"* and *"a carload of beer"*: *Huntington Papers,* Series 1, Reel 22 (Coolidge to Huntington, May 10, 1881); for a detailed study of Pullman and his car designs, see Liston Edgington Leyendecker, *Palace Car Prince: A Biography of George Mortimer Pullman* (Niwot, Colo.: University of Colorado Press, 1992). George Mortimer Pullman did not invent the sleeping car, but through numerous refinements, he took the concept of a straight-backed chair or a cramped fold-down bunk to a palatial experience deserving of the Pullman's Palace Car Company name. Pullman's overarching concept was that one might dine, sleep, relax, and even conduct business with as much comfort on the rails as in the best hotels of the land. Among Pullman's innovations were fold-down seats and couches, private drawing rooms that converted to sleeping quarters, dining cars with refrigeration, and more pleasing and separate lavatory facilities for ladies and

gentlemen. As for the cars themselves, in addition to plush furnishings, Pullman put more wheels on the undercarriage and added shock absorbers that reduced sway and made for a smoother ride. Sometimes Pullman leased its cars to railroads along with continuing service contracts, and sometimes they were sold outright.

CHAPTER 12: WEST ACROSS TEXAS

1. Handbook of Texas Online, under the word "Railroads," www.tsha.online.org/handbook/online/articles/RR/eqr1.html (accessed September 27, 2007); "Galveston, Harrisburg and San Antonio Railway," www.tsha.online.org/handbook/online/articles/GG/eqg6.html (accessed September 27, 2007); "Texas and Pacific Railway," www.tsha.online.org/handbook/online/articles/TT/eqt8.html (accessed September 27, 2007). The Texas and Pacific acquired the faltering attempts of the Memphis, El Paso, and Pacific and another road's 60-mile stretch of track between Longview and Waskom, Texas. By 1873, it had built north from Marshall to Texarkana, Texas, and west from Longview to Dallas. Construction west from Dallas was halted at Eagle Ford by the panic of 1873, but by 1876, the Texas and Pacific reached Fort Worth.

2. Klein, *Union Pacific, Birth,* pp. 275–77, 285–89, specifically, "*an able man*" and "*was not worth that,*" p. 287; "*the vaunted Pennsylvania connection,*" p. 286.

3. This summary of Gould's early career is from his most balanced and insightful biographer, Maury Klein, *The Life and Legend of Jay Gould,* specifically, "*He never disclosed,*" p. 67; Erie election and *Boston Herald* quote, p. 79; "*quite depressed,*" p. 113; Erie ouster, p. 125; entry into the Union Pacific, pp. 139–41.

4. "*You know I never had much respect*" and "*the reverse of Scott*": Huntington Papers, Series 4, Reel 3 (Colton to Huntington, October 15, 1877); "*You write that you*": ibid. (Huntington to Colton, February 2, 1875).

5. "*Disagreeable as the medicine*": Huntington Papers, Series 4, Reel 3 (Colton to Huntington, October 15, 1877); Gould buys out Scott in Klein, *Gould,* p. 265.

6. Lavender, *The Great Persuader,* p. 336.

7. "*our line down*" and "*It seems to me*": Huntington Papers, Series 1, Reel 21 (Crocker to Huntington, January 3, 1881); Lavender, *The Great Persuader,* p. 327, 420n14.

8. "*I do not suppose*": Huntington Papers, Series 1, Reel 21 (Crocker to Huntington, January 8, 1881).

9. "*They really damage*": Huntington Papers, Series 1, Reel 22 (Crocker to Huntington, April 9, 1881); "*We crossed the bridge*": ibid. (Crocker to Huntington, May 9, 1881).

10. Lavender, *The Great Persuader,* p. 336; "*should be ours*" and "*I am afraid*": Huntington Papers, Series 1, Reel 22 (Crocker to Huntington, April 27, 1881).

11. "*If one man builds*" and "*there is no local business*": Klein, *Gould,* p. 270.

12. "*I do not believe*": Huntington Papers, Series 1, Reel 22 (Crocker to Huntington, May 13, 1881, No. 309); "*we shall go right*": ibid. (Crocker to Huntington, May 13, 1881, No. 310); "*My own opinion*": Devine, *Slavery, Scandal, and Steel Rails,* p. 208, quoting Huntington to Crocker, May 12, 1881.

13. "*as little to do*": Klein, *Gould,* p. 269; "*do more watching*" and "*Their friendship is*": ibid., p. 271.

14. "*At our last meeting*": Huntington Papers, Series 1, Reel 25 (Gould to Huntington, November 1, 1881); Klein, *Gould,* p. 271.

15. William S. Greever, "Railway Development in the Southwest," *New Mexico Historical Review* 32, no. 2 (April 1957): 158–59; see also Lavender, *The Great Persuader,* pp. 336–37.

16. Last spike ceremony and *"What should have been"*: *Lone Star* (El Paso, Texas), December 3, 1881.

17. *"such as will sooner"* and *"in making the owners"*: *Huntington Papers,* Series 1, Reel 21 (Stanford to Huntington, February 1, 1881).

CHAPTER 13: TRANSCONTINENTAL AT LAST

1. *" a matter of detail"*: *Congressional Globe,* 30th Cong., 2nd sess. (February 7, 1849), pp. 470, 472; for details of these early predecessors to the St. Louis and San Francisco Railroad, see H. Craig Miner, *The St. Louis–San Francisco Transcontinental Railroad: The Thirty-fifth Parallel Project, 1853–1890* (Lawrence: University Press of Kansas, 1972).

2. *U.S. Statutes at Large,* 39th Cong., 1st sess., chap. 278, 1866, pp. 292–99.

3. Bradley, *Santa Fe,* pp. 142–45; Miner, *St. Louis–San Francisco,* pp. 93–95; *"The new company is"*: *Railroad Gazette,* September 1, 1876.

4. Miner, *St. Louis–San Francisco,* pp. 104, 115–16; Bryant, *Atchison, Topeka and Santa Fe,* p. 85; annual report in Bradley, *Santa Fe,* p. 140.

5. Bradley, *Santa Fe,* pp. 147–48; Miner, *St. Louis–San Francisco,* p. 121; *"As a county we agreed"*: *Wichita City Eagle,* October 9, 1879.

6. Bryant, *Atchison, Topeka and Santa Fe,* p. 83.

7. Van Law, "Four Years on Santa Fe Railroad Surveys," pp. 7–9.

8. James Garrison et al., *Transcontinental Railroading in Arizona, 1878–1940: A Component of the Arizona Historic Preservation Plan,* prepared for the Arizona State Historic Preservation Office, December 1989, by Janus Associates, Phoenix, pp. 17–18; *"on railroad business"*: *Weekly Arizona Miner,* July 9, 1880.

9. Land grant application and construction in Bradley, *Santa Fe,* pp. 148–49; wages and workforce in Bryant, *Atchison, Topeka and Santa Fe,* pp. 87, 90; *"The directors of the 35th Parallel R.R."*: Garrison, *Transcontinental Railroading in Arizona,* p. 18, quoting *Weekly Arizona Miner,* March 25, 1881; *"The whole country"*: *Weekly Arizona Miner,* April 8, 1881.

10. Garrison, *Transcontinental Railroading in Arizona,* pp. 19–20; *"thread-like rill"* and *"for a railroad"*: Whipple, *Report, Pacific Railroad Reports,* vol. 3, p. 78; Whipple initially named the location "Cañon Diablo," and it retained its Spanish spelling until 1902, when the Santa Fe anglicized the spelling of *cañon* all along its line; David F. Myrick, *Railroads of Arizona,* vol. 4, *The Santa Fe Route* (Wilton, Calif.: Signature Press, 1998), pp. 27–29, 106. The original Cañon Diablo bridge served until 1900, when it was replaced by a newer single-track structure. This second bridge was replaced in 1947 by a massive double-track steel arch bridge that eliminated the last bottleneck of single track between San Bernardino, California, and Belen, New Mexico.

11. *"the town at present"*: *Weekly Arizona Miner,* January 27, 1882; Garrison, *Transcontinental Railroading in Arizona,* pp. 19–20; Myrick, *Railroads of Arizona, The Santa Fe Route,* p. 29.

12. *"in the United States"*: Miner, *St. Louis–San Francisco,* p. 122; *"Owing to changes"*: Bradley, *Santa Fe,* p. 149.

13. Bradley, *Santa Fe,* p. 150; *"Do not be afraid"*: Evans, *Huntington,* p. 5; *"to Gould as a client"*: Miner, *St. Louis–San Francisco,* p. 131.

14. *"a matter of indifference"*: New York Times, January 31, 1882; *"Mr. Huntington today informs me"*: Huntington Papers, Series 1, Reel 26 (Gould to Strong, copy with note to Huntington, February 5, 1882).

15. *"Your desire to secure"*: Huntington Papers, Series 1, Reel 26 (Strong to Gould, February 8, 1882).

16. *"sagacity and good sense"* and *"a pleasing idea"* and *"to discriminate"*: Commercial and Financial Chronicle, March 4, 1882.

17. Agreement in Bradley, *Santa Fe,* pp. 150–51; *"strong backers in Boston"*: Grodinsky, *Transcontinental Railway Strategy,* p. 194, quoting Crocker to Huntington, April 27, 1882; financial statistics from Bradley, *Santa Fe,* pp. 290, 294–95.

18. Garrison, *Transcontinental Railroading in Arizona,* pp. 20–22; Myrick, *Railroads of Arizona, The Santa Fe Route,* pp. 30–31, 70.

19. Garrison, *Transcontinental Railroading in Arizona,* p. 22; Miner, *St. Louis–San Francisco,* p. 138. Portions of the 1883 trestle at Needles washed out the following year even as a stronger replacement was under construction. Passengers and freight were ferried across the river while the new bridge was completed.

CHAPTER 14: BATTLING FOR CALIFORNIA

1. Waters, *Steel Trails,* pp. 71–72.

2. *"You could knock"* and *"try and break"*: Grodinsky, *Transcontinental Railway Strategy,* p. 168.

3. *"a brawling stream"*: William Henry Bishop, "Southern California," Harper's New Monthly magazine (December 1882): 63–64; high water line story from Kurt Van Horn, "Tempting Temecula: The Making and Unmaking of a Southern California Community," Journal of San Diego History 20, no. 1 (Winter 1974), accessed online at www.sandiegohistory.org/journal/74winter/temecula.htm.

4. Waters, *Steel Trails,* pp. 72–73.

5. Waters, *Steel Trails,* pp. 131–33.

6. Fogelson, *Fragmented Metropolis,* p. 60.

7. *"They [the Southern Pacific] are expected"*: Miner, *St. Louis–San Francisco,* p. 138; Bryant, *Atchison, Topeka and Santa Fe,* pp. 90, 92, specifically, *"freight often became,"* p. 92; revenue figures from Bradley, *Santa Fe,* p. 295.

8. Van Horn, "Tempting Temecula," accessed online.

9. Bradley, *Santa Fe,* pp. 161–63; Lavender, *The Great Persuader,* pp. 338–41.

10. Donald Duke, *Santa Fe . . . The Railroad Gateway to the American West,* vol. 1, Chicago-Los Angeles-San Diego (San Marino, Calif.: Golden West Books, 1995), pp. 17, 58–59, 72. The Cajon Pass route has remained a critical artery to rail traffic. In the summer of 2007, the Burlington Northern–Santa Fe added a third line to its corridor and daylighted two short tunnels on its northbound leg. The Union Pacific maintains a fourth line, its Palmdale Cutoff, across the pass.

11. Grodinski, *Transcontinental Railway Strategy,* p. 218.

12. *"San Diego is"*: San Diego Union, October 16, 1885; *"a period of moderate expansion"*: Bryant, *Atchison, Topeka and Santa Fe,* p. 102.

13. *"San Diego should have"* and *"San Francisco is"*: *Los Angeles Times,* January 12, 1886; *"It doesn't stand to reason"*: *Los Angeles Times,* November 29, 1885.

14. *"Railroading is a business"*: *Annual Report of the Board of Directors of the Atchison, Topeka and Santa Fe Railroad Company to the Stockholders for the Year Ending December 31, 1884,* p. 36.

CHAPTER 15: GOULD AGAIN

1. Maury Klein, "In Search of Jay Gould," *Business History Review* 52, no. 2 (Summer 1978): 167. This article predates Klein's landmark biography of Gould and may be the best analysis of his reputation. There is an anecdotal story about these fierce competitors from a meeting that occurred at J. P. Morgan's New York home late in 1890. Among those present were Gould, Huntington, Palmer, and Allen Manvel of the Santa Fe. "You are all gentlemen here," noted the president of a much smaller Midwest road. "In your private capacity as such, I would trust any of you with my watch, and I would believe the word of any of you, but in your capacity as railroad presidents, I would not believe one of you on oath, and I would not trust one of you with my watch." Indeed, each knew that the others would look after their own interests first and foremost, but in their own way and time, Gould, Huntington, Palmer, and many others at that meeting were generous philanthropists with the largesse of their success (Klein, *Gould,* pp. 460–61, quoting *New York Herald,* December 16, 1890).

2. *"I know there are"* and *"I have always"*: Klein, "In Search of Jay Gould," p. 172.

3. J. R. Perkins, *Trails, Rails, and War: The Life of General G. M. Dodge* (Indianapolis: Bobbs-Merrill Company, 1929), p. 263.

4. *"I appreciate your friendship"*: Klein, *Gould,* p. 264; for family, see ibid., pp. 74–76.

5. Klein, *Union Pacific, Birth,* pp. 398–99. The Denver Pacific was included with the Kansas Pacific sale. The transaction left Denver wondering about John Evans's promises that the Denver Pacific and Kansas Pacific would never pass from local control. Palmer and his Denver and Rio Grande also weighed Gould's moves, first tolerating him as a short-term savior in the midst of the Royal Gorge war and then as a potential customer for a western extension of the Missouri Pacific.

6. Klein, *Union Pacific, Birth,* pp. 432, 444; Athearn, *Rebel of the Rockies,* pp. 133–35; Klein, *Gould,* p. 270.

7. Colorado Central construction dates from Wilkins, *Colorado Railroads,* pp. 4, 7, 9, 11, 19; *"that the Colorado Central"*: Robert C. Black III, *Railroad Pathfinder: The Life and Times of Edward L. Berthoud* (Evergreen, Colo.: Cordillera Press, 1988), p. 79. Part of the Colorado Central's problem was a continuing battle between Loveland's commercial interests centering around Golden, and Denver's own rail interests championed by John Evans. Seeking an independent link to the Union Pacific main line, the Colorado Central further diffused its focus by pushing multiple lines in too many directions in both standard and narrow gauges. Its Golden-Denver artery was built in 1870 to standard gauge. Two years later, the railroad laid narrow gauge tracks west up Clear Creek to its forks and up the north fork to the mining town of Black Hawk, a distance of 20 miles. Just before the panic of 1873, it extended the three-foot line from the forks several miles to Floyd Hill and laid standard gauge tracks from just east of Golden northerly to Boulder and Longmont, reaching out to the Union Pacific.

8. Black, *Railroad Pathfinder*, pp. 96–99; Cornelius W. Hauck, *Narrow Gauge to Central and Silver Plume, Colorado Rail Annual*, no. 10 (Golden, Colo.: Colorado Railroad Museum, 1972), pp. 74, 77. Interestingly enough, when the Union Pacific reorganized the Georgetown, Leadville and San Juan Railroad in 1881, the geography of its name got shorter, not longer: It became the Georgetown, Breckenridge and Leadville.

9. Robert Brewster Stanton, *Down the Colorado* (Norman: University of Oklahoma Press, 1965), pp. xiv–xv, 20–22.

10. Hauck, *Narrow Gauge to Central and Silver Plume*, pp. 77–79; Gould visit in *Georgetown Courier*, October 18, 1883; "The bridge builders say": *Georgetown Courier*, November 29, 1883; "'Tis done at last": *Georgetown Courier*, January 24, 1884. Construction costs for this extension, including the loop, were $254,700.

11. Grodinsky, *Transcontinental Railway Strategy*, pp. 172–73; Lavender, *The Great Persuader*, p. 336.

12. Grodinsky, *Transcontinental Railway Strategy*, pp. 299–300.

13. Waters, *Steel Trails*, pp. 76–83; Bryant, *Atchison, Topeka and Santa Fe*, pp. 126–34. As early as 1881, Charles Crocker encouraged Huntington to buy the Gulf, Colorado and Santa Fe as a defense against Gould, but at the time, Huntington was momentarily making peace with Gould and fixated with the continued eastward growth of his own empire. Meanwhile, the Santa Fe's Southern Kansas Railway had also completed a line from Kiowa, Kansas, across the Cimarron and Canadian rivers and on to Panhandle City in Texas. Critics were quick to say that this road started nowhere and ended nowhere, but Strong undertook the route to counter John Evans's Gulf-to-Rockies route and ensure that the Santa Fe maintained an edge in shipping Texas beef to Kansas City.

After their sale of the South Park, Evans and some of his investors incorporated the Denver and New Orleans Railroad to run from Colorado to the Gulf of Mexico. Its initial goal was to link up with the Fort Worth and Denver City under the leadership of General Grenville Dodge. This Texas road hoped to build northwest from Fort Worth. Not surprisingly, Evans's sale of the South Park to Gould and Dodge's work for Gould on other construction ventures raised the opposition's cry that Evans was actually building the Denver and New Orleans for Gould.

The line stalled at Pueblo for the better part of five years. When it renewed construction southeast from Trinidad in 1887 as the Denver, Texas and Gulf Railroad, it did so only because of trackage rights on the Denver and Rio Grande between Pueblo and Trinidad, now laid as standard gauge. About this time, William Barstow Strong tried to acquire the road for the Santa Fe as its independent entry into Denver. Evans said no and pushed on to meet up with Dodge in northeast New Mexico.

The story of this Gulf-to-Rockies line is not directly related to the struggle for the southern transcontinental corridor, but it must not be overlooked. By varying degrees, this route interacted as a north-south feeder among the Union Pacific, Kansas Pacific, Missouri Pacific, Santa Fe, and Texas and Pacific. With connections south from Fort Worth, it reached into Mexico. While the road ran increasingly eastward the farther south it got from Denver, it essentially emulated with standard gauge rails the north-south feeder line between Denver and El Paso that Palmer originally envisioned for the Denver and Rio Grande. In 1890 the Gulf-to-Rockies line became part of the Union Pacific. See Richard C. Overton, *Gulf to Rockies: The Heritage of the Fort Worth and Denver–Colorado Southern Railways, 1861–1898* (Westport, Conn.: Greenwood Press, 1970).

CHAPTER 16: TO THE HALLS OF MONTEZUMA

1. For the construction history of the Mexican Railway see David M. Pletcher, "The Building of the Mexican Railway," *Hispanic American Historical Review* 30, no. 1 (February 1950): 26–62. The American Civil War interrupted plans for an American-backed railroad across the Isthmus of Tehuantepec, and Mexico endured its own internal strife before France attempted to profit from the confusion and seize Mexico under the pretense of collecting foreign debts.

2. David M. Pletcher, "General William S. Rosecrans and the Mexican Transcontinental Railroad Project," *Mississippi Valley Historical Review* 38 (March 1952): 657–58.

3. Pletcher, "Rosecrans and the Mexican Transcontinental Railroad Project," pp. 659–64; Fisher, *A Builder of the West*, pp. 213, 217–22.

4. Pletcher, "Rosecrans and the Mexican Transcontinental Railroad Project," pp. 662, 670–72, specifically, "*Mr. Lerdo is,*" pp. 670–71, note 30; "*is opposed to our gauge*" and "*The General as usual*": Palmer Collection, Box 9, FF 711 (Palmer to Queen Palmer, January 2, 1873); generally, see also the chapters on Rosecrans and Plumb in David M. Pletcher, *Rails, Mines, & Progress: Seven American Promoters in Mexico, 1867–1911* (Ithaca, N.Y.: Cornell University Press, 1958).

5. "*This business in Mexico*" and "*wanted to know*": Palmer Collection, Box 9, FF 711 (Palmer to Queen Palmer, January 6, 1873).

6. "*General Rosecrans*": Palmer Collection, Box 9, FF 713 (Palmer to Queen Palmer, May 15, 1873); Fisher, *A Builder of the West*, pp. 229–35; Pletcher, "Rosecrans and the Mexican Transcontinental Railroad Project," p. 673.

7. Bryant, *Atchison, Topeka and Santa Fe*, pp. 80–83; "*William is looking*": Cleaveland, *The Morleys*, p. 203.

8. Gerald M. Best, *Mexican Narrow Gauge* (Berkeley, Calif.: Howell-North Books, 1968), pp. 11–12. Palmer assured himself of a suitable entry into the capital by acquiring the struggling Mexico, Toluca, and Cuautitlan, a narrow gauge short line. Its thirty-five-pound rails were deemed too light, so the line was relaid with forty-five-pound rail.

9. Klein, *Gould*, pp. 274–75, 306. Gould consolidated his interests with the Mexican Southern Railroad, the chief promoter of which was former president Ulysses S. Grant.

10. *Gunnison Review*, July 30, 1881, quoting the *Denver Tribune*.

11. Best, *Mexican Narrow Gauge*, pp. 12–13, 16; two versions of Morley's accident are Waters, *Steel Trails*, pp. 107–8n and Cleaveland, *The Morleys*, pp. 212–15, including "*one of the most able,*" p. 215; "*that so far as*": Klein, *Gould*, p. 275.

12. Best, *Mexican Narrow Gauge*, pp. 14, 16.

CHAPTER 17: CALIFORNIA FOR A DOLLAR

1. *Railway Review*, June 5, 1886, p. 286.

2. Grodinsky, *Transcontinental Railway Strategy*, pp. 280–85; "*the people along*": Fifteenth

Annual Report of the Board of Directors of the Atchison, Topeka and Santa Fe Railroad Company to the Stockholders for the Year Ending December 31, 1886, p. 28.

3. Bradley, *Santa Fe*, pp. 177–81; *"two streaks of rust"*: Bryant, *Atchison, Topeka and Santa Fe*, p. 136.

4. Bradley, *Santa Fe*, pp. 181–83. The bridges and their approaches were major structures. The longest crossed the Missouri River at Sibley, Missouri, just east of Kansas City. The Sibley Bridge was composed of seven girder sections—three of them 400 feet long—that totaled 2,000 feet and were supported by eight masonry piers. It was accessed on the east by an additional 1,900-foot viaduct. The main span of the Grand River structure between Carrollton and Marceline, Missouri, was 459 feet long; the Des Moines River crossing southwest of Fort Madison was 900 feet; and the Illinois River crossing at Chillicothe had a main span of 752 feet. That left the Mississippi bridge at Fort Madison. Completed in early December 1887, the structure cost $580,000 and had a total length of 2,963 feet. The crossing consisted of eight spans: four each of 237.5 feet, one of 275 feet, two of 150 feet, and one drawbridge span of 400 feet. An additional 1,038 feet of viaduct made up the eastern approach over seventy-four 14-foot spans.

5. Bradley, *Santa Fe*, pp. 181, 184; Bryant, *Atchison, Topeka and Santa Fe*, pp. 138–39; Miner, *St. Louis–San Francisco*, pp. 166–67.

6. Franklin Hoyt, "San Diego's First Railroad: The California Southern," *Pacific Historical Review* 23, no. 2 (May 1954): 145–46.

7. *"to keep peace"* and *"We have done"*: Grodinsky, *Transcontinental Railway Strategy*, p. 318.

8. Bryant, *Atchison, Topeka and Santa Fe*, pp. 102–3; Franklin Hoyt, "The Los Angeles and San Gabriel Valley Railroad," *Pacific Historical Review* 20, no. 3 (August 1951): 237.

9. Census figures from 1880 U.S. Census; dollar equivalents based on CPI from measuringworth.com; *"say they can purchase"*: Fogelson, *The Fragmented Metropolis*, p. 65, quoting *Los Angeles Herald*, November 5, 1880, and *"It seems almost impossible"*: p. 66, quoting *Los Angeles Evening Express*, September 1, 1884.

10. *"Like birds of passage"*: Fogelson, *The Fragmented Metropolis*, p. 66; dollar story from Wilson and Taylor, *Southern Pacific*, p. 86.

11. Fogelson, *The Fragmented Metropolis*, p. 67.

12. *"The history of Western railroad"*: *Seventeenth Annual Report of the Board of Directors of the Atchison, Topeka and Santa Fe Railroad Co. to the Stockholders for the Year Ending December 31, 1888*, p. 16; 1888 trackage from Bradley, *Santa Fe*, p. 290.

CHAPTER 18: MAKING THE MARKETS

1. Miner, *St. Louis–San Francisco*, p. 148.

2. Walter R. Borneman, *Marshall Pass: Denver and Rio Grande Gateway to the Gunnison Country* (Colorado Springs, Colo.: Century One Press, 1980), pp. 39, 48, 50, specifically, *"of this line,"* p. 48. The wording "Scenic Line of the World" in reference to Marshall Pass appeared as early as a travel account in the *Gunnison Review* of June 11, 1881.

3. *"Never mind, my dear"*: Walter R. Borneman, "Ride the Historic Georgetown Loop," *American West* 24, no. 3 (June 1987): 44.

4. Dow Helmers, *Historic Alpine Tunnel* (Colorado Springs, Colo.: Century One Press, 1971), *"highest point reached,"* p. 70, *"It is something to know,"* p. 41. The Central Pacific established the first major altitude record in the United States by crossing 7,085-foot Donner Summit. The Santa Fe's crossing of 7,834-foot Raton Pass was a clear watershed on the line's westward advance, but the crossing did not garner an altitude record. By the time the Santa Fe built across Raton, the Denver and Rio Grande had pushed its narrow gauge rails over 9,390-foot La Veta Pass en route from Cuchara Junction to the San Luis Valley. In May 1879, the Denver, South Park and Pacific captured the altitude record by building over Colorado's 9,991-foot Kenosha Pass en route to the Alpine Tunnel. Late in 1880, the Rio Grande completed a spur line over 11,318-foot Fremont Pass northeast of Leadville, but the South Park snatched the title back when it finally opened the Alpine Tunnel in 1882 at an elevation of 11,538 feet. In the fall of 1887, the Colorado Midland completed the standard gauge Hagerman Tunnel at 11,528 feet between Leadville and the Roaring Fork Valley. The Hagerman Tunnel held the altitude record after the Alpine Tunnel was temporarily shut down between 1888 and 1895, although the Hagerman Tunnel itself was abandoned for the lower Busk-Ivanhoe Tunnel (10,953 feet) in 1893.

Any contest between the gauges for the altitude record was firmly settled when David Moffat's standard gauge Denver, Northwestern and Pacific crossed 11,680-foot Rollins Pass in 1904. Rollins Pass (also called Corona) held the record until it was abandoned for the lower Moffat Tunnel (9,239 feet at apex) in 1928, although the track was not torn up until 1937. The record then fell to the narrow gauge line over Marshall Pass, with its elevation of 10,846 feet. When the Marshall Pass line was abandoned in 1955, the Rio Grande standard gauge over Tennessee Pass captured the record with a crossing of 10,424 feet. (Elevations and dates from Wilkins, *Colorado Railroads.*)

5. Myrick, *New Mexico's Railroads,* pp. 15–16.

6. Donald Duke, *Santa Fe . . . The Railroad Gateway to the American West,* vol. 2, *Passenger and Freight Service, et al.* (San Marino, Calif.: Golden West Books, 1997), pp. 306–8.

7. Bryant, *Atchison, Topeka and Santa Fe,* p. 111.

8. For a thorough history of the Harvey girls, see Lesley Poling-Kempes, *The Harvey Girls: Women Who Opened the West* (New York: Paragon House, 1989), specifically, *"no ladies west of Dodge,"* p. 52; *"We didn't have,"* p. 56; and *"they used to say,"* p. 99.

9. For the coat rule, including the Harvey sons' continuation of it despite litigation, see Waters, *Steel Trails,* pp. 277–78; the cup code is discussed in Poling-Kempes, *The Harvey Girls,* pp. 58, 217n.

10. Dining car service in Bryant, *Atchison, Topeka and Santa Fe,* p. 118; for a complete list of Harvey facilities, see Poling-Kempes, *The Harvey Girls,* pp. 233–34; *"had more friends"*: Bryant, *Atchison, Topeka and Santa Fe,* p. 106. From 1930 to about 1970, there was a Fred Harvey lunch counter and restaurant in Cleveland's Terminal Tower, at one time the tallest building outside of New York City. On trips to downtown Cleveland from the west side in the late 1950s, the author's grandmother took him to Fred Harvey for ice cream. Gram's talk of "Fred Harvey" left a five-year-old quite expecting to see the man himself walk out from the kitchen.

11. Brooke Kroeger, *Nellie Bly: Daredevil, Reporter, Feminist* (New York: Times Books, 1994), pp. 4–5, 43–44, 75, 85–86, 168–73, specifically, "*I am off for New York,*" p. 75; "*Start the man,*" p. 140; "*For Nellie Bly,*" p. 161; "*On the line out to this point,*" p. 165; reports of Nellie's progress across Kansas in *State Journal* (Topeka), January 23, 1890; the bridge incident in *State Journal,* January 24, 1890.

CHAPTER 19: CANYON DREAMS AND SCHEMES

1. Wilkins, *Colorado Railroads,* pp. 81, 85. The Rio Grande Western standard gauge built from Cisco, Utah, up the Colorado River through spectacular Ruby Canyon, and met its original narrow gauge right-of-way about 20 miles west of Grand Junction.

2. David Lavender, *Colorado River Country* (New York: E. P. Dutton, 1982), pp. 151–53, specifically, "*I have given up,*" p. 153. The *Black Betty* was portaged by wagon across sagebrush flats to avoid Westwater Canyon and its test-piece rapid, the Skull.

3. Lavender, *Colorado River Country,* pp. 152–56. The author paddled the length of the Grand Canyon, including Soap Creek Rapid, with David Lavender in 1986.

4. David Lavender, *River Runners of the Grand Canyon* (Tucson: Grand Canyon Natural History Association and the University of Arizona Press, 1985), pp. 25–27, specifically, "*cut my salary off,*" p. 27.

5. Lavender, *Colorado River Country,* p. 157; "*a living, moving*": Lavender, *River Runners,* p. 30.

6. Lavender, *Colorado River Country,* p. 158; Lavender, *River Runners,* pp. 30–31; "*not one word*": Robert Brewster Stanton, *Colorado River Controversies* (Boulder City, Nev.: Westwater Books, 1982), p. 110.

7. Worster, *A River Running West,* pp. 527–28.

8. C. Gregory Crampton, *Ghosts of Glen Canyon* (Salt Lake City, Utah: Cricket Productions, 1986), p. 80.

9. While it is heavily steeped in legend, the Cañon Diablo train robbery is best analyzed in Paul T. Hietter, " 'No Better Than Murderers': The 1889 Canyon Diablo Train Robbery and the Death Penalty in Arizona Territory," *Journal of Arizona History* 47, no. 3 (Autumn 2006): 273–98. In another incident, two robbers pulled their guns on the Santa Fe station agent at Glorieta in December 1888 and took $90 in cash and a $53.65 company check. The *Las Vegas Daily Optic* was less than sympathetic in opining, "any man who cannot defend himself from two assailants ought to be robbed."

10. Myrick, *Railroads of Arizona, The Santa Fe Route,* pp. 155–58, specifically, "*All this hullabaloo,*" p. 158.

CHAPTER 20: THE BOOM GOES BUST

1. *Historical Statistics of the United States, Colonial Times to 1970,* pt. 2 (Washington: U.S. Department of Commerce, 1975), p. 731.

2. Bradley, *Santa Fe,* pp. 187, 191–93; labor issues in Waters, *Steel Trails,* pp. 313–15.

3. Bradley, *Santa Fe,* pp. 195, 214–22, specifically, "*amply and satisfactorily*" and "*are in such condition,*" p. 218; "*a success in every,*" p. 220; "*pending negotiations*" and "*is amply able,*" p. 222.

4. Bradley, *Santa Fe,* pp. 226–34, specifically, "*no foundation in fact,*" p. 228; for "off bal-

ance sheet" example, see pp. 231–32, indictment, p. 233. Reinhart was acquitted after the government failed to prove that he knew of the transactions.

5. Bradley, *Santa Fe,* pp. 236–40, 246–49, specifically, *"to rid the company,"* p. 236. The new debt was structured with 4 percent bonds and an assortment of preferred stock and income bonds. Interest payments on the latter vehicles were tied to revenues and thus served to reduce fixed costs. Santa Fe stockholders were assessed 10 percent for every $100 of common stock, with these assessments becoming preferred stock. A pool of European investors agreed to buy out those shareholders who opposed the assessment.

6. *Denver Republican,* December 22, 1893, quoting *Railway Age,* December 21, 1893.

7. Bradley, *Santa Fe,* pp. 249–51, specifically, *"believed in the good old doctrine,"* p. 249.

8. Bradley, *Santa Fe,* pp. 252, 258–61. The final end to the Atlantic and Pacific as a separate entity came after another round of foreclosures, when the Frisco purchased the old Central Division, some 112 miles largely in Indian Territory.

9. Bradley, *Santa Fe,* pp. 263, 266, 286, 291, 298–300, 311.

10. Bryant, *Atchison, Topeka and Santa Fe,* pp. 173–76. San Francisco *Examiner,* January 30, 1895. Frank Norris published *The Octopus* in 1901. Although purportedly fiction, there was no mistaking the ugly characterization of the Southern Pacific in the best muckraking style of that day. Fortunately, histories such as Richard Orsi's *Sunset Limited* offer a much more balanced view.

11. Bryant, *Atchison, Topeka and Santa Fe,* pp. 178–81; *"the same thing"*: Treadway, *Cyrus K. Holliday,* p. 243 (quoting Holliday to Strong, October 10, 1896).

CHAPTER 21: STILL WEST FROM DENVER

1. Bradley, *Santa Fe,* pp. 209–10, 246, 315; Athearn, *Rebel of the Rockies,* pp. 171, 173–74; John Lipsey, "How Hagerman Sold the Midland in 1890," *Denver Westerners Brand Book, 1956,* pp. 267–85, specifically, *"I do not suppose,"* p. 271, and *"it enables me,"* p. 283. See also John Lipsey, "J. J. Hagerman, Building of the Colorado Midland," *Brand Book of the Denver Posse of the Westerners for 1954,* pp. 95–115. The Santa Fe's purchase price of the Midland was $2.4 million in stock and $1.6 million in cash.

2. *"Such another opportunity"*: *Denver Republican,* January 12, 1900.

3. *"We have bought"*: George Kennan, *E. H. Harriman: A Biography,* vol. 1 (Freeport, N.Y.: Books for Libraries Press, 1967), pp. 240–41.

4. Athearn, *Rebel of the Rockies,* pp. 194–95. Palmer's generosity was first described in Fisher, *A Builder of the West,* pp. 303–4. There was apparently no public announcement of this generosity at the time, but Fisher reported a round of thank-you letters in the Palmer papers. These are not found in the Palmer Collection, but there is a letter from a Palmer crony, George Foster Peabody, that certainly captures the spirit: "I am however most heartily in favor of much ampler figures for all of them—for we are greatly indebted to their steadfast loyalty." Palmer Collection, Box 5, FF 330 (Peabody to Palmer, unclear date; possibly November 5, 1900).

5. Maury Klein, *The Life and Legend of E. H. Harriman* (Chapel Hill: University of North Carolina Press, 2000), p. 220.

6. Athearn, *Rebel of the Rockies,* pp. 197, 199–200; Spencer Crump, "Western Pacific:

The Railroad That Was Built Too Late," *Railway History Quarterly* 1, no. 1 (January 1963): 3, 20; Klein, *Harriman,* pp. 321–22.

7. Crump, "Western Pacific," pp. 20, 26, 30; *"The policies, ambitions"*: *Wall Street Journal,* April 14, 1906; *"still had light"*: Klein, *Harriman,* p. 322. The Western Pacific's other problem was competition from the Los Angeles and Salt Lake Railroad. A promoter named R. C. Kerens cobbled together 28 miles of line between Los Angeles and the port at San Pedro and spent the better part of the 1890s trying to interest the Union Pacific in acquiring it as the western terminus of a beeline route from Salt Lake City to Los Angeles. The Union Pacific gave Kerens's proposal a low priority, largely because any entrance into Los Angeles would have faced the wrath of the Southern Pacific.

In the spring of 1899, Kerens sent yet another proposal to the Union Pacific, but this time he was a buyer. Instead of promoting the sale of his Los Angeles Terminal Railway, Kerens sought to buy or lease the assortment of Union Pacific–controlled lines running south from Ogden. This got the Union Pacific's immediate attention. "I infer from his conversation," a sharp lieutenant telegraphed Harriman, "that W. A. Clark of Montana is behind him."

There was good reason for Harriman to be alarmed. William Andrews Clark was the proverbial loose cannon, an eccentric with enough money to do just about anything he set his mind to do. Born on a Pennsylvania farm in 1839, Clark taught school for a few years in Missouri and ended up in the rough-and-tumble gold camps of Montana's first mining rush. He struggled as a merchant, moved into banking, and then, in 1872, got in on the ground floor of a little place called Butte. The mineral there proved to be copper, and a mine and a smelter later, W. A. Clark was one of the copper kings of Montana.

Whether Clark sought a distraction in the deserts of Nevada or his sharp nose for the next deal led him there is debatable. Regardless, W. A. Clark was indeed the man backing R. C. Kerens in his Los Angeles–to–Salt Lake plans, and Huntington's death suddenly made the venture all the more feasible. In March 1901, Clark incorporated the San Pedro, Los Angeles, and Salt Lake Railroad and acquired the Los Angeles Terminal Railway as his western anchor.

The key to the middle portion of the route lay in control of the canyon of Meadow Valley Wash, a 110-mile slot extending southward from Caliente on the Nevada-Utah border to an expanse of desert that would soon become the railroad town of Las Vegas. While Harriman rushed Union Pacific–backed construction crews south from Ogden, Clark's men blocked the northern end of the Meadow Valley Canyon with a barricade and feverishly graded as many miles as possible at the other end. Clark was eventually able to enjoin Harriman from doing any work in the canyon, but both he and Harriman soon decided that it was time to talk things out.

After much posturing, Harriman concluded that what Clark really wanted was the glory of being involved with a major railroad construction. For Harriman, who was at the height of his Union Pacific–Southern Pacific empire, glory for others was a relatively cheap commodity as long as he held ultimate control. In fact, given his other designs on the West, Harriman didn't mind that Clark boasted publicly that he was to be a sole owner of the Los Angeles–Salt Lake line and planned to link the road with George Gould's system. Clark's bravado was a great smoke screen. Behind the scenes, Harriman was secure in an agreement to own one-half of both the San Pedro, Los Angeles, and Salt Lake and its construction company. As one of Harriman's advisors put it privately, "Mr. Clark is very sensitive on the point of his road being built as a San Pedro proposition. We are less tenacious about sentimental considerations but are looking to the final result."

The road secured trackage rights from the Santa Fe over Cajon Pass and rapidly filled in the gap from Barstow through Meadow Valley Wash, a stretch that required numerous tunnels. The new beeline was opened for business in May 1905 and immediately became a critical western artery because it had much the same characteristics as the Santa Fe's 35th parallel main line: relatively gentle grades, generally less snow, and a direct route. It became the Union Pacific's route of choice into Southern California. In 1916 "San Pedro" was dropped from its name because Los Angeles had effectively expanded to annex that onetime little port, and the road became simply the Los Angeles and Salt Lake Railroad. Clark finally sold his half interest in the line to the Union Pacific in 1921, four years before he died. (Klein, *Harriman*, pp. 243–49; for Clark's background, see Michael P. Malone, *The Battle for Butte: Mining and Politics on the Northern Frontier, 1864–1906* [Seattle: University of Washington Press, 1981], pp. 13–15, 126–27; Kennan, *Harriman*, vol. 1, pp. 344–46.)

8. Athearn, *Rebel of the Rockies*, pp. 201, "*As to the D. and R. G.*" 210–11, 285, 295; Fisher, *Builder of the West*, pp. 312–18.

CHAPTER 22: TOP OF THE HEAP

1. Maury Klein, *Union Pacific: The Rebirth, 1894–1969* (New York: Doubleday, 1989), pp. 119; Bryant, *Atchison, Topeka and Santa Fe*, pp. 184–85; tobacco story in Waters, *Steel Trails*, p. 348n.

2. Klein, *Harriman*, pp. 318–19.

3. Klein, *Harriman*, pp. 251–52; Klein, *Union Pacific: The Rebirth*, pp. 119, 144.

4. "*not adopted at first*": Palmer, *Report of Surveys Across the Continent*, p. 13; Bryant, *Atchison, Topeka and Santa Fe*, pp. 194–99, 201; gradients in Waters, *Steel Trails*, p. 354. A 19-mile cutoff was also completed west of Belen to link directly with the route west from Albuquerque and speed east-west trains across the Rio Grande Valley with barely a pause.

5. Virginia L. Grattan, *Mary Colter: Builder upon the Red Earth* (Grand Canyon, Ariz.: Grand Canyon Natural History Association, 1992), specifically, "*a decorator who knew,*" p. 8; "*the first building,*" p. 10; "*to give up,*" p. 25; "*Her buildings,*" p. 2.

6. Scotty's story should be taken with a grain of salt. This information is mostly from Dorothy Shally and William Bolton, *Scotty's Castle: Death Valley's Fabulous Showplace* (Yosemite, Calif.: Flying Spur Press, 1973), pp. 7–9.

7. This synopsis and the quotes are from an undated, reproduced publication entitled "Record Breaking Run of the Scott Special," which may have been produced by the Santa Fe in 1955 for the fiftieth anniversary of the run. Some references suggest that it was originally done shortly after the run. Another anniversary celebration was the reenactment of the Scott Special for a segment of the popular TV western of the 1950s

and 1960s, *Death Valley Days*. Santa Fe locomotive 1010, which pulled the original train between Needles and Seligman, was fired up for the run. Today it is at the California State Railroad Museum.

8. *"loves a good time"*: Shally and Bolton, *Scotty's Castle*, p. 9; *"Scott repays,"* ibid., p. 8.

9. *Eleventh Annual Report of the Atchison, Topeka and Santa Fe Railway Company, 1906*, p. 20.

10. *"virtual miracle"*: Bryant, *Atchison, Topeka and Santa Fe*, pp. 200–1; *"blue chip"*: ibid., p. 204.

11. *"the Pennsylvania of the West"* and *"The Pennsylvania policy"*: Carl Snyder, *American Railways as Investments* (New York: Moody, 1907), p. 81.

12. *"the road had become"*: "Fifty Years of Santa Fe History," *Santa Fe Magazine*, January 1923, p. 43.

CHAPTER 23: DUELING STREAMLINERS

1. Duke, *Santa Fe, Passenger and Freight Service*, pp. 312–16.

2. Duke, *Santa Fe, Passenger and Freight Service*, pp. 326–27.

3. Donald J. Heimburger and Carl R. Byron, *The American Streamliner: Prewar Years* (Forest Park, Ill.: Heimburger House, 1996), pp. 24–27, 33–34. Later in 1934, this Pioneer Zephyr was put into regular service between Lincoln and Kansas City via Omaha. It ran until 1960, when it was given to Chicago's Museum of Science and Industry.

4. Heimburger and Byron, *American Streamliner: Prewar Years*, pp. 22–24, 88. The Union Pacific took delivery of its streamliner on February 25, 1934—ahead of the Zephyr by two months—and also sent it on a national tour, but the train did not enter regular service as the City of Salina between Kansas City and Salina, Kansas, until January 31, 1935. The San Francisco leg of the City streamliners was made possible by a partnership with the Southern Pacific west of Ogden, while the Union Pacific owed its competition in the Los Angeles market to the wholly owned Los Angeles and Salt Lake Railroad.

5. Heimburger and Byron, *American Streamliner: Prewar Years*, pp. 73–80; Duke, *Santa Fe*, pp. 339–45; Bryant, *Atchison, Topeka and Santa Fe*, p. 345. In an effort to make the entire Santa Fe system run faster, passenger and freight operations were put on a unified schedule. Rather than shuttle freights onto sidings to clear the main line for passenger trains, high-speed freights—which could indeed roll right along thanks to diesel motive power—were often run as second sections of passenger trains a few minutes behind.

6. Bryant, *Atchison, Topeka and Santa Fe*, pp. 344–45.

7. Bryant, *Atchison, Topeka and Santa Fe*, pp. 272–75, 278, 312, 315–16. The war also provided the Santa Fe with a long-sought entry into the sprawling harbor at Long Beach, California. When nearby aircraft plants and defense industries swelled that city's population to 250,000, wartime traffic prompted the ICC to grant it equal access to the port along with the Union Pacific and Southern Pacific. By the time Santa Fe tracks were laid, the war was over, but the railroad was not about to give up any hard-won concessions. Similar wartime situations across the country strengthened the Santa Fe's postwar profile.

Other wartime improvements reduced operational bottlenecks, such as the 1890 crossing of the Colorado River near Needles. There, a new double-tracked, seven-pier, 1,500-foot span eliminated sharp approach curves, permitted higher speeds across the bridge, and reduced freight schedules by twenty minutes. A similar effort was begun at Cañon Diablo, although that new bridge was not completed until after the war.

At the close of the war, there were 1,567 steam locomotives, 103 road diesels, and 144 diesel switchers on the Santa Fe roster. Five years later, even as the Santa Fe continued to rely on steam for a time, the trend was irreversible: 1,199 steam engines and 627 road diesels. By 1956, there were only 96 steam locomotives left in operating condition on the railroad that had used them to become a transcontinental lifeline.

8. Frederic Wakeman, *The Hucksters* (New York: Rinehart, 1946), p. 275.

9. Joseph Borkin, *Robert R. Young: The Populist of Wall Street* (New York: Harper and Row, 1969), p. 89.

10. Athearn, *Rebel of the Rockies,* p. 335.

11. Donald J. Heimburger and Carl R. Byron, *The American Streamliner: Postwar Years* (Forest Park, Ill.: Heimburger House, 2001), pp. 142–43, 150–51. The California Zephyr wasn't as fast as the Union Pacific, but what it lacked in speed, it made up for in scenery. Eleven cars—all with the adjective *Silver* before their names—carried passengers through the most scenic sections of the Rockies and California's Feather River Canyon during daylight hours. "Promise yourself . . ." advertisements encouraged, "Next trip between Chicago and the Coast, it's the California Zephyr for me!"

12. Heimburger and Byron, *American Streamliner: Postwar Years,* pp. 89–90. The Union Pacific first teamed up with the Chicago and Northwestern and later the Milwaukee Railroad for service on the eastern leg of the trip between Omaha and Chicago.

13. Heimburger and Byron, *American Streamliner: Postwar Years,* pp. 108, 114; *"the top of the Super"*: Bryant, *Atchison, Topeka and Santa Fe,* p. 351; Robert Strein, John Vaughan, and C. Fenton Richards, Jr., *Santa Fe: The Chief Way* (Santa Fe: New Mexico Magazine, 2001), p. 1; for an example of the "Meeting of the Chiefs" advertisement, see *Saturday Evening Post,* December 17, 1949, and note that most other ads are black and white and less than a full page. And when it came to *affordable* luxury, El Capitan, while coach only, ran twelve to eighteen cars and carried about four hundred passengers between Chicago and Los Angeles. Round-trip fares in the 1950s were about $90. The Santa Fe billed this service as "America's New Railroad" and had the perfect arrival solution. "When you get there," read a tiny box in the advertisements, " . . . rent a car."

14. Bryant, *Atchison, Topeka and Santa Fe,* pp. 276, 283, 296–97; *Time,* May 23, 1955, pp. 94–95. The converse of the Super C was the unit trains that the Santa Fe assembled to move single commodities on a slow but reliable schedule to serve one customer. Coal was the obvious example, but the Santa Fe also hauled unit trains of sulfur from the plains of Texas and potash from southeastern New Mexico.

Bibliography

BOOKS

Anderson, George. *General William J. Palmer: A Decade of Colorado Railroad Building*. Colorado Springs: Colorado College Publication, 1936.

Athearn, Robert G. *Rebel of the Rockies: The Denver and Rio Grande Western Railroad*. New Haven, Conn.: Yale University Press, 1962.

Bain, David Haward. *Empire Express: Building the First Transcontinental Railroad*. New York: Penguin Books, 1999.

Bell, William A. *New Tracks in North America: A Journal of Travel and Adventure Whilst Engaged in the Survey for a Southern Railroad to the Pacific Ocean in 1867–1868*. London: Chapman and Hall, 1870.

Best, Gerald M. *Mexican Narrow Gauge*. Berkeley, Calif.: Howell-North Books, 1968.

Black, Robert C., III. *Railroad Pathfinder: The Life and Times of Edward L. Berthoud*. Evergreen, Colo.: Cordillera Press, 1988.

———. *The Railroads of the Confederacy*. Chapel Hill: University of North Carolina Press, 1952.

Borkin, Joseph. *Robert R. Young: The Populist of Wall Street*. New York: Harper and Row, 1969.

Borneman, Walter R. *Marshall Pass: Denver and Rio Grande Gateway to the Gunnison Country*. Colorado Springs, Colo.: Century One Press, 1980.

Bowers, John. *Chickamauga and Chattanooga: The Battles That Doomed the Confederacy*. New York: Avon Books, 1995.

Bowles, Samuel. *Across the Continent: A Summer's Journey to the Rocky Mountains, the Mormons, and the Pacific States, with Speaker Colfax.* Springfield, Mass.: Samuel Bowles & Company, 1865.

Bradley, Glenn D. *The Story of the Santa Fe.* Revised and expanded second edition of 1920 original. Palmdale, Calif.: Omni Publications, 1995.

Bryant, Keith L., Jr. *History of the Atchison, Topeka and Santa Fe Railway.* New York: Macmillan Publishing Co., 1974.

Burgess, George H., and Miles C. Kennedy. *Centennial History of the Pennsylvania Railroad Company, 1846–1946.* Philadelphia: The Pennsylvania Railroad Company, 1949.

Chaffin, Tom. *Pathfinder: John Charles Frémont and the Course of American Empire.* New York: Hill and Wang, 2002.

Chase, C. M. *The Editor's Run in New Mexico and Colorado.* Fort Davis, Tex.: Frontier Book Company, 1968.

Clark, Ira G. *Then Came the Railroads: The Century from Steam to Diesel in the Southwest.* Norman: University of Oklahoma Press, 1958.

Cleaveland, Norman, with George Fitzpatrick. *The Morleys—Young Upstarts on the Southwest Frontier.* Albuquerque: Calvin Horn Publisher, 1971.

Crampton, C. Gregory. *Ghosts of Glen Canyon.* Salt Lake City, Utah: Cricket Productions, 1986.

Daggett, Stuart. *Chapters on the History of the Southern Pacific.* 1922. Reprint, New York: Augustus M. Kelley, 1966.

Davis, Elmer O. *The First Five Years of the Railroad Era in Colorado.* Golden, Colo.: Sage Books, 1948.

DeArment, Robert K. *Bat Masterson: The Man and the Legend.* Norman: University of Oklahoma Press, 1979.

Deverell, William. *Railroad Crossing: Californians and the Railroad, 1850–1910.* Berkeley: University of California Press, 1994.

Devine, David. *Slavery, Scandal, and Steel Rails: The 1854 Gadsden Purchase and the Building of the Second Transcontinental Railroad Across Arizona and New Mexico Twenty-five Years Later.* New York: iUniverse, 2004.

Dodge, Grenville M. *How We Built the Union Pacific Railway, and Other Railway Papers and Addresses.* Washington: GPO, 1910.

Ducker, James H. *Men of the Steel Rails: Workers on the Atchison, Topeka & Santa Fe Railroad, 1869–1900.* Lincoln: University of Nebraska Press, 1983.

Duke, Donald. *Santa Fe . . . The Railroad Gateway to the American West,* Vol. 1, *Chicago-Los Angeles-San Diego.* San Marino, Calif.: Golden West Books, 1995.

———. *Santa Fe . . . The Railroad Gateway to the American West,* Vol. 2, *Passenger and Freight Service, et al.* San Marino, Calif.: Golden West Books, 1997.

Duke, Donald, and Stan Kistler. *Santa Fe . . . Steel Rails Through California.* San Marino, Calif.: Golden West Books, 1963.

Evans, Cerinda W. *Collis Potter Huntington.* Newport News, Va.: Mariners' Museum, 1954.

Fisher, John S. *A Builder of the West: The Life of General William Jackson Palmer.* Caldwell, Idaho: The Caxton Printers, 1939.

Fogelson, Robert M. *The Fragmented Metropolis: Los Angeles, 1850–1930.* Cambridge, Mass.: Harvard University Press, 1967.

Glaab, Charles N. *Kansas City and the Railroads.* Madison: State Historical Society of Wisconsin, 1962.

Goetzmann, William H. *Army Exploration in the American West, 1803–1863.* Lincoln: University of Nebraska Press, 1979.

Gordon, Sarah H. *Passage to Union: How the Railroads Transformed American Life, 1829–1929.* Chicago: Ivan R. Dee, 1996.

Grattan, Virginia L. *Mary Colter: Builder upon the Red Earth.* Grand Canyon, Ariz.: Grand Canyon Natural History Association, 1992.

Grodinsky, Julius. *Transcontinental Railway Strategy, 1869–1893.* Philadelphia: University of Pennsylvania Press, 1962.

Hauck, Cornelius W. *Narrow Gauge to Central and Silver Plume. Colorado Rail Annual.* No. 10. Golden, Colo.: Colorado Railroad Museum, 1972.

Hauck, Cornelius W., and Robert W. Richardson, eds. "The Santa Fe's D&RG War No. 2." *Colorado Rail Annual.* Golden, Colo.: Colorado Railroad Museum, 1965.

Heimburger, Donald J., and Carl R. Byron. *The American Streamliner: Postwar Years.* Forest Park, Ill.: Heimburger House, 2001.

———. *The American Streamliner: Prewar Years.* Forest Park, Ill.: Heimburger House, 1996.

Helmers, Dow. *Historic Alpine Tunnel.* Colorado Springs, Colo.: Century One Press, 1971.

Hofsommer, Don L. *The Southern Pacific, 1901–1985.* College Station: Texas A&M University Press, 1986.

Jacobs, Timothy. *The History of the Pennsylvania Railroad.* Greenwich, Conn.: Bonanza Books, 1988.

Kelsey, Harry E., Jr. *Frontier Capitalist: The Life of John Evans.* Denver: State Historical Society of Colorado and Pruett, 1969.

Kennan, George. *E. H. Harriman: A Biography.* Vol. 1. Reprint of 1922 edition. Freeport, N.Y.: Books for Libraries Press, 1967.

Klein, Maury. *The Life and Legend of E. H. Harriman.* Chapel Hill: University of North Carolina Press, 2000.

———. *The Life and Legend of Jay Gould.* Baltimore: Johns Hopkins University Press, 1986.

———. *Union Pacific: The Birth of a Railroad, 1862–1893.* New York: Doubleday, 1987.

———. *Union Pacific: The Rebirth, 1894–1969.* New York: Doubleday, 1989.

Kroeger, Brooke. *Nellie Bly: Daredevil, Reporter, Feminist.* New York: Times Books, 1994.

Lavender, David. *Bent's Fort.* New York: Doubleday, 1954.

———. *Colorado River Country.* New York: E. P. Dutton, 1982.

———. *The Great Persuader.* New York: Doubleday, 1970.

———. *River Runners of the Grand Canyon.* Tucson: Grand Canyon Natural History Association and the University of Arizona Press, 1985.

Lewis, Oscar. *The Big Four: The Story of Huntington, Stanford, Hopkins, and Crocker, and of the Building of the Central Pacific.* New York: Alfred A. Knopf, 1938.

Leyendecker, Liston Edgington. *Palace Car Prince: A Biography of George Mortimer Pullman.* Niwot, Colo.: University Press of Colorado, 1992.

MacGregor, Bruce A., and Ted Benson. *Portrait of a Silver Lady: The Train They Called the California Zephyr.* Boulder, Colo.: Pruett, 1977.

Malone, Michael P. *The Battle for Butte: Mining and Politics on the Northern Frontier, 1864–1906.* Seattle: University of Washington Press, 1981.

Martin, Albro. *Railroads Triumphant: The Growth, Rejection, and Rebirth of a Vital American Force.* New York: Oxford University Press, 1992.

McLuhan, T. C. *Dream Tracks: The Railroad and the American Indian, 1890–1930.* New York: Harry N. Abrams, 1985.

Middleton, William D. *Landmarks on the Iron Road: Two Centuries of North American Railroad Engineering.* Bloomington: Indiana University Press, 1999.

Miner, H. Craig. *The St. Louis–San Francisco Transcontinental Railroad: The Thirty-fifth Parallel Project, 1853–1890.* Lawrence: University Press of Kansas, 1972.

Myrick, David F. *New Mexico's Railroads: A Historical Survey.* Albuquerque: University of New Mexico Press, 1993.

———. *Railroads of Arizona.* Vol. 1. *The Southern Roads.* Berkeley, Calif.: Howell-North Books, 1975.

———. *Railroads of Arizona.* Vol. 4. *The Santa Fe Route.* Wilton, Calif.: Signature Press, 1998.

———. *Railroads of Arizona.* Vol. 5. *Santa Fe to Phoenix.* Berkeley and Wilton, Calif.: Signature Press, 2001.

Norris, L. David, James C. Milligan, and Odie B. Faulk. *William H. Emory: Soldier-Scientist.* Tucson: The University of Arizona Press, 1998.

Ormes, Robert M. *Railroads and the Rockies: A Record of Lines in and near Colorado.* Denver: Sage Books, 1963.

Orsi, Richard J. *Sunset Limited: The Southern Pacific Railroad and the Development of the American West, 1850–1930.* Berkeley: University of California Press, 2005.

Osterwald, Doris B. *Rails Through the Gorge: A Mile by Mile Guide for the Royal Gorge Route.* Hugo, Colo.: Western Guideways, 2003.

Overton, Richard C. *Gulf to Rockies: The Heritage of the Fort Worth and Denver–Colorado Southern Railways, 1861–1898.* Westport, Conn.: Greenwood Press, 1970.

Palmer, William J. *Report of Surveys Across the Continent, in 1867–'68, on the Thirty-fifth and Thirty-second Parallels, for a Route Extending the Kansas Pacific Railway to the Pacific Ocean at San Francisco and San Diego.* Philadelphia: W. B. Selheimer, printer, 1869.

Perkins, J. R. *Trails, Rails, and War: The Life of General G. M. Dodge.* Indianapolis: Bobbs-Merrill Company, 1929.

Pletcher, David M. *The Diplomacy of Annexation: Texas, Oregon, and the Mexican War.* Columbia: University of Missouri Press, 1973.

———. *Rails, Mines, & Progress: Seven American Promoters in Mexico, 1867–1911.* Ithaca, N.Y.: Cornell University Press, 1958.

Poling-Kempes, Lesley. *The Harvey Girls: Women Who Opened the West.* New York: Paragon House, 1989.

Saunders, Richard, Jr. *Main Lines: Rebirth of the North American Railroads, 1970–2002.* DeKalb: Northern Illinois University Press, 2003.

———. *Merging Lines: American Railroads, 1900–1970.* DeKalb: Northern Illinois University Press, 2001.

Shally, Dorothy, and William Bolton. *Scotty's Castle: Death Valley's Fabulous Showplace.* Yosemite, Calif.: Flying Spur Press, 1973.

Signor, John R. *The Los Angeles and Salt Lake Railroad Company: Union Pacific's Historic Salt Lake Route.* San Marino, Calif.: Golden West Press, 1988.

———. *Tehachapi: Southern Pacific–Santa Fe.* San Marino, Calif.: Golden West Books, 1983.

Snyder, Carl. *American Railways as Investments.* New York: Moody, 1907.

Spearman, Frank H. *The Strategy of Great Railroads.* New York: Charles Scribner's Sons, 1904.

Sprague, Marshall. *The Great Gates: The Story of the Rocky Mountain Passes.* Boston: Little, Brown and Company, 1964.

Stansbury, Howard. *An Exploration to the Valley of the Great Salt Lake of Utah.* Philadelphia: Lippincott, Grambo & Co., 1852.

Stanton, Robert Brewster. *Colorado River Controversies.* 1932. Reprint, Boulder City, Nev.: Westwater Books, 1982.

———. *Down the Colorado.* Norman: University of Oklahoma Press, 1965.

Strein, Robert, John Vaughan, and C. Fenton Richards, Jr. *Santa Fe: The Chief Way.* Santa Fe: New Mexico Magazine, 2001.

Treadway, William E. *Cyrus K. Holliday: A Documentary Biography.* Topeka: Kansas State Historical Society, 1979.

Wakeman, Frederic. *The Hucksters.* New York: Rinehart, 1946.

Ward, James A. *J. Edgar Thomson: Master of the Pennsylvania.* Westport, Conn.: Greenwood Press, 1980.

Waters, L. L. *Steel Trails to Santa Fe.* Lawrence: University of Kansas Press, 1950.

Wilkins, Tivis E. *Colorado Railroads.* Boulder, Colo.: Pruett, 1974.

Williams, John Hoyt. *A Great & Shining Road.* New York: Times Books, 1988.

Wilson, Neill C., and Frank J. Taylor. *Southern Pacific: The Roaring Story of a Fighting Railroad.* New York: McGraw-Hill Book Company, 1952.

Winther, Oscar Osburn. *The Transportation Frontier: 1865–1890.* New York: Holt, Rinehart and Winston, 1964.

Worster, Donald. *A River Running West: The Life of John Wesley Powell.* New York: Oxford University Press, 2001.

Wright, Lyle H., and Josephine M. Bynum, eds. *The Butterfield Overland Mail.* San Marino, Calif.: The Huntington Library Press, 1942.

ARTICLES

Barnes, Lela, ed. "Letters of Cyrus Kurtz Holliday, 1854–1859." *Kansas Historical Quarterly* 6 (August 1937): 241–94.

Bishop, William Henry. "Southern California." *Harper's New Monthly* magazine (December 1882): 45–65.

Borneman, Walter R. "Ride the Historic Georgetown Loop." *American West* 24, no. 3 (June 1987): 42–47.

Chappell, Gordon. "Scenic Line of the World." *Colorado Rail Annual* 8 (1970): 3–96.

Crump, Spencer. "Western Pacific: The Railroad That Was Built Too Late." *Railway History Quarterly* 1, no. 1 (January 1963): 1–48.

Ellis, David M. "The Forfeiture of Railroad Land Grants, 1867–1894." *Mississippi Valley Historical Review* 33 (June 1946): 27–60.

Farley, Alan W. "Samuel Hallett and the Union Pacific Railway Company in Kansas." *Kansas Historical Quarterly* 25, no. 1 (Spring 1959): 1–16.

BIBLIOGRAPHY

Farnham, Wallace D. "The Pacific Railroad Act of 1862." *Nebraska History* 43 (September 1962): 141–67.

———. "The Weakened Spring of Government." *American Historical Review* 67 (April 1963): 662–80.

Fels, Rendigs. "American Business Cycles, 1865–79." *American Economic Review* 41, no. 3 (June 1951): 325–49.

Greever, William S. "Railway Development in the Southwest." *New Mexico Historical Review* 32, no. 2 (April 1957): 151–203.

Hietter, Paul T. " 'No Better Than Murderers': The 1889 Canyon Diablo Train Robbery and the Death Penalty in Arizona Territory." *Journal of Arizona History* 47, no. 3 (Autumn 2006): 273–98.

Hoyt, Franklin. "The Los Angeles and San Gabriel Valley Railroad." *Pacific Historical Review* 20, no. 3 (August 1951): 227–39.

———. "San Diego's First Railroad: The California Southern." *Pacific Historical Review* 23, no. 2 (May 1954): 133–46.

Klein, Maury. "In Search of Jay Gould." *Business History Review* 52, no. 2 (Summer 1978): 166–99.

Lawrence, George C. "The Western Pacific." *Railroad Age Gazette* 45, no. 15 (September 11, 1908): 902–10.

Le Massena, Robert A. "The Royal Gorge." *Denver Westerners Monthly Roundup* 21, no. 11 (November 1965): 3–17.

Lesley, Lewis B. "The Entrance of the Santa Fe Railroad into California." *Pacific Historical Review* 8, no. 1 (March 1939): 89–96.

———. "A Southern Transcontinental Railroad into California: Texas and Pacific Versus Southern Pacific, 1865–1885." *Pacific Historical Review* 5, no. 1 (1936): 52–60.

Lipsey, John. "How Hagerman Sold the Midland in 1890." *Brand Book of the Denver Westerners, 1956*: 266–85.

———. " J. J. Hagerman, Building of the Colorado Midland." *Brand Book of the Denver Posse of the Westerners for 1954*: 95–115.

Lyman, Edward Leo. "From the City of Angels to the City of Saints: The Struggle to Build a Railroad from Los Angeles to Salt Lake City." *California History* 70 (Spring 1991): 76–93.

Mock, S. D. "Colorado and the Surveys for a Pacific Railroad." *Colorado Magazine* 17, no. 2 (March 1940): 54–63.

———. "The Financing of Early Colorado Railroads." *Colorado Magazine* 18, no. 6 (November 1941): 201–9.

Overmeyer, Philip Henry. "George B. McClellan and the Pacific Northwest." *Pacific Northwest Quarterly* 32 (1941): 3–60.

Pletcher, David M. "The Building of the Mexican Railway." *Hispanic American Historical Review* 30, no. 1 (February 1950): 26–62.

———. "General William S. Rosecrans and the Mexican Transcontinental Railroad Project." *Mississippi Valley Historical Review* 38 (March 1952): 657–78.

Snell, Joseph W., and Don W. Wilson. "The Birth of the Atchison, Topeka and Santa Fe Railroad." *Kansas Historical Quarterly* 34, no. 2 (Summer 1968): 113–42.

————. "The Birth of the Atchison, Topeka and Santa Fe Railroad—Concluded." *Kansas Historical Quarterly* 35, no. 3 (Fall 1968): 325–56.

Spitzzeri, Paul R. "The Road to Independence: The Los Angeles and Independence Railroad and the Conception of a City." *Southern California Quarterly* 83, no. 1 (Spring 2001): 23–58.

Van Horn, Kurt. "Tempting Temecula: The Making and Unmaking of a Southern California Community." *Journal of San Diego History* 20, no. 1 (Winter 1974), accessed online at www.sandiegohistory.org/journal/74winter/temecula.htm.

Ward, James. A. "Image and Reality: The Railway Corporate-State Metaphor." *Business History Review* 55 (Winter 1981): 491–516.

Zega, Michael E. "Advertising the Southwest." *Journal of the Southwest* 43, no. 3 (Autumn 2001): 281–315.

GOVERNMENT DOCUMENTS

Butterfield Overland Mail–The Pinery. Guadalupe Mountains National Park brochure, 1988.

Emory, W. H. *Notes on a Military Reconnaissance from Fort Leavenworth, in Missouri, to San Diego, in California, Including Parts of the Arkansas, Del Norte, and Gila Rivers*. 30th Cong., 1st sess, Ex. Doc. 41.

————. *Report on the United States and Mexican Boundary Survey*. 34th Cong., 1st sess., H.R. Exec. Doc. 135.

Garrison, James, et al. *Transcontinental Railroading in Arizona, 1878–1940: A Component of the Arizona Historic Preservation Plan*. Prepared for the Arizona State Historic Preservation Office, December 1989, by Janus Associates, Phoenix.

Reports of the Explorations and Surveys, to Ascertain the Most Practicable and Economical Route for a Railroad from the Mississippi River to the Pacific Ocean. 33rd Cong., 2nd sess., H.R. Ex. Doc. 91 (cited as *Pacific Railroad Reports*).

The War of the Rebellion: A Compilation of the Official Records of the Union and Confederate Armies (cited as *Official Records*).

PERSONAL PAPERS AND CORPORATE RECORDS

Atchison, Topeka and Santa Fe Railroad Collection, Stephen H. Hart Library, Colorado Historical Society, Denver; cited as Santa Fe Collection by box and file folder (FF).

William A. Bell Collection, Stephen H. Hart Library, Colorado Historical Society, Denver; cited as Bell Collection by box and file folder.

Denver and Rio Grande Western Railroad Collection, Stephen H. Hart Library, Colorado Historical Society, Denver; cited as Denver and Rio Grande Collection by box and file folder.

John Evans Collection, Stephen H. Hart Library, Colorado Historical Society, Denver; cited as Evans Collection by box and file folder.

Timothy Hopkins Transportation Collection, Green Library, Stanford University Libraries, Stanford, California.

Collis P. Huntington Papers, 1856–1901, microfilm edition in Western History Department, Denver Public Library, Denver; cited as Huntington Papers by series and reel number.

David Sievert Lavender Papers, Norlin Library, University of Colorado, Boulder.

William Jackson Palmer Collection, Stephen H. Hart Library, Colorado Historical Society, Denver; cited as Palmer Collection by box and file folder.

Robert F. Weitbrec Collection, Stephen H. Hart Library, Colorado Historical Society, Denver.

UNPUBLISHED DISSERTATIONS AND PAPERS

Benson, T. Lloyd, and Trina Rossman. "Re-assessing Tom Scott, the 'Railroad Prince.' " A paper given for the Mid-America Conference on History, Furman University, September 16, 1995.

Storey, Britt Allan. "William Jackson Palmer: A Biography." Unpublished PhD dissertation, University of Kentucky, 1968.

NEWSPAPERS

Arizona Daily Citizen/Arizona Weekly Citizen (Tucson)

Arizona Daily Star (Tucson)

Arizona Sentinel (Yuma)

Boston Herald

Colorado Tribune (Denver)

Colorado Weekly Chieftain (Pueblo)

Commercial and Financial Chronicle

Congressional Globe

Daily Alta California (San Francisco)

Denver Republican

Denver Times

Emporia (Kansas) *News*

Engineering News

Georgetown (Colorado) *Courier*

Gunnison (Colorado) *Review*

Hutchinson (Kansas) *News*

Kansas Daily Commonwealth (Topeka)

Kansas State Record (Topeka)

Las Vegas (New Mexico) *Daily Optic*

Las Vegas (New Mexico) *Gazette*

Lone Star (El Paso, Texas)

Los Angeles Evening Express

Los Angeles Herald

Los Angeles Times

Mountain Mail (Salida, Colorado)

New York Herald

New York Times

New York Tribune

New York World

Osage (Kansas) *Chronicle*

Railroad Gazette

Railway Times

Rocky Mountain News

San Diego Union

San Francisco Bulletin

San Francisco Examiner

Thirty-four (Las Cruces, New Mexico)

Wall Street Journal

Weekly Arizona Miner (Prescott)

Index

Page numbers in italics refer to illustrations.

About the Author

WALTER R. BORNEMAN is the award-winning author of eight works of nonfiction, including the *New York Times* bestseller *The Admirals, American Spring, 1812, The French and Indian War,* and *Polk*. He lives in Colorado.